Post-liberalism
Studies in political thought

John Gray

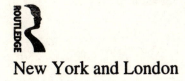

New York and London

First published 1993
by Routledge
11 New Fetter Lane

Simultaneously published in the USA and Canada
by Routledge
29 West 35th Street, New York, NY 10001

Reprinted 1993

Typeset in Times by LaserScript, Mitcham, Surrey
Printed in Great Britain by
Antony Rowe Ltd, Chippenham, Wiltshire

British Library Cataloguing in Publication Data
A catalogue reference for this book is available from the British Library
ISBN 0–415–08873–9

Library of Congress Cataloging in Publication Data
Gray, John, 1948–
    Post-liberalism: studies in political thought/John Gray.
    p. cm.
    "Companion volume to . . . Liberalisms: essays in political
    philosophy (Routledge, 1989)" – Pref.
    Includes bibliographical references and index.
    ISBN 0–415–08873–9: $39.95
    1. Liberalism. 2. Liberty. 3. Communism. 4. Socialism.
I. Gray, John, 1948– Liberalisms. II. Title.
JC585.G7365   1993
320.5′1 – dc20   92-23117
                                                                        CIP

ISBN 0–415–08873–9

Contents

Preface

This collection of twenty essays, articles and reviews, which is a selection of pieces of work I have published or written over the last ten years, is intended as a companion volume to my earlier collection, *Liberalisms: Essays in Political Philosophy* (Routledge, 1989). In that earlier collection, I brought together a selection of papers written over a dozen years on the foundational aspects of liberalism. The upshot of the line of thought pursued in those essays was that doctrinal or fundamentalist liberalism, according to which a liberal regime is the only ideally legitimate one for mankind, is indefensible and has no claim on our reason. The earlier collection ended on a sceptical note, both in respect of what a post-liberal political theory might look like, and with regard to the claims of political philosophy itself.

The present, further selection of my work is intended to give a post-liberal theory a more definite content. It does so, by considering particular thinkers in the history of political thought, by criticizing the conventional wisdom, liberal and socialist, of the Western academic class, and, most directly in the collection's last essay, by trying to specify what remains of value in liberalism. The upshot of *this* line of thought is that we need not regret the failure of foundationalist liberalism, since we have all we need in the historic inheritance, spreading now to various parts of the world where it was suppressed or unknown, of the institutions of civil society. It is to the practice of liberty that these institutions encompass, rather than to the empty vistas of liberal theory, that we (as post-moderns no longer animated by the illusions of the Enlightenment project) should repair.

This collection could not have been brought together without the help of many people. The Principal and Fellows of Jesus College accorded me periods of sabbatical leave in which to think and write. A period as Distinguished Visiting Professor at the Murphy Institute of Political Economy enabled me to develop my thoughts in an environment as conducive to reflection as to enjoyment. Conversations, formal and informal, over many years at colloquia convened by Liberty Fund of Indianapolis have honed my thoughts on civil society and limited government. I am sure that the present collection could never have been put together without the support given me by the Social Philosophy and Policy Center in Bowling Green, Ohio. Without my recurrent periods of residence there, my thoughts could not have had the freedom to germinate and find embodiment in many of the essays collected here. For that freedom I thank the Directors and staff of the Center. I wish particularly to thank Mary Dilsaver and Tammi Sharp, who patiently and impeccably transformed my execrable script into a bona fide manuscript.

Finally, I wish to thank my wife, Mieko, without whose devotion this collection, and much else, would undoubtedly never have come to pass.

John Gray
Jesus College

October, 1991

Acknowledgements

'Hobbes and the modern state' and 'Santayana and the critique of liberalism' appeared in *The World and I* (Washington, D.C.) in March 1989 and February 1989. 'Hayek as a conservative' and 'Oakeshott as a liberal' appeared in *The Salisbury Review* (London) in July 1983 and January 1992. 'Buchanan on liberty' appeared in *The Journal of Constitutional Political Economy*, vol. 1, no. 2 (Spring/Summer 1990), 149–68. The following appeared in the *Times Literary Supplement:* 'Berlin's agonistic liberalism', 5 July 1991; 'The system of ruins', 30 December 1983; 'The delusion of *glasnost*', 21 July 1989; and 'The academic romance of Marxism', 24 February 1989. 'Philosophy, science and myth in Marxism' appeared in *Marx and Marxisms*, ed. G. H. R. Parkinson, Royal Institute of Philosophy Lecture Series, vol. 14 (Cambridge: Cambridge University Press, 1982). 'Against Cohen on proletarian unfreedom' appeared in *Social Philosophy & Policy*, vol. 6, issue 1 (Autumn 1988), 77–112. 'Totalitarianism, reform and civil society' appeared in *Totalitarianism at the Crossroads*, ed. E. F. Paul (New Brunswick: Transaction Books, 1990), 97–142. 'Western Marxism: a fictional deconstruction' appeared in *Philosophy,* no. 64 (1989), 403–8. 'Post-totalitarianism, civil society and the limits of the western model' appeared in *The Reemergence of Civil Society in Eastern Europe and the Soviet Union*, ed. Zbigniew Rau (Boulder, San Francisco and Oxford: Westview Press, 1991), 145–60. 'Political power, social theory and essential contestability' appeared in *The Nature of Political Theory*, ed. D. Miller and L. Siedentop (Oxford: Clarendon Press, 1983). 'An epitaph for liberalism' appeared in the *Times Liberary Supplement*, 12 January 1990. 'The end of history – or of liberalism?' appeared in *The National Review* (New York), 27 October 1989, 33–5. 'The politics of cultural diversity' appeared in *Quadrant*, November 1987, 29–38, and in *The Salisbury Review*, September 1988, 38–45. 'Conservatism, individualism and the political thought of the New Right' appeared in *Ideas and Politics in Modern Britain*, ed. J. C. D. Clark (London: Macmillan, 1990). 'What is dead and what is living in liberalism' is published for the first time in this volume.

Part I
Thinkers

1 Hobbes and the modern state

Thomas Hobbes lived in, and wrote for, an age of civil and religious wars. For this reason, it may seem that we have little to learn from him today that we do not already know. To be sure, anyone who reflects upon the intractable religious conflicts of Northern Ireland or the Middle East will see that wars of religion are as much an evil of our age as they were of Hobbes's, and civil peace as precious a good. Beyond these commonplace reflections, it would appear that Hobbes has indeed little to teach us. His entire system of thought, conceived and developed at a time when the scientific revolution was barely under way, may have the aspect of an anachronism, of an intellectual construct whose terms and postulates are so far removed from our own that we are hard put to make sense of it, and cannot put it to work to illuminate the dilemmas that confront us today. On this conventional view, we may read Hobbes's writings as literature (for he is one of the greatest prose stylists in English) or as history, but we will not turn to them for instruction or enlightenment.

Much as might be said in support of this conventional opinion, it is radically misguided. It is true that Hobbes's system of ideas encompasses extravagances we find hard to credit, and that his entire mode of thought has an archaic character, recalling medieval ways of reasoning more than the methods of modern science by which he supposed his theorizing was governed. Yet there is an arresting contemporaneity about many of Hobbes's insights that we can well profit from. Nor is this relevance to our age a matter of surprise, for Hobbes wrote at the start of the modern age (he was born in 1588 and died in 1679), and few have seen further to the bottom of the dilemma of modernity than he. By comparison or contrast with Hobbes, John Locke is truly a remote thinker, Kant hollow and Burke not much more than a nostalgist. Far from being an anachronistic irrelevance, Hobbes's thought is supremely relevant to us, who live at the end of the modern era whose ills he sought to diagnose. With all of its limitations and its excesses, Hobbes's thought goes far to account for the maladies of the modern state, and does so in ways that are as surprising and paradoxical as they are instructive. The lesson of Hobbesian theory for us is that the modern state is weak because it aims too high and has grown too large. Worse, the modern state has failed in its task of delivering us from a condition of universal predation or war of all against all into the peace of civil society. Modern democratic states have themselves become weapons in the war of all against all, as rival interest groups compete with each other to capture government and use it to seize and redistribute resources among themselves. In its weakness the modern state has recreated in a political form that very state of nature from which it is the task of the state to deliver us. In this political state of nature, modern democratic states are riven by a *legal and political war of all against all*, and the institutions of civil society are progressively enfeebled. And the conflicts which rack the modern state are not merely economic in origin. All modern democracies, but especially the United States, have transformed the state into an arena of doctrinal conflicts, wherein under the banners of fundamental rights or social justice contending political movements vie for supremacy. Worst of all, the totalitarian states of the Communist world have created a monstrosity that even Hobbes (for all his vaunted, and genuine, pessimism) could not have envisaged – a political order in which the state of nature and a lawless Leviathan are inextricably intertwined. Distracted from its true purposes by the political religions of our time, Communism and liberalism, the modern state has become a burden on civil society, sometimes (as in Communist regimes) a burden that is too heavy to bear. Even in the Western democracies, it has become more of an enemy of civil society than its guardian. We have been delivered from the lawless chaos of society without the state into an anarchic servility of unlimited government.

That modern governments are weak because they do too much and claim authority they do not have, and so are at the furthest remove from Hobbesian states, is a paradox, but like every genuine paradox it is a truth expressed in the form of an apparent contradiction. We can discern the reasons for this truth, and the outlines of an Hobbesian critique of the modern democratic state, if we look again, with fresh eyes, at Hobbes's chief doctrines about man, society and government. Consider first Hobbes's conception of human nature. What is most distinctive in it is its departure from the classical conception of man, most notably theorized by Aristotle and given a Christian rendition by Aquinas. In the classical conception, man is like everything else in the world in having a natural end, *telos* or perfection, which it is his vocation to realize. By comparison with Hobbes's view, the content of this perfection – a life of contemplation in Aristotle and salvation in Aquinas – is less important than its affirmation. In Hobbes's view, mankind has no supreme good which it is called to achieve, no *summum bonum*, but only a *summum malum*, a supreme evil, which we aim to elude. A good life for a human being consists, not in possessing any final or supreme good, but simply in satisfying our restless desires as they spring up. Hobbes tells us that

> Continual success in obtaining those things which a man from time to time desireth, that is to say, continual prospering, is what men call Felicity; I mean the Felicity of this life, for there is no such thing as perpetual tranquility of mind, while we live here; because Life itself is but Motion, and can never be without Desire, nor without Feare, no more than without Sense.[1]

For Hobbes, as his most distinguished twentieth-century interpreter, Michael Oakeshott, has put it, human fulfilment is to be found,

> not in pleasure – those who see in Hobbes a hedonist are sadly wide of the mark – but in Felicity, a transitory perfection, having no finality and offering no repose.[2]

As Hobbes puts this view emphatically:

> the Felicity of this life, consisteth not in the repose of a mind satisfied. For there is no such *finis ultimus* (utmost aim) nor *summum bonum* (greatest good) as is spoken of in the Books of the old Moral Philosophers. . . . Felicity is a continual progress of the desire, from one object to another; the attaining of the former, being still but the way to the later. The cause whereof is, that the object of man's desire is not to enjoy once only, and for one instant of time; but to assure forever, the way of his future desire.[3]

For Hobbes, then, the human good is life in movement, which is pursuit of one's passing desires. For human beings, it follows, the greatest evil can only be immobility, or death, since that is the cessation of all movement and all desire. It is indeed Hobbes's view that men avoid death, and above all a violent and painful death, before all else. Just as Epicurus had seen in the absence of pain rather than in pleasure the good for men, so Hobbes gave the avoidance of death and not life itself as the pre-eminent human end. What do these claims imply for man in society? They suggest an incessant competition for the means whereby death can be avoided, or delayed. Human life, Hobbes avers, can be compared to a race – a race which has no other 'goal' or 'garland' than 'being foremost'.

> In it to endeavor is appetite; to be remiss is sensuality; to consider them behind is glory; to consider them before is humility . . . to fall on the sudden is the disposition to weep; to see one outgone when we would not

is pity; to see one outgo when we would not is indignation; to hold fast by another is love; to carry him on that so holdeth is charity; to hurt oneself for haste is shame . . . continually to be outgone is misery; continually to outgo the next before is felicity; and to forsake the course is to die.[4]

The consequence of this competition, as well as its primary cause, is

a general inclination of all mankind, a perpetual and restless desire of power after power, that ceaseth only in Death. And the cause of this, is not always that a man hopes for a more intensive delight, than he has already attained to; or that he cannot be content with a moderate power: but because he cannot assure the power and means to live well, which he hath present, without the acquisition of more.[5]

Hobbes's master thesis is that, in the absence of a sovereign power which binds them to peace, men's natural condition is a condition of conflict or war. As he famously sums up his chain of reasoning:

Whatsoever is consequent to a time of Warre, where every man is Enemy to every man; the same is consequent to the time, wherein men live without other security, than what their own strength, and their own invention shall furnish them withall. In such conditions, there is no place for Industry; because the fruit thereof is uncertain; and consequently no culture of the earth; no navigation, nor use of the commodities that may be imported by Sea; no commodious building; no instruments of moving, and removing such things as require much force; no knowledge of the face of the Earth; no account of time; no Arts; no Letters; no Society; and which is worst of all, continual fear, and danger of violent death. And the life of man, solitary, poor, nasty, brutish and short.[6]

No less famous than this passage is Hobbes's conclusion: human beings can be delivered from their natural condition of war, only by the creation of 'an artificial man', a sovereign authority which is empowered to do all that is necessary to bring into being, and keep, a civil peace. This sovereign must be unlimited in his powers of action, and must be a unitary authority, since otherwise dispute will be engendered as to the limits of the sovereign's authority, and peace will be put in jeopardy. The Hobbesian political remedy for the natural misery of mankind is then a state whose authority is unlimited, save by its task of keeping the peace. More, Hobbes believed that his analysis would find support among men, who would be driven by prudence and experience of the fearful consequences of weak or divided government to enter into a covenant which instituted Leviathan, the Hobbesian state.

What is to be said of Hobbes's argument? The overwhelming preponderance of critical opinion goes against his analysis at almost every point. Hobbes has remained what he was for his contemporaries, a scandal and a scapegoat for the false consciousness of his critics. As Oakeshott delightfully observes,

> Against Hobbes, Filmer defended servitude, Harrington liberty, Clarendon the Church, Locke the Englishman, Rousseau mankind and Butler the Deity.[7]

Much, if not most in the traditional criticisms of Hobbes's doctrine represents it crudely, and so goes astray. It is said, truly enough, that human behaviour is not governed predominantly by the imperative of death-avoidance. If it were, how could we explain the heroic resistance of the Afghans against Soviet conquest in our own day, and many another similar instance in history? It is suggested that Hobbes held to another falsehood about human nature, the theory of *psychological egoism*, according to which whatever any man does he does at the behest of his own interests. And it has even been alleged that the model of a Hobbesian state is a totalitarian government, from which civil society and autonomous institutions have been extirpated. Despite occasional inadvertencies in Hobbes's writings, all of these charges are wide of the mark. As a recent commentator[8] has shown beyond reasonable doubt, Hobbes held not that all human conduct was motivated by self-interest, but only that self-interest was a powerful human passion, and sheer concern for others, especially those who are not near to us in our affections, is rare and politically insignificant. More precisely, it is the interest in self-preservation that Hobbes supposes to be decisive in human conduct – and, most precisely, the interest in avoiding a violent death at the hands of other men. This last point is not clear in Hobbes's literary masterpiece, *Leviathan*, where it is death itself that is specified as the supreme human evil, but it is explicit in his *De Homine*, where Hobbes observes:

> the greatest of goods for each is his own preservation. For nature is so arranged that all desire good for themselves. . . . On the other hand, though death is the greatest of all evils (especially when accompanied by torture), the pains of life can be so great that, unless their quick end is forseen, they may lead men to number death among the goods.[9]

Hobbes's is not, then, the mechanistic theory in which an egoistic account of human nature is conjoined with the claim that merely avoiding death is the passion which most decisively governs men. Nevertheless, Hobbes is certainly open to criticism for his neglect of the moral and political importance of *collective identification* – the pervasive human phenomenon in virtue of which personal identities are constituted by membership in some nation, religion, tribe or other collectivity. The fact is that the man who conceives himself as a solitary individual, whose identity is unencumbered by any collective identification, though he is real, is vanishingly rare. As the novelist and aphorist, Elias Canetti, author of a fascinating study in Hobbesian political psychology, *Crowds and Power*, has said of Hobbes:

> He explains everything through selfishness, and while knowing the crowd (he often mentions it), he really has nothing to say about it. My task, however, is to show how complex selfishness is: to show how what it controls does not belong to it, it comes from other areas of human nature, the ones to which Hobbes is blind.[10]

Hume had rightly criticized Hobbes for his radical individualist picture of human beings as solitaries, who contract as much into society as into government. Such a picture must be a distortion, he urged, since we are born into families, which are social institutions, and come to consciousness speaking a language, which presupposes that we have a common life and a shared history. Anticipating the twentieth-century arguments of Ludwig Wittgenstein for the impossibility of a private language,[11] Hume pointed out that our ability to contract into government presupposes that we already have the practice of promising. Hume's point against Hobbes is that we are social beings *au fond*. Canetti's is the subtler one that our identities as persons are not natural but artifactual and are formed in a matrix of collective identifications (of which the crowd is perhaps the crudest). Because we derive our self-conception from membership in common forms of life, self-interest cannot be a primordial motivation in our lives in even the qualified way we have seen Hobbes make it so. The extravagant individualism of Hobbesian psychological theory, which flies in the face of much in experience and historical knowledge, comes in part from the method he sought to adopt in political theorizing, which aimed to be rigidly deductive. As he avows in *De Homine*,

> politics and ethics (that is, the sciences of just and unjust, of equity and inequity) can be demonstrated *apriori*; because we ourselves make the principles – that is, the causes of justice (namely laws and covenants) whereby it is known what justice and equity, and their opposites injustice and inequity, are. For before covenants and laws were drawn up, neither justice nor injustice, neither public good nor public evil, was natural among men any more than it was among beasts.[12]

Hobbes, like many another rationalist after him, here neglects the origins in natural social relationships of the moral and legal norms that sustain and constitute the state. He neglects, in other words, the natural roots of the artificial virtues, whose relations with each other are theorized so well by Hume. Like subsequent rationalists, such as his near-contemporary Spinoza, Hobbes's project was a sort of *moral geometry*, whereby moral theory (if not moral life) could be purged of all that was merely contingent, historical local and ephemeral. His adoption of the geometrical method encouraged him to ignore, when he did not altogether deny, the historicity of the various forms of moral and political life – a truth about them whose implications for philosophy were not elaborated upon until Hegel developed them (though they are prefigured in the work of Vico[13]).

Even though traditional criticism of Hobbes is misplaced, it is true that his thought is disabled by a rationalism which obscures the social and historical character of the phenomena which are the subjects of his investigations. It is far from being the case, however, that Hobbes's rationalism – which he may have derived from Descartes, and which is in sharp contrast with the empiricism of the nascent scientific revolution of the seventeenth century – leads him to a conception of government that anticipates twentieth-century totalitarianism. As Oakeshott has again put it,

> It may be said . . . that Hobbes is not an absolutist precisely because he is an authoritarian. His scepticism about the power of reasoning, which applied no less to the 'artificial reason' of the Sovereign than to the reasoning of the natural man, together with the rest of his individualism, separate him from the rationalist dictators of his or any age. Indeed . . . Hobbes, without being himself a liberal, had in him more of the philosophy of liberalism than most of its professed defenders.[14]

Oakeshott's observations are much to the point here. Hobbes was not a proto-totalitarian just because the task of the state was for him the limited, but crucial one of securing the peace of civil society. Though he denies that subjects possess fundamental rights to liberty of conscience (or to anything else, apart from self-preservation), Hobbes is insistent that the control of belief by the promotion of an orthodoxy is no part of the duty of a sovereign, and may well run counter to his only duty of keeping the civil peace. The sovereign *cannot* in any case (and here Hobbes is at one with Spinoza) control belief, since belief is not a matter of will. The sovereign *ought not* (because it is beyond the purposes of government) to interfere with opinion or expression, except in so far as it may threaten peace. Nothing could be further from Hobbes's intention (or more remote from anything he could have imagined) than the thought-police of twentieth-century totalitarian states, with their vast propaganda machines and interminable investigations into the ideological probity of their hapless subjects.

The paradox of the Hobbesian state is that, whereas its authority is unlimited, its duty is minimal – the maintenance of civil peace. Civil peace here comprehends more than merely the absence of civil war – it encompasses that framework of civil institutions whereby men may coexist in peace with one another, notwithstanding the diversity of their beliefs and enterprises and the scarcity of the means whereby these are promoted. Civil peace, that is to say, embraces the institutions of private property and contractual liberty, it presupposes a rule of law and it entails that the subjects of a civil society are bound to no common purpose but instead enjoy the freedom to pursue their own purposes. The liberties of the subjects of a civil society are not, as Hobbes conceives of them, absolute or inalienable rights, since they may be circumscribed by the requirements of a civil peace in the absence of which they are altogether extinguished. The liberties of the citizens of a civil society are not, in other words, preordained constraints on the authority of the state. They are intimated by the spirit of civil society itself, which is held together only by recognition of the authority of the sovereign and lacks any common purpose into whose service citizens might be coercively pressed. Maximal and indeed unlimited as the discretion of the Hobbesian state (or its ruler, which might be a person or an assembly) certainly is, its authority derives entirely from its contribution to the renewal in peace of civil society. It should be clear enough that the Hobbesian conception of the state in no way prefigures or models the *dirigiste* regimes which litter our century with their ramshackle institutions and wayward projects. What *does* the Hobbesian conception have to say, then, as to the character and condition of the modern state? Let us see.

The first and cardinal truth about the state in Hobbes's conception of it is that it possesses no resources of its own. It is sustained by a tax on consumption, which is used to pay for a volunteer army, to defray the costs of the legal system and to fund useful public works. The Hobbesian state is not a minimum state of the doctrinaire sort theorized in the writings of Herbert Spencer or Robert Nozick, and it does not exist to protect an imaginary set of inalienable (and incorrigibly empty) natural rights of the kind postulated in the philosophies of Locke and Kant. Hobbes's state has in common with the minimum state of classical liberalism, nevertheless, the crucial attribute that, since it has no assets of its own, it is not in the business of distributing resources to its subjects. As with the classical liberal state, the task of the Hobbesian state with regard to the institution of private property is finished when it has specified the practices and conventions which are to govern its acquisition and transmission and the procedures for arbitrating disputes about it. The task of the Hobbesian state, accordingly, is the demarcation or definition of property rights and the institution of a rule of law for their adjudication. Once that task has been discharged, nothing more remains to be done. Now consider the contrast with the modern state. Every modern state owns or controls vast assets and most modern states make a claim on approximately half of the wealth produced by the civil societies which it is their task to protect. Above and beyond the income required to fund national defence, the legal system and necessary charitable and public works, all modern states operate vast redistributional taxation and welfare systems, whereby income and wealth are transferred coercively across a welter of interests and pressure groups. Further, all modern states have entered into the business of wealth creation itself. By an array of tariffs and subsidies, unsound banking practices, and a plethora of regulations and regulatory authorities, modern states have invaded the wealth-creating activities of civil society to a profound degree, moulding and shaping the environment in which business enterprise functions, and in effect becoming vast business enterprises themselves. Finally, every modern state owns massive assets of its own, in nationalized or federally owned business, and in land and plant of all descriptions. As a result of the awesome economic power of the modern state, it pre-empts far more of the income and wealth of its citizens than ever feudal rulers were allowed (restricted as typically they were to one day in three of their serfs's labour) and it exercises an invasive influence on every area of social life unheard of since the absolutist monarchies of early modern Europe.

As to the causes of the growth of the modern state, we may speculate reasonably that much may be accounted for by the advent of mass democracy. The contemporary neo-Hobbesian theorists of the Virginia Public Choice School[15] have added much to our understanding of the expansionist imperative of modern states by their analysis of *the economics of political life*. The insight developed by the Virginia theorists is that, if we attribute to political actors the same sort of profit-maximizing motivation ordinarily ascribed to actors in the market-place, and if the environment in which political actors operate is that of a mass democracy in which powerful coalitions of interests form, then there will be an extremely powerful tendency for the size of government to grow, and its control over civil society to increase. For it will almost always be advantageous for politicians to extend benefits to existing and new interest groups rather than to curtail or withdraw them, since the losses to concentrated and collusive groups of such defunding will always be politically more significant than gains to widely dispersed groups. In modern mass democracies, accordingly, states tend overwhelmingly to service private interests rather than protect or promote the public interest. Contrary to the classical theory of the state as the provider of public goods – goods, that is to say, which in virtue of their indivisibility and non-excludability must be provided to all or none – *modern states are above all suppliers of private goods*. Whereas in the Hobbesian conception, the state exists to supply the pure public good of

civil peace, the modern state exists in practice to satisfy the private preferences of collusive interest groups. In so doing, it has become distracted
from, and has largely defaulted on its central functions of keeping the peace
and keeping in good repair the institutions of civil society.

The transformation of the modern state from a guardian of the public
interest and supplier of public goods – which it was, in Britain and the
United States, substantially until the First World War – has had profound
implications for civil society. Its chief impact has been to weaken the
vitality of the autonomous institutions which are the life-blood of civil
society. Charitable organizations, trade unions, educational institutions,
and large sectors of cultural life, which had hitherto enjoyed a significant
measure of independence from government have been increasingly drawn
within the influence or control of the state. The sphere of free individual
activity, the sphere of contractual liberty, has waned, as the sphere of
hierarchical organizations, the sphere of status, has waxed. This is the
baleful process identified by such classic writers as Maine and Acton, and
illuminated in our own time (in different but mutually enriching idioms) by
Hilaire Belloc's *The Servile State* and F.A. Hayek's *The Road to Serfdom*.
It is the process – well advanced in all modern states, but reaching its
terrifying completion in the totalitarian states of the Communist blocs,
which I shall consider at the close of these reflections – whereby the free
subjects of civil society are transformed into dependent functionaries or
vassals of the state.

The consequences in modern democracies of the erosion of civil society
by an expansionist state has everywhere been the outbreak of *a political
war of redistribution*. From being an umpire which enforces the rules of the
game of civil association, the state has become the most potent weapon in
an incessant political conflict for resources. Its power is sought, in part
because of the vast assets it already owns or controls, but also because no
private or corporate asset is safe from invasion or confiscation by the state.
From being a device whereby the peaceful coexistence of civil association
is assured, the state becomes itself an instrument of predation, the arena
within which a legal war of all against all is fought out. The rules of the
game of civil association – the laws specifying property rights, contractual
liberties and acceptable modes of voluntary association – are now themselves objects of capture. Corporate interests and pressure groups are
continuously active, by lobbying, colonization or cooption of regulatory
authorities, or just plain corruption, to mold these rules to suit their own
interests. Often enough, they are constrained to do so defensively, in the
sure knowledge that if they do not alter the legal and regulatory framework
to their advantage, their competitors will amend it against their interests.
Civil life soon comes to resemble the Hobbesian state of nature from which

it was meant to deliver us. As it has been restated by several recent commentators,[16] Hobbes's state of nature has many of the characteristics of the Prisoner's Dilemma explored in game theory, in that in it agents are compelled to act against their own interests because of the uncertainty they confront about the future conduct of others and the likelihood that others will be similarly constrained to adopt self-destructive policies. Most typically, agents in a Prisoner's Dilemma are constrained to attack or cheat others because of the rational suspicion they have of others' future conduct towards them. The Hobbesian state is the classical solution of the Prisoner's Dilemma in that the Hobbesian contract, by providing for agreed-upon coercion to obey known rules, releases its covenanters from destructive conflict into the peace of civil life. In the modern state this order of things is reversed. Individuals and enterprises are constrained to organize collusively so as to capture the interventionist state, if only because they know that if they do not, others will. As a result, their energies are distracted from production, and displaced into the political struggle for redistribution. The end result of this metamorphosis, in its extremity, can only be the impoverished and brutish life portrayed by Hobbes in the state of nature.

Matters have not yet gone so far in the major Western democracies. The examples of Argentina under the Peronist dictatorship, or of Britain under the last Labour Government, should however caution us against over-complacency. Indeed, in subtler and less obvious ways, the stagnation produced by the weakening of civil society and the overexpansion of the state are increasingly evident as the United States follows Europe into a sort of economic sclerosis, the result of which can only be further ill-judged interventionism. The transformation of the modern state from a guardian of civil association, whose conflict and best theorizing is found in Hobbes's *Leviathan*, into a corporatist Behemoth, has implications which extend far beyond the economic realm. The political war of redistribution is itself only a facet, if the most insistent and easily perceptible one, of the debility and weakness of modern government. The other arena of conflict in the modern state is doctrinal rather than economic, and manifests itself in the pathology of contemporary legalism. Once again a contrast with the Hobbesian conception is instructive. In civil society as theorized by Hobbes – and, for that matter, though less lucidly and profoundly, by Locke and Burke – all subjects possess the same liberties under the rule of law. Only the sovereign itself, as maker of law, may go beyond it, when the necessities of his responsibility as keeper of the civil peace so dictate. The liberties embedded in civil association are the old liberal freedoms – the freedoms of occupation, conscience, contract, association and so on. In exercising these freedoms, citizens create a myriad of intermediary associations and spontaneous institutions in which the life of civil society is expressed.

Whether they be working men's friendly societies, gentlemen's clubs, monastic retreats, missionary societies or eleemosynary organizations, these spontaneous formations can each embody their own *ethos* while keeping to the letter and spirit of civil association. They depend for their existence and renewal solely on the commitment of their members, and none enjoys any special privileges over the rest. At any rate, this was the situation in England, the United States and most of Europe for most of the time from the late seventeenth century until the First World War. In the modern state, what intermediary institutions and voluntary associations seek from government is not equal freedom under the rule of law, but political recognition and legal privilege. More, they seek a political endorsement of the values and norms which their organizations embody and express. What is most profoundly characteristic of social life in the modern state relates to that aspect of human nature most conspicuously neglected by Hobbes – its propensity to collective identification. In the civil societies of nineteenth-century Europe and America, it seemed that this propensity could be fully satisfied, without recourse to political coercion, through the spontaneous formations of voluntary association. (Perhaps personal identities were more sturdy in those days, and less in need of the dubious sustenance of political recognition.) In twentieth-century democratic states, we see the need for collective identification finding overtly political expression in the form of *contending projects for the political protection of cultural identity*.

This is the true significance of the manifold exercises in affirmative action, anti-discrimination policy and minority rights which disfigure and devalue much contemporary legislation. They are only incidentally, if at all, remedies against injustice or past wrongs. They are projects of collective self-assertion, which seek to entrench and privilege a specific identity by legal and political means. My expression 'legal and political means' should be noted here, for it is intended to mark one of the most characteristic vices of the modern state, which is the politicization of legal process. In the United States, this has occurred through a ruinous inflation of the rhetoric of rights, whereby every moral and political dispute and debate is cast in the legalistic idiom of rights discourse. Accordingly, the courts, and for that matter, the entire procedure of judicial review, have become theatres of doctrinal conflict, in which rival political and cultural movements contend through the medium of an intellectually bankrupt tradition of rights discourse as to the proper content (never the appropriate extent) of state intervention in civil life. Conflicts of interests and ideals which were hitherto reconciled – as they still are reconciled, in the few benighted polities (such as Great Britain and New Zealand) where the virus of rights discourse has not yet become endemic – by bargaining, compromise and the political arts are in the United States intractably contested through the processes of law. Distinct communities and ways of life which had once been constrained to such a mutual accommodation by moderating their claims on each other and on government have an incentive to engage in all-out legal and political conflict. Litigation substitutes for political reasoning, and the matrix of conventions, subterfuges, and countervailing powers on which any historic civil society must stand is weakened or distorted. This, it is worth repeating, is the real significance of the incessant contestation in universities, churches, municipalities and federal courts as to the 'rights' of ethnic minorities, 'alternative lifestyles' and feminist women. They concern, not the rightful extension to individuals denied them of the liberties and immunities enjoyed by others in equal freedom under the rule of law, but rather the political self-assertion of collective identities, each of which seeks privileges and entitlements which cannot in their nature be extended to all. So far gone is the United States in this degradation of law – which is the capital on which civil society must draw for its daily support – that it is not hard to envisage the United States as heading for an Argentine-style nemesis, in which economic weakness, over-extended government and doctrinal excess compound with each other to lay waste the inheritance of civility.

The worst nemesis of the modern state is not to be found in the Western Democracies. It is not even that found in the so-called developing or Third World, where arbitrarily constructed nation-states have completed the dis-location of traditional ways of life under the aegis of a Eurocentric ideology of modernization. It is in the Communist world that the true contrary to a Hobbesian state has come about. There the overriding imperative is not peace, but ideological uniformity and the totalitarian reconstruction of social life according to Marxist-Leninist dogma. Under such circum-stances, there cannot be the autonomous institutions which make up a civil society, nor any sphere of individual liberty under the rule of law. The coercive power of the state invades every nook and cranny of social life, penetrating and weakening even the family, perhaps the ultimate unit on which civil society stands. Two points are especially noteworthy when contrasting the Hobbesian state with Communist states. First, and most often neglected, is the *lawlessness* of life in Communist states. In the absence of an independent judiciary and of proper legal procedures, and given the ubiquitous presence of agencies prepared to wield extra-legal coercion at their own discretion, no one can be sure of protection by the law, or even know what the law may be. As an inexorable consequence, not only are civil liberties impossible to exercise securely, but even the pre-requisites of modern economic lifestyle – well-defined property rights and reliably enforced contracts, for example – are ill-provided for. It is these deprivations, as much as the extravagant Titanism of its central planning apparatus, which account for the intractable waste, malinvestment and sheer poverty which distinguish Soviet life.

Soviet totalitarianism is distinguished not only by the poverty it inflicts on its subjects but by the war it compels them to wage upon each other. This war of all against all among Soviet subjects is only the reverse side of the civil war – the war on civil society – that the Soviet power has waged since it struck the first blow in the Bolshevik *coup d'état*.[17] Since wealth, education and health care are all in Soviet society *positional goods* – goods whose radical scarcity means that their enjoyment or possession by one entails their exclusion from others – each subject of the Soviet order must contend with others in struggling to obtain them. In this respect Soviet society, like Hobbes's state of nature, is a vast Prisoner's Dilemma, with each being constrained to act against his own interest and, thereby, directly or indirectly, to reproduce the order (or chaos) in which he is imprisoned. Thus Soviet subjects are compelled to compete with each other in climbing the rungs of the *nomenklatura*, pursuing the ordinary goods of life by party activism or, *in extremis*, by informing or denouncing one another, and so renewing daily the system that keeps them all captives. If cooperation is found anywhere in Soviet society beyond the enclaves in which traditional values of love, family piety and religious devotion are still alive, it is perhaps in the enormous black, informal or parallel economy, where much that permits the ordinary subject to stay afloat is transacted. Yet even this nexus of voluntary exchanges has its dark side in that, by mitigating the depredations of the Soviet planning system, it enables it (with the indispensable nourishment of repeated inputs of Western capital and technology) to reproduce and perpetuate it. The promises offered by Gorbachev's project of *perestroika* are in all probability entirely delusive. Every material incentive of the Soviet economy constrains its subjects to collaborate in recreating it, with all of its unavoidable poverty and repression. It is a salutary thought for the Western liberal mind that no Communist state has yet definitely tolerated the re-emergence of civil society. In Poland the countervailing authority of the Church may have for the time being succeeded in forcing a retreat on the part of the totalitarian state, and in China we witness a genuinely bold experiment whose outcome, however, remains unknowable. So far, alas, we have no unequivocal reason for supposing that the indissoluble linkage between a state of nature and a lawless government, once it has been forged, is other than stable and self-perpetuating.

What of the prospects of the Western democracies? It cannot be said that recent projects of streamlining overextended government and returning many of its powers to the autonomous institutions of civil society, have done more than slow or retard the twentieth-century tendency to ever-more extensive government intervention. Neither the Thatcher government nor the Reagan administration has succeeded in its project of withdrawing government decisively from economic life and so restoring vitality to independent institutions. Their project, like that of similar governments elsewhere in the world, has been hampered by the inheritance of interventionism which they have faced in a burden of debt, overregulation and persistent inflation. The ultimate obstacle to the restoration in practice of a Hobbesian form of government may, however, not be economic at all. The resistance of the modern state to confinement within the Hobbesian functions of keeping the peace and maintaining civil society has its origin in the humanistic hubris which animates the political religions of our time. Given the waning of genuine transcendental faith, and its supplanting by secular orthodoxies or religions from which the transcendent content has been all but emptied, the modern liberal mind cannot accept that the state is a desperately modest device, which does not offer salvation, but only a barrier against the worst impediments to a tolerable human life. In the Hobbesian conception, the state is but a makeshift shelter against the primordial evils of the human lot. In its protective shadow, we may hope for many forms of excellence to thrive. But the peace of civil association in a limited state conceived on Hobbesian lines can only make such excellence a possibility, it cannot guarantee it. It is in the attribution to it of the character of *a political providence* that the dilemma of the modern state lies. Its resolution requires the relinquishment of the liberal illusion that the state can be more than a necessary precondition of a good life whose excellences will always be at risk.

> Here, in civil associations, is neither fulfillment nor wisdom to discern fulfillment, but peace. . . . And to a race condemned to seek its perfection in the flying moment and always in the one to come, whose highest virtue is to cultivate a clear-sighted vision of the consequences of its actions, and whose greatest need (not supplied by nature) is freedom from the distractions of illusion, the Leviathan, that *justitiae mensura atqua ambitionis elenchus*, will appear an invention neither to be despised nor over-rated.[18]

The *new Hobbesian dilemma* of the modern state is that, in becoming the prey of liberal dogma and the focus of a political war of redistribution, it has become weak even as it has grown larger, and has neglected its true tasks as it has become the servant of impossible dreams. It remains to be seen whether a reversion to a Hobbesian humility, in which the state is at once small and strong, is itself only a nostalgic vision, a dream that haunts an age, like Hobbes's, that is deafened by the clamour of barbarous religions and possessed by a longing for peace.

2 Santayana and the critique of liberalism

The thought of George Santayana has never had a wide influence. Both the style and the substance of his philosophy go against the current of twentieth-century sensibility and whatever echoes his philosophical writings had among his contemporaries have long since faded into silence. Neglect of Santayana's work by professional philosophers and by educated opinion is unfortunate for many reasons. His prose style – condensed, aphoristic and ornate at the same time – is beautiful and unique in twentieth-century philosophical writing, bearing comparison only with that of such earlier, and very different philosophical stylists as David Hume. Again, though his work never formed part of any recognized tradition or school, Santayana's contributions to a range of philosophical disciplines – the theory of knowledge and scepticism, metaphysics and ethics – still contain something from which we can learn, if only we are ready to read him with intellectual sympathy. His contributions to these subjects have been ignored, partly as a result of the vulgar academic prejudice according to which anyone who can write exquisitely must be a *belle-lettrist* or prose poet rather than any sort of serious thinker, and partly because the idiom of Santayana's writings consorts badly with that of the analytic schools which have dominated Anglo–American philosophy for most of our century. The chief reason for neglect of his thought, however, probably lies in the circumstances of his own life. It is in any case lamentable that his works are rarely seriously studied nowadays, since we are thereby deprived of his thoughts on society and government, which encompass one of the most profound and incisive critiques of liberalism ever developed. It is a symptom of the intellectual temper of our times that one of the very few systematic studies of Santayana's philosophy to be published in recent years omits altogether any consideration of his political philosophy.[1] It is hard to resist the suspicion that Santayana's political thought is not only unknown to modern opinion, but (where it has even been heard of) deeply unfashionable and indeed thoroughly uncongenial. For this reason alone, it may well have much to teach us of the ironies and limitations of the ruling liberal world view.

The circumstances of Santayana's life were uncommon, and are more than usually relevant to the understanding of his thought. Born in Spain in 1863 of Spanish parentage, Santayana retained his Spanish nationality throughout his life and (though in fact he left Spain at the age of nine) always regarded himself as a Spaniard. He was nevertheless educated in the United States, wrote all his philosophical works and his poetry in English, and had his only long-term association with a university, as a student and later a professor, at Harvard. Santayana's intellectual temperament, aloof, ironical and poetic, had little in common with that which, then as now, dominated American culture, and he became increasingly disaffected with American life. His distance from, and even disdain for, American culture was evident to his colleagues at Harvard, and reciprocated by his polar opposite there, William James, whose earnest, optimistic and sermonizing outlook was outraged by Santayana's detachment, and who expressed his condemnation of the style and substance of Santayana's thought famously when he called it 'the perfection of rottenness'. Santayana's colleagues were stupefied and outraged, when in 1911 he acted upon his estrangement from American life and academic culture by resigning his professorship at Harvard and departing forever for Europe, where he lived the life of an independent scholar, residing in hotels and eventually a convent, and remaining productive until the year of his death in 1952. There can be little doubt that Santayana's repudiation of the academic milieu in which philosophical inquiry had become professionalized and institutionalized, together with his indifference to the moralistic and world-improving sensibility which animated much in American thought and life during his lifetime, reinforced the neglect of his work engendered by its peculiarities of tone and content.

Immensely erudite though he was in the history of philosophy, Santayana appears to have been uninfluenced by any of the thinkers he studied. In his later years, he tended to represent himself as a spokesman for a human orthodoxy, as sceptical as it was naturalistic, which had hitherto rarely found a voice, and then chiefly in poets, such as Lucretius. His philosophical development is easily summarized. Aside from his doctoral dissertation on Lotze's philosophy, his first significant publication was in aesthetic theory. *The Sense of Beauty*, published in 1896,[2] contains many of the themes which were to pervade his writings over the next half-century and more – and, most particularly, an analysis of a spiritual value in naturalistic, bodily and partly sexual terms which at no point descends to a crude reductionism. The distinctive Santayanian conjunction of a sturdy

Lucretian materialism about that which exists with a strong affirmation of the spiritual reality of a realm of essences, is already manifest in this very early work, and is worked out in systematic detail in Santayana's first major philosophical statement, *The Life of Reason*,[3] published in five volumes in 1905–6. Santayana's metaphysical doctrine, a rather obscure and perhaps ultimately incoherent combination of a materialist ontology with a pluralist theory of essences, was further elaborated in the four volumes of his *Realms of Being*,[4] published between 1927 and 1942. In addition to these major treatises, Santayana published many collections of essays, of which *Winds of Doctrine* (1913)[5] and *Soliloquies in England and Later Soliloquies* (1922)[6] are among the most notable. *Winds of Doctrine* contains Santayana's coruscating and devastating assessment of the early philosophy of his friend Bertrand Russell, in which he comments on Russell's belief – derived from G.E. Moore, and later abandoned by Russell under the impact of Santayana's criticism – that there are objective moral qualities in no way dependent upon the constitution of human beings for their content – by observing that

> For the human system whisky is truly more intoxicating than coffee, and the contrary opinion would be an error; but what a strange way of vindicating this real, though relative, distinction, to insist that whisky is more intoxicating in itself, without reference to any animal; that it is pervaded, as it were, by an inherent intoxication, and stands dead drunk in its bottle![7]

Santayana's Soliloquies are noteworthy in that they contain some of his most penetrating analyses of the failings of liberalism, and of the transformations of opinion wrought by the catastrophe of the First World War. The main themes of Santayana's political philosophy are scattered throughout these and other essays, but it receives a complete and magisterial statement in his *Dominations and Powers*, which appeared a year before he died.

What are the most essential elements in Santayana's political thought, and how do they bear on his critique of liberalism? We find the very kernel of Santayana's rejection of liberalism in his observation that

> this liberal ideal implies a certain view about the relations of man in the universe. It implies that the ultimate environment, divine or natural, is either chaotic in itself or undiscernible by human science, and that human nature, too, is either radically various or only determinable in a few essentials, round which individual variations play *ad libitum*. For this reason no normal religion, science, art or way of happiness can be prescribed. These remain always open, even in their foundations, for each man to arrange for himself. The more things are essentially

unsettled and optional, the more liberty of this sort there may safely be in the world and the deeper it may run.[8]

Santayana here illuminates the central dogma of modern liberalism, unreflectively and stubbornly held – the dogma that human nature is a fiction, a chaos or an unknowable thing, so that it is not unreasonable for each generation to start life afresh, to try every experiment in living again and await what comes of it. The sceptical dogmatism of the modern liberal mind is at the furthest remove from the outlook of the ancients, for whom human nature was in most essential respects knowable and fixed, a stable matrix within which variations among individuals and peoples might safely occur. For the ancients, accordingly, liberty was not a fundamental right to indeterminacy, founded on chaos, but a very definite thing:

> When ancient peoples defended what they called their liberty, the word stood for a plain and urgent interest of theirs: that their cities should not be destroyed, their territory pillaged, and they themselves sold into slavery. For the Greeks in particular liberty meant even more than this. Perhaps the deepest assumption of classic philosophy is that nature and the gods on the one hand and man on the other, both have a fixed character; that there is consequently a necessary piety, a true philosophy, a standard happiness, a normal art. . . . When they (the Greeks) defended their liberty what they defended was not merely freedom to live. It was freedom to live well, to live as other nations did not, in the public experimental study of the world and of human nature. This liberty to discover and pursue a natural happiness, this liberty to grow wise and to live in friendship with the gods and with one another, was the liberty vindicated at Thermoplyae by martyrdom and at Salamis by victory.[9]

Classical liberty, for Santayana, was the freedom of self-rule, in which civilized peoples pursued the arts of life in the assurance that knowledge of the human good was (within limits, like everything else) achievable. Liberal freedom, on the contrary, is the freedom of inordinacy, an hubristic compound of antinomian individualism with a sentimental humanism which the Greeks would have despised had they been decadent enough to be able to imagine it. The contrast between classic freedom and the freedom of liberal modernity is clear enough, but it should not lead us into misinterpreting Santayana's moral vision and political perspective. Santayana, like the Greeks, believed human nature to be a stable and knowable thing, with definite limits and a bounded range of variations. He differed radically from the Greeks – at least, from the dogmatists among them, such as Aristotle – in his conception of the status and content of the human good. For Santayana, the human good was as various as the diverse kinds of human beings who achieved it or failed to realize it. There is not one supreme good for all men – contemplation, say, as Aristotle would have it, or a life of work and prayer, as for Aquinas – nor is there a single form of collective life, such as that of the *polis*, in which human flourishing may occur. Instead there is a constrained but legitimate diversity of goods, individual and collective, and it is a tyrannous impulse in political philosophy (well exemplified in modern liberalism) to elevate any of them to the status of *summum bonum*. Just as the good life for an individual may be one of bourgeois productivity or aristocratic leisure, religious piety or the pleasures of the senses, so monarchy and republicanism, free enterprise or the feudalism of a traditional social order may be equally lawful facets of the human good. What the human good encompasses in any one time or place is a matter for study and deliberation, not legislation, and there is always a margin of contingency and caprice in it, which no theory can tame. What is definitely excluded by Santayana's moral outlook is not the partial relativity or indeed the limited subjectivity of the good, which he affirms, but instead its infinite variability, its unknowable openness to unheard-of novelty, its plasticity and malleability by human will and the utopian or reformist imagination.

What is excluded by Santayana's moral conception is, in short, *progress*. It is not that Santayana, in a spirit of misanthropic perversity, denies that human arrangements are ever improvable. Nor does he subscribe to radical relativism: he does not deny, but affirms, that there are better and worse forms of government, virtues and vices that are common to all men. Santayana departs from the parochial dogmatism of the classic Greek moralists when, in the tradition of Democritus and Lucretius, he insists on a legitimate variety of mores and ways of life, but he nowhere endorses the heresy of liberal toleration – the heresy that there is nothing to choose between traditions and cultures. His rejection of progress has other and more reasonable grounds. In the first place, even when incontestable improvement takes place in human affairs, there is nothing inevitable about it; it occurs as a matter of chance or human will, and it is always reversible. As Santayana puts it:

> Progress is often a fact: granted a definite end to be achieved, we may sometimes observe a continuous approach towards achieving it, as for instance towards cutting off a leg neatly when it has been smashed; and such progress is to be desired in all human arts. But *belief* in progress, like belief in fate or in the number three, is a sheer superstition, a mad notion that because some idea – here the idea of continuous change for the better – has been realized somewhere, that idea was a power which realized itself there fatally, and which must be secretly realizing itself everywhere else, even where the facts contradict it.[10]

The idea of a law of progress, or of an all but irresistible tendency to general improvement, is then merely a superstition, one of the tenets of the modernist pseudo-religion of humanism. Even if such a law or tendency existed and were demonstrable, the liberal faith in progress would for Santayana be pernicious. For it leads to a corrupt habit of mind in which things are valued, not for their present excellence or perfection, but instrumentally, as leading to something better; and it insinuates into thought and feeling a sort of historical theodicy, in which past evil is justified as a means to present or future good. The idea of progress embodies a kind of *time-worship* (to adopt an expression later used by Wyndham Lewis) in which the particularities of our world are seen and valued, not in themselves, but for what they might perhaps become – thereby leaving us destitute of the sense of the present and, at the same time, of the perspective of eternity. The idea of progress has yet another radical fault. It supposes that there is a constant standard by which improvement may be measured, or at any rate a consecutive series of such evolving standards. Now it is true that human beings, like other animal species, have certain needs in common, and their lot is improved the better these needs are satisfied. But in the human species, if not in other species, the satisfaction of these basic needs evokes others, and changes the standards whereby future improvement may be measured. Nor is this self-transformation of mankind by the satisfaction of its needs a linear or one-dimensional process, since different individuals and peoples in different historical and cultural milieux suffer it differently. And its effects are not always beneficent in terms of human well-being:

> It is perhaps only in transmissible arts that human progress can be maintained or recognised. But in developing themselves and developing human nature these arts shift their ground; and in proportion as the ground is shifted, and human nature itself is transformed, the criterion of progress ceases to be moral to become only physical, a question of increased complexity or bulk or power. We all feel at this time the moral ambiguity of mechanical progress. It seems to multiply opportunity, but it destroys the possibility of simple, rural or independent life. It lavishes information, but it abolishes mastery except in trivial or mechanical efficiency. We learn many languages, but degrade our own. Our philosophy is highly critical and thinks itself enlightened, but it is a Babel of mutually unintelligible artificial tongues.[11]

Whereas it pervades modern culture, especially in America (where it animates much that passes there for conservatism), the idea of progress is naturally most at home in liberalism. It is the central irony of modern liberalism that a political creed devoted to liberty (as it was with the classical liberals, with Tocqueville, Constant, Madison and the Scottish

Enlightenment) should by way of the idea of progress come to subordinate liberty to the promotion of general welfare. 'The most earnest liberals', as Santayana observes, 'are quickest to feel the need of a new tyranny: they are the first to support vast schemes of world improvement, reckless of their concomitant effects on the liberty which an earlier generation of wiser liberals prized'. 'They [the most earnest liberals]' Santayana tells us, 'save liberal principles by saying that they applaud it [the new tyranny] only provisionally as a necessary means of freeing the people. But of freeing the people from what? From the consequences of freedom'.[12] Nothing in Santayana's analysis suggests that this metamorphosis in liberalism from a creed of liberty to a creed of progress through a new tyranny was avoidable, or is somehow (as latter-day classical liberals such as Hayek imagine) now reversible. Nor does he suppose the present regime of welfare-state or corporate-capitalist liberalism (as we would now call it) to be stable or enduring. 'They [the liberals] were no doubt right', he says, 'to be confident that the world was moving toward the destruction of traditional institutions, privileges and beliefs; but the first half of the twentieth century has already made evident that their own wealth, taste and intellectual liberty will dissolve in some strange barbarism that will think them a good riddance.'[13] The liberal age is, then, for Santayana most definitely a transitional one: its ruling conceptions of progress and liberty degraded, confused or incoherent, its benefits in the growth of wealth and knowledge doubtful and precarious, and the stability of the social order on which this expansion of human powers depended fragile. The question arises: by what, in Santayana's view, might liberalism be replaced?

Whatever he thought might supplant liberalism, Santayana was clear that it would not be an extension of liberalism in some other form: for, as he says, 'if any one political tendency kindled my wrath, it was precisely the tendency of industrial liberalism to level down all civilisations to a single cheap and dreary pattern'.[14] A post-liberal epoch, if one were to come about, and mankind not simply relapse into barbarism, would not be the anarchic Utopia that has always been a temptation of liberalism, and which is naively theorized in the writings of those ultra-liberals, the anarchists, such as Fourier and Proudhon, and, in our own day, the epigones of libertarianism. If anything, a post-liberal age would be the exact opposite of such a play-filled Utopia. It would, to start with, shed itself of that spirit of individuality, virtually unknown among the Greeks and Romans, which is the gift of Judaism and Christianity to our civilization. Santayana perceives, what is repressed in modern culture, that liberalism and the other political religions of our age are only the illegitimate offspring of the Judeo-Christian tradition, itself only the repression (in precisely the Freudian sense) of our religious needs and sensibility, while political religions – liberalism just as much as Communism – are only the return of the repressed needs for transcendence and the sacred. If, as the *philosophes* of the French Enlightenment hoped and projected, European culture were to shed its Christian inheritance, it would likely shed its individualism along with it, and the result would be far from that dreamt of by liberal theory:

> Health and freedom . . . if recovered against the lingering domination of Christianity, may reserve some surprises to the modern mind. The modern mind is liberal and romantic; but a state of society and a discipline of the will inspired by pure reason would be neither romantic nor liberal. It would be sternly organic, strictly and traditionally moral, military, and scientific. The literary enemies of Christianity might soon find reason to pine for that broad margin of liberty and folly by which Christianity, in merry Christian times, was always surrounded. They could have played the fool and the wit to better advantage under the shadow of the Church than in the social barracks of the future; and a divided public allegiance, half religious and half worldly, might have left more holes and cracks to peep through than would the serried economy of reason.[15]

Santayana himself seemed hardly to regret the passing of that spirit of individuality which Christian faith had nurtured and sheltered. Without sharing the primitive fantasies of Enlightenment rationalism, he inclined to welcome a sort of ideal paganism in which religions would be candidly accepted as local varieties of poetry, and the relativity of piety would become a commonplace. The political form of this post-liberal epoch would be a universal empire. Himself entirely a marginal man, through the prism of whose thought were refracted many national cultures – Spanish, English and American, among others – Santayana rightly abominated the tribalistic passions associated with the modern nation-state. The form of economic and social life he commended, one simpler, more local and more frugal than that of liberal societies, was to be protected by the framework of a global peace. His political ideal, and his prescription for a post-liberal order, is an idealized version of the ancient polity, and is well characterized in an essay of 1934, 'Alternatives to liberalism':

> The ancients were reverent. They knew their frailty and that of all their works. They feared not only the obvious powers bringing flood, pestilence or war, but also the subtler furies that trouble the mind and utter mysterious oracles. With scrupulous ceremony they set a watchtower and granary and tiny temple on some gray rock above their ploughed fields and riverside pastures. The closed circle of their national economy, rustic and military, was always visible to the eye. From that little

stronghold they might some day govern the world; but it would be with knowledge of themselves and of the world they governed, and they might gladly accept more laws than they imposed. They would think on the human scale. . . . In such a case, holding truth by the hand, authority might become gentle and even holy.[16]

Santayana's conception of a post-liberal regime, which has great strengths as well as disabling weaknesses, has been criticized from a variety of standpoints, some more vulgar than others. It has been attacked as proto-Fascist, but this is surely a baseless criticism, with nothing to support it save that Santayana was living in Fascist Italy at the time he published 'Alternatives to liberalism', and may have thought the Mussolini regime preferable to the realizable alternatives. The criticism of Santayana's post-liberal vision as proto-Fascist is indefensible, if only because there are unequivocal evidences in his writings of his repudiation of Fascist doctrine and practice. It is hard to interpret the following passage from *Dominations and Powers* as other than an explicit critique of the vulgar Nietzchean pretensions of the Fascist leaders:

> Can it be that these *Realpolitiker* have forgotten the rudiments of morals, or have never heard of them? Are these supermen nothing but ill-bred little boys? . . . The oracular Zarathustra, become prime minister, will sit at his desk in goggles, ringing for one secretary after another. . . . Poor superman! As things get rather thick about him, will he regret the happy irresponsible days when, in the legend of a Borgia, he could publicly invite all his rival supermen to a feast, in order to have them poisoned at his table? Or will he remember how, distracted by the heat and nobly fearless, he drank the poisoned wine by himself, and perished instead most horribly? Ah, those bold romantic crimes were not really more satisfactory than the entanglements of this official slavery. Both are vanity. And in that case, what follows? It follows that these wild ambitions (though some lovely thing may be summoned by them before the mind) are themselves evil, at least in part; and that the misguided hero, like a Damocles or like a poor ghost-seeing and witch-hunting Macbeth, will lose his soul in gaining a sorry world, and his wishes, once attained, will horrify him. These are trite maxims, and elementary: but I am talking of children, to children: a pack of young simpletons led by some young scoundrel.[17]

The real criticisms of Santayana's vision lie elsewhere. There is in the first place a decidedly arcadian quality about his conception of a post-liberal order. It is not only post-liberal but also post-industrial. It is an obvious, but also a decisive objection to such a conception, that it is incompatible with the maintenance of the world's existing population. A less crowded world might well be a better one, our present population may indeed be unsustainable over the long run; but it is clear that it will be reduced only by a catastrophe in whose wake not only the industrialism Santayana despised, but also the possibility of a post-industrial order on the lines Santayana envisaged, would be effectively destroyed. There are also deep difficulties in Santayana's account of the imperial framework within which the local and rustic economies he prized would be sheltered. His idea of a liberal universal empire has many attractions. It acknowledges, what contemporary liberal thought cannot admit, that it is the empire, and not the nation-state, that is the most appropriate political order for the realization of the goals of individual liberty, the rule of law and peace among diverse communities. As Santayana, outlining the idea of a universal liberal empire, asks rhetorically:

Why not divorce moral societies from territorial or tribal units, so that membership in these moral societies, as in a free Church, should be voluntary, adopted only by adults with a full sense of their vocation for that special life, and relinquished, without any physical hindrance, as soon as that vocation flagged, or gave place to some other honest resolution?[18]

Again, he observes:

Under such a Roman peace, as we call it, a further development is possible. Not only may each nation, within its territory, preserve its language and laws and religion under the imperial insurance, but where different nations have intermingled, as often happens in great cities or in provinces vaguely open to any immigrant, each may preserve all its moral idiosyncrasy, its speech, dress and domestic life, side by side with the most alien races.[19]

Santayana's conception has the decisive merit of acknowledging the political form of empire to be that best suited to maintaining the condition of cultural pluralism – the variety of traditions and ways of life – advocated, but everywhere discouraged, by modern liberalism. There is nevertheless a vast unreality in his speculations on how this liberal universal empire might come about. He rejects the idea that it might be a Pax Americana, on the plausible ground that the very virtues of American culture – its evangelizing reformism and incorrigible optimism – ill fit the United States for an imperial role. More disputably, he rejects the British Empire (as it existed when he first wrote in 1934 what later became a chapter in *Dominations and Powers*[20]) as a model for a Roman peace on the ground that the British had a contemptuous indifference to the customs of their subjects that rendered them odious as rulers. (The observation may be correct, but the British attitude to their subjects had many points of affinity with that of the Romans to theirs – and it at least protected the British from the folly of a messianic liberalism.) Most absurdly, Santayana – not perhaps without a motive of perversity – suggests that 'Perhaps the Soviets might be better fitted than any other power to become the guardians of universal peace'. With the utmost naivete (or disingenuousness), he goes on:

> In regard to tenure of land, and to the management of industry and communications, if the management were competent, a universal communism, backed by irresistible armed force, would be a wonderful boon to mankind. . . . The Soviets would . . . have to renounce all control of education, religion, manners and arts. We are proletarians and unwilling Communists only in the absence of these things; in their presence, we all instantly become aristocrats. Everything except the mechanical skeleton of society . . . must be left to free associations, to inspiration founding traditions and traditions guiding inspiration. The local attachments of such culture are important, and a just universal government would not disturb them. Each nation or religion might occupy, as private property under the common law, its special precincts or tracts of lands; or it might live locally intermingled with other nations and religions; but each in its own home would be protected from annoyance, and free to worship its own gods with the homage of a complete life fashioned in their image.[21]

Here Santayana's enmity to liberal culture has led him radically astray. It was evident to any judicious observer by the mid-thirties, and certainly by the time *Dominations and Powers* was published, that the Soviet system was perhaps the most destructive of local traditions, and above all of religious practices, in human history, and everywhere implemented a revolutionary Communist messianism incomparably more tyrannous than any identified by Santayana's strictures against the United States. For this reason, if we were ever to fall under a *Pax Sovietica*, it would be the peace of universal impoverishment and barbarism, and not the just liberal empire of which Santayana dreamt.

In truth, Santayana was unable to give an account of any plausible alternative to liberal society. He comes very close to admitting this, when in 'Alternatives to liberalism' he identifies liberal society as a transitional state, but cannot specify its successor:

> liberalism presupposes very special conditions. It presupposes a traditional order from which the world is to be emancipated. It presupposes heroic reformers, defying that order, and armed with a complete innate morality and science of their own by which a new order is to be

established. But when once the new order has been thoroughly destroyed, that kind of heroic reformer may well become obsolete. His children will have no grievances and perhaps no morality. Even the abundance of their independent sciences, without an ultimate authority to synthesize or interpret them, may become a source of bewilderment. Add interracial war and a breakdown in industry, and there may seem to be occasion for turning over a new leaf. As to what may be found, or may come to be written, on the next page, no political programme can give us any assurance.[22]

If this diagnoses sapiently the ills of the liberal condition, Santayana is here (confessedly) unable to offer us a panacea for them. His *critique of liberalism*, however, retains considerable value. Santayana illuminated the chief danger to liberal society in liberalism itself – in a political religion of *man-worship* which had lost the humility, and indeed the scepticism, that informs the historic Western religions. With its incoherent doctrine of progress, its inordinate and antinomian individualism, and its ultimate subordination of the claims of liberty to those of an imaginary general welfare, liberalism has at length become the enemy of the civil society it once sought to theorize. As Santayana puts it in his *apologia pro mente sua*:

> My naturalism and humanism seemed to them [Santayana's liberal readers] to give *carte blanche* to revolution: and so they do, if the revolution represents a deeper understanding of human nature and human virtue than tradition does at that moment; but, if we make allowance for the inevitable symbolism and convention in human ideas, tradition must normally represent human nature and human virtue much better than impatience with tradition can do; especially when this impatience is founded on love of luxury, childishness, and the absence of any serious discipline of mind and heart. These are the perils that threaten naturalism and humanism in America.[23]

Santayana's political thought, despite his hopes of it, does not encapsulate any continuing amount of a post-liberal order. What it most powerfully suggests is the necessity (if the historical inheritance of liberal society which is our patrimony is to be preserved and not squandered) of abandoning the romantic culture of limitless hubris for a classical ethos of limitation and constraint. We are not, each of us, as our liberal culture encourages us to imagine, limitless reservoirs of potentiality, for whom the past is an incumbrance and the future a blank sheet of possibility. We are finite, mortal selves, burdened by the evils of our history and the miseries natural to the human condition, who achieve excellence and a measure of well-being only in so far as we accept the disciplines of civilization.

Political wisdom is the sad business of prescribing for ordinary mortals, not a recipe for adventures in infinite freedom. This humble view was not unknown to the early theorists of liberalism, but it has been repressed and obliterated by modern liberalism, with its hallucinatory perspectives of open-ended world improvement and global betterment. We conceive government aright, if we conceive it as Hobbes did, and as some of the early liberals did, as a shelter against the worst of evils, civil war and the reversion to nature. It is the limited government which we inherit as our tradition – now far gone in desuetude – which protects us against such misfortune, and which thereby allows the emergence of civil society as the artificial remedy for our natural imperfections. Santayana reminds us, in his remarkable essay on Freud, that

> The human spirit, when it awakes, finds itself in trouble; it is burdened, for no reason it can assign, with all sorts of anxieties about food, pressures, pricks, noises and pains. It is born, as another wise myth has it, in original sin. And the passions and ambitions of life, as they come on, only complicate this burden and make it heavier, without rendering it less incessant or gratuitous.[24]

Political wisdom lies in accepting this human lot, not in seeking to wish it away by vast projects of reform. We alleviate the human lot as best we can by repairing and renewing the traditional institutions we have inherited, where these are themselves founded on a sane awareness of the human condition. For us, this means returning to the minute particulars of the liberal inheritance of civil society that we are at present frittering away in crazed fads and fashionable experiments. Our danger is that, like an ageing debauchee who has grown used to drawing on his patrimony, we may not realize until it is too late that it has largely been consumed. It is such a condition of which Santayana wrote when he observed that

> we sometimes see the legislator posing as a Titan. Perhaps he has got wind of a proud philosophy that makes will the absolute in a nation or in mankind, recognising no divine hindrance in circumstances or in the private recesses of the heart. Destiny is expected to march according to plan. No science, virtue or religion is admitted beyond the prescriptions of the state. . . . Here is certainly an intoxicating adventure; but I am afraid a city so founded, if it could stand, would turn out to be the iron City of Dis. These heroes would have entombed themselves in hell, in scorn of their own nature; and they would have reason to pine for the liberal chaos from which their satanic system had saved them.[25]

The final insight of Santayana's critique of liberalism is not that liberal society is inherently a transitional state of things. It is that the nemesis of liberal society is its self-destruction by liberal ideology – by a frenzy of theorizing which is willing to lay waste the inherited institutions of a liberal order – limited government, private property, the rule of law – for the sake of an imagined improvement of the human condition. Santayana's insight – an insight he did not always himself grasp, captivated as he sometimes was by delusive visions of radical alternatives to liberal society – is that the preservation of the liberal inheritance has as its most necessary condition a comprehensive disenchantment with liberal theory. Unless we can shake off the hubristic illusions of liberalism, the spiralling decline in our civilization is unlikely to be arrested, and may well end in the collapse of liberal society itself.

3 Hayek as a conservative

Is Hayek a conservative? Many conservatives will quickly deny that he can be anything of the kind. They will cite the famous Postscript to his *Constitution of Liberty*,[1] 'Why I am not a Conservative', in which Hayek disavows the characteristically conservative project of using the power and authority of the state to protect endangered moral traditions and to shore up threatened social hierarchies, and argues instead for a version of the classical liberal view, that the primary task is the curbing of all such political power. Conservatives often invoke this and other evidence in support of a picture of Hayek as a doctrinaire defender of liberty, whose general outlook is little different from that of Nozick, or a partisan of *laisser-faire* such as Milton Friedman. It is a short step from radical libertarianism to an ideology which, while centred on the defence of the market economy, is neglectful of the moral tradition which makes a market economy possible. Hayek's conservative critics take this step on his behalf, and condemn him accordingly.

It is not hard to show that the standard conservative view of Hayek's thought is ill-founded. Hayek's position is distinctive, to be sure. It embodies the best elements of classical liberalism and also suggests a criticism of many conventional conservative positions. At the same time it derives from some of the most profound insights of conservative philosophy, and puts them to work in an original and uncompromising fashion.

We must recall Hayek's birth and education in the last two decades of the Hapsburg Empire, in whose defence he fought as an aircraftman, and remember that his formative intellectual influences were not those of English-speaking empiricist philosophy. Central among these influences were the philosophies of Immanuel Kant and Ernst Mach, variants of which dominated the intellectual life by which Hayek was surrounded in his youth. Hayek's thought also bears the imprint of the Viennese critics of language: of Karl Kraus, of the now almost forgotten Fritz Mauthner, and of Hayek's half-cousin, Ludwig Wittgenstein. The reflections of these men on the decay of intelligence wrought by the perversion of language have always inspired Hayek, and have played a part in many of his later writings. (Hayek's devastating analysis of the expression, 'social justice',[2] in which he illuminates its workings so as to make clear its lack of definite sense, may be best understood as continuing the Krausian tradition of resisting the modern idolatry of general words.)

Most importantly, though, Hayek's writings reflect his lifelong aspiration to come to terms with the debacle of the First World War, when the high civilization and the rule of law established in Hapsburg Austria-Hungary gave way to chaos and barbarism. As a result of this weakness, Europe has been engulfed by vast movements dedicated to the repudiation of the European inheritance. Hayek's attempt to synthesize the deepest insights of conservatism with the best elements of classical liberalism merits our closest scrutiny, if only because the experience which inspired it – the experience of an apparently inexorable drift to dissolution and barbarism in all the central institutions of society – may not be so far from our own. His researches into the ultimate sources of the current malaise of civilized authority led him deeply into the theory of knowledge and into philosophical psychology: for it is Hayek's view that the impossible ambitions spawned by contemporary culture arise from a false understanding of the human mind itself.

The well-spring of all Hayek's work in social philosophy and in economic theory is, then, a conception of human knowledge. Hayek's theory of knowledge can be understood, in the first place, as a sceptical variant of Kantianism. For Hayek, as for Kant, our knowledge is not based in incorrigibly known sensations,[3] and the empiricist attempt so to reconstruct it is forlorn. Our minds are no more passive receptacles for sensory data than they are mirrors for reflecting the necessities of the world: they are creative powers, imposing order on a primordial chaos by way of a built-in set of categories. Philosophy cannot hope to step outside these categories so as to attain a transcendental point of view, or to reach an Archimedean point of leverage from which to assess or reform human thought. For Hayek, as for Kant, philosophy is reflexive and critical rather than transcendental or constructive: it plots the limits of the human understanding but cannot hope to govern it.

Hayek's sceptical Kantianism has features, however, which take it far from anything that Kant could have accepted and which give to it a wholly distinctive turn. The organizing categories of the human mind are, for Hayek, neither immutable nor universal; rather they express evolutionary adaptations to a world that is in itself unknowable. Hayek's thought has here a real point of affinity with that of his friend Sir Karl Popper, who has long expounded a naturalistic and evolutionary theory, in which human knowledge is regarded as continuous with animal belief. More decisively, however, Hayek differs from Kant in denying that the governing principles of our minds are fully knowable to us. We will always be governed by rules of action and perception, which structure our experience and behaviour down to their last details, and some of which will necessarily elude our powers of critical inquiry. In recognizing these elements of our mental life – these 'meta-conscious rules' of action and perception, as he calls them[4] – Hayek identifies a limit to the powers of reason more severe than any Kant could have admitted. For if such rules exist, then (though we can at no point learn their content), we can be sure that critical thought itself is governed by them. Hence our own minds, no less than the external world, must in the end remain a domain of mystery for us, being governed by rules whose content we cannot discover.

Hayek is a Kantian, then, in denying that we can know things as they are in themselves, or can ever step out from the categories which govern our understanding. He goes further than Kant, in seeing the categories of our understanding as mutable and variable, and in some major degree un-knowable to us. Most distinctive in Hayek's sceptical and Kantian theory of knowledge, however, is his insight that all our theoretical, propositional or explicit knowledge presupposes a vast background of tacit, practical and inarticulate knowledge. Hayek's insight here parallels those of Oakeshott, Ryle, Heidegger, and Polanyi; like them he perceives that the kind of knowledge that can be embodied in theories is not only distinct from, but also at every point dependent upon, another sort of knowledge, embodied in habits and dispositions to act. Some of this practical knowledge is found in rules of action and perception imprinted in the nervous system and transmitted by genetic inheritance. But much of the most significant part of the practical knowledge expressed in our dealings with each other is passed on mimetically, in the cultural transmission of traditions or practices, some of which are bound to be inaccessible to critical enquiry. In all our relations with the social world we are informed and sustained by these elements of tacit knowledge, which we know to be pervasive in our thought and conduct, but whose content we can scarcely guess at.

In his own view, and surely rightly, Hayek's conception of the human mind as governed by rules, some of which must escape conscious scrutiny, has the largest consequences for social philosophy. For it entails the bank-ruptcy of the rationalist project, undertaken in different ways by Bacon, Descartes, and Spinoza, of subjecting the mind to a systematic purge of tradition and prejudice. We can never know our own minds sufficiently to be able to govern them, since our explicit knowledge is only the visible surface of a vast fund of tacit knowing. Hence the rationalist ideal of the government of the mind by itself is delusive. How much more of a mirage, then, is the ideal of a society of minds that governs itself by the light of conscious reason. The myriad projects of modern rationalism – constructivist rationalism, as Hayek calls it – founder on the awkward fact that conscious reason is not the mother of order in the life of the mind, but rather its humble stepchild. All of the modern radical movements – liberalism after the younger Mill as much as Marxism – are, for Hayek, attempts to achieve the impossible. For they seek to translate tacit knowledge into explicit theory and to govern social life by doctrine. But only tacit knowledge can engender government, and tacit knowledge may be lost by its translation into overt, propositional form. Hayek is here developing, in its political implications, a version of the thesis of the primacy of practice in the constitution of human knowledge. The thesis has a distinguished pedigree in the writings of a number of contemporary philosophers, of whom Oakeshott, Wittgenstein and Heidegger are perhaps the most notable.

The thesis of the primacy of practice leads Hayek to refine the argument that rational resource-allocation under socialism is impossible – an argument which Hayek inherited from his colleague L. von Mises. In his disputes with socialist economists, Mises had contended that, in the absence of market-pricing of all factors of production, chaos in calculation was bound to ensue, and could be avoided only be relying on world capitalist markets and domestic black markets. (Saul Kripke has noted[5] an interesting analogy between this argument of Mises's and Wittgenstein's arguments against the possibility of a private language – an analogy I can only remark upon, but not pursue here.) Hayek sees, as his colleague Mises did not, that the knowledge which is yielded by market pricing cannot be collected by a central authority or programmed into a mechanical device, not just because it is too complex, nor yet because it is knowledge of a fleeting reality (though this is closer to the nub of the matter), but rather because it is knowledge given to us only in use. It is knowledge stored in habits and in practice, displayed in entrepreneurial flair, and preserved in the countless conventions of business life. Unhampered markets transmit this knowledge, which is otherwise irretrievable, dispersed in millions of people. One may almost say that, for Hayek, this practical knowledge achieves a full social realization *only* when market-pricing is not interfered with. For – like much traditional knowledge – it is holistic, a property of the entire society, and not the private possession of any of its separate elements or members.

Hayek's case against socialist planning, and in favour of the unhampered market, rests upon these considerations rather than upon any Lockean theory of property rights, or upon a fanaticism for *laisser-faire*. The impossibility of socialism, and of successful intervention in the economy, is an *epistemological* impossibility (as well as a moral impossibility). His differences with Keynes, for example, are imperfectly understood if one does not grasp that the Keynesian macroeconomic manager must claim knowledge which Hayek insists is available to no one. The Keynesian planner may indeed achieve temporary successes, by exploiting money illusion and manipulating business confidence, but this is bound to be a short-lived victory. Such Keynesian policies work only in so far as they are contrary to established expectations which they cannot help eroding. Moreover, they take no account of the inevitable discoordination of relative prices and incomes. Governments can do next to nothing to remedy these consequences, since it is given to no one to know what is the correct relative price-structure. Hayek nowhere suggests that market failure is an apodictic impossibility; but he is surely on firm ground in arguing that it is in the unhampered operation of the market process itself that we have the best assurance of economic coordination.

Socialism and interventionism, then, are but long shadows cast by a false philosophy of mind. The order we find in society, no less than that which prevails in our own minds and bodies, is an undesigned order, and not a product of rational planning. The dominant superstition of the Age of Reason is the belief that vital social institutions – the law, language, and morality, as well as the market – must be or can become products of conscious contrivance and control, if they are effectively to serve human purposes. This modern superstition results from an anthropomorphic transposition of mentalistic categories to the life of society. Hayek's criticism echoes a distinguished line of antirationalist thinkers, of whom Pascal is perhaps the closest to him, in his celebrated distinction between *l'esprit de géométrie* and *l'esprit de finesse*. It is because the rational principles of social life are immanent in its practices that we cannot trust our reason in its speculative projections for reform.

This is why, especially in his later writings, Hayek attaches so great an importance to the spontaneous development of the law in the institution of an independent judiciary. He goes so far as to see, in the contemporary recourse to legislation, a major threat to liberty and to social stability. There is, indeed, an important analogy between Hayek's arguments for the impossibility of comprehensive economic planning and his criticism of a legal system that is dominated – as all now are – by statute. Just as no economic plan can approach the sensitivity and subtlety of the market process in integrating men's plans and achieving coordination in the use of resources, so statutory legislation cannot match the sensitivity of the common law in responding to and adjudicating the concrete problems of man's social existence. But the common law, which relies on the doctrine of precedent, cannot survive without a strong, independent and decentralized judiciary.

It is not that Hayek supposes that a modern state can altogether forswear legislation,[6] any more than it can wholly dispense with economic policy; but in both cases the balance needs to be redressed, in favour of spontaneous order, whether that of the market or that of the judicial process. The two issues of economic planning and the rule of law are therefore inseparably connected for Hayek. He sees clearly that the rise of the administrative state, together with the prevalence of grandiose projects for redistribution and social welfare, pose a major threat to the rule of law, and therefore to individual liberty. A government which seeks to regulate prices and incomes is bound to transfer large powers to administrative authorities. In the nature of things these authorities will exercise a terrifying discretion over the lives and fortunes of the citizens. Such authorities may clothe their arbitrariness in an ideology of social justice, or they may attempt to revive the doctrine of the Just Wage. But their decisions cannot be contained within the rule of law, for they crucially depend upon a claim to knowledge which no one possesses – a claim which, in the nature of things, cannot be adjudicated.

Aside, then, from the fact that policies of intervention in the market and in the provision of social goods tend to expand as their failures are recognized, such policies necessarily involve a transfer of authority over our lives to administrators effectively unconstrained by law, and often uninhibited by common moral sentiments. Hayek's criticism of the ambitions of the administrative and welfare states should be less implausible in conservative circles than it was when his *Road to Serfdom*[7] appeared. We can see now the accuracy of his prediction that the expansionist state will be captured by movements and professions whose outlook and interests are deeply at odds with the preservation of established ways of life.

What in turn may conservatives learn from Hayek's thought? His chief importance, I think, is that he has freed classical liberalism from the burden of an hubristic rationalism. He has thereby produced a defence of liberty which aims to reconcile the modern sense of individuality with the claims of tradition. Hayek shows that we are bound to rely primarily on inherited traditions of thought and conduct in all our dealings with each other. The inarticulate character of the great submerged part of our knowledge means that we always know far more than we can ever say. It also means, crucially, that the rational criticism of social life must come to a stop when it reaches the tacit component of our practices.

There is an uncomfortable lesson here for conservatives, since Hayek's diagnosis condemns the attempt to retard or reverse the flood of social change, no less than it undermines the reformer's desire to remodel society, according to some more 'rational' plan. Hayek would heartily endorse

Wittgenstein's remark, that trying to salvage damaged traditions by wilful effort is like trying with one's bare hands to repair a broken spider's web. The most we can do is to remove those artificial impediments to the vitality of our traditions which have been imposed by the state. And with its policies in education and housing, the state has surely been a far greater destroyer of traditions and communities than has the market.

Hayek's chief lesson for conservatives, then, is that it is a delusion to think that conservative values can be protected by a successful capture of the expansionist state. The damage done to social life by an invasive state is integral to its existence, and conservative governments are better occupied during their tenure of office in whittling down the state and in restoring initiative to the people, than in the futile enterprise of trying to convert the state's bureaucracies to a conservative view of things.

This is not to say that Hayek's thought is not open to legitimate conservative criticism. At times he seems to subscribe to a doctrine of historical progress which, though it was accepted by such conservatives as Burke and Hegel, cannot be endorsed by any twentieth-century conservative. Here I think we must turn to Michael Oakeshott's writings[8] for the insight that human history is not to be construed as a single evolutionary process, but rather as a series of distinct adventures in civilization. Although Hayek is perhaps right to see the conquest of the world by European individuality as an historical fate, which it is idle to wish away, he may be too ready to see this as a stage in a global progressive development. There is a faint echo in his writings, which a conservative would wish could not be heard, of the historical theodicy of the Enlightenment. This theodicy is an indefensible and indeed pernicious part of the inheritance of classical liberalism, which in most other respects we are wise to cherish.

Finally, Hayek's thought poses a dilemma for conservatives which few of them have yet come to recognize. The dilemma is found in his perception, especially in his later writings, that the modern development of age-old European moral and intellectual traditions has produced an outlook that is deeply destructive of civilized institutions. The peculiarly modernist outlook – a combination, I should say, of homeless moral passion with rationalist fantasy – is now so pervasive as to have acquired deep roots in popular sentiment and a secure place in virtually all the disciplines of thought. It results in what Hayek calls 'unviable moralities'[9] – systems of moral thought and sentiment incapable of sustaining any stable social order; in the bizarre intellectual constructs of contemporary sociology; and even, as in architecture, in a corruption of the practical arts. Taken together, these developments create a climate of culture which is profoundly hostile, not only to its traditional inheritance, but even to its own continued existence. We confront the phenomenon of a culture permeated throughout by a hatred of its own identity, and by a sense of its purely provisional character. This culture is not without sources in our most ancient religious and moral traditions – for example, in Platonic rationalism and in Christian moral hope.[10] In his writings on Mandeville, Hayek has made clear that the defence of the market economy may demand a far from conservative revision of ordinary morality.[11] His latest thoughts on the phenomenon of intellectual and moral inversion[12] suggest that he has illuminated what is, from a conservative viewpoint, an even greater problem: since much of contemporary culture is possessed by a death-wish brought on by pathological developments in some of our oldest traditions, a modern conservative must also be a moral and intellectual radical.

4   Oakeshott as a liberal

What may now be meant by the word 'liberal' is anyone's guess.
Michael Oakeshott[1]

The claim that the conception of political life that animates the thought of Michael Oakeshott, clearly one of the most original and profound British political philosophers since Hume and certainly this century's greatest conservative writer, is a liberal conception may seem unacceptably paradoxical or even wilfully perverse. Yet it is far from being novel. Commentators such as W. H. Greenleaf and Samuel Brittan have seen in Oakeshott's thought deep affinities with the intellectual tradition of classical liberalism; an entire paper (greatly admired by Oakeshott himself[2]) has been devoted to interpreting Oakeshott as a liberal theorist; and both of the two recent book-length studies of Oakeshott's work[3] characterize his outlook on politics as at least akin to that of a liberal. For all that, it still remains unclear just what sort of liberal Oakeshott might have been, what it was that he took from liberal thought and what he rejected, and how the liberal element of his thought coheres with the rest.

It is not too hard to be clear about what Oakeshott rejected in liberal thought. The liberal project of fixing, by way of a doctrine or a theory, the proper scope and limits of the authority of government, determinately once and for all, as it was attempted by Locke or Kant, J. S. Mill or, in our own time, by Rawls and Nozick, Oakeshott rejected as a prime example of rationalism in politics. From this point of view, liberalism is (or was) merely a species of ideology – of that rationalist abridgement of the contingencies and vicissitudes of practice that aspires to be, but can never succeed in becoming, an authoritative, prescriptive guide for practice. The proper tasks and limits of government cannot be determined by reasoning from first principles (supposing there could be such things); they can be established, always provisionally and never indisputably, only by reasonings that are circumstantial and which invoke precedents, judgements and practices that are already present in current political life. Oakeshott's rejection of the rationalist (or fundamentalist) element in liberalism expresses one of his most profound insights – that political deliberation and political discourse are closer in their character to conversation than they are to any sort of demonstrative reasoning. For Oakeshott, as for Aristotle, political discourse is a form of practical reasoning, and in virtue of that character can never issue in, or rest upon, the certainty found (according to Aristotle, at any rate) in the theoretical disciplines. Political discourse, then, though it may contain passages of argument, is not an argument, but a conversation.

Oakeshott's repudiation of this aspect of liberalism – perhaps its most definitive or constitutive – has far-reaching implications for the current understanding (or confusion) we have of the relations of political philosophy with political practice, and it contains lessons which, if we could learn them, might at least temper the barbarism into which political life has long since fallen among us. The first lesson is that the hubristic project of doctrinal or fundamentalist liberalism – the project attempted by all the liberal thinkers mentioned earlier of fixing the boundaries of government action by some principle or doctrine, be it *laissez-faire*, a specification of allegedly natural (but patently conventional) rights, or a list of basic liberties derived (as in Rawls and Dworkin[4]) from a conception of justice rooted only in the fleeting local knowledge of the American academic *nomenklatura* – embodies a mistaken conception of philosophy itself. Whereas philosophy can clarify the presuppositions or postulates of practice, and thereby perhaps in some degree illuminate it, it can neither found practice nor govern it. For it is practice that is always primordial. Accordingly, if philosophical inquiry has any practical effects or benefits, they are oblique, indirect and prophylactic. (And, of course, philosophy need have no other goal than the pursuit of understanding.) Oakeshott's conception of philosophy radically undermines the liberal foundationalist project, which seeks to circumscribe the authority of government by a theory. It also serves to chasten the ambitions of philosophers, who seem always to have been astonished that political life could proceed without their constant supervision.

Oakeshott's conception of political life as a conversation may have a prophylactic role to play in respect of the barbarization of political discourse and practice that in our day is far gone. The tendency of much in recent thought and practice has been to try to assimilate political discourse to some other, supposedly superior mode, and thereby to deny to political life its autonomy. This decline is, perhaps, farthest gone in the United States, where in the context of a common culture whose resources are fast depleting every political question is now couched in legalist terms. The idea of politics as a conversation in which the collision of opinions is moderated and accommodated, in which what is sought is not truth but peace, has been almost entirely lost, and supplanted by a legalist paradigm in which all political claims and conflicts are modelled in the jargon of rights. In such a context, not only is civilized political discourse virtually extinguished, but the legal institutions into which it is transplanted are corrupted. The courts become arenas for political claims and interests, each of them inordinate and resistant to compromise, and political life elsewhere becomes little more than bargaining and log-rolling. The result of the American assimilation of politics to law has, then, been the corruption of both. In the course of this development, the profound insights of the authors of *The Federalist Papers* into the limitation of government, not primarily by constitutional devices, but by the civic virtues of a free people that has in common a devotion to the culture and practice of liberty and which understands the ground of that practice to be the imperfectibility of our species, have been almost lost. In Europe, and in Britain, the virus of legalism has been less pervasive, but the presence of other ideologies more powerful. If socialism is everywhere on the wane, other ideologies are waxing – including ideological strands within conservative thought and practice, which ascribe to governments the objectives of restoring a lost moral consensus, of reviving a fragmented national integrity, or promoting maximal wealth-creation. Here the autonomy of political life is compromised by its attempted assimilation to the modes of discourse of history, economics or industrial management. If we could recover the understanding of political discourse Oakeshott has theorized for us, that understanding might – far more than the institution of what Oakeshott, in the magnificent and invaluable new edition of *Rationalism in Politics* published by Liberty Press of Indianapolis[5] and edited by Timothy Fuller, calls 'the absurd device of a Bill of Rights' – protect us from the inordinacies and invasiveness of the modern state.

What we have seen so far is that the rationalist projects of doctrinal liberalism, spawned by a false philosophy that pretends to govern rather than merely to struggle to understand practice, have had the effect of corroding our historical inheritance of civil society and of weakening traditional constraints on the activities of government. We have yet to see what Oakeshott retains of liberal thought. We find this, if I am not mistaken, in the understanding of civil life he develops in his conception of *civil association*, which may be taken to be the living kernel of liberalism, and the chief element in Oakeshott's thought in virtue of which it deserves the appellation 'liberal'. In his account of civil association, Oakeshott (as Wendell John Coats, Jr, shows in his admirable paper[6]) synthesizes a variety of seemingly disparate understandings, Aristotelian and Ciceronian, Roman and Norman, Lockean and Hegelian, to yield an account of that form of human association – emerging distinctively only in late medieval Europe, and never without opposition in any modern European state – in which men live together, not under the aegis of any common end or hierarchy of ends, but instead by their subscription to a body of non-instrumental rules, whereby they can (in all their variety and conflicting purposes) coexist in peace. Civil association has, from the first, had a rival in *enterprise association* – that mode of association constituted by shared adherence to a common objective, the mode of association animating an industrial corporation, say. What distinguishes a civil association from an enterprise association, most fundamentally, is that the former is purposeless in having no projects of its own, whereas the latter is constituted by its projects. For Oakeshott, this is to say that civil association is a form or mode of association that is non-instrumental and moral, whereas the latter's authority derives solely from the projects that animate it.

Oakeshott is clear that modern European states have always partaken of both modes of association. Rarely, if ever, has such a state been merely a guardian of civil association. As he observes: 'Modern history is littered not only with visions, in various idioms, of a state as a purposive association, but also with projects to impose this character upon a state'.[7] Like the minimum state of classical liberalism, civil association is an ideal type, or a limiting case, not found in the real world of human history. In historical fact, all modern European states have had elements – managerialist, mercantilist or corporatist – in virtue of which they have acquired the character of enterprise associations, and their role as custodians of civil association has accordingly been compromised. Indeed, it may be said of twentieth-century totalitarian states that they are nothing but enterprise associations, committed for that reason to the destruction of civil association. And one of the inheritances of liberal ideology, the idea of progress in history, has made it hard for any modern state not to claim for itself the role of an agent of world-betterment. Indeed civil association itself has been defended as a means to prosperity – a complete misunderstanding of it in Oakeshott's terms. One may say, in fact, that, though it has never been altogether silenced, the voice of civil association has in our century never been very loud: it has, most of the time, been shouted down by all those ideologies and movements that perceive the authority of he state only in its success in exploiting the earth's resources. It is this Baconian conception of the office of government that, in Oakeshott's view, pervades all contemporary conceptions of the state-as-enterprise-association, be they Fascist or Fabian, Marxist or Manchesterist in inspiration.

We can now see what Oakeshott's thought has in common with classical liberalism. For the classical liberal, the authority of the state did not depend on its contribution, if any, to economic growth, any more than it depended on the local cultural identity of its subjects. It depended on its being recognized, not in terms of desirable projects or particular cultural values, but in terms of law or justice – of *lex*. As Robert Grant has put it, in what is by far the most perceptive and illuminating account of Oakeshott's thought we possess, 'A *civitas* (or civil association) need not be culturally homogeneous (thought doubtless a degree of homogeneity will help). The only homogeneity which counts, and which is essentially "cultural", consists in a common disposition to value *lex* above one's local cultural identity.'[8] It is in his account of the authority of the office of rule as being formal or abstract in this fashion, then, not in his eloquent defence of individuality, that the most fundamental affinity between Oakeshott and classical liberalism is to be found. It shows him to have more in common with Kant, in the end, than with Burke or Hegel.

It may well be that it is precisely in its kinship with classical liberalism on the nature of the authority of the state that the Achilles heel of Oakeshott's political thought lies. Both assert that the authority of a modern state depends neither on its success in any substantive purpose nor on its relationship with the cultural identity of its subjects. Both claims are profoundly questionable. As to the former, less fundamentally important claim, it is a matter of brute historical fact that no government can, in any modern democratic state, long survive if it does not preside over sustained economic growth. For this reason, every modern government is inexorably drawn into the dreary business of aligning the economic with the electoral cycle: all are in some significant measure mercantilist or corporatist in practice. In short, all modern states are to a considerable degree enterprise associations. The project of effecting a radical disseveration of government from the conduct of economic life, which Oakeshott shared with the classical liberals, has in common with classical liberalism a quality otherwise entirely absent from Oakeshott's thought – namely, its Utopian character. The project of denying to the modern state its character as, in significant part, an enterprise association, is hardly a conservative one; if it could be achieved, the transformation of political arrangements thereby wrought would be little short of revolutionary. This is, in effect, tacitly acknowledged by Oakeshott, when in his most overtly political essay, 'The political economy of freedom',[9] he endorses the radical proposals advanced by the Chicago economist Henry Simons, in his *Economic Policy for a Free Society*.[10] More typically, the debacles of Thatcherism and Reaganism suggest that, for us, the enterprise-association state is an historical fate, which we may indeed strive to temper, but which we cannot hope to overcome.

The second claim – that the authority of a modern state does not depend on its subjects having a common cultural identity – is yet more questionable, and more importantly so. It is the claim, found in Kant and in much recent American constitutional theory, that the recognition of the state as embodying abstract or formal principles of law or justice is all that is needed for its authority. Recent history does little to support this claim. On the contrary, it may be observed that, in so far as a polity is held together by little else than allegiance to abstract principles or procedural rules, it will be fragmented and unstable, and its authority weak. The point may be made in another way. The idea that political authority could ever be solely or mainly formal or abstract arose in times when a common cultural identity could be taken for granted. For Kant as for the framers of the Declaration of Independence, that common cultural identity was that of European Christendom. In so far as this cultural identity is depleted or fragmented, political authority will be attenuated. We may see this ominous development occurring in microcosm in Britain, where a minority of fundamentalist Muslims that is estranged from whatever remains of a common culture, and which rejects the tacit norms of toleration that allow a civil society to reproduce itself peacefully, has effectively curbed freedom of expression about Islam in Britain today. We may see the same somber development occurring on a vast scale in the United States, which appears to be sliding inexorably away from being a civil society whose institutions express a common cultural inheritance to being an enfeebled polity whose institutions are captured by a host of warring minorities, having in common only the dwindling capital of an unquestioned legalism to sustain them. Oakeshott himself observes that

> the authority of an office of rule remains always a delicate matter of current belief. It must be able to survive a rainy day; it must be proof against disapproval and ridicule of the performances of the office and it cannot be bought with good works; it hangs like a drop of dew upon a blade of grass.[11]

For us, who live in an age of mass migrations and fundamentalist convulsions, and who are witness of the dependency of political allegiances on resurgent local cultural identities, ethnic and religious, in the post-Communist world, it is clear that the authority of a state that (however inevitably compromised by its engagements as an enterprise association) acts as a custodian of civil association is frailer even than Oakeshott perceived, and cannot long do without the support given it by a common culture.

It may be that what Oakeshott has taken from the liberal tradition about the authority of the state is not, finally, his most important borrowing from it. It is his conception of civil association, in which the historical European inheritance of civil society is cleansed of its theoretical accretions, such as notions of natural rights, *laissez-faire* and the minimum state, that is likely to be his most enduring gift to political philosophy, and it is one that can plausibly be termed liberal. In Oakeshott's writings on education,[12] again, one finds a conception of education that is liberal in the best sense of that term – a view of education, not as the inculcation of an orthodoxy, the acquisition of information or the transmission of useful skills, but as initiation into a cultural inheritance in the course of which we learn to become civilized conversants. If, in very unOakeshottian vein, we were to ask which element in his thought has most contemporary relevance, it would perhaps be his idea of a liberal education as an unchartered intellectual adventure, with no goal beyond its own inner *telos* – an idea which some of us may recognize in our pasts, but which is threatened now on every side, as much by managerial conservatism as by left-wing ideologues.

Of Oakeshott as a philosopher and as a man I have so far said nothing. As to his philosophy, ably and comprehensively expounded by Paul Franco[13] (himself a pupil of Timothy Fuller, America's best Oakeshott scholar), it is his pluralist affirmation of the diversity of modes of discourse and experience, of moralities as vernacular languages whose nature it is to be many and divergent, and of the miscellaneity of practice, which no theory can hope to capture, that embodies his most distinctive contribution to philosophy. It is only in the later Wittgenstein (whose thought, though influenced by Spengler, lacks the deep historical consciousness of Oakeshott's) that we find a comparable critique of traditional rationalism and contemporary positivism. It is a comment on the current state of academic philosophy that Oakeshott's contribution to it has gone almost unnoticed.

If one had to express the spirit of Oakeshott's thought in a single phrase, one might say that it is *a critique of purposefulness*. The image of human life that Oakeshott conveys to us is not that of a problem to be solved or a situation to be mastered, it is the poetic (and religious) image of our being lost in a world in which our vocation is to play earnestly and to be earnest playfully, living without thought of any final destination. For those of us lucky enough to have known the man, Oakeshott's writings will always evoke the memory of his conversation, in which intellectual passion commingled with a fathomless gaiety, and the dry reasonings of philosophy became, as in the dialogues of Socrates, dialectical, and at last lyrical.

5 Buchanan on liberty

INTRODUCTORY REMARKS

It may appear that I utter a truism when I say that the thought of James Buchanan is a contribution to political economy. What is intended by that remark, however, is far from truistic: it is that Buchanan's thought is political economy in the classical sense – the sense in which it was practised by the Scottish School, and in which it encompasses social philosophy as well as positive or explanatory economic theory. For, as with Smith, Ricardo or indeed Marx, Buchanan's thought composes a system of ideas and comprehends a distinctive perspective on man, government and society. This is to say that, even without regard to its specific content, Buchanan's thought is distinguished by its resistance to contemporary disciplinary fragmentation and has thereby helped to reconstitute political economy in its classical sense.

Buchanan's system of ideas is an original contribution to political economy, synthesizing elements from a diversity of traditions – Wicksellian, Austrian, and Chicagoan – into a powerful and coherent body of theory. It is not my brief here to attempt to assess Buchanan's system as a whole – a task that is in any case well beyond my powers. My brief is the narrower, but nonetheless fundamental one of explicating and assessing the place of liberty in Buchanan's work. For, whereas Buchanan's thought diverges from classical liberalism in ways that are important and instructive, there can be no doubt that, like classical liberal thought, Buchanan's is animated by a profound moral concern for the fate of free men and free peoples. Indeed, if one were to characterize Buchanan's thought as a research programme in the Lakatosian sense, one would most appropriately characterize it, at any rate in its normative dimension, as an inquiry into the constitutional preconditions and constraints on individual liberty.

My examination of Buchanan on liberty will have six elements, or phases. I shall, first, consider Buchanan's *indeterminate contractarianism*, a form of contractarian political theorizing that has decisive advantages over the more prescriptive theories of Gauthier and Rawls. Second, I shall discuss Buchanan's *critical constructivism* – his version of critical rationalism and his critique of libertarian and Hayekian conceptions of spontaneous order and institutional evolution. Third, I will examine his *subjectivist conception of economic value*, together with his associated criticism of welfare economics and his general repudiation of notions of efficiency in resource allocation as the principal functional value of market institutions. Fourth, I shall investigate the foundational ethical values of Buchanan's theory of liberty, arguing that the ethical foundation of his system is not value subjectivism but a species of *value individualism*. Fifth, I shall explicate Buchanan's *perspectivist epistemology*, in terms of which he is able to defend the utility of the construct of *Homo economicus* without attributing to it total explanatory or predictive power. Sixth, and last, I shall address the most explicitly normative aspect of Buchanan on liberty, when he tries to specify the conditions under which we may move 'from Hobbesian despair to Humean hope'.

I shall not here attempt to summarize my conclusions, except in their most general respects. The proceduralist character of Buchanan's indeterminate contractarianism has three sources, in his mitigated scepticism and critical constructivism and in his value-individualism. This value-individualism, in turn, is the ethical postulate on which his defence of liberty stands. The postulate of value-individualism (the content of which I later try to specify) is a distillation of the Western historic experience of individuality. For this reason, Buchanan's contractarianism, like that of the later Rawls, presupposes the cultural inheritance of Western individualism, with its roots in Christianity and Stoicism. I shall argue that it is this cultural context of Buchanan's individualism – a context which both shapes and constrains the liberal individual – that enables him to make the hazardous passage from Hobbesian despair to Humean hope. In the last context, I shall argue that even the gossamer-thin veil of ignorance or uncertainty which Buchanan's contractarian constitutionalism comprehends is unnecessary when we come to theorize the real-world attempts of people in specific historic contexts to contract new constitutional settlements and institutions.

INDETERMINATE CONTRACTARIANISM

Much recent contractarian theorizing suffers from a fundamental incoherence. On the one hand, contractarian theorists expose evaluative individualism, seeing in the autonomy of the individual the ultimate, foundational postulate of contractarian political philosophy, and they conceive of agreement under appropriately characterized circumstances as necessary and sufficient for legitimate authority. At the same time, most recent contractarian theorists, notably Rawls and Gauthier, have made a requirement of strict determinacy in the upshot of contractarian deliberation a major part of the agenda of contractarianism as a distinctive method in political philosophy. In Rawls, indeed, the requirement is for unique determinacy, as well as fixity, in the principles that emerge from the original position. As I have argued elsewhere,[1] this agenda of determinacy, which figures prominently in all of Rawls's work, coheres badly with the recognition, explicit in his later work, that both the *telos* and the content of contractarian reasoning arise against the background of a specific, historically concrete cultural and political tradition – roughly, the liberal tradition of constitutional democracy, with its underlying matrix of individualist moral culture. For, if the content of contractarian methods is given by an evolving and mutable historical tradition, it is hard to see why the upshot of the method should be unalterably fixed, nor how it can reasonably be expected to be uniquely determinate in its central results (such as the specification of the basic liberties).

There is a basic incoherence in Rawlsian contractarianism, however, that applies to it in all of its versions, and not only in its later, Deweyan-historicist variety. This is an incoherence in its attempt to combine a conception of justice as *au fond* purely procedural with the requirement that contractarian method yield principles that are strictly, if not uniquely determinate solutions to the dilemma of contractarian choice. The fusion of these irreconcilable demands gives to Rawlsian contractarianism an inherent instability, marked by many observers, and commits Rawls to a member of questionable, arbitrary and often plainly *ad hoc* manoeuvers (such as the attribution of extreme risk-aversion to the hypothetical contractors) in the effort to derive the principles (such as the Difference Principle) on which he has independently settled. A methodological agenda having these incompatible desiderata also opens his entire enterprise to rival interpretations, such as the cognitivist and voluntarist interpretations developed in Sandel's useful critique.[2] This ambiguity in the interpretation of Rawls's theory derives directly from its methodological contradictions, and has subversive implications for Rawls's attempt to achieve a vantage point of neutrality in respect of questions of realism in moral epistemology.

The ambiguities and difficulties in Rawls's work I have specified are in no way intended to undermine Rawls's achievement in reviving contractarian political philosophy as a systematic discipline. They are meant to underscore the inappropriateness of the requirement of determinacy in outcome for a methodology that is contractarian and individualist in political philosophy. It is here, I believe, that Buchanan adheres more faithfully than Rawls to the individualist value theory that is the ultimate postulate of contractarian theorizing, when he explicitly disavows any agenda of determinacy for the output of contractarian deliberation. As Buchanan has stated his rejection of determinacy in canonical form:

> *Any* distribution of tax shares generating revenues sufficient to frame the relevant spending project passes Wicksell's test, provided only that it meets with general agreement. Analogously, *any* set of arrangements for implementing fiscal transfers, in-period, meets the constitutional stage Wicksellian test provided only that it commands general agreement.

> This basic indeterminacy is disturbing to political economists or philosophers who seek to be able to offer substantive advice, over and beyond the procedural limits suggested. The constructivist urge to assume a role as social engineer, to suggest policy reforms that 'should' or 'should not' be made, independently of any revelation of individuals' preferences through the political process, has simply proved too strong for many to resist. The scientific integrity dictated by reliance on individualist values has not been a mark of modern political economy.[3]

And, as Buchanan has stated of the divergence between his contractarian perspective and other, more constructivist perspectives:

> The whole contractarian exercise remains empty if the dependence of politically generated results upon the rules that constrain political action is denied.[4]

The superior consistency of Buchanan's indeterminate contractarianism gives it a decisive advantage over others, whether (as in Rawls) they seek to specify an egalitarian upshot constrained by a classical liberal prioritizing of liberty, or whether, as in Narveson's recent work,[5] they seek to ground a minimal state, devoid of distributional functions, in contractarian reasonings. Buchanan's approach is at once more internally rigorous and at the same time less methodologically hubristic, in leaving the upshot of contractarian deliberation to practice, as constrained by appropriate rules.

CRITICAL CONSTRUCTIVISM

Buchanan's approach resists the uncritical constructivism, with its implied posture of godlike omniscience, that animates much in current political economy and political philosophy, even in some of their contractarian varieties. It differs from these uncritical constructivist approaches in leaving to practice the upshot of contractarian choice at the post-constitutional level. It differs from them, also, in working with a veil of ignorance that is gossamer-thin,[6] screening out only knowledge of the contractors's final social state, and in taking the status quo distribution of assets as its point of departure.

Buchanan rejects uncritical constructivism, even in the forms in which it animates some contractarian theorizings, for the reasons I have given, and to this extent he shares with Hayek a common conception of the species of rationalism – ultimately Cartesian in inspiration, perhaps – that he wishes to reject. Buchanan's evaluation of constructivism differs from Hayek's, however, in several essential and fundamental respects. In the first place, as an economist versed in public goods theory, the Prisoner's Dilemma and free-rider problems, Buchanan perceives that in the absence of mutually agreed and enforced constraints there is no guarantee, and indeed no plausible prospect, of consistently cooperative behaviour. The spontaneous coordination of human activities, manifest in the market-place, for example, is not a primordial phenomenon; it is an artefact of legal and political institutions that protect private property and facilitate contractual exchange. Buchanan recognizes, in a way that Hayek only rarely does, that there is little or nothing that is spontaneous in the social orders from which we benefit; they are institutions, built up over the generations, often with great difficulty, and they stand in need of recurrent repair and reform. As a good scholar of Hobbes, Buchanan is more than sceptical about the spontaneity of social order: without denying that cooperative conventions may evolve without design or intention, he is emphatic that social interaction in the absence of clearly demarcated property rights formulated and enforced by a common power is likely to result in a *spontaneous disorder* that is wasteful and harmful to all. This point may be made in another way. Buchanan recognizes that the undesigned coordination of the market-place presupposes the public goods of peace and law – goods that, because of their public character, can be provided only by the state. In this he is at one with Hobbes, who rightly saw peace as the necessary condition, not only of commodious living, but of liberty.

Buchanan's difference from Hayek may be stated in another, and perhaps more radical way. Buchanan refuses to follow Hayek in generalizing the observed phenonemon of undesigned coordination in market exchange and extending and developing that observation into a theory of cultural evolution or institutional Darwinism. For Buchanan, as for myself, such generalization and extension are misguided, since they neglect the institutional conditions under which alone an undesigned order that is beneficent may be expected to emerge. The undesigned coordination that manifests itself as order in the market does so in virtue of specific tendencies in markets, and it is beneficent because voluntary exchange is not typically zero-sum. Once the institutional framework to the market is absent, however, we have no reason whatever for supposing that competition – be it competition of individuals for resources, or tradition or practice, or of states – should be beneficent. To argue that it is so, is to assume or presuppose an entire body of functionalist social theory that is at odds with the methodological individualism Hayek elsewhere expouses. It is to presuppose both a unit of selection, and a mechanism for selection, akin to those in Darwinian evolutionary theory, which have no real analogies in social theory. With Hayek, Buchanan avows a mitigated scepticism, akin to Hume, and with Hayek's friend Popper, he conceives of reason as in essence critical and fallibilist rather than apodictic or axiomatic. Unlike Hayek (or Polanyi), Buchanan is unwilling to allow that our historical inheritance of received institutions should be exempt from critical appraisal. In fact, he maintains, we have no option, we are bound, given the desuetude of many of our institutions, and their colonization by collectivist interests, to subject them to critical assessment. Only an historical theodicy could give man's random walk in historical space the aspect of an orderly progression, when what is disclosed to the critical eye are rare episodes of freedom surrounded by long stretches of barbarism and tyranny. None of this is meant (by me or Buchanan) to deny Hayek's massive achievement in illuminating the epistemic role of the market in generating and utilizing dispersed (and often tacit) knowledge. It is simply to assert that we cannot rely uncritically on the tacit wisdom of inherited institutions, but must instead try to reform them with the aid of our best theorizing, when these institutions are in disrepair, and perhaps embody the tacit error or ignorance of generations of collectivism.

These methodological objections to the Hayekian synthetic philosophy, and to notions of spontaneous social order, have pertinent applications to contemporary political developments. In the relations between market capitalist orders and totalitarian command economies, there are game-theoretic predictions, and ample historical evidences, that competition may not promote market institutions, but may instead result in stable relations of parasitism which serve to reproduce, and even to strengthen, the totalitarian command economies. The limitations of institutional Darwinism are, however, perhaps most clearly evident in current developments *within* the Communist blocs. For there – in Poland, Hungary, the Baltic States, China, and perhaps in the Soviet Union – the inherited (or imposed) institutions of central planning are collapsing without the evolutionary emergence of successor institutions. True, in Poland and elsewhere, elements of civil society that were formerly repressed by totalitarian bureaucracy have successfully reasserted themselves in a spontaneous fashion, but the legal, political and economic framework of civil society cannot there emerge as a property of institutional evolution; it must be constructed, or else reconstructed in the wake of revolution. The would-be covenantors of the Soviet bloc countries are, in some respects, akin to the covenantors in Hobbes's state of nature, save that (as Z. Rau has noted[7]) it is a state of enslavement that they seek to escape from. (I have myself argued elsewhere that the dilemma of the subjects of a totalitarian order resembles the Hobbesian dilemma in that one of the constitutive features of totalitarianism, which it shares with the Hobbesian state of nature, is lawlessness[8]). Hayekian institutional Darwinism has, then, no application to historical contexts – like that of the Soviet bloc states – where extant institutions are bankrupt and lack even latent successors. Admittedly, also, public choice dilemmas may thwart the construction of new institutions, as conflicts of interest emerge within the opposition and in the nascent civil society; but it is still only the project of constructing a new social contract, as embodied in new or reconstructed institutions, that offers hope of exit from totalitarianism to a stable post-totalitarian order. In such circumstances, we cannot intrust ourselves to the providential designs of Burkean or Hayekian institutional evolution. Rather, armed with the best theory we can find, we must wager on a new social contract.

ECONOMICS, SUBJECTIVISM AND VALUE

The undesigned coordination of the market, together with its consequent contribution to human well-being, are to be explained by the fact that voluntary exchange – exchange, that is to say, conducted against a background of institutions defining and protecting private property rights and enforcing the terms of contractual agreements – is typically positive-sum. Without these background institutions, which are the matrix of the spontaneous order we observe in the market process, there is no reason to suppose that competition, or exchange, should be other than zero-sum, or even negative-sum. Indeed, it is precisely the character of the pre-legal state of nature, in which most resources apart from those consumed for subsistence are devoted to self-defence or to mutual predation, that such exchange as occurs need not be, and often is not, a benefit to both parties. In a market order that is constituted by the legal framework I have mentioned, on the other hand, there is a very strong presumption, grounded both in theory and history, that the constantly iterated act of exchange will benefit all parties to it.

To say this is to say that the market economy can be justified by its contribution to the well-being of the individuals who participate in it. It is of the utmost importance, both in my own judgement and in Buchanan's, as I understand him, that this defence of the market in terms of its contribution to human well-being not be conflated with a consequentialist or utilitarian conception of the market as maximizer of collective or aggregate welfare. We should resist this conflation, according to Buchanan, for several reasons. In the first place, the idea of aggregate or collective well-being involves a fallacy of conceptual realism – it confuses what is at best an heuristic fiction with reality, in this case the reality of discrete human individuals, each with their own distinctive desires, preferences and projects. This suggests a second reason for resisting the move from a well-being-based justification of the market to an aggregative consequentialist justification – which is the impossibility of aggregating individual preferences and satisfactions. Whereas comparative, on-balance judgements of social welfare may be feasible in limiting cases, Buchanan rightly insists that the pretensions of welfare economics founder on the incommensurability of the various components of the well-being of persons. To say this is not merely to reaffirm the classical (and in general insoluble) problems of making well-founded interpersonal utility comparisons. It is also to note the incommensurabilities that may arise among the components of even a single person's well-being.

Aggregative, consequentalist justifications of the market have had, as Buchanan has constantly reminded us, baleful results for theory and policy. In theory, they have sponsored the conception of economic science as having to do with wealth-maximization, or maximal allocative efficiency, or productivity, reinforcing the Communistic fiction that views the catallaxy of the market as akin to an hierarchical organization or household. In other words, aggregative conceptions have reproduced the disabling equation of market exchange with conceptions of maximization or economizing that weakened the foundations of the classical economics of the Scottish School. It is for this reason, among others, that Buchanan is an unequivocal subjectivist as to economic value. As against the classical economists, including Marx, Buchanan insists that economic value is not an inherent property of any sort, it is subjective – an aspect of the choices and experiences of individuals. And, since these choices encompass a multitude of incommensurables, there is no way of summing up subjective economic value into any judgement of collective or aggregate welfare.

In its uses in welfare economics, the aggregative conception has had a damaging effect on policy. Like the fiction of perfect competition, the aggregative models of welfare economics have encouraged policy-makers to consider intervention and regulation wherever markets depart from some theoretical norm of efficiency or maximization. They have thereby reinforced the vulgar academic perception of markets as impersonal processes, sometimes chaotic or defective but having a logic of their own, and of political processes as highly voluntaristic activities, barely constrained by economic interests or situational logic. Welfare economics has thus contributed to the neglect of the economics of bureaucracy, government and political life, and has tended to underestimate the importance of government failure. In the most general terms, it has seen market failure as an occasion for government intervention rather than for the reform of market institutions (by, for example, the creation of property rights where none have hitherto existed). The aggregative method of macroeconomics, and, in particular, of welfare economics, has an inherent collectivist bias, in that it seeks to enhance imaginary maxima rather than to reform or extend markets so as better to enable individuals to achieve their diverse and incommensurable goals. Buchanan has performed a signal service in setting theory and policy on the very different individualist agenda of reforming rules and institutions the better to facilitate the conditions of voluntary exchange.

VALUE INDIVIDUALISM

The result of Buchanan's subjectivism about economic value is that, taking market exchange as a system or process of reiterated transactions rather than as any single act, the efficiency of market institutions is redefined in procedural terms. It is the voluntaristic character of market exchanges, and not any assumptions about maximization or equilibrium, that assure their beneficent contribution to the human good. It is here that I advance, tentatively and provisionally, an interpretation of Buchanan's normative theory that diverges somewhat from his often repeated affirmation of a general value-subjectivism. Such subjectivism, with its distinguished Hobbesian and Humean pedigree, is eminently apposite, not only in economic theory, but also in political theory – at least, in the latter, as a counterbalance to the conception of politics as an activity devoted to the pursuit of truth on the model of truth-seeking and inquiry in the natural sciences. It is more questionable whether a Hobbesian value-subjectivism is presupposed or implied by Buchanan's political thought. Plausibly, the foundational value is not that of preference-satisfaction (in which the good is what is desired), but individual autonomy, conceived as an intrinsic good. This, Kantian or Spinozistic, interpretation of Buchanan's system is entirely consilient with subjectivism as to economic value. It is also compatible with a version of realism or objectivism as to the status of the value of autonomy – although, as I shall later argue, this value is best interpreted in Buchanan's thought as a distillate of our cultural tradition. My principal point here, however, is that there is a position in normative theory, value-individualism, that is distinct from value-subjectivism but consistent with a subjective view of economic welfare. This individualist view, which regards persons as themselves ultimate values (and not, as in utilitarianism, passive receptacles of impersonal value) allows for a defence of the market in terms of its contribution to the autonomy and well-being of individuals. And it does so without making any concession to the aggregative fiction of consequentalism. For as in Hume, where this argument has its classical formulation, the market benefits each, and thereby all – not, as in Bentham, benefitting a spurious collectively and so (fallaciously) each.

In this account, the value of preference-satisfaction is not (as in some varieties of value-subjectivism) ultimate, but derivative. It derives from the value of autonomy, or, more precisely perhaps, of the autonomous person. Buchanan favours market freedom under the rule of law, ultimately, as I interpret him, not because preferences are most often satisfied under such institutions, but because such institutions best protect and respect autonomous individuals. That this distinction is not a trifling one is seen when we consider those circumstances when populations appear not to value the autonomy they may enjoy as individuals, and instead prefer the security they expect (and regularly fail to receive) from arbitrary and unconstrained government. It will be a later argument of mine that the normative basis of Buchanan's political thought presupposes an inheritance of individualist moral culture that may be on the wane. At this stage, I wish only to comment that, whereas value-individualism may be affirmed in a way that is neutral as to questions of moral epistemology, it is for that reason compatible with a form of moral realism of the sort that Buchanan has rightly rejected in other contexts.

EPISTEMOLOGICAL PERSPECTIVISM

Buchanan's resistance to macroeconomic modelling, and his extension of microeconomic theory to political and other behaviours and institutions, involves his invoking as an explanatory and predictive construct the conception of *Homo economicus*. In terms of the methodology of the Virginia School of Public Choice, of which he is the principal expositor, this entails the adoption of a principle of parity of motivation in the economic and the political realms, where 'economic' designates the sphere of explicit market exchanges. Another way of expessing this methodological move is to say that using the model of *Homo economicus* results in the development of an economic theory of human behaviour in bureaucratic and political institutions. It comprehends specifying and theorizing the incentive structures, time preferences and goals of agents within these 'non-economic' contexts and institutions, employing the postulate that their motives and deliberations differ in no essential respects from those of participants in regular market exchanges – buyers, sellers, entrepreneurs, and so forth.

The result of this methodological move is to demystify the political process and to theorize it in terms of the interests of the individuals and groups (often acting collusively) who engage in it. Especially when applied in conjunction with the theory of rent-seeking to such phenomena as industrial regulation and occupational licensure, this methodology has had considerable explanatory and predictive power and has come closer than any other to establishing a genuine positive political science. Having said this, it is important to note that Buchanan has never subscribed to the economic imperialism of those, such as Becker, who claim that the entirety of human behaviour can be captured in the terms of economic theory. Buchanan's differences from this approach are, as I understand his work, severalfold. It is in the first place unclear from his writings whether he accepts the specific content of Becker's methodology (such as the fixity or stability of preferences) or whether he would endorse Becker's claim that apparently non-deliberative behaviour, such as unreflective rule-following, can always be explained as a strategic response to the information costs of calculation. Buchanan's many sympathetic references to Austrian economics suggest that the positivistic model of human action, and indeed of economic theory, embodied in this Beckerite research programme would be uncongenial to him.

The real difference between Buchanan's methodological commitment to *Homo economicus* and Becker's is far more fundamental: it is epistemological. For, unlike Becker, Buchanan has explicitly disavowed the claim that the content of *Homo economicus* captures the whole of human behaviour, even in its political and catallactic dimensions. For Buchanan, the public choice perspective is a window on the human world, a lens through which much may be perceived and understood that which would otherwise remain invisible or unintelligible, but it is not a mirror of social reality, aiming to reflect it in its totality and within a single, holistic explanatory scheme. The epistemological position or standpoint which best characterizes Buchanan's view of public choice is *perspectivism*, a term often employed in the interpretation of Nietzsche's theory of knowledge. Within the analytical tradition in epistemology, the closest approximation to Nietzscheam perspectivism is perhaps found in Nelson Goodman's *irrealism*,[9] although anticipations may be discerned in the pragmatist epidermologies of William James, C. S. Pierce and indeed Quine. What are the central elements of perspectivism in epistemology, and how do they affect the scope and limits of the utility of *Homo economicus* in public choice theory?

Using the book *The Reason of Rules*,[10] which Buchanan co-authored with Geoffrey Brennan, as our principal authority, we may infer that the per- spectivist epistemology of public choice has three important elements. There is, first, the thesis that theory – clearly in the human sciences, but also perhaps in the natural sciences – is underdetermined by evidence so that the idea of science as a mirror of nature, a recorder of objective facts, them-selves identified in a theory-independent fashion, is rejected. This under-determination thesis is, in other words, *a rejection of naive empiricism*, or at any rate, a statement of its severe limitations. There is, second, the thesis that in theorizing the human world we may profitably have recourse to a diversity of perspectives, none of which captures everything we wish to understand. Thus, in social theory, the construct of *Homo economicus* may be complemented by the Hayekian conception of man as at bottom a rule-follower, and not a calculator, reckoner, or maximizer. This *pluralist* aspect of perspectivist epistemology may allow for fruitful research into questions having to do with the pre-reflective or non-calculational conditions of market exchange in Western societies, and it may assist us to conceive of the possibility that in some societies (perhaps Japan) straightforward maximization may be an exceptional incident in economic life that is otherwise comprehensively governed by cultural norms. The third element of a perspectivist epistemology in public choice would be in the proposition that our choice of a methodological perspective will be informed, at least in part, by pragmatic concerns having to do with prediction and control. In the specific context of public choice theorizing of government failure, our programmatic concerns may also be ethical, normative concerns, in that we deploy the construct of *Homo economicus* to attempt to understand, and so to predict and through constitutional reform to control, the behaviours and incentive structures that recurrently give rise to government failure. In its combination of the rejection of naive empiricism, pluralism and methodological pragmatism, I see the perspectivist epistemology of Buchanan as a *tertium quid* or *via media* between wholesale relativism or instrumentalism and the full-blown realism of Popper.

I do not aim here to attempt a philosophical assessment of perspectivist epistemology, although I find it an attractive and plausible position, especially in the human sciences. My concern is rather to note that, because it is advanced in this perspectivist fashion, and lacks the aprioristic character of other research programmes for the extension of economic explanation into 'non-economic' areas of life, Buchanan's version of public choice in no way commits him to denying the existence, or indeed the theorizability, of phenomena such as Kantian principled behaviour, patriotism, moral vision or altruism – even in political contexts. Indeed, it may be that the kind of constitutional revolution needed in order to restore limited government depends upon the existence, in leaders and segments of the population, of motivations and commitments of sorts that *Homo economicus* does not possess and which public choice does not aim to theorize. It is to the prescriptive dimension, or implication, of Buchanan's thought that I now turn, when I consider the necessary preconditions of a theory of individual liberty in an historical context of inordinate government operating under the imperatives of unconstrained majoritarian democracy.

FROM HOBBESIAN DESPAIR TO HUMEAN HOPE

The normative *telos* of Buchanan's work is the renovation of limited democratic government, constrained in its taxing, transfer and spending powers by a stiff regime of conventional rules. He has not engaged in advocacy of specific measures, but instead regards this normative goal as at once animating, and at the same time a natural implication, of his work in developing constitutional political economy as a distinct discipline. Constitutional political economy is distinctive, in Buchanan's conception of it, not only in virtue of its methodology, but also because as a practitioner of it Buchanan has consistently repudiated the role, so commonly assumed by economists, of policy adviser to supposedly benevolent governments with large directionary powers. Buchanan's role has been that of communicating the importance of the rule-governed polity, of constitutionalism in its Madisonian variety, and of showing its natural harmony with constitutional political economy as a theoretical perspective.

What is Buchanan's account of the means whereby we move from the Leviathan of unconstrained (or inadequately constrained) majoritarian democracy to limited government? I do not mean to ask what are the political steps to this end, but rather how that passage is to be theorized. Several points are salient here. In the first place, Buchanan is clear that we must take the *status-quo* distribution of assets as our starting point. (Where else, after all, could we start?) Working, as do Gauthier and Rawls, with hypothetical baselines of equality or Lockean rights imparts into contractarian method non-procedural, or pre-procedural standards of justice which are difficult, if not impossible, to defend in philosophical terms. This is to say that, in adopting a *status-quo* baseline, Buchanan, like Hume, accepts the historic distribution of titles without making fruitless inquiries into its history or justice as appraised by controversial, questionable and often conflicting standards. But second, Buchanan applies this rejection of non-procedural conceptions of justice by arguing for a redistributional dismantlement of the currently overextended state which satisfies the criterion of Pareto-optimality: no one is left worse off. This is a most important feature of his approach, since it presupposes the vital, but often neglected point that redistribution is not always a zero-sum transaction. It need not be so, when the redistribution effected involves dismantling most existing transfer payments schemes, along with their bureaucracies, and disbursing the resources so released to the public. This redistributional Parietianism is interesting and important for many reasons, not least of which is that the buying-off of rent-seekers which it incorporates is now an explicit part of the policy of privatization and marketization now under way in Poland, Czechoslovakia, Hungary and elsewhere in the post-Communist world.

On the theoretical side, Buchanan's account of the renegotiation of entitlements incorporates the methodological device of a thin veil of ignorance, screening out only knowledge of one's final social situation. I will now suggest as a further development of Buchanan's thought, consistent with his adoption of a *status-quo* baseline, that the device of the veil of ignorance – even in the thin form he adopts along with other contractarian theorists such as Kavka – is unnecessary in his system, and possibly indefensible. For, if one is allowed knowledge of one's existing assets and position, what is the rationale for being denied information as to one's ultimate situation? A different way of expressing this thought is that the actual risks of real-world renegotiation of property titles are what will inform the contractors, and not any hypothetical uncertainty generated by the thought experiment of the veil of ignorance. My suggestion is also motivated by the fact that hypothetical circumstances cannot – despite all that Rawls and Gauthier have to say – generate reasons for action for persons in their actual circumstances. As Jeffrey Paul has persuasively argued,[11] there is an is–ought gap in all hypothetical contractarianism for just this reason. A natural development of Buchanan's thought, accordingly, is to eliminate from it its last hypothetical or counterfactual component, the veil of ignorance, and reconstitute his contractarianism as entirely of the actual-contract variety.[12] His public choice theorizing would then fuse with his normative philosophy in providing a most powerful tool for those in the real world who are seeking to achieve a new social contract or constitutional settlement.

We come now to the crux of our entire inquiry: what is the place of liberty in Buchanan's indeterminate contractarianism? Unlike Rawls's, Buchanan's contractarian method does not privilege liberty from the start, and it does not issue in a determinate list of basic liberties that are fixed and unalterable. Nor is this altogether surprising, given the Hobbesian pedigree of his political philosophy. Again, and for the same reason, Buchanan is clear that, in any plausible real-world situation, contractarian choice would not (contrary to Narveson) yield a Nozickian or Spencerian minimum state, and would not necessarily issue in unencumbered Lockean rights at every point. Indeed, he has argued forcefully that a limited government would surely have some redistributional functions in providing for reasonable equality of opportunity and inhibiting concentrations of wealth that might prove inimical to liberty. In Buchanan's system, then, liberty is not given the apodictive priority it has in Kantian-inspired contractarianism, nor is it the case that the role of the state is defined by the protection of Lockean rights.

Nevertheless, it is plain that Buchanan's contractarianism is bound to issue in most real-world contexts in the enhancement and protection of individual liberty, and will in virtually all contexts protect central economic liberties. It does so in virtue of his opposition to aggregative theorizing and his exploitation of the classical insight that voluntary exchange is mutually beneficial. It does so, again, because his defence of the market economy is in terms of its contribution to human autonomy rather than to any abstract conception of general well-being or collective welfare. And it does so, finally, in virtue of his insight that, provided there is a suitable framework of law, the undesigned coordination of the market is superior to any that could be generated by command or coercion.

It is true, however, that, so far as I can see, Buchanan's contractarianism cannot give universal protection to the personal or civil liberties that are central in Western individualist tradition. This apparent cultural limitation of his method seems to me to be both inevitable and not undesirable. It is far from self-evident, and sometimes plainly false, that the institutions and civil liberties of even limited democratic government are always and every-where appropriate and defensible. It may well be, for example, that in some circumstances the transition from a totalitarian command economy can be negotiated, and a stable post-totalitarian civil society achieved, only under the aegis of an authoritarian state that protects market freedoms under a rule of law, but in which the full panopoly of democratic and civil liberties is absent. It is a strength, rather than a weakness, of Buchanan's system that it can accommodate this possibility.

The dependency of Buchanan's social philosophy on the moral culture of Western individualism seems to me, also, at once unavoidable and not necessarily a weakness in it. Some aspects of Buchanan's thought, as of Hobbes's, may have universal or near-universal scope and validity, in so far as they concern the status of peace as a condition of any other political good. Beyond the limits of Western individualist cultures, or of cultures undergoing a process of modernization that involves assimilating Western values, however, there is no guarantee that contractarian choice will issue in anything more than the legal and economic framework of a market order. We may go further. We may need to confront the disturbing prospect that, in our own cultures, the morality of individuality has been so weakened by generations of collectivism and governmental profligacy that contractarian choice may not protect all of the liberties we associate with our tradition, nor restore all of those currently curbed by interventionism and collec-tivism. This disquieting possibility seems to me an inexorable result of the virtue of Buchanan's contractarianism – its indeterminacy as to outcome.

Within Buchanan's system of ideas, there are resources which sustain hope that a restriction of limited government is a possibility. Like Oake-shott,[13] Buchanan recognizes that, stated it its starkest form, wherein men are theorized wholly in *Homo economicus* or egoistic terms, the Hobbesian problem is insoluble. The problem is solved in Hobbes, only by the *deus ex machina* of the proud or gallant man, who chooses to exit from the indignities of the state of nature, and becomes first performer in the social contract from a sense of honour. Another solution is suggested by Hume, who (while acknowledging all the realities of conflict theorized by Hobbes) perceives that human beings are not the solitary predators hypothesized in the state of nature, but social beings, born in families, bound together by sexual and familial love, speakers of common languages in which common forms of life are expressed.[14] Against this background conception of human nature, Hume is able to illuminate the emergence of conventional norms which allow men to act cooperatively and to mutual benefit. Such norms or conventions are the submerged structure of any viable society, and they cohere to form a common culture, of which legal and conventional rules are the visible part. Where the common culture has been desolated by generations of collectivism, as perhaps in some of the countries of Latin America (Brazil, Argentina), there can be little hope that a constitutional revolution in the direction of limited government could be successful or stable. (Perhaps the best that can be hoped for in those circumstances is that the government will remain weak and ineffectual and allow the real business of society to be transacted in the informal economy.) This is to say that, in some historical contexts, the ruin of civil society is irreversible, and the Hobbesian dilemma as insoluble as it is in the starkest account of the Hobbesian state of nature.

In the Western constitutional democracies, with all their tendencies to omnicompetent government, we are far from such a nemesis. Along with the tacit error ingrained in the population by half a century or more of overextended government, there is still a common stock of individualist moral culture, which is the capital or patrimony, the historic inheritance, on which a constitutional revolution in the direction of individual liberty under the rule of law of a limited government can draw. (This common cultural inheritance is possessed far more securely by the populace than by the intellectual élites, whose work has not been to theorize but more often to corrode or destroy it.) The forms in which we may hope that governments withdraw from their current inordinacy will necessarily be various, as will the new constitutional settlements that emerge. In states with written constitutions, they will involve constitutional amendments (such as an amendment mandating a balanced budget) via a constitutional convention. In states, such as New Zealand and the United Kingdom, whose constitutions are unfixed and unwritten, the return to limited government will involve a reforging of the tacit economic constitution overturned by the disciples of Keynes against the background of a politically irreversible shift of resources from government to civil society. In the post-Communist blocs, where the inordinacies of unlimited government have been most catastrophic, we may witness the inspiring spectacle of civil society triumphing over totalitarian bureaucracy, and the reinstitution of a civil society under the aegis of a social contract and a constitutional settlement that guarantees market freedom, private property and civil liberty.

CONCLUDING REMARKS

None of these developments has the slightest degree of inevitability. In the real world of insuperable unknowledge (to use a Shacklean neologism),[15] the future is always dark and hazardous. At no point in his work has Buchanan engaged in the hubristic exercise of forecasting the fate of liberty. But if liberty has a future, it will have been fortified by Buchanan's work. For the final message of Buchanan's thought, as I have interpreted it, is that if we wish to preserve the precious heritage of Western individuality, we are bound to engage in the project of theorizing the world as it is, without illusion or groundless hope, even as Buchanan's teacher, Knight, did in his writings. And then, armed with the theoretical understanding we have achieved, we must wager on liberty by seeking, in all the vicissitudes and contingencies of practice, a new constitutional settlement on limited government in which free men and women may live in voluntary association – in liberty under the rule of law.[16]

6 Berlin's agonistic liberalism

It is often said of Izaiah Berlin – not least, by Berlin himself – that he abandoned philosophy for intellectual history, when (after a conversation with the logician, H.M. Sheffer) he became convinced that he could not make a truly significant contribution to the two areas of philosophy, logic and psychology, which Sheffer has persuaded him would henceforth be at the centre of the discipline. There is, no doubt, something to be said for this common view. That Berlin has made an enduring, and thoroughly original contribution to the history of ideas is not in any question. His essays in intellectual history, brought together and published in five volumes (so far) by his editor, Dr Henry Hardy of Wolfson College, Oxford, develop an interpretation of modern European thought that is novel and profound. In his work on the history of ideas, Berlin has exhibited a gift of imaginative empathy with thinkers whose view of the world is deeply alien to his own – thinkers such as de Maistre and Sorel, for example – in which he has no peer among his contemporaries, and which is, perhaps, comparable only with the imaginative clairvoyance whereby Keirkegaard was able to enter into experiences and forms of life he had never himself known. More particularly, our understanding of our intellectual inheritance has been altered, and altered irreversibly, by Berlin's work on the thinkers of what he calls the Counter-Enlightenment – those Romantics, fideists, and solitaries, such as Vico and Herder, who broke into pieces that system of ideas, rationalist and universalist, transmitted from the ancient to the modern world, and embodied in the French Enlightenment, that formed the bedrock of the Western tradition.

Endorsed as it has been by Berlin himself, this common interpretation of his work seems to me nevertheless mistaken. For Berlin's essays in intellectual history make a contribution to moral and political philosophy, begun in the essays on liberty, that is of the first importance, subverting as it does the ruling orthodoxies in those subjects, and raising an interrogation mark over the very foundations of the Western tradition. The idea that animates all of

Berlin's work, both in intellectual history and in political theory, is one which, if true, as I take it to be, strikes a death-blow to the central, classical Western tradition – and, it must be added, to the project of the Enlightenment. Berlin's master idea is that ultimate values are objective and knowable, but they are many, they often come into conflict with one another and are uncombinable in a single human being or a single society, and that in many of such conflicts there is no overarching standard whereby the competing claims of such ultimate values are rationally arbitrable. Conflicts among such values are among incommensurables, and the choices we make among them are radical and tragic choices. There is, then, no *summum bonum* or *logos*, no Aristotelian mean or Platonic form of the good, no perfect form of human life, which we may never achieve but towards which we may struggle, no measuring rod on which different forms of human life encompassing different and uncombinable goods can be ranked. This assertion of the variety and incommensurability of the goods of human life is not, it is worth noting, the Augustinian thesis that human life is imperfect, and imperfectible: it is the thesis that the very idea of perfection is incoherent. Nor are the conflicts among goods illuminated by Berlin's value-pluralism occasioned, principally or merely, by such contingencies as the brevity of human life, or the scarcity of worldly resources: they are to be accounted for by the very natures of the goods themselves. The incommensurabilities invoked by Berlin, and by which the notion of perfection is destroyed, are what Joseph Raz – in his *The Morality of Freedom*,[1] the only major work in political philosophy thus far in which Berlin's pluralism is developed and applied – has termed *constitutive incommensurabilities*. Consider an example from the arts. It makes no sense to try to rank the excellence of the plays of Shakespeare, say, against that of the French classicists, Corneille and Racine, or to put the beauty of the Parthenon in the balance with that of Notre Dame. We lack the scales on which these goods might be weighed. For this reason, though there may be improvement or decline within specific artistic traditions, there can be no progress in the arts that spans divergent and incommensurable traditions. On Berlin's view, the same is true in ethics. The virtues of the medieval Christian ruler cannon coexist, in one man, with the *virtu* of the Renaissance prince; nor can the virtues recognized in Homeric Greece flourish in harmony with those of Whig England. In our own day, the virtues of a devoted family man are incompatible with those of the man devoted to pleasure. Within cultures, as within individual lives, we confront an ineradicable moral scarcity, veiled or denied in most philosophies, which it is our fate as humans to endure.

The distinctiveness and radicalism of Berlin's species of objective pluralism are easily missed. Its distinctiveness was missed by Leo Strauss

when, with characteristic obtuseness and perversity, he condemned Berlin
as a relativist for whom all values were culture-specific and, in the end,
subjective. Throughout his writings, Berlin has constantly stressed that,
though their embodiments in specific forms of life will vary across cultures,
ultimate values are objective and universal – as are conflicts among them.
Berlin's variety of pluralism is a species of value realism, not of scepticism,
subjectivism or relativism. As Berlin puts it in his most recent collection of
essays, *The Crooked Timber of Humanity: Chapters in the History of Ideas*:

> Incompatible these (human) ends may be; but their variety cannot be
> unlimited, for the nature of men, however various and subject to change,
> must possess some generic character if it is to be called human at all.[2]

Berlin's affirmation of generically human values that, despite their different embodiments in different cultures, are universal, gives the lie to
Michael Ignatieff's claim, made in his otherwise powerful contribution to
the current collection, that 'When Berlin speaks of universal values, he
means European values'. This interpretation, though it may indeed have
some slight textual support, runs flatly counter to the realist orientation of
Berlin's theory of value, and runs the risk of banalizing Berlin's standpoint
as in the end a variant of relativism. Everything suggests that Berlin's thesis
of value-incommensurability is meant to have universal force and that it is,
if anything, especially subversive of distinctively Western traditions of
rationalism and monism.

The implications of Berlin's value-pluralism for political philosophy
have gone curiously unnoticed by most, partly, no doubt, because they
undermine so much in recent liberal thought. It is a key feature of Berlin's
argument in his seminal 'Two concepts of liberty'[3] that, just as there are
conflicts among ultimate values that are incommensurable – between
liberty and equality, equality and general welfare, say – so there are
conflicts no less radical within liberty itself – conflicts among distinct
liberties having incommensurable value. When the liberty of privacy competes with freedom of information, a trade-off must be made and a balance
struck; but there is no comprehensive theory – no theory of the sort John
Stuart Mill thought he possessed when he sought to found the 'one very
simple principle' of *On Liberty*[4] in the requirements of general utility – by
which such conflicts among liberties might be arbitrated. This is to say that
the legalist or constitutionalist project, which animates so much in recent
Anglo–American theorizing, of specifying a unique set of rights or basic
liberties that dovetail in an harmonious compossibility, the project – which
finds a clear expression in the work of Rawls, late and early – is grounded
in an illusion. (Is it subversion of this illusion that explains the fact,
otherwise extraordinary, that as yet no book-length study of Berlin's

thought has been published?) Among liberties, as among equalities, there may be, and are, radical choices to be made; gains made in one class of liberties may be at the expense of losses in others; and there is no theory or overarching principle whereby these hard choices can be made easy, or the conflicts they express conjured away.

It is, perhaps, in injecting value-pluralism into the ideal of liberty itself, rather than in its defence of the negative liberty of non-interference against the claims of the positive liberty of self-mastery, that the true significance of Berlin's 'Two concepts of liberty' may come to be seen. In insisting in that essay that the liberty to live as one pleases and the freedom to have a voice in collective deliberation are two things, not one, and that individual freedom and political democracy need not, and do not, always complement one another, Berlin uttered a truth, much against the current of the age, that remains thoroughly unfashionable and fundamentally important. Again, his distinction between negative and positive liberty remains a vital one, even if one believes (as I do myself) that the chief value of freedom from coercion by others is the contribution it makes to individual autonomy. The permanent value of that essay may nonetheless lie elsewhere. It may be found in the fact that, in founding the value of freedom in the opportunity it gives us of navigating among incommensurable options and forms of living, Berlin at the same time cuts the ground from under those doctrinal or fundamentalist liberalisms – the liberalism of Nozick or Hayek no less than of Rawls or Ackerman – which suppose that the incommensurabilities of moral and political life, and of liberty itself, can be smoothed away by the application of some theory, or tamed by some talismanic formula. It is, perhaps, the chief virtue of a liberal society, as Berlin conceives of it, that in it conflicts among values, including conflicts among liberties, are perceived as ultimate truths about the human world, not to be suppressed or explained away by spurious theorizing. It is in taking its stand on incommensurability and radical choice as constitutive features of the human condition that Berlin's liberalism most differs from the panglossian liberalisms that have lately enjoyed an anachronistic revival. Unlike these, Berlin's is an agonistic liberalism, a stoic liberalism or loss and tragedy. For that reason alone, if there is any liberalism that is now defensible, it is Berlin's.

Berlin is a philosopher of history as much as of liberty. His rejection of historical inevitability is of a piece with his more general repudiation of human determinism. In the restatement of the ideas of Vice and Herder, he has done much to restore plausibility to the idea that there is a mode of understanding, peculiar to history and perhaps the other humane studies, which is irreducible to that appropriate in the natural sciences. And he has given contemporary plausibility to the view that, whereas human beings share in a common fund of capacities and dispositions that constitutes their nature, among these are the capacity to transform themselves – their needs, their views of the world and their self-understandings – and the disposition to constitute for themselves distinct and typically[5] exclusive identities – as Jews or Arabs, Frenchmen or Englishmen, and so on. It is here that a crux emerges in Berlin's thought. It was a cardinal tenet of the Enlightenment that, whatever cultural variety the future of mankind would encompass, it was reasonable to expect convergence on a universal civilization under-girded by a shared, rational morality. If the upshot of Berlin's value-pluralism is to undermine the idea of a rational morality, the effect of his work on nationalism is to jettison the prospect that a time may come when men's dominant allegiance is to the norms of a universal civilization. The crux in Berlin's thought goes yet deeper than this. It is in a tension between the idea of a common human nature and the idea of human self-creation and self-transformation. If, as Vico, Herder and Berlin maintain, we are a highly inventive species whose forms of life are radically underdetermined by our common humanity, what reason is there to share the hopes of the Enlighten-ment for an eventual convergence of liberal and humanistic values? Why not expect, instead, endemic conflict among human beings, as they con-stitute themselves into distinct and incommensurable cultures, each com-mitted to its identity, and not all animated by anything resembling liberal values? Do not recent developments in the Soviet Union, and in the beleaguered state of Israel, suggest that this latter prospect is all too likely? It is at this point that the kinship of Berlin with David Hume, remarked upon in notable contributions to this collection by Richard Wollheim and Stuart Hampshire, breaks down. For all his scepticism, Hume believed that the moral and political judgements of men whose minds were unclouded by enthusiasm or false philosophy would come to rest in a general con-vergence. If only because of his conviction of the constancy of human nature, he could think of human history only as an alternation of civilization and barbarism – not as the exfoliation of incommensurably divergent civilizations. Yet it is precisely that prospect, so threatening to the hopes and expectations of the Enlightenment, that Berlin's radical value-pluralism opens up. There is, then, a paradoxical kinship between the two thinkers, after all: both are profoundly civilized men, defenders of the values that animated the Enlightenment, whose philosophies render foun-dationless the enlightened societies to whose defence they remain stead-fastly committed.

One of the many merits of Edna and Avishai Margalit's rich and reward-ing collection on Berlin and Berlinian themes[5] is the sense – very im-perfectly conveyed here – it transmits of the tone of Berlin's writings and conversation, of the multiplicity of his interests and the variety of his achievements. The fifteen sections of the book – encompassing essays by Sidney Morgenbesser and Jonathan Lieberson, David Pears, Charles Taylor, Richard Wollheim, Leon Wieseltier, Ronald Dworkin, G.A. Cohen, Stuart Hampshire, Michael Ignatieff, Yael Tamir, Francis Haskell, Bernard Williams, Alfred Brendel and Joseph Brodsky, together with a delightful poem by Stephen Spender – touch on most aspects of the thought of this many-sided thinker, only a few of which (though the most fundamental and important ones) have been addressed here. The essays testify to the character of Berlin's mind as a luminous prism, in which the cultural traditions of Russia, England and Judaism are marvellously refracted. It is their plurality of traditions in Berlin's own intellectual life that ultimately prevents any assimilation of his voice to that of Hume. For, in the end, one cannot help feeling that, with all that he shares with him in learning and cultivation, Berlin's voice as it echoes through these pages is not Hume's. If it shares with Hume's a profound intellectual gaiety and a relish for the contingencies of history; it has in it resonances that come from other aspects of Berlin's plural inheritance, altogether absent in the genial Hume. The voice we hear is one that cleaves to mortal men and women in all their unconsoled sorrow, and which refuses with a passion the mocking harmonies of any theodicy. It is Job's.

Part II
Critiques

7   The system of ruins

As it has been disclosed to us in twentieth-century political history, the fate of Marxism is to be the first world-view in human history that is genuinely self-refuting. To be sure, all systems of general ideas about man and society have unintended consequences when they are given practical effect, and it is a commonplace that the distance between doctrine and practice is nowhere wider or harder to bridge than in political life. Further, it is a familiar theme in political thought that social institutions may over the long run have a self-destroying tendency in so far as they cannot help breeding expectations they must fail to satisfy.

None of these traditional themes succeeds in capturing the thoroughly paradoxical role of Marxian ideas in contemporary political life. The distinctive achievement of Marxism, peculiarly ironical in a system of ideas committed *au fond* to the unity of theory with practice, is that its most spectacular victories in the real world have afforded the most devastating criticisms of its fundamental tenets. Accordingly, in installing in Russia and in much of Asia new economic and political institutions to which nothing in the old orders corresponded, the Communist régimes have exhibited unequivocally that radical autonomy of general ideas in the political realm which their official doctrine, no less than classical Marxism, tirelessly denies. The stupendous successes of Communism in the real world have given a practical self-refutation of the Marxian system, since in every case the actual result of a revolutionary socialist victory has been to flout the aspirations of the revolutionaries as it demonstrates once again the impossibility of Communism as Marx conceived it.

The self-refutation in practice of Marxism over the past half century was not unanticipated in the theoretical writings of Marx's critics. In a rare moment of realistic insight, the great Russian anarchist, Bakunin, predicted that the outcome of a Marxian socialist revolution would be a form of dictatorship more repressive and more exploitative than the bourgeois political order it replaced. In a far more systematic fashion, Böhm-Bawerk in his *Karl Marx and the Close of his System* (1896)[1] dissected the errors of Marx's economic theory and showed how they debilitated his account of market capitalism, while Böhm-Bawerk's successors in the Austrian School of Economics, L. von Mises and F.A. von Hayek, developed in the 1920s and 1930s powerful theoretical arguments explaining the failures in resource-allocation of socialist systems. Apocalyptic though it has been, the history of Marxism in practice over the past half-century has served only to give concrete historical exemplification to criticisms of Marx's ideas that were developed during his lifetime and in the first fifty years after his death.

The ruin of Marx's system by the events of the past half-century has in no way inhibited the production of Marxian theoretical literature in Western societies. Throughout the past hundred years, Marxian ideas have served in capitalist societies as weapons in the armoury of cultural criticism, as tools in projects for revisionary history, and as postulates for sociological research. In fulfilling this role of promoting self-criticism within Western society, Marxian thinkers have been compelled to refine the central notions of Marx's system beyond anything he could have recognized or endorsed, and in so doing they have often obfuscated important questions in the interpretation of his writings. It is one of the few hopeful features of the flurry of activity surrounding the anniversary of his death that a handful of books has appeared that give Marx's life and work the benefit of a detached and scrupulous historical analysis. In this connection, the *Dictionary of Marxist Thought*[2] edited by Tom Bottomore is an invaluable aid in identifying the key terms in Marx's own work and distinguishing their force in Marx from the uses made of them by later writers. Bottomore's *Dictionary* is usefully complemented by Gérard Bekerman's *Marx and Engels: A conceptual concordance*,[3] in which the crucial ideas of the two writers are illustrated by quotations from their writings, carefully chosen by Bekerman and skilfully translated by Terrell Carver. These works of reference will prove indispensable to anyone who wishes to form a reasoned judgement about the currently fashionable thesis that it was Engels who made of Marx's subtle and eclectic thought a crude and mechanical system.

A very different, but equally valuable service is performed by David Felix's *Marx as Politician*.[4] Felix's method is unique in Marxian scholarship inasmuch as he develops his incisive criticism of Marx's theories through the medium of a demystifying political biography. His strategy is to deconstruct Marx's chief theoretical claims by illuminating their force as acts in his struggles for political power over the emergent working-class movements of nineteenth-century Europe and their rivalrous leaders. Nowhere in Felix's elegantly and acidulously written book does he suggest that understanding Marx's theories in this way, as aspects of his political practice, by itself devalues their claims to truth, but he shows convincingly that we can best account for the manifest incoherences of Marx's system by viewing it as a makeshift, constantly reworked according to the political necessities of the moment. Again, without ever replicating the vulgarities of psychohistory, Felix gives a psychological gloss to his political reading of Marx's theoretical activity by displaying its roots in an ungovernably assertive and domineering personality. Marx's virulent contempt for ethical socialism, his rigid posture of opposition to all existing social orders and his cynical dismissal of the claims of small nations and vanquished classes are given a compelling interpretation by reference to his anomic and obsessional fascination with power. Felix's final assessment of Marx's political vision grasps firmly a truth that has been stubbornly resisted by all of his conventional biographers when he writes, '"Nazi" was the simplified acronym for National Socialist German Workers Party. It was an accurate name for the party Marx would like to have led in Germany in 1848–9, nationalistic, socialistic, and as anti-Semitic as tactically useful'.

The many affinities between Marx's political vision and the ideas and movements of the radical Right which Felix identifies are profoundly explored in Ernst Nolte's important collection of essays, *Marxism, Fascism, Cold War*.[5] Since his seminal study, *Three Faces of Fascism*,[6] Nolte has been widely misread as a theorist of Fascism who conceives it in Marxian terms as the radical anti-socialist response to capitalist crisis and who seeks the elimination of the liberal category of totalitarianism in the explanation of both Communism and Fascism. The discursive and wide-ranging essays assembled in this volume should lay to rest any such interpretation of Nolte's work, which is distinctive in representing contemporary Marxist practice as having authentic origins in Marxian doctrine and instructive in perceiving the structural similarities of Marxian and Fascist contestations of bourgeois society. Thus in identifying, in his brief essay on 'The conservative features of Marxism',[7] the character of Marxism (understood here to mean the doctrines held in common by Marx and Engels) as a critique of modernity, Nolte helps us towards an explanation of the encrusted cultural conservatism of all actual Communist régimes that is more adequate than any to be found in the strained apologetics of Western Marxian writers. The enmity of Communist governments to all the most radical expressions of the modern spirit – in art and philosophy as well as lifestyle and popular culture – is correctly perceived as emanating directly from the anti-individualist animus which pervades the thought of Marx and Engels alike. The repression in Communist states of all modernist movements is not, then, an aberration or even an unintended consequence of Marx's doctrine, but simply an expression of its original intent. In its application to the fascist phenomenon, Nolte's analysis is conclusive in linking the Rousseauesque primitivism of Marx's fantasy of ending the social division of labour with the Fascist rebellion against commercial society. As Nolte drily observes:

> Fascism can be directly compared with Marxism of the Soviet nature only in its radical form, in respect of its inner solidarity and its appeal to comrades of like mind in all countries; Italian fascism, in its phase as a development dictatorship, and more than ever the Croatian Ustase and the Romanian Iron Guard were in fact, on the contrary, more like many of today's 'national liberation movements' than like late National Socialism . . . ; there is nothing more grotesque than a 'theory of Fascism' which denounces capitalism with much sincere indignation as the root of Fascism, at the same time overlooking that the theory identifies itself with conditions which show all the formal characteristics of Fascism. It is not astonishing that the liberal capitalist system produces Fascism under certain circumstances, but it is astonishing that in the great majority of cases Fascism has not succeeded in gaining power in spite of certain circumstances. The explanation can only lie in the fact that this social system with its peculiar lack of conception, its deep-rooted divergencies, its inborn tendency to self-criticism, its separation of economic, political and spiritual power obviously offers strong resistance to a transformation to fascist solidarity, and is aware that the deliverance which is promised would at the same time be loss of self. Thus capitalism is indeed the soil of Fascism, but the plant only grows to imposing strength if an exorbitant dose of Marxist fertilizer is added to the soil.[8]

The most important essay in Nolte's collection deals not with the question of Fascism, however, but with errors in the historical interpretation of early industrial capitalism which have been widely disseminated by Marxian writers. Along with radical Tories such as Oastler, Sadler, Southey and Disraeli, Marx and Engels associated the Industrial Revolution with the pauperization of the masses and the devastation of their traditional ways of life. By comparison with the factory system as it developed under *laisser-faire* capitalism, pre-industrial life was pictured in almost Arcadian terms of satisfying work, harmonious community and a reasonable sufficiency of material goods. Nolte is assiduously specific in documenting how Marx and Engels and the reactionary and Romantic critics of industrialism and the factory system neglected the filth, squalor and waste of human life endemic in pre-industrial society. In this Nolte's analysis parallels that of a number of contemporary economic historians, among whom the most distinguished is R.M. Hartwell, whose researches have gone far to establish that the

Marxian immiseration thesis is as false in respect of early industrialism as it is of our own capitalist economies. An explosion of population involving a massive decline in infant mortality rates, increasing consumption of commodities hitherto regarded as luxuries, and many other empirical factors point to the early industrial period in England as one of much-enhanced popular living standards.

At the same time, Nolte is careful to specify the background of this explosion in living standards in several centuries of European and, above all, English political and cultural development, which preceded it. Noting that 'European society is, from its beginnings in the early middle ages onward, the society of a functioning or dynamic pluralism whose several relatively autonomous powers, such as royalty and the aristocracy, the state and the church, and also the individual states restrict each other, and yet they remain even in sharpest struggle, related to each other and subject to mutual influence', Nolte inverts the historical materialist thesis of the primacy of technological and economic factors in accounting for social and political changes and explains the technological development of early industrialism as a variable dependent upon pluralist legal and political institutions. In so doing he is concerned to stress particularly the importance of the English example, wherein the Industrial Revolution was the culmination of several centuries of agrarian development on a market model. His account of the background and conditions of the Industrial Revolution in England converges at several points with that given by Alan MacFarlane in his fascinating *Origins of English Individualism*,[9] and it would be encouraging to suppose that Nolte's book will do something to subvert the legend, which the writings of Karl Polanyi and C.B. Macpherson have made a central element in academic folklore, that the seventeenth and eighteenth centuries in England encompassed a radical transition from communitarian to individualist forms of social life.

The upshot of Nolte's analysis is that European capitalism is a historical singularity, in no way the necessary or inevitable outcome of human social development taken as a whole. It was as a lucky chance, the unlikely outcome of a serendipitous conjunction of events, that market processes were able to spread in the early Middle Ages and thus to lay down the necessary conditions for the emergence of large-scale capitalist production. This conclusion goes against one of the central tenets of Marx's thought, and allows us to pinpoint one of its most disastrous errors. For all his insistence on the particularities of specific cultures and on the unevenness of economic development in different nations, Marx (and Engels after him, albeit with fewer saving reservations) subscribed to a belief in something like a law of the increasing development over human history of productive forces. He asserted this not just as a brute historical fact nor yet as a mere trend, but as the unifying principle of human history. It is such a principle, something midway between the statement of a trend and the enunciation of a law that G.A. Cohen terms the Development Thesis in his *Karl Marx's Theory of History: A Defence*.[10] It is one of the most noteworthy features of Cohen's book, which sets standards of competence and rigour in argument which have been matched by few twentieth-century Marxian thinkers and which non-Marxian philosophers would do well to try to emulate, that his defence of the Development Thesis is feeble and admittedly unsuccessful. In the end Cohen is driven to invoke in its support a starkly Benthamite, and for that reason wholly un-Marxian, conception of man as an economizer of his efforts.

This move has to confront, however, the inconvenient fact that the systematic and continuous expansion of productive forces over many centuries appears to have occurred within capitalist Europe and its offshoots and nowhere else. Explaining the singularity of capitalist development generates a most fundamental criticism of the Marxian scheme of historical interpretation. For, contrary to Cohen's attempted reconstruction of historical materialism in Darwinian functionalist form, a mechanism for filtering out inefficient productive arrangements exists *only within the capitalist mode of production*. Within a capitalist market economy, there is a powerful incentive for enterprises to innovate technologically, and to adopt innovations pioneered by others, since firms which persist in using less efficient technologies will lose markets, reap dwindling profits and eventually fail. Nothing akin to this selective mechanism of market competition existed to filter out inefficient technologies in the Asiatic mode of production, and it has no replica in existing socialist command economies. Cohen's defence of the Development Thesis is bound to fail because it attempts to account for the replacement of one productive mode by another by invoking a mechanism which features internally in only a single mode of production, market capitalism.

Cohen's argument has the virtue of confronting a central difficulty in Marxian historical materialism which most Marxian writers prefer to pass over. Thus the problem is mentioned by Alex Callinicos neither in his propagandist tract, *The Revolutionary Ideas of Marx*,[11] nor in his more reflective and self-critical *Marxism and Philosophy*.[12] None of the writers in David McLellan's *Marx: The first hundred years*[13] takes it up, even when (as in the essays by Raymond Williams, Ernest Mandel and Roy Edgley) their contributions focus more or less directly on problems and applications of historical materialism. This omission is striking and lamentable, but eminently understandable, since any recognition of the inadequacy of the Marxian scheme of historical development is bound to undermine the viability of Marxian socialism itself. If we acknowledge, as did Marx, the essentially unconservative character of capitalist enterprise, we will find it incongruous that he and his followers imagine that the prodigious virtuosity of capitalism can be retained while its central mechanism, market competition, is abolished. There is, in fact, no reason to think that the productive achievements of capitalism will even be maintained, still less surpassed, once market mechanisms for allocating resources are removed. It is this insight which explains the vast chaos and colossal malinvestments which are typical of all existing socialist command economies. In Marx's own writings, in accordance with his refusal to engage in utopian speculations, no proposal is ever advanced for the coordination of economic activity in socialist or Communist societies: it is simply assumed, with the utmost naïveté, that an acceptable allocation of resources to particular uses will emerge spontaneously, without the need for markets or pricing, from the collaborative discussions of socialist citizens. It was indeed to this gigantic evasion that Lenin referred obliquely, when he confessed that the principal task of the Bolsheviks in the USSR was the construction of state capitalism. Aside from the fact that it entails inexorably a concentration of power in bureaucratic institutions which Marx always sought to avoid, but which was realized fully in the Stalinist period, Lenin's project of a state capitalist régime was bound to founder on the absence within it of the central capitalist institution for resource-allocation.

In the event, the Soviet experience amply confirmed the predictions of those economists of the Austrian School, particularly von Mises and von Hayek, who argued for the impossibility of rational resource allocation under socialist institutions. In the Soviet Union, working-class living standards after over sixty years of state capitalist construction are probably lower than in Brazil, while elsewhere, in Hungary and in China, only the expedient of reintroducing capitalist institutions is allowing wealth to grow and incomes to rise. These developments exemplify in concrete historical contexts the theoretical insights with which the Austrian economists prevailed over their socialist opponents in the great debates of the inter-war years. Yet, despite their intellectual victory, the Austrian arguments have been ignored by generations of economists and their relevance to the Soviet experience has been expounded in depth only by Paul Craig Roberts in his vital and neglected book *Alienation and the Soviet Economy*.[14] It is entirely characteristic that in his contribution to the McLellan collection, Mandel, after showing an awareness of the calculation debate that distinguishes him from the bulk of his professional colleagues, should demonstrate his inability to grasp the nature of the problem at issue when he remarks innocently of von Mises's argument that it has 'in the meantime been taken care of by the computer'. As it has turned out, history has forced back on to the intellectual agenda a debate which the intelligentsia for several generations consigned to the memory hole.

The ruin of Marxism both as a scheme of historical interpretation and as a theory of economic organization has evoked a variety of responses among contemporary Marxian writers. The great majority has tried to prevent the destruction of the doctrine by intractable facts through the elaboration of protective *ad hoc* hypotheses. Accordingly, an effort has been made to explain the catastrophic impact of Marxism in Russia by seeking out continuities between the political culture and institutions of Tsarism and those of the Soviet power, with the underlying insinuation that in Russia an enlightened Western European creed of democracy and freedom was corrupted by contact with tyrannous native traditions. Its culturally racist features aside, this argument misrepresents Tsarism, which for the last sixty years of its history was an open, progressive authoritarian system, far less inhumane or repressive of individual liberty than the great majority of member states in today's United Nations, and evolving in a context of extraordinary economic growth and brilliant cultural achievement. The real Russian tragedy was the reverse of that imputed by the conventional and complacent view in that the blossoming civic traditions of Tsarism were in 1917 barbarized and destroyed by the incursion of a totalitarian ideology of Western European origins.

On a more general level, this sort of protective manoeuvre within Marxism must be criticized on the Popperian ground that it has the effect of transforming what was in Marx's hands a living and corrigible body of thought into an intellectual deadweight of reinforced dogmatism. Thus every contribution to the Norman Fischer volume on *Continuity and Change in Marxism*[15] (with the partial exception of a cryptic and suggestive piece by Kostas Axelos) reveals an abandonment of the empirical content of Marx's thought in favour of a reassertion of its Hegelian essentialist metaphysics. This metamorphosis of Marxism from a body of empirical social theory and of historical interpretation into a self-enclosed meta-physical system is most evident in the Frankfurt School, but despite all protestations to the contrary it characterizes Althusser's Cartesian re-construction of Marx's thought as well as Marcuse's Heideggerian varia-tions on Marxian and Hegelian themes.

In fairness it must be said that the multiple ironies involved in this retreat to metaphysical inquiry from a system of thought which at its height promised an end to philosophy have not gone unnoticed by all Marxian thinkers. The tension between the metaphysical turn in recent Marxism and the anti-philosophical bent of Marx's own mature thought is at the heart of Callinico's *Marxism and Philosophy* and it motivates Susan Easton's search for affinities and convergences in *Humanist Marxism and Wittgen-steinian Social Philosophy*.[16] Easton's intriguing project of linking up a form of Marxism in which human activity and not historical law is central, with the Wittgensteinian conception of knowledge as embodied in social practices, does not face its hardest difficulty in the biographical fact that Wittgenstein's own political views were conservative, not to say reactionary, and were never seen by him to conflict in any way with his developed philosophical outlook. The most serious difficulty for this kind of Marxian theorizing is its irresistible tendency to slip into an Idealist constructivism about the social world of precisely the sort that Marx repudiated in his attacks on Hegel and on Stirner. The metaphysical turn of humanist Marxism is sure to be a dead end because it begins by shedding the realist commitments which Marx himself rightly thought to be most distinctive of his view of social life.

In their retreat from empirical theorizing to essentialist metaphysics, the Hegelian Marxists forgo one of Marx's most ambitious projects: the development of a comprehensive theory of ideology. Any theory of ideology, and above all a Marxian theory, incorporates a distinction between appearance and reality in society which the Idealist implication of humanist Marxism tends to occlude. Further, the abandonment of the claim to scientific realism in Marx's thought suggests an obvious question about the ideological character of humanist Marxism itself. This is a question that haunts Jorge Larrain's meandering and inconclusive discussions in *Marxism and Ideology*,[17] but which is posed decisively at several points in Jean Cohen's *Class and Civil Society: The limits of Marxian critical theory*.[18] Cohen's is a luminously intelligent investigation of the limitations of Marxian class theory which takes seriously the criticism of socialist and Marxist thought as itself having the mystifying and repressive functions of an ideology. She considers in this context not only the theory of Konrad and Szelenyi, which echoes the predictions of the late nineteenth-century Polish anarchist, Waclas Machajski, in representing Marxism in the Soviet bloc as the instrument of a novel form of domination, but also Western theorists of the new class such as Irving Kristol and Alvin Gouldner.

Cohen's own attitude to Szelenyi's class analysis of the Eastern bloc societies – a most useful exposition of which Szelenyi gives himself in his contribution to M. Burawoy and Theda Skocpol's *Marxist Inquiries*[19] – is not free from ambiguity. She recognizes the truth in Szelenyi's and Konrad's claims regarding the existence of an exploitative social stratum which has arisen in the Communist régimes via its control of education and of access of information, but she goes on to criticize their approach as flawed because it adopts a strategy of analysis whose limitations are those of Marx's class theory. The opposite situation seems to me to be the true one: the theory of the new class in its control of education and of access of information cannot be stated in Marxist terms, but she goes on to criticize their approach with Marxian class theory. That the new class is not a Marxian class is a criticism of the theory of Szelenyi and Konrad only in so far as they see themselves as completing Marxian social theory rather than abandoning it whenever new forms of injustice and exploitation elude its grasp.

The general relevance of the theory of the new class is that it encourages us to look at the ideological function of socialist thought itself. In so doing we harness the critical intent which motivated Marx's analyses of the classical economists to examine Marxian and other socialist system of ideas as vehicles for the protection and promotion of the interests of specific social groups. Essential to the theory of ideology, after all, is not only the identification of a distance between reality and appearance in society, but the demonstration that this distance is functional in enabling some social interest to prevail over some other. Ideology, in short, facilitates domination and exploitation as ongoing social relationships. Not only in its manifestations in the Soviet bloc, but also in Western societies, socialist thought invites ideological analysis as an instrument in the social struggle among competing groups for access to state power and thereby to the resources the modern interventionist state commands. Whereas a theory of the ideological functions of the socialist system promises much in the illumination of the chronic legitimation crisis of the Communist régimes and of the conflicts in our own societies, the project of developing fully such a theory is one that even independent critical thinkers of the stature of Jean Cohen seem to retreat from.

The undefended assumption that socialist goals stand in need of no ideological demystification, even if socialist régimes sometimes do, is an outstanding feature of Barry Smart's able exploration of the relations of Foucault's thought with Marxism,[20] and the inherent progressiveness of the socialist ideal figures as a presupposition of analysis, inhibiting fundamental criticism, equally in George G. Brenkert's *Marx's Ethics of Freedom*.[21] It seems that the stance of radical criticism does not extend, so far as these writers are concerned, to the socialist conventional wisdom of the Western academic class.

A re-emergence of Marxism as a progressive research programme in social theory may be predicated upon several rather exacting conditions. A new Marxism worthy of serious critical attention would have to confront the Austrian thesis that market competition and bureaucratic command structures are together the mutually exhaustive means of resource-allocation in complex industrial societies, with command economies having ineradicable tendencies to vast waste and malinvestment. It would have to consider the possibility that the economic chaos and political repression characteristic of all socialist command economies are not mere aberrations, but structurally inseparable results of such economies. It would, above all, need to confront the repressed possibility that the Gulag represents an unavoidable phase in socialist construction rather than a contingent incident in Soviet (and Chinese) experience. In order to face these hard questions, a new Marxism would demand a purer and more self-critical method of thought than any variety of Marxism has so far achieved. It would need to engage directly with the moral theory of justice and exploitation and to abandon the forlorn pretence that it can deploy some special, dialectical logic to circumvent contradictions within its own theories. The central concern of such a new Marxism – to link normative exploitation theory with empirical class analysis – is in fact the subject matter of a powerful new school of Analytical Marxism, led by such figures as G.A. Cohen, Jon Elster and John Roemer, with whose works the future of Marxism, if it has any, must henceforth be associated.

It is hard to imagine that the version of Marxian theory which looks like being developed by these thinkers will do more than generate a few scattered insights which are easily absorbed into normal social science. Once the spurious claim to esoteric insight and omnicompetent method is given up, Marxian thought confronts the same intractable difficulties in the theory of justice and in the philosophy of social science which have bedeviled non-Marxian thought, and it has little that is special of its own to offer. The attraction of Marxism to the Western intelligentsia was, in any case, never that of an analytically superior theoretical system in social science. It was rather the appeal of a historical theodicy, in which Judeo–Christian moral hopes were to be realized without the need for a transcendental commitment which reason could not sanction. In the Communist societies where Marxism has been institutionalized as the official ideology, its mythopoeic elements have not indeed been especially prominent. For all the paraphernalia of the Lenin cult, Marxist ideology has functioned there in Hobbesian fashion, as an instrument of political discipline, and has had no role in spiritual life. If anything, the inability of Communist Marxism to function as a comprehensive view of the world has added a new twist to the history of its practical self-refutation, as when the Soviet Buryat Mongols appropriate the official legend of the Paris communards and pray to their spirits, which have come to rest in the home of the Buryat's traditional objects of worship under Lake Baikal. Yet the irony of Marxism's self-effacement in the Soviet Union is unlikely to be altogether evaded in the liberal intellectual cultures of the West, even if it does not take the beautiful form of a Shamanistic metamorphosis of Marxist piety. Western analytical Marxism will flourish and expand just in so far as it possesses those mythic elements in Marx's thought that it is committed to shedding.

At the same time, eliminating the mythic content of Marxism will rob it of its distinctive power and speed its recuperation by bourgeois social science. The final dilemma of Western Marxism is that, unless it represses in the interests of criticism and objective knowledge the mythopoeic impulse which explains its appeal over the past century, it can only present to the rest of us the spectacle of an esoteric and barely intelligible cult, whose devotees pass their time picking reverently among the shards and smithereens of a broken altar.

December, 1983

8 The delusion of glasnost

Two world-historical tendencies are presently converging in Central Europe – the rapid and inexorable dissolution of the post-war global settlement and the continuing decomposition, as yet local, partial and reversible, of socialism on the Soviet model. These are developments for which Western policy and opinion are ill prepared. The revelations of *glasnost* confound the certainties of generations of Western opinion-formers. In the Soviet Union, in Poland and now in Hungary and the Baltic states, official sources have revealed a spectacle of economic catastrophe, ecological devastation, hideous social problems and massive popular estrangement – phenomena long familiar to those who have ever lived in Eastern Europe, but on which the Western mind has hitherto turned a senile and incurious eye, clouded by fading images of a new socialist order. The inescapable implication of such disclosures is that the prognostications of Western scholars and journalists, who perceived in the States of Eastern Europe blemished but progressive regimes bent on a task of constructive economic and social planning, have proved to be (as Vladimir Bukovsky has said of Western Sovietology) simply trash, less reliable and far more removed from reality than the wildest tales of the most embittered émigrés. Nor has Western conventional wisdom been noticeably upset by the harrowing news now released daily. Instead, and entirely predictably, the profound crisis to which *glasnost* and the reform movements attest is interpreted by *bien-pensant* Western opinion as further evidence (if such were needed) of the corrigibility of Soviet-style institutions, not as proof of their bankruptcy. In the Soviet Union itself, *glasnost* has served only to reveal intractable and perhaps insoluble economic problems, but this has not prevented Western observers from discerning signs of large-scale restructuring. In our times, *perestroika*, like socialism, is in the eye of the beholder.

The unravelling of the post-war settlement poses similar conundrums for Western opinion. In a sort of political relativization of geography, the division of Europe at Yalta resulted in a loss of the sense of Europe's historic boundaries. On the map, Prague is west of Vienna, and in cultural and historical terms it is at the very heart of Europe; but Czechoslovakia did not have the good fortune Austria had in being neutralized, so it is now part of Eastern Europe, which is to say, hardly part of Europe at all. As far as Western opinion is concerned, Central Europe disappeared down an Orwellian memory hold at Yalta – it is no longer even a geographical expression. Those who live in the forgotten lands of Central Europe may be forgiven if they find the *status quo* less than entirely congenial. It is, in any case, by now scarcely a *status quo*. With extraordinary subtlety and boldness, Soviet policy has sought (and achieved) a return of the repressed memory of the common cultural inheritance among the peoples of Central Europe. It has done so, above all, in West Germany, which is the hinge on which turns the future of Central Europe, and much else. Whatever the immediate outcome of current negotiations, it is safe to assert that neither the division of Germany in its present form, nor West Germany's current relationship with NATO, can be sustained for long. As it stands, the political and military posture of West Germany disregards both the realities of history and legitimate German aspirations for reunification; and the pressures for a separate settlement between West Germany and the Soviet Union are probably irresistible. Such a Soviet–German understanding would not be without precedent. It is, perhaps, not altogether fanciful to see in today's accelerating *rapprochement* a repeat run of the Treaty of Rapallo, under the secret terms of which Germany helped to train and arm the Red Army, and which inaugurated a major programme of German economic aid to the ruined Soviet economy. History was not kind to that particular understanding, but everything suggests that the movement to detach West Germany from its NATO allies cannot now be reversed.

The shape of a new German settlement is thoroughly obscure. We may nevertheless ask, what would any such settlement portend for the nations of Central Europe? Here differences in the conditions prevailing in the different countries are of considerable importance. In Poland, the regime has abandoned the vain attempt to maintain a classic Communist *weltanschauung*-state, thereby becoming the first authentic example of post-totalitarianism, and is now embarking on an experiment in controlled democracy. Developments in Poland have occurred principally in response to crises within Polish society: they have been engendered by the ruination of the economy and by the organized resistance of Solidarity and have been facilitated by the alternative authority structures existing in the Catholic Church. In Hungary, though it is also a response to economic catastrophe, the reform movement has followed a different path, being initiated from within the Party, itself doubtless responding to exogenous forces. Whereas in Poland the institutions of civil society have achieved a measure of autonomy by asserting themselves successfully against the totalitarian bureaucracy, in Hungary civil society is emerging in the wake of a project of economic and political reform initiated from above. Again, the geo-political environments of the two countries are manifestly different, with neutrality on the Austrian model and EEC membership an outcome con-ceivable for Hungary but unthinkable in the case of Poland, for which Finlandization remains the utmost that can reasonably be hoped for.

Such differences between the two countries that are presently at the cutting edge of reform in Central Europe should not lead us to overlook no less significant features they have in common. Both are burdened by an overwhelming foreign debt, which in all likelihood can never be repaid, and which overshadows the faltering and inconsistent reform process in their economies. In both countries, the ruling Communist parties are making systematic efforts to contain and co-opt the oppositional movements, which in each case are deeply divided and increasingly fragmented. Each country has a powerful and gifted intelligentsia, which has a distinguished pedigree of pre-Communist theorists of liberty and civil society, such as Istvan Szechenyi and Jozsef Eötvös in Hungary, while in Poland the independent journal *Res Publica* has given voice to a diversity of conservative and liberal thinkers, Polish and foreign, contemporary and historical. Most fundamentally, the two countries have in common what differentiates them from their East European neighbours, where a bloodless totalitarianism still rules: a project of reform which, in virtue of the intractable realities of economic bankruptcy and popular estrangement, threatens constantly to metamorphose into revolution. This is the truth concealed by slogans such as market socialism – an inherently unstable equilibrium which can only mutate into the politically explosive direction of the reinvention of the central institutions of market capitalism, or else back into the repressive machinery of the command economy.

The ambiguities, ironies and paradoxes of the reform movements in the Soviet Union and parts of Eastern Europe are well explored in Jeffry C. Goldfarb's timely and thoughtful *Beyond Glasnost: The post-totalitarian mind.*[1] Discussing such diverse figures as Havel, Kundera, Baranczak, Michnik, Haraszti and Konrad, Goldfarb finds in them all manifestations of a post-totalitarian culture which, he claims, it is the strategy of *glasnost* to emulate, denature and emasculate. It pursues this objective via the inven-tion of yet another Newspeak, in which the rudimentary truthtelling that distinguishes many of the thinkers and spokesmen of the oppositional movements is distorted and corrupted. Elements of Goldfarb's analysis are problematic and questionable. For one thing, the reality of a post-totalitarian *culture* is at present clearly discernible only in Poland. It does not exist in Czechoslovakia (where, however, a pretotalitarian mind has never disappeared, but has merely been repressed) and as for Hungary, where the memory of a culture of fear remains recent and vivid, it is too early to essay a judgement. What is important and profound in Goldfarb's book is his depiction of the nations of Eastern and Central Europe as locked in a chronic crisis in which, in various fashions and to different degrees, the autonomous institutions of civil society constantly assert themselves against totalitarian administration. This analysis marks a significant advance on the conventional Western perception of the reform movements as expressions of self-criticism by the enlightened despots of the Soviet bloc.

The two movements which bring Central Europe back on to the agenda of history – the unravelling of the post-war settlement and the disintegration of Soviet-style Communism – are interrelated at every point. The historic injustice perpetrated by the Allies at Yalta was a necessary condition of the imposition of Stalinism on Eastern Europe, just as earlier intervention in the service of Wilsonian notions of national self-determination and global democracy had given the *coup de grâce* to the Habsburg Empire. As a consequence of Europe's two civil wars, no institutional framework is easily conceivable within which Central Europe could become again a political reality. The empire of the Habsburgs is a nostalgist's dream, and many questions surround the prospect of a neutral, unified Germany: what would be its borders? And its relations to Poland and Czechoslovakia? The darker side of the dissolution of the post-war settlement is in the prospect of most of Eastern Europe remaining in the vice of an atavistic neo-Stalinism, with a permanent legitimation crisis in Hungary and Poland, and West Germany prized loosed from NATO only to inherit the rusting industries and indigent pensioners of the GDR. The Soviet bloc would then face an indefinite period of decline, its reform movements stifled by spasms of repression and economic collapse staved off by recurrent injections of Western credit and technology.

It is a scenario on these lines – in which the Western powers throw their weight behind the neo-totalitarian project of *perestroika* and the posture of openness in the Soviet Union is abandoned – that seems the most likely, as the economies of the Soviet bloc lurch into the abyss and nationalist movements threaten to become uncontrollable. In this scenario, in which the Soviet bloc is refinanced by the West without guarantees of real economic reform in the direction of a full market economy, the prospect of a rebirth of Central Europe will prove to have been a seductive mirage and post-totalitarianism (except perhaps in Poland and Hungary) an ephemeral phantom. The possibility of a genuine civil society, which the profound crisis of the Communist regimes has briefly generated, will then have been extinguished. This will have come to pass, in part, because of the intractable domestic problems of the East European economies, which cannot move to market institutions without imposing costs on their populations that are bound to test to destruction the fragile institutions of controlled democracy. Even in long-established Western democracies, such as New Zealand and the United States, the project of limiting government and reviving market institutions has itself been limited by democratic pressures. (In the United Kingdom, the upshot of Thatcherism is likely to be no different.) How can we expect the long-suffering workers of Eastern Europe, condemned to forty years of poverty by the socialist command economy, to consent to decades of austerity as the condition of its dismantling? And is it reasonable to expect the solidarity of workers and peasants to survive the conflicts of interest that will emerge between them with the adoption of a market economy?

Faced with such dilemmas, Western policy and opinion are likely to react, not with constructive engagement, but with their characteristic mixture of inept Machiavellianism and guileless credulity, and will opt for the delusive stability of *perestroika* without *glasnost*. They will opt, in other words, for economic reconstruction by authoritarian means. If they do, they will be disappointed, since it is the lesson of China that economic reconstruction founders when it is not accompanied by a commitment to political accountability and the rule of law, and recourse to repression is a permanent possibility. In respect of Poland and the Baltic States, in any case, it is far from clear that a return to repression is a realistic possibility. Even if the present movement to civil society be reversed, it will not (as many in the West continue to hope) inaugurate a period of stability in Central and Eastern Europe, but only stave off change until a worse crisis cannot be prevented. For, in truth, the situation in Eastern Europe is not one in which orderly reform can be effected, it is more akin to a revolutionary situation – but that is a truth which transgresses the limits of Western *glasnost*.

July, 1989

9   The academic romance of Marxism

The claim that the real history of the twentieth century can be illuminated by the intellectual history of Marxism is, perhaps, one that could now only be made in the United States. From the perspective of most Europeans, including the vast majority of those living in the Soviet bloc and virtually all who may once have been Marxists, any such claim will seem at best heavily ironical, and at worst a piece of academic frivolity. For in none of its many varieties did Marxist thought anticipate (nor has it yet even begun to explain) the most decisive developments which occurred in Europe and elsewhere in our century. It was paralysed by the trauma of the First World War, in which the proletarian classes of Europe exhibited national and not class allegiances, and it recovered for a decade only by retreat into millenarian fantasy about the new society (and, let us not forget, the new humanity) which it supposed to be under construction in Russia in the aftermath of the Bolshevik Revolution. The lessons of War Communism, in which a systematic attempt to operate an economy without market exchange may have cost as many lives as the later experiment in socialist agriculture conducted by Stalin, were lost on the Marxian theorists of revolutionary socialism – if, indeed, they troubled themselves to inquire into these events. Instead, Marxist thought between the wars oscillated uncertainly between witless Sovietism and self-deceiving piety towards revolutionaries not compromised by collaboration in Stalinist terror, such as the ineffectual and romantic Rosa Luxembourg and the vain and pitiless opportunist Trotsky. Marxist thought was utterly unprepared for the successive catastrophes of the destruction of social democracy in Europe, the Nazi–Soviet pact and the Holocaust. Equally, the role of slave labour in the Gulag during the period of rapid industrialization under the Five Year Plans in the Soviet Union was repressed for a generation or more in Western Marxism, whose exponents found in the convulsions of the Cultural Revolution in China (which probably cost more lives than the Stalinist terror, and encompassed a cultural genocide in Tibet) an alternative solace for their oppositional energies.

The *coup de grâce* to Marxism in Western Europe has been given by developments during the past generation, which have comprehended the repression of a popular revolution in Hungary, an aborted reform from above in Czechoslovakia, the attempted destruction by way of a Pinochet-style military dictatorship of the autonomous institutions of the Polish working class in its project of asserting civil society (including the Roman Catholic Church) against the totalitarian bureaucracy and, last but not least, the strategy of dismantling the institutions of central economic planning and engaging Western finances in a project of capitalist economic development which, with varying degrees of consistency, is currently under way in the Soviet bloc and in People's China. Not one of these world-historical developments was predicted, nor has any of them been theoretically accommodated, by Western Marxism, which has preferred to devote its attention to the question why no socialist revolution has yet occurred in any capitalist society.

Like Marx's thought itself, the proposition that the intellectual history of Marxism might be deployed to illuminate the crises of our time finds little reception in contemporary Europe. If in Paris it would be greeted with bored indifference, in Warsaw and Leningrad it will meet with incredulity and downright contempt. It will command intellectual interest, if at all, only on condition that it focuses on the causal relations between Marxian theory and the catastrophes that have disfigured the societies in which Marxism has acquired political hegemony – a topic virtually passed over in silence by Martin Jay. How, then, does Jay attempt to justify the research programme advanced in *Fin-de-Siècle Socialism*?[1] He tells us that it may be 'instructive to consider the possible parallels between the late nineteenth century and the waning years of our own. For in so doing', he asserts, 'we may find some suggestions for the socialism that is likely to develop in the 21st century'. His statement is arresting, inasmuch as the suggestion that the near future will offer a future to socialism in any of its radical variants is likely to be other than risible only in a society which (like the United States and unlike most of Europe) lacks any historical experience of revolutionary socialism.

There is a deeper reason for the incongruity of Jay's project. For the most part, American radical intellectuals in recent decades have, in default of theorizing their own history, traditions and institutions, aped the spent intellectual fashions of Europe. In general, American intellectual life in this century has given evidence of prodigious vitality and originality, with American philosophers developing the seminal work in pragmatism of such thinkers as C.S. Peirce and William James, and American philosophy coming to dominance in much of the rest of the world. Again, American thought has produced profound reflections on the American political experience in the work of thinkers such as John Rawls, whose theory of liberal justice embodies an unsurpassed distillation of American constitutionalism, and the socialist historian Eugene Genovese, whose work on the antebellum South has delineated the structure and dynamic of an anticapitalist economy and culture in its relations with the commercial civilization of the North.

By contrast, the American radical intelligentsia over the past decades has typically been preoccupied with the ephemera of the European culture market, whose most grotesque manifestations have enjoyed in American academia a sort of stilted after-life – as evidenced in deconstructionist literary theory and in the applications to law by the Critical Legal Studies Movement of the banalities of the participatory democratic theory of the 1960s. Jay's project becomes intelligible, if not justifiable, when we note its background conditions – an intellectual culture insulated from political experience of radical socialism and an academic class which uses the rhetoric and theorizing of the radical intelligentsia of Europe a decade or a generation ago to legitimate its estrangement from its own culture. For these reasons alone, we may confidently predict that the academic institutions of capitalist America will be the last redoubt of Marxian theorizing when it has long since been repudiated wholesale by the peoples and rulers of the states where once it commanded power.

It must be acknowledged at once that Jay's intellectual history of Marxism is always scholarly and is for the most part written felicitously and in civilized tones. At times, indeed, he charmingly throws off intimations of the absurdist aspects of his own project. Thus, as an aside, he notes that

> the bizarre spectacle of autocratic rulers like Joseph Stalin, Josip Tito and Mao Tse Tung holding on to power for life suggests, in fact, that monarchy is a far more likely prototype for socialist politics in certain 20th century regimes than anything remotely derivable from the democratic tradition.

Inexplicably, Jay here omits any reference to Romania and North Korea, where the institution of Communist autocracy promises (or promised) to become hereditary – an even more delightful inversion of Marxian expectations. Again, when Jay writes of Laclau and Mouffe's book, *Hegemony and Socialist Strategy* [2], that they 'argue for a revised version of Gramsci's notion of hegemony filtered through a post-structuralist critique of the possibility of an identitarian subjectivity', it is impossible to believe that he is not satirizing the exotic argot spoken only by Western academic Marxists at governmentally funded international conferences. Most centrally, though, Jay's treatment in the four central chapters of the book of two key figures in post-War Western Marxian theorizing – Jurgen Habermas and Alvin Gouldner – betrays an intermittent awareness of the political marginality, social and economic context and inherent redundancy of Marxian thought in the contemporary world.

Very properly, Jay observes that (in an authentic Marxian tradition) Habermas has disavowed as utopian any effort at giving substantive content to a post-capitalist order and has instead concentrated on the procedural conditions of human self-transcendence and emancipation – conditions comprehending an 'ideal speech situation' of unmanipulated communicative rationality, a reduction in the role of scientific-technological reason and an enhancement of the aesthetic dimensions of human life. As Habermas puts it, tersely: 'A reified everyday praxis can be cured only by creating unconstrained interaction of the cognitive with the moral-practical and the aesthetic-expressive elements'. Commenting on this and similar statements, Jay remarks mildly that 'Habermas owes us a more explicit explanation of the aesthetic-practical rationality he wants to defend in modernism. It is difficult enough', he goes on, 'to grasp what a mediated relationship among cognitive-instrumental, moral-practical and aesthetic-expressive rationalities would look like, even if they all might be simultaneously reintegrated with the life-world. It is even harder if the rational status of the third remains somewhat of a mystery.' Jay's comments on Habermas may be put in somewhat less hermetic terms. The idea of full communicative rationality in an ideal speech situation among people is an opaque one in Habermas's thought. Whatever it means, it is associated with the Enlightenment expectation that in an undistorted dialogue human beings will come to convergence in their values, projects and perspectives. At no point in his prolix and voluminous theorizings does Habermas give this expectation any foundation in reason. It hovers in mid-air, foundationless, like the Cheshire Cat's smile, its supportive body detached and destroyed by the very modernism Habermas is so anxious to defend. Nor is his expectation of convergence on values and perspectives as the outcome of dialogic rationality sustained by the actual circumstances of modern societies, which all in varying degrees harbour a diversity of cultural traditions. An open dialogue among these traditions is far more likely to result in the emergence of powerful rivals to Habermas's modernist humanism than to reinforce it. In reposing his faith in open dialogue, he has the character of a sort of *bien-pensant* Pascal, laying a wager on reason which nothing in our (or his) experience warrants.

Jay comes closest to confronting the insuperable limitations and social functions of Marxian thought in his two chapters on Gouldner, the 'outlaw marxist' sociologist. In his *Against Fragmentation*[3], Gouldner sought to develop earlier analyses in which he attempted to bring to consciousness what Jay calls 'the suppressed secret of Marxism's embarrassing social origins in the radicalized bourgeois intelligentsia'. It is Gouldner's embarrassing thesis that the radicalization of the intelligentsia is a response to a blockage in their upward social mobility rather than the expression of any commitment to critical reason. Jay puts it thus:

> As blocked ascendants, radical intellectuals from Jacobins onward often looked to state service as a possible way to salvage their positions, while at the same time serving the general cause of social rationalisation. Ironically, even the culture of critical discourse harboured its own form of potential elitism. For although selfconsciously egalitarian in terms of its adherents, it was hierarchically related to those outside its own boundaries. The absolute commitment to rationality, at least as a regulative ideal, could easily conflict with the specific material interest of the non-intellectual agents. . . . Indeed, the very notion of a material interest suggested an undiscussable given outside the realm of rational discourse.

This is far from being a novel position, being anticipated by the Polish syndicalist theorist, W. Machajski and, as Gouldner himself notes, by Marx's arch enemy, Bakunin. But it is entertaining to find it advanced by a Marxist.

Predictably, Jay is concerned to defend Marx against Bakunin's claim that Marxism expresses the class interest of a nascent *pedantocracy*, but Bakunin's claim is well borne out by the history of American academic Marxism. In the United States, a radical intelligentsia which perceives its social status to be lower than that of business, which is accordingly estranged from the dominant values of its parent culture, and which is substantially marginalized from the political process, has attempted to legitimate its interests and objectives by the adoption of an anti-market ideology. This stratagem may be better theorized in the terms of the Virginia School of Public Choice as a classic instance of rent-seeking, or in the Paretian categories of residues and derivations, but that it has many affinities with the practices analysed in the Marxian theory of ideology needs little elaboration. It is, perhaps, the chief point of interest in Jay's book that, whereas he considers Gouldner's application to the radical socialist intelligentsia of the Marxian theory of ideology, he is enough of a spokesman for Western radical academics to refrain from pursuing Gouldner's demystificatory critique.

John Roemer's Marxism[4] is in a very different vein from that predominantly inspired by the Frankfurt School which Jay seeks to chronicle and interpret. It is a species of analytical Marxism, which aims to dispose of the Hegelian inheritance which encumbers Marx's own thought and to reconstruct the central propositions of the Marxian critique of capitalism using only the tools of mainstream ('bourgeois') economics and philosophy. In the writings of G.A. Cohen and Jon Elster, this analytical school within contemporary Marxism has produced work of considerable intellectual quality, even if it is sometimes doubtful how far Cohen and Elster still deserve (or wish) to be called Marxists. By contrast, Roemer in both methodological and political terms is a far more orthodox Marxist, in that he aims with the help of game theory to rehabilitate the notion of exploitation, if not in the technical Marxist sense – a project which Cohen has apparently abandoned. Further, unlike Elster, he endorses the classical Marxist critique of capitalism as chaotic and inefficient and (apart from a few nervous references to the pros and cons of market socialism) makes few concessions to the allocative efficiency of markets and seems to conceive of Marxian socialism in the traditional terms of central economic planning. Although he is ready to abandon the technical Marxian idea of exploitation and with it the labour theory of value, Roemer's project is to reconstruct the hard core of the Marxian critique of capitalism with the resources of standard micro-economics and neo-classical equilibrium theory.

The first point to be made about Roemer's reconstruction is that, just like the neo-classical model it deploys, it stands at a very great distance from any real-world economy. Indeed, Roemer's distance from reality is signalled before he even begins to develop his model, when on the first page of the book he tells us that Marxism has achieved 'intellectual hege-mony' across a third of the world, in that 'the world-view of Marxism based on class, exploitation and historical materialism is pervasive in these (com-munist) societies'. This sordid piece of intellectual flatulence, which betrays an inability to distinguish between cultural and political hegemony, will provoke hollow laughter in Budapest and Prague (not to mention Bucharest and Peking), where oppositional movements and indeed ruling élites are publicly or privately contemptuous of Marxism even if they sometimes remain socialist in outlook. Such bizarre statements are clues to the basic weakness of Roemer's project, which arises from its borrowings from the most abstract and least realistic portions of conventional economic theory. Along with the majority of his fellow economists who are not Marxists, Roemer works with an equilibrium model of economic life which abstracts from its most fundamental features – the scarcity and dispersal of knowledge and the role of market institutions in transmitting and utilizing it via the price mechanism. Because it assumes full knowledge of others' preferences and resources on the part of economic agents, general equili-brium theory models no possible state of the world. It is not an ideal type, but a barely coherent fiction whose centrality in economics has served only to distract attention from the actual workings of market processes.

Using this model, Roemer can demonstrate that under certain formally statable conditions resources will be allocated more efficiently by planning than in any real-world market system, and he is able to point to features of markets in the real world which explain their failures. Nothing in these reasonings tells us anything of value as to the comparative allocative efficiency of markets and central planning as alternative institutional arrangements. Roemer tells us that, for a variety of reasons, capitalist economies exhibit 'a vast mizallocation of resources'. The invisible-hand properties of market systems presuppose a tendency in them to reach equilibrium, he asserts, and this is frustrated by the uncertainties about the future that market participants confront – uncertainties that cause people to behave irrationally. Now equilibrium in markets is, doubtless, an asymptote, which they will not always have even a tendency to move towards, but what justifies Roemer's implicit confidence that economic planning will be any improvement on markets? (If 'people' behave irrationally in the face of uncertainty, will not *planners* do likewise? Or will they abolish the uncertainty arising from our ignorance of the future?) When we return from the dream world of Roemer's theorems to history and common experience, we discover that every market failure present in capitalist systems, such as environmental pollution, discoordination, worker alienation and underemployment, is replicated on a far greater scale (though often covertly) under socialist central planning institutions. These facts, which are commonplaces under the Soviet *glasnost*, are as yet too subversive to be mentioned by Roemer.

The chaos, waste and malinvestment characteristic of central economic planning, which is the common historical experience of those socialist states which are now attempting to resurrect market institutions, was accurately predicted in the writings of Mises and Hayek and others in the Austrian School. The Austrian argument was always that, for the very same reasons that a perfectly competitive market is a fiction, so central economic planning is an impossibility. No government can possess the information about relative scarcities, time preferences and consumer tastes that is transmitted (however imperfectly) through price signals, but without which economic planning is an exercise in disaster. Nor do moves in the direction of market socialism much mitigate these dilemmas, as the Yugoslav and Hungarian examples show. In practice, socialist economies behave exactly as Austrian theory predicts – they rely on historic and capitalist prices, they depend crucially on recurrent injections of Western capital and technology and on a parallel economy of which the official economy is only the visible tip. It is probably unnecessary to note that Roemer's references to the failings of Communist economies are scanty and evasive. In general, he proceeds as if the moves towards reinvention of market institutions in

China and elsewhere are irrelevant to his argument. In this, and in the fetishistic formalism of his entire method, he fails to take his own advice, when he remarks apropos of invisible-hand theorems: 'Models are simplifications of reality, and judgement must be exercised before boldly claiming that the simplifications are appropriate for the policy question at hand'.

It is in regard to exploitation that Roemer's theorizing is most resistant to contact with history and social reality. As he defines it, 'a person is exploited if the labour that he expends in production is greater than the labour embodied in the goods he can purchase with the revenues from production'. What is most significant here is not whether he is successful in formulating a conception of exploitation that serves the Marxist critique of capitalism without incorporating the defects of Marx's own conception, but that Roemer's conception makes the actual economic well-being of the worker a matter of theoretical and moral indifference. This is to say that, even if we envisage a socialist economy that is not disfigured (as all actually existing socialisms are) by networks of graft and corruption, by Third World levels of proletarian housing and medical care and by an exploitative *nomenklatura*, the worker who is not exploited will almost certainly have a lower level of economic well-being than a comparative worker under capitalist institutions – a result that flows inexorably from the disastrous allocative influences of central economic planning. This result is the more significant if we recognize that exploitation exists under socialist institutions. Roemer goes so far as to admit this, but assures his readers that much socialist exploitation is an inevitable and 'socially necessary' incident in socialist construction, while the 'questionable' forms of socialist exploitation which arise from differential status are no worse than those found in capitalist societies. It does not occur to him to ask whether such an outcome is worth the millions of lives lost during the most active periods of socially necessary socialist exploitation. The upshot of Roemer's neglect of the real world is that, with all its gimmick-ridden formalism, his reconstruction of Marxian economic philosophy has the intellectual relevance of a dated crossword puzzle.

Taken together, the books of Jay and Roemer exemplify the poverty of American academic Marxism – a Marxism innocent of history, politically irrelevant and marginal in its own culture. That these characteristics are not confined to American Marxism is shown by the work of Roberto Unger, with its hare-brained schemes for the transfer of productive assets to 'rotating capital funds' – schemes whose practical implementation would rapidly transform the United States into a replica of Unger's native Brazil. It is in regard to American Marxism, however, that the character of academic radicalism in the United States is most readily apparent – its function as the ideology of an aspirant intellectual *rentier* class, an ideology despised in every society that has had the misfortune to be subject to its political hegemony, and which in the United States compensates for its manifest political nullity by seeking hegemony within academic institutions.

10 Philosophy, science and myth in Marxism

INTRODUCTION

> Feuerbach resolves the religious essence into the human essence. But the human essence is no abstraction inherent in each single individual. In its reality it is the ensemble of social relations.[1]

It is a common belief, shared both by Marxists and by critics of Marxism, that differences in the interpretation of this statement have important implications for the assessment of Marx's system of ideas. How we read it will affect our view of the unity of Marx's thought and of the continuity of its development over his lifetime, and it will bear crucially on our appraisal of the epistemological status – metaphysical, scientific or mythopoeic – of the various elements of the Marxian system. Among Marxists, members of the Frankfurt School have emphasized the paternity of Marxian metaphysical humanism in Hegel's conception of man as a self-creating being, while Althusser and his disciples have seen in the extrusion from Marx's later work of any such 'anthropomorphic' notion a guarantee of the scientific character of his historical materialism. Among Marx's liberal critics, it is widely agreed that he espoused an essentialist view of man and, often enough, it is thought that this alone is sufficient to disqualify his system from scientific status. No consensus exists, however, as to the cognitive standing of the several components of Marx's thought. That agreement should be lacking as to the place in it of a conception of human nature is hardly surprising. Different construals of the role of a view of man will reflect divergent commitments, not only in the philosophy and methodology of social and historical inquiry, but in moral and political thought as well.

I do not aim to canvass systematically all the salient philosophical problems posed by Marx's assumptions about man. More modestly, I aim to offer an assessment of the epistemic status and mutual relations of the principal parts of Marx's system, but to do this indirectly and obliquely by way of a discussion of the contributions to Marxist thought of three important writers. Each of these writers is in a genuine Marxian tradition in that he develops a theme which is undeniably present in Marx himself, and each of them presents the Marxian system as a totality belonging to a different mode of discourse. First, I shall consider some aspects of the writings of Herbert Marcuse. Against the attribution by Althusser of an epistemological rupture in the evolution of Marx's ideas, I shall contend that a definite metaphysical view of man runs consistently through all of Marx's writings. Not only does evidence from the body of Marx's later writings show that he never abandoned the philosophical anthropology he endorsed in the *Economic-Philosophic Manuscripts*: it can easily be shown that some such doctrine is presupposed by his materialist conception of history. But whereas Marx's historical materialism depends upon his metaphysic of human nature, the latter cannot adequately support the former. Indeed, Marcuse's writings suggest that emphasizing Marx's metaphysical humanism tends to undermine the claim of his system to be a theory of world history. In Marcuse's case, it yields an elegiac Marxism, from which class struggle has been all but eliminated, in which social revolution has the character of an improbably Pascalian wager, and whose primary uses seem to be those of a weapon in the armoury of cultural criticism. This result is to be accounted for, not by reference to the metaphysical status of the central postulate of Marcuse's system, but in terms of specific incoherences in its philosophical anthropology.

Second, I shall consider G.A. Cohen's recent defence of historical materialism in functionalist terms. Important weaknesses in Cohen's argument suggest the conclusion that, if Marx's system contains a theory of universal history and not just an explanatory model of capitalist development, it must trade on teleological explanations of a sort which social science cannot countenance. Thus Hegel's view that human history has an overall intelligibility deriving from the fact that it has a telos or end-state, a view which Cohen expounds sympathetically in the first chapter of his book (see note 21 to this chapter) but whose bearing on Marx's historical materialism he does not systematically examine, is actually indispensable to it in so far as it contains a theory of the development of human productive powers through successive economic systems. The collapse of historical materialism as a theory of world history carries with it the ruin of its central thesis about the primacy of productive forces in explaining social change. The upshot of my criticism of Cohen's book is that, whatever incidental contributions to social science it may contain, Marx's system does not in its main elements belong to the scientific mode of discourse.

Finally, I turn briefly to examine the interpretation of Marxism developed by Georges Sorel, a neglected Marxist thinker rightly described by Croce as the most original and important Marxist theorist after Marx himself. In Sorel we find a construction of Marx's system, in which Marx's own activist and Promethean conception of man and his doctrine of class struggle are fully preserved, but in which his historicist and scientistic pretensions have been decisively abandoned. In Sorel's writings, the mythopoeic character of Marxism as the ideology of proletarian class struggle is explicitly acknowledged and its source in a definite moral tradition identified. Sorel's Marxism is not without the difficulties connected with any form of relativism in social and political theory. It appears to be involved in paradoxes of self-reference, and I shall touch on a couple of these whose implications are serious for Sorel's idiosyncratic version of Marxism. I shall point to a tension in Sorel's thought between its mythopoeic and its scientific or diagnostic aspects and I shall suggest that developing a realist science of society involves abandoning some of the most distinctive claims of Sorel's Marxism.

The programmatic conclusion of the paper, whose cogency I do not aim to demonstrate but merely to support indirectly by way of a survey of three Marxian writers, is that Marx's is an explosively unstable system of ideas each of whose components has a distinct epistemological status and stands in need of a different kind of support. Elaborating each of these strands in Marx's thought produces such radically diverse varieties of Marxism that we are justified in regarding talk of Marx's 'system' as little more than a *façon de parler*.

MARXISM AS METAPHYSICS: MARX AND MARCUSE ON MAN AS A SELF-CREATING BEING

> The practical creation of an objective world, the fashioning of inorganic nature, is proof that man is a conscious species-being. . . . It is true that the animals also produce. They build nests or dwellings, like the bee, the beaver, the ant, etc. But they produce only their own immediate needs or those of their young; they produce one-sidedly, while man produces universally; they produce only themselves, while man reproduces the whole of nature; their products belong immediately to their physical bodies, while man freely confronts his own product. Animals produce only according to the standards and needs of the species to which they belong, while man is capable of producing according to the standards of every species. . . .
>
> It is therefore in the fashioning of the objective world that man really proves himself to be a species-being. Such production is his active species-life. Through it nature appears as his work and his reality. The object of labour is therefore himself, not only intellectually, in his

consciousness, but actively and actually, and he can therefore contemplate himself in a world he has himself created.[2]

It is clear from this and from other, similar passages, scattered throughout the corpus of Marx's writings, that when Marx asserts that man's nature is that of a maker, he intends his reader to understand far more than that man is a tool-using and a tool-fashioning animal. Certainly, that man's reliance on tools in the reproduction of his life-activity is part of what distinguishes him from other animals is never contested by Marx: it is a distinctive feature of human life to which he often refers. It may be supposed that when, in a well-known passage in *The German Ideology*,[3] Marx observes that men may be distinguished from animals by their consciousness, their religion or anything else, but '[they] distinguish themselves as soon as they produce their means of subsistence', this is what he has in mind. The greater part of Marx's meaning is more plainly evident, however, when he returns to the question of man's *differentia specifica* in *Capital*,[4] declaring that 'what distinguishes the worst of architects from the best of bees is this: that the architect raises his structure in imagination before he erects it in reality'. In such statements Marx appears to be insisting on a sharp contrast between human life and that of other animals:

> The animal is immediately one with its life-activity. It is not distinct from that activity; it *is* that activity. Man makes his life-activity itself an object of his will and consciousness. He has conscious life-activity. It is not a determination with which he directly merges. Conscious life-activity directly distinguishes man from animal life-activity. Only because of that is he a species-being.[5]

What separates the life of men and women from the life of other animals, it seems, is the element of Hegelian negativity, itself dependent on the capacity for abstract thought, which allows them to distance themselves from the behaviour, instinctual or conventional, which they inherit directly from nature or society. It is this negativity and critical reflexivity which forbids any inference from man's fixed characteristics as a biological species to his essential life-activity, and which licenses the claim that man's nature is that of a self-creative being.

It is only this understanding of the claim that man is the producer of himself and of his world which enables us to see how Marx could contrast his own standpoint with that of the old, 'contemplative' materialism. For, whereas he speaks of man as being a part of nature, Marx's standpoint is far from the caricature of German positivism preserved in the writings of Engels and Lenin. It is more akin to the Hegelian and radically anti-naturalist standpoint, in which nature is given to man only as an artifact that he has himself produced. In this perspective, the relation between man and nature is theorized, not as a process in which a domain of inert objects confronts a passive subject in whose consciousness it is reflected, but as a transaction in which it is their own practice which gives nature all those of its features which are recognizable by men. Far from subordinating men's lives and history to laws given independently of their purposes or self-interpretations, Marx tends to treat the whole domain of nature as a precipitate of human activities. So strong does this tendency become, so powerful the influence of the mystical idea (derived by Hegel from Böhme) of nature as man's larger body, that there is some basis for Kolakowski's imputation[6] to Marx of a species-relativism. In general, of course, Marx is far from an Idealist denial of the independent reality of the external world. Rather, in standard pragmatist fashion, he tends to regard the concepts and categories embodied in any view of nature as artifactual, useful fictions whose truth-value derives wholly from their contribution to the success of human struggles with the world. This is not to deny that man comes to self-consciousness to find himself situated in a natural order. It is to say that his picture of the world is not something given to him as a datum, but merges in his practical struggles with it, which in their turn contribute to the progressive humanization of the world in an objective and factual sense. I shall call the thesis that man is in this radical respect his own maker and the shaper of his world Marx's *activist* thesis.

So far Marx's view of the nature of man would seem to be largely a development of some of the main preoccupations of German Idealism. Marx also picked out as among man's *differentiae specificae* another feature, owing more to the Romantic movement, according to which man is distinguished by a vital need for productive labour, going well beyond anything required in the struggle with brute scarcity. For Marx, the estrangement of labour in class and, above all, in capitalist society, consists, not only or primarily in the expropriation of its product, but in the fact that men's life-activity is governed by the autonomous power of the commodity. It is not just that men must work in order not to starve that constitutes labour's estrangement. After all, a *rentier* who does not have that necessity is judged by Marx to be no less disabled as a productive being than is a proletarian. Marx's view, rather, is that labour ceases to be estranged only when it is the direct expression of man's nature, only when its character is poetic or artistic. This aspect of Marx's view of man is *productivist*, not only in the sense that he acknowledges that human beings must secure the means of their survival before they can do anything else, but crucially in that self-expressive labour is conceived to be an endogenous imperative of man's nature. This feature of Marx's conception distinguishes his thought sharply from the outlook of the ancient world, in which human fulfilment was believed to lie in contemplative absorption in a natural or divine order. It separates him no less clearly from the Classical Economists, by whom labour was conceived typically as a distasteful incident *en route* to consumption, and whose social ideal is best epitomized in J.S. Mill's 'gospel of leisure'.

The expressive view of labour (which I have termed Marx's productivist thesis about man) is easily seen as a corollary or entailment of his activist view of man as in essence self-determining. Thus far Marx might seem little more than a radical individualist, a liberal humanist opposed to the fossilization of social life in oppressive institutions. To construe the Marxian system in this way, however, would be a grievous misunderstanding. For, in a drastic extension of the Hegelian tradition, Marx supposed that self-determination for man involves the suppression or dissolution of all distinct, autonomous spheres of social activity and modes of intellectual life. He states this view unambiguously in *Capital*:[7]

> The religious reflex of the real world can . . . only then finally vanish when the practical relations of everyday life offer to man none but perfectly intelligible and rational relations to his fellowmen and to nature.
>
> The life-process of society, which is based on the process of material production, does not strip off its mystical veil until it is treated as production by freely associated men, and is consciously regulated by them in accordance with a settled plan.

Here Marx asserts that man's self-determination is inhibited just in so far as the objects and relationships of the social world have a life and laws of their own. It is not too much to say that, for Marx, social science withers away with the ending of alienation, precisely because its subject-matter – a densely textured ambience of autonomous institutions, conventions and practices – has ceased to exist. Similarly, it is only mankind's pre-history that can on this view be law-governed. To acknowledge that for human beings the social world must always remain a world that is not of their own making, that men's identities will always be constituted by the roles and activities in which they find themselves, would be for Marx to acquiesce in an utter loss of human freedom. It is not easy, all the same, to envisage what the end of estrangement would be like, given that so much that is constitutive of our lives as we know them would vanish. There is no doubt that the Marxian conception of a de-alienated community would have been resisted by Hegel himself as asocial and abstract to the point of virtual emptiness. However this may be, Marx's view that full human self-determination is incompatible with the survival of any independent spheres of social life yields an important clue to his central understanding of capitalism and of its dialectical negation. It is not in virtue of the distribution of income or the form of property that it involves that capitalism is regarded by Marx as the supremely dehumanizing mode of production. It is because capitalist production has the character of an impersonal process by which human subjects are constrained, and in which their transactions are frozen or crystallized into reified forms of the species-life, that Marx sees it as the radical loss or negation of the human essence. The alienation of labour cannot survive the end of commodity-production just because estranged labour is defined as that which occurs whenever productive exchanges fail to be the direct expression of organized human will.

What defines socialism, accordingly, is the overcoming of commodity-production and its replacement by planned production for use. It is planned production for the direct satisfaction of human needs (including the vital need for expressive labour), production no longer mediated by monetary exchanges or by impersonal laws of supply and demand, which is definitive of the socialist order.[8] It was taken for granted by Marx, no doubt, and it is a natural implication of his account of self-determination, that economic planning in a socialist order would be democratic. (I leave to one side here difficult questions about the decision-procedures, majoritarian or other-wise, appropriate to the democratic planning of a whole economy, and I refrain from commenting on the Arrow-type logical dilemmas such pro-cedures would certainly generate.) It is crucially important to grasp, how-ever, that the self-regulation of a socialist economy is in every respect diametrically opposed to that which obtains in a market order or catallaxy.[9] For, whereas the order that emerges from a series of market exchanges, though it has its source in human actions, owes its most important properties to the fact that it is *not* the result of human design, the order of a socialist economy in the Marxian conception of it is supposed to embody only the intentions of its constituent subjects. It is a fundamental criticism of Marx's idea of a socialist economy that, even supposing human pre-ferences and purposes could in the absence of class stratification attain a measure of compossibility sufficient to obviate serious conflicts over the allocation of resources, the suppression of market processes would deprive economic planners of much information useful to the rational imple-mentation of agreed projects. Whatever its difficulties, it is in the idea of the subordination to collective human will of spontaneous economic processes that the thrust of Marxian socialism is contained, and it is this thesis about the economic consequences of human self-determination that I propose to call Marx's *anti-autonomist* thesis.

Each of these three facets of Marx's conception of man is fully preserved in Herbert Marcuse's version of the critical theory of the Frankfurt School. The activist thesis is expressed in Marcuse's constant emphasis on the creative role of man as the subject of history, the agent of the creation and continuous transformation of the forms of his social life, and his rejection of any image of man's self-development which pictures it in terms of submission to the necessity of historical laws. Like Marx, Marcuse argues that it is the reduction of human relations to relations between things and, in particular, to relations between commodities, that constitutes the essential inhumanity of capitalist society, and which, in reducing proletarian life-activity to a commodity on the labour market, generates the 'determinate negation' of the capitalist order. In Marcuse, as in Marx himself, the conceptual foundation of historical materialism is a form of metaphysical humanism, which conceives of history as the progressive disclosure of man's defining species-powers, but which acknowledges that the activities of empirical social groups and individuals may conceal as much as they reveal of man's essential nature and possibilities. Marcuse is in Marx's own authentic tradition in his strong emphasis on the functions of ideological false consciousness in inhibiting men's reflection on their circumstances as alienated labourers and thus in reproducing an irrational social order. In elaborating an ambitious theory of ideology, Marcuse follows Marx in presupposing a set of species-powers whose flourishing it is precisely the role of false consciousness to prevent. Like Marx and Hegel, Marcuse takes for granted that these powers of critical reflection remain latent in most societies, and are manifestly present only in relatively highly complex societies; but he is in no doubt that some such account of man's species-being is presupposed by any theory of ideology. His work shows clearly enough that both the logic of historical materialism and its development as a theory of ideology require a philosophical anthropology of just the sort Althusser's disciples seek to suppress from Marxism. In Marcuse, too, finally, we find Marx's productivist emphasis on the intrinsic value of self-expressive labour, and the anti-autonomist conception of a rationally reconstructed and holistically administered economic order.

In laying emphasis on the metaphysical humanist aspect of the Marxian system, however, Marcuse retreats from its historicist claims and abandons some of its most distinctive theses about the role of proletarian class struggle in the transition to socialism. The dilemma in which Marcuse's abandonment of Marxian historicism places him is well illustrated in his characteristic combination of repeated emphatic statements of the invincibly totalitarian character of modern capitalism with frequent affirmations of the real possibility of total social revolution and reconstruction. On the one hand, Marcuse has declared that 'the vital need for revolution no longer prevails among those classes that as the "immediate producers" would be capable of stopping the capitalist production'.[10] 'Marx's conception of revolution', he continues 'was based on the existence of a class which is not only impoverished and dehumanized, but which is also free from any vested interest in the capitalistic system and therefore represents a new historical force with qualitatively different needs and aspirations'.[11] According to Marcuse, the emergence of such an 'internal negative force' is blocked in advanced industrial society – 'not by violent suppression or by terroristic modes of government, but by a rather comfortable and scientific coordination and administration'.[12] As a result of contemporary society's 'highly effective scientific management of needs, demands and satisfaction',[13] 'the internal historical link between capitalism and socialism ... seems to be severed',[14] so that 'the idea of the available alternatives evaporate into an utterly utopian dimension in which they are at home'.[15] Here Marcuse is asserting that, owing to the success of modern techniques of demand management, in which even the unconscious needs and instincts of the population become liable to manipulation, the traditional oppositional class in capitalist society has become attached to the circumstances of its servitude. Thus alienated labour may, with the perfection of industrial relations techniques, come to be experienced as rewarding and fulfilling. On the other hand, social groups exist which will seek to exploit the utopian possibilities which Marcuse believes to be inherent in modern capitalism. In *One-Dimensional Man*, Marcuse discovered the last vestiges of revolutionary protest within 'the substratum of the outcasts and outsiders, the exploited and persecuted of other races and other colours, the unemployed and unemployable'.[16] In *An Essay on Liberation*, Marcuse opines that, as a result of the advance of automation, 'a general unstructured, unorganized and diffused process of disintegration may occur'.[17] Marcuse proposes that an intellectual vanguard exploit the new contradictions of late capitalist society by implementing a policy of discriminating tolerance toward conservative and reactionary forces and forge an alliance with other oppositional groups. The new society will be inaugurated by a government consisting of an educational dictatorship of free men and women which, guided by a radical transvaluation of values and inspired by a new sensibility, can take advantage of the vast technological resources of modern society and avoid the repression which has disfigured all previous revolutions. In Marcuse's last writings, the social revolution powered by the entry into radical politics of a minority of powerless outsiders, which in *One-Dimensional Man* he had described as 'nothing but a chance',[18] is again treated as a utopian possibility against which virtually all existing institutions and social forces militate.

Marcuse's thought clearly illustrates the tensions inherent in any revision of the Marxian system in which metaphysical postulates are given epistemological priority over social theory and historical interpretation. Socialism becomes a free-floating possibility, an abstract and avowedly utopian prospect, grounded only in a speculative distillation of the human essence. Shorn of the Marxian theory of transition, in which the proletariat is acknowledged to be the class in which mankind's universal interests are embodied, Marcuse's Marxism resembles nothing so much as a Left Hegelian radical humanism. In detaching the transition to socialism from any sort of proletarian activity, again, Marcuse (like Stalin) revives a pre-Marxist Jacobin tradition in which workers become passive objects of their own liberation. The dilemma of Marcuse's thought results from his recognition of the superannuation of the Marxian system conceived as a theory of capitalist development and a scheme for the interpretation of history coupled with his refusal to regard any empirical development as constituting any sort of criticism of Marxism's metaphysical core. Against this criticism, no doubt, it will be urged that Marcuse is at once more and less authentically Marxian than I have pictured him as being. Thus he has always maintained that working-class activity and initiative are indispensable to socialist revolution, just as Marx did. On the other hand, his theory of human nature owes much to Freud, and his theory of a 'technological eros' is oriented around the concept of play rather than that of labour. In reply, I would point out that Marcuse's writings contain some of the same tensions that haunt Marx's work. Like Marx, Marcuse seems to vacillate between a conception of man as *Homo laborans* whose nature has been thwarted by millennial class exploitation and a view of man in which his possibilities are realized only by emancipation from labour into playful freedom. In the one case, the ending of economic alienation is seen as necessarily involving some sort of self-management and transformation of daily labour into an inherently valuable experience, while in the other the emphasis will be laid on the progressive reduction of labour time. Both strands of thought about work are authentically Marxian, and it is unnecessary to invoke Freud's influence on Marcuse to account for the latter's emphasis on the intrinsic virtues of playful activity.

With regard to Marcuse's insistence on the necessity of working-class initiative in the making of a socialist revolution, it must be said that this has never carried much credibility. If the working class has any active role in Marcuse's scenario, it is *after* the socialist revolution – in the period of socialist construction. In denying to the working class any important role in the earlier phases of socialist revolution, Marcuse is merely reasserting his conviction of the integration of working-class people in advanced capitalist society. Surely, however, even a sympathetic critic of Marcuse will feel that a more perceptive response to evidences of this integration would have been to undertake a revision of some of his most fundamental Marxian commitments.

Now I do not mean here to invoke any naive falsificationist criterion of the adequacy of Marcuse's (authentically Marxian) metaphysic of human nature. To call Marcuse's view of man a metaphysical view, after all, is to say that no criticism of it which appeals solely to experience can ever be decisive; it is to say that it is a view which structures experience and which gives a framework to empirical evidence. This is not to deny that empirical evidences can have salience to a criticism of Marx's view of man, which may be evaluated in Lakatosian fashion as being part of a progressive or a degenerating research programme. Such an evaluation will not be attempted here, but an outline of it is easily sketched. We will have reason to regard the conception of man expressed in Marx's writings, and in such of his followers as Marcuse, as being part of a degenerating research programme, if there are philosophical reasons for revising it which bear on available empirical evidence. To put the point dogmatically, Marx's view of man as in essence an unconditioned and self-determining agent brings with it all the confusion of Idealist logic and ontology. Kamenka's criticism of Marx on this point is worth quoting:

> Man, as Marx in his metaphysical moments portrays him, is (potentially) the unconditioned being of the scholastics (i.e. God), whose unconditionedness is one of his perfections, essential to his (true) nature, and therefore to be deduced from it. It is from the scholastic view of God that Marx unconsciously derives the conception of man as (properly) always a subject and never a predicate. It is from scholastic logic that he gets the otherwise unsupported notion that the self-sufficient, the self-determined, the always active, is morally superior to the conditioned, the determined, the also passive.[19]

More plausibly, perhaps, Kolakowski has suggested[20] that Marx's view of man is bound up inextricably with a Platonist ontology in which the world is conceived as a great chain of being, in which degrees of reality are recognized and are conflated with degrees of goodness, and in which the human species recapitulates in an historical theodicy the return to an undifferentiated unity pictured as the destination of Spirit in neo-Platonic and Hegelian writings. The objection to Marx's view of man, then, is not the crass empiricist objection that its content has an essentialist or metaphysical aspect, but rather a philosophical objection of a substantive sort. It is not one that can be defended here, and I will not try to defend it. Perhaps it will suffice to say that the claim that Marxism constitutes a degenerate research programme rests on a conjunction of philosophical criticism of its underlying logic and ontology with evidences and reasonings about political life which suggest the incoherence of the Marxian idea of a return to a lost unity in a conflict-free union of civil and political society. The crucial objection here has been well put by Kolakowski in his critique of the myth of human self-identity as foundational in the Marxian project of a post-political society. This is a criticism which need not draw directly on philosophical reasonings, since it may be argued that the transcendence of self-division, which is the project of Marx no less than of Rousseau, is unachievable except at a price which Rousseau acknowledged but Marx did not – namely, a retreat to much lower levels of critical self-awareness in a far simpler social order. This suggests an ironical criticism of Marx's historical interpretation in virtue of its failing to take seriously the irreversibility of cumulative conceptual enrichment through the increasing moral complexity and cross-cultural sensibility of human society. There is a further strand of criticism salient here too, one which draws on the writings of Durkheim and Weber, in which it would be argued that role-occupance of the constraining sort Marx condemns is not merely functionally indispensable to industrial societies, but actually largely constitutive of human self-identity in any conceivable society. Despite their abstractness, these are quasi-empirical rather than straightforwardly philosophical propositions and ones we are in a better position to evaluate than Marx was. This is to say merely that, if we are correct in judging Marx's system to embody a degenerate research programme in our own context, nothing follows directly as to its credentials in Marx's own time.

MARXISM AS SOCIAL SCIENCE AND THEORETICAL HISTORY: COHEN ON HISTORICAL MATERIALISM AS A SPECIES OF FUNCTIONALISM

In G.A. Cohen's recent restatement of Marx's historical materialism in functionalist terms, the dependency of Marx's system on a view of human nature is explicitly acknowledged, though its metaphysical content is largely suppressed. Cohen notes that there is 'a Marxist tradition to deny that there exists an historically invariant human nature', but insists that there are 'enduring facts of human nature'[21] – facts which Marx's system depends upon, and which are not controverted by the insistence on the partial self-transformation of man in history. As Cohen puts it, 'man is a mammal, with a definite biological constitution, which evolves hardly at all in some central respects throughout millennia of history'.[22] How does Cohen construe the place of a view of human nature in Marx? He states as the central claim of historical materialism what he calls the *primacy* thesis, which asserts that 'the nature of a set of productive relations is explained by the level of development of the productive forces embraced by it (to a far greater extent than vice versa)'.[23] He tells us that the primacy thesis is associated with a second thesis, which he calls the *development* thesis and which he states as follows: 'The productive forces tend to develop throughout history'.[24] He specifies this as entailing more than that productive forces *have* developed. For, whereas this might have happened 'for a miscellany of unco-ordinated reasons',[25] the development thesis asserts a universal tendency to development of the productive forces. It does not entail that the forces *always* develop, since, as Cohen notes, citing the decline of imperial Rome as an example, there are 'exceptions to the generalization that the productive forces, though indeed capable of stagnation, do not, barring natural disaster, go into reverse'. Thus, as Cohen puts it succinctly, the development thesis 'predicate[s] a perennial tendency to productive progress, arising out of rationality and intelligence in the context of the inclemency of nature'.[26] As to apparent counter-examples, a theory of history is not answerable to abnormal occurrences, Cohen tells us, though he admits that there is an as yet unsatisfied need for criteria of normalcy for human societies.

Cohen tells us that the development thesis, for which criteria for abnormality in society or history seem to be indispensable, is itself a necessary support for the primacy thesis. What then supports the development thesis? Cohen declares that 'we put it as a reason for affirming the development thesis that its falsehood would offend human rationality'.[27] The development thesis gains plausibility, he says,[28] if we note three facts about men: that they are somewhat rational; that their general historical situation is one of scarcity; and that they possess intelligence of a kind and degree which enables them to improve their lot. Cohen observes that the thesis that men are irrational if they fail to exploit the opportunity to expand productive forces whenever the growth of knowledge allows this has two difficulties. We do not know 'the relative magnitude of man's material problem and consequent interest in its solution, by comparison with other human problems and interests. . . . Whether the falsehood of the development thesis would offend rationality demands a judgment of the comparative importance of potentially competing interests'.[29] Cohen identifies a second difficulty when he observes that 'it is not evident that societies are disposed to bring about what rationality would lead men to choose. There is some shadow between what reasons suggests and what society does'.[30] Cohen says of his defence of the development thesis that it is 'not conclusive, but it may have some substance'.[31] This modest disclaimer fails to do justice to the difficulties in which Cohen puts himself. They all arise from the fact that the conception of rationality with which Cohen works, though it is intended by him to have a universal application, has the content he needs only if the values of some elements of our own culture are fed into it. Otherwise, it is an almost completely empty, indeterminate and programmatic conception, and the thesis that productive relations tend to alter to allow for the most efficient use of productive forces becomes vacuous rather than contingently false. The notion of more or less efficient uses of productive forces makes sense only when, as in problems of engineering, there is agreement on objectives. Even within our own culture, it is a salient feature of social problems, including problems of production, that typically they arise from conflicts of ways of life rather than from the kind of technical disagreement that might occur between engineers charged with the completion of a common project.[32] Consider in this regard current controversy about factory farming and about the elimination and replacement of small family farms by large agricultural corporations.[33] To suppose that discussion of the merits of rival forms of agricultural enterprise can proceed by reference to some common standard of efficiency is to suppose what is patently false, that farming has a single undisputed purpose. Understanding current controversy in this area involves recognizing that rival conceptions of farming are at issue, each of which is bound up with the defence of a broader way of life. An appeal to some over-arching standard of efficiency in satisfying express preferences could settle such dispute only if there were a common market to which all demands could be brought and a reasonable bargain struck.[34] No criterion of efficiency could be at the same time neutral in a conflict of this sort and yet authoritative for all parties to it. For, while contending social movements and ways of life often come to a working compromise, such a settlement is wholly different in character from a market-place bargain, since it often represents only an abatement in the struggle between incommensurable claims.

These difficulties are even more formidable when an appeal to efficiency is made, not to settle practical conflicts within a given culture, but to help to explain transitions from one social order or historical epoch to another. When capitalist enterprise emerged from feudal societies in Europe, protagonists of the rival forms of economic life did not self-evidently share objectives and problems for which capitalism proved to be the most cost-effective solution. Those who think that human history as a whole can be understood as a movement from less to more efficient uses of expanding productive forces take for granted a common standard of efficiency where one is not even conceivable. None of this is to suggest that immanent criticism of a culture or a way of life cannot proceed by invoking efficiency. It is not to endorse some quasi-Parsonian view in which the rationality of any social arrangement is indistinguishable from its sheer persistence. It is to say that a standard of efficiency is lacking which can be applied cross-culturally or even (within a single society) between ways of life expressive of incommensurable values.

These difficulties are not met by Cohen's observation that the development thesis depends on a judgement about the relative importance in men's lives of material and other interests. A sharp distinction between material and other interests is apt only in a secular and post-traditional society of just the sort in which capitalist enterprise is typically dominant. Even within a society of this sort, applying such a distinction presents problems, not of imprecision or of open texture, but of sheer indeterminacy. If an affluent but harassed businessman relinquishes a high income for a more relaxed and leisurely life in the country, is he settling a conflict between his material and his non-material interests in favour of the latter? If workers object to the introduction of Taylorian techniques of time-management into the life of the factory, and their opposition is not dampened by a credible offer of higher wages, is this a case where material interests are foregone for the sake of other goods? And are we to understand that the path of rationality lies in always favouring material interests, supposing a rough and ready demarcation criterion between these interests and others is available? If not, what sense is there in the claim that the falsity of the development thesis would be an impeachment of human rationality? Invoking criteria of normalcy in history or in society (there is a disturbing slippage here) is unhelpful, since we lack criteria which satisfy Cohen's requirement of yielding the development thesis without question-beggingly presupposing it. Finally, even if a workable classification of human interests existed, and it were true that men always tended to favour their material interests over others, still the development thesis would not follow. Cohen alludes to Marx's apparent belief that it was population growth which, in disrupting the balance between needs and natural resources distinctive of primitive Communism,[35] spurred the adoption of what he calls 'a more aggressive technology'. An equally effective way of remedying the imbalance caused by demographic growth, and a way which has been favoured by the overwhelming majority of traditional societies, is the institution of population controls. Unless a parochially European preoccupation with human mastery of the natural environment is written into the conception of rationality with which Cohen works, I do not see how such a response can be disqualified as irrational. The conception of *Homo economicus* which Cohen's conception of rationality comprehends has, in fact, no tendency to support Marxian productivism.

That Cohen works with an ahistorical, unMarxian and almost Benthamite conception of rationality emerges from his cursory consideration of the problematic aspects of any criterion for the assessment of productive power. Productive power, he tells us, is 'the amount of surplus production the forces (of production) enable', where surplus production is understood in this context to signify 'production beyond what is necessary to satisfy the indispensable physical needs of the immediate producers, to reproduce the labouring class'. Thus, he declares, 'the development of the productive forces may be identified with the growth of the surplus they make possible, and this in turn may be identified with the amount of the day which remains after the labouring time required to maintain the producers has been sub-tracted'.[36] Now it is no news to Cohen, any more than it was to Marx, that criteria for 'subsistence' inescapably contain cultural elements: for, apart from anything else, differing forms of social life will make differing demands on men's bodies, and so necessitate differences in diet and so on. Further, it is not obvious on the face of it what time-span is to be used in assessing a productivity increase. These are problems of which Cohen is clearly aware, and which might be thought to pose no fatal threat to his proposed criterion. The real difficulties lie elsewhere. First of all, the efficiency or productivity criterion he suggests needs to be argued for: why adopt this criterion rather than any other? It is not a criterion whose salience is *self-evident*. Men have nowhere consistently regarded a shortening of the working day, or an increase in their capability to support ever larger numbers of human beings, as constitutive of their welfare. How could the priority of such goals over other goals – over goals to do with national grandeur, spiritual development and the preservation of ancient traditions, for example – possibly be constitutive of rationality? Second, in pre-supposing our ability to make on-balance aggregative judgements about socially necessary labour time, Cohen's proposed productivity criterion evidently involves just that weighing of incommensurables which it was its purpose to circumvent.[37] The key point, however, is that, even if Cohen's productivity criterion can be coherently spelt out, he has said nothing to show that increasing productivity is always (or paradigmatically) rational. He needs to do this, given the distance between the productivity criterion and ordinary (culturally and historically variant) conceptions of rationality, if his proposal is to have any intuitive forcefulness.

It may be from an awareness of these difficulties that Cohen affirms that 'the fact that capitalism did not arise spontaneously outside of Europe is a serious problem for historical materialism'.[38] Unless we begin by ascribing to human history an end-state for which capitalism is an indispensable condition, there seems no reason why capitalism should not be regarded as a unique episode. This view of the matter is given added plausibility when we recall that Marx himself regarded the expansionist and productivist imperatives which Cohen deploys in an attempt to develop a scheme of universal historical interpretation as distinctive of and peculiar to the capitalist system.[39] The dynamism which capitalism displays as a system cannot be used to account for its emergence in the first place, given what Marx describes[40] as the essential conservatism of all pre-capitalist modes of production. On one occasion, indeed, Marx apparently disavows any generalization of an explanatory model which is in place when it is applied to the workings of the capitalist system to the domain of human history as a whole. If this statement of Marx's[41] is taken as an authoritative evidence of his intentions, we have reason to regard historical materialism as a theory of capitalism rather than a scheme of historical interpretation.

If the development thesis lacks rational support, what of the primacy thesis which Cohen rightly takes to be the corner-stone of Marx's historical materialism? Cohen specifies the explanatory relation postulated in historical materialism as holding between productive forces and productive relations as being a functional rather than a causal relation. In part this claim, along with the construal of the Marxian model of society as tripartite rather than bipartite in which it is embedded, is intended as a rebuttal of some criticisms of historical materialism. Cohen aims to answer, especially, writers such as Acton, Plamenatz and Nozick, who maintain that historical materialism's explanatory pretensions are nullified by the conceptual impossibility of making the sorts of distinctions it presupposes. Thus he maintains against such critics that a characterization of production relations is available which is *rechtfrei* in that it does not contain those very things (normative or superstructural aspects of social life) that it purports to explain. It is still unclear, I think, that Cohen's description of the rights and powers of proletarians in a capitalist order, for example, is *rechtfrei* in the sense he needs if capitalist production relations are to be describable independently of the legal and ideological forms in which they are found. Cohen is probably right, then, when he contrasts his own account of production relations with that which Engels stigmatized as the 'force theory' in *Anti-Dühring*,[42] but it may be doubted if the force theory (whose absurdity is manifest when it is assessed as an account of the production relations characteristic of a whole epoch or mode of production) can be avoided without embracing an account which remains open to the criticisms Cohen is concerned to rebut. I do not want to pursue these questions here, however, since nothing in my argument turns on how they are answered, but merely to look more closely at the functionalist reformulation of the primacy thesis which Cohen advances.

To say that production relations and legal and political institutions have a functional connection with productive forces is to say that they allow the latter to develop and expand according to their potential powers. This is a technological reformulation of Marx's materialism which captures at least a part of Marx's meaning, and which allows for critical discussion. It does not treat technological innovation as explanatory of all great social changes but as itself beyond explanation, but asserts that, once the disposition of human beings to conquer natural scarcity has brought about a new set of productive forces, production relations and the rest of society will adjust so as to permit their most efficient deployment. What is lacking in the account so far is any elaboration of the mechanism whereby this is supposed to occur. Cohen tries to supply this with an Engels-type argument that the explanatory form of Marx's materialism is akin to that of Darwin's evolutionary theory,[43] but the argument has two crippling disabilities. One of them has been noticed by Peter Singer,[44] when he points to the misconception of Darwin's theory contained in Cohen's statement of it. Darwin did not (as Cohen suggests) explain the long necks of giraffes by saying that long necks have the function of enabling giraffes to survive, for to say that would be to say nothing. Darwin's explanation of the long necks of giraffes was in terms of the action of natural selection on giraffes with necks of varying lengths – an explanation which displaces any functional explanation. Contrary to Cohen, a theory of evolution by the natural selection of the products of random genetic mutations renders any functional explanation otiose in these domains.

More fundamentally, Cohen's reformulation identifies no mechanism, akin to that of natural selection of genetic accidents in Darwinian theory, whereby more efficient uses of productive forces replace less efficient ones. To be sure, such a mechanism exists within capitalist economies in which firms behave as Marx, following the Classical Economists, thought they would behave. In a competitive capitalist environment, it may well be true (as Cohen suggests) that adopting more efficient methods for the exploitation of available productive forces may be a condition of a firm's survival. The same competitive pressure may indeed account for technological innovation and the spread of new technologies throughout the economy as well as for firms seeking to make the best use of existing technology. (This latter is a point Cohen does not make.) Where the mechanism of market competition is lacking, we have no reason to expect that productive forces will gravitate to their most efficient uses. Cohen tells us that this might take place in the absence of market competition, if, for example, the central planners of a socialist economy were to decide to take advantage of economies yielded by increases in the scale of production. That this *could* happen cannot be disputed, but – as the complaints of dissenting Soviet-bloc economists confirm – socialist economies contain no mechanism in virtue of which it is bound to happen, or which generates any persisting tendency in favour of such a development. When Cohen speaks of this, the only case he mentions of a move to more efficient uses of productive forces happening in the absence of competitive pressure, he gives the game away by calling it a *purposive* elaboration of a functional explanation. It clinches the suspicion that, except when its subject matter is purposive behaviour and its cybernetic simulations, functional explanation is out of place in social science. A crypto-Darwinian (but not a functional) explanation may be given for technological innovation and for production by another which is more efficient. The productive efficiency of a metropolitan capitalist economy may enable it to overwhelm less efficient peripheral economies by a variety of means, including military force, but that is another matter. Consideration of productive efficiency cannot account for the emergence of the capitalist mode in the first place, and it would be fanciful to suppose that they explain its extension into hitherto traditional economies. More unblinkingly than Marx himself, Cohen mistakes an imperative of the capitalist system for a universal tendency. There is nothing in Cohen's argument which adequately supports his claim that Marxian functionalism lacks the conservative complications of functionalism's non-Marxian variants.

I do not claim that the corpus of Marx's writings contains nothing of interest or importance in the way of scientific analysis of the capitalist system. Marxian trade-cycle theory, for example, though it remains eminently controversial, is part of a theory of capitalist crisis and breakdown which may still be worth studying, but nothing in it warrants the belief that capitalism's successor will be a more efficient mode of production. Even the full validity of the Marxian theory of capitalist crisis would not guarantee the development thesis. All this suggests that, quite apart from any of the difficulties I have mentioned in specifying the exact content of Cohen's functionalist statement of Marx's historical materialism, the scientistic and positivistic version of the Marxian system which Cohen develops cannot support its role as a theory of history. It might be replied that the weakness of Cohen's defence lies in the view of human nature with which he works – a view which he admits[45] is not to be found elaborated in Marx's writings, though he claims they contain much that is consonant with it. It might be thought in other words, that Cohen's failure is to write into his view of human nature a strong endogenous productivist imperative. Even if this were done, however, it would not yield anything like an historical law, or even a persisting tendency, unless other, competing human dispositions were reliably defeated. This could be thought to be so, I suggest, only if the expansion of human productive powers were an end-state ascribed to human history as a whole. Unless human history has an immanent goal or purpose, unless teleological explanation is appropriate in respect of vast multigenerational changes, the Marxian theory of history fails. The conclusion is irresistible that historical materialism has the character of an historical theodicy and not of a contribution to a science of society.

MARXISM AS THE IDEOLOGY OF PROLETARIAN CLASS STRUGGLE: SOREL ON MYTH AND MORAL REGENERATION IN THE SOCIAL REVOLUTION

In Sorel's Marxism we find a species of revolutionary socialist ideology which, as Isaiah Berlin has observed in a luminously perspicuous essay,[46] breaks with two of the most fundamental beliefs of the Western intellectual tradition – the Greco–Roman belief that knowledge liberates and the Judaeo–Christian belief in an historical theodicy – that inform and shape Marx's own thought to its very foundations. Yet Sorel's claim to be a follower of Marx was neither fanciful nor perverse. In at least two important respects, Sorel develops distinctive and valuable features of Marx's thought.

First, Sorel expounds in a sharp and clear form the metaphysical conception of man as a creative and self-creative being which I have claimed is a logical presupposition of historical materialism. Against the thinkers of the French Enlightenment, against Bentham and his followers among the Philosophic Radicals, Sorel affirmed a view of man as active rather than passive, struggling rather than enjoying, doing and making rather than contemplating or absorbing sense-data. Human action he seems to have conceived as erupting from an inner necessity to imprint a unique mark on the world. Nothing could be further removed from the inertial conception of human action as a response to external stimulus or internal deprivation, which we find in Hobbes, Bentham or Holbach. Sorel greatly valued natural science, which he pictured in Marxian pragmatist fashion as a weapon in which human order is imposed on an inherently formless natural world, but he had nothing but disdain for projects for a social science wherein human conduct would be subsumed under the intelligibility of impersonal and abstract laws. Sorel takes from Marx, then, his view of man as a creature standing apart from the objects of the natural order, as distinct from other animals in that his life is, first and foremost, an expression of a primordial creative impulse.

Sorel takes from Marx, second, what I might call an agonistic view of society. It is viewed, not as a perpetual-motion machine in which a rational harmony of interests produces continuing progress in the satisfaction of wants, but as an arena of conflicting classes, moralities and world-views. One implication of the pluralistic and conflictual model of social development Sorel derived from Marx is that, for Sorel as for Marx, socialist revolution has a social rather than a political character. It is not a *coup d'état* or a putsch, the fruit of a conspiracy of *déraciné* intellectuals, but the culmination of a long period of class struggle. More radically than Marx, Sorel attributed an anti-political character to the social revolution. It was not just that revolutionary syndicalism, as Sorel imagined it, repudiated the prudent and temporizing politics of the Third Republic, but that social revolution was construed as an expressive and not a purposive act, a gesture of independence and solidarity to the assessment of which its consequences were virtually irrelevant. In his strong emphasis on the internal moral qualities of class struggle, Sorel is doubtless influenced by Proudhon, but his anti-Utopian indifference to blueprints for a future socialist order is authentically Marxian. More decisively than either of the two Marxist writers I have discussed, Sorel grasps Marx's distinctive insight that social development is the story of conflict between distinct social groupings, with different places in society's productive apparatus and having contending moral outlooks and views of the world. He develops Marx's accent on class struggle – an aspect of the Marxian system which tends to fall out of Marcuse's and Cohen's reformulation of it.

So far, I have maintained that Sorel adopts Marx's activist view of man and the pragmatist view of knowledge that goes with it in Marx. He develops Marx's doctrine of class struggle into an anti-Utopian critique of ideas of social unity and rational harmony among men which goes well beyond Marx's own intentions. He shares with Marx an anti-instrumental and expressive interpretation of human action and, above all, of human labour, whose centrality in men's lives he doubted as little as Marx did. Where Sorel departs from Marx he is, in my view, on his strongest ground. He relinquishes any historiosophical pretensions for his conception of class struggle and goes so far as to condemn Marx for an excessively determinist account of social development. Sorel's voluntarism is related to a deeper difference from Marx, namely the primacy he gave to will over intellect in human affairs. In insisting on the importance of myth as a non-rational moving force in society and history, and in belittling the role of prudence and of rational calculation of self-interest, Sorel broke decisively with the intellectualist psychology Marx inherited from the Enlightenment and which he attempted (somewhat incongruously) to marry with the expressive conception of action he borrowed from Hegel. Sorel is influenced by Schopenhauer and by Nietzsche in treating the conceptions men form of their social circumstance as being moulded primarily, not by disinterested reflection on an available body of evidence which is neutral as regards conflicting purposes, but by their hopes and needs. Sorel's conception of myth is akin to Marx's conception of ideology and to Freud's notion of illusion in that the truth content of beliefs, images and symbols so characterized is not denied but regarded as irrelevant to their function in the overall economy of human activity. Sorel's departures from the intellectualist psychology of the Enlightenment, however, lead him to view myth in a fashion radically divergent from anything that can be teased out of Marx's writings on ideology. In Marx, one of the criteria whereby a belief or conception is judged to have an ideological function is that, apart from its supportive role in rationalizing men's interests, it is typically distortive of their real circumstances and conceals from them the true character of their activities. A distinction between appearance and reality in society is the hinge on which any authentically Marxian theory of ideology turns. In

Sorel's thought, on the contrary, the idea that there is a true or essential state of society to knowledge of which men can attain, if it is present at all, is extremely subdued. Sorel comes close to the view that men's social relations are so constituted by their ideas and beliefs, and especially by myths which make an appeal to the will, that any idea of a science of society must be rejected as incoherent. Revolutionary socialism could not then be a part of such a science: it must be viewed rather as a moral outlook and a conception of the social world, evolved obscurely (like its rivals) from the unknowable depths of the minds of human beings sharing a common lot.

Sorel's construal of socialist thought as the conceptual form of proletarian class struggle was, of course, a direct influence on Lukács's *History and Class-Consciousness*,[47] where (as in Sorel) it gives rise to well-known difficulties and paradoxes. All these problems turn on a paradox of self-reference. For the claim that socialism, like all other ideologies, is a perspective on society generated at a specific vantage-point, and serving specific interests, seems itself to have the aspect of a cognitively absolute claim formulated at a point of neutrality between competing interests and their associated world-views, whose very possibility the general theory of ideology denies. Another way of stating the difficulty is to say that judgements that such-and-such a belief is ideological in character are always theory-dependent. Further, the theory presupposed by any such judgement must itself be given a privileged immunity from the relativization which it confers on its subject matter if it is not to have a self-defeating effect. These difficulties are, if anything, more prominent in Sorel's theory of myth than in Marx's account of ideology.

I do not propose to comment directly here on these questions, but one observation is worth making about the way in which Sorel's successors developed his thought. It is in the writings of Michels and his school that we find both a continuation of Sorel's work and a resolution of some of its difficulties which at the same time embodies an incisive criticism of some of Sorel's excesses. The substantive burden of Michels's criticism of Sorel is, of course, contained in his denial that the revolutionary syndicates could reasonably be supposed to be agents of the moral regeneration or *ricorso*, the renewal or recursion from decadence, that Sorel hoped for. In so far as the syndicates acted as organs of genuine class struggle, with intermediate as well as long-term aims demanding a consideration of strategic and tactical advantage, their anti-instrumental and anti-political integrity was inevitably compromised. The pressure of a quasi-military struggle itself generates élitism and an oligarchy with interests distinct from those of the proletarian majority. In short, Michels saw that there was no reason to think the revolutionary trade unions were exempt from the fate that had befallen the social-democratic parties.

Michels' criticism exposes an epistemological tension in Sorel's thought as much as it reveals its practical weakness. The tension is between those areas of his writings in which Sorel acts merely as the exponent of a proletarian world-view and morality and those in which he is the theorist of its emergence and conditions. The latter role is arguably presupposed by much of what Sorel says in the former capacity. Further, its culmination is precisely a realist science of power and of social movements of just the sort Sorel despised. Since these aspects of Sorel's thought, the diagnostic and the prophetic, were never clearly distinguished, the one frequently corrupted the other. Thus we find nowhere in Sorel any theoretical recognition of the historical limitation of the proletarian outlook whose governing myths he had poetically explored. Nowhere does Sorel acknowledge that the outlook he is expounding is that of certain social groupings at a certain stage of their development, in a specific (and soon to be transformed) economic and political environment. This is the price of Sorel's abstention from grand theories of history – that his account of the working-class movement and its morality is hopelessly unhistorical. If the delusive character of Sorel's hopes for the proletariat is ever conceded by him, it is only implicitly in his late flirtation with radical nationalist groups whose anti-bourgeois stance seemed to him to offer some prospect of the *ricorso* and cultural renaissance which to the end of his days he continued to conceive in political (if highly idiosyncratic) terms.

CONCLUSION

Each of the three Marxian thinkers I have discussed and criticized recalls elements of Marx's thought and develops them in a legitimate and in some respects a fruitful direction. Like Marx's thought as a whole, each of these thinkers elaborates upon an aspect of Marx's contribution, and it turns out under pressure to disintegrate into several categorically distinct segments. The upshot of my criticism of each of these writers is that the epistemological instability of the Marxian system of ideas is such as to ruin it as a contribution to rational inquiry. If it liberates thought from some forms of absolutist limitation, it at the same time creates new obstacles to unfettered inquiry in their place.

It may be asked, at this point, what conclusion may be reached as to the place in the Marxian scheme of a conception of human nature? Much that I have said might seem to support a view akin to Alasdair MacIntyre's,[48] when he denies that social and moral conflicts can ever be arbitrated by appeal to a view of human nature. No view of human nature can have practical authority, he suggests, because each moral tradition carries with it its own view of human nature. We will, each of us, see ourselves in terms of the moral practices in which we stand, and our conception of human nature will itself be constituted by the moral practices to which we belong. This radical sceptical view, though it may seem to be supported by what I have said in criticism of Cohen about the incommensurability of different cultures and forms of life, is not entailed by it. It would be Idealism of just the sort against which Marx (and Cohen[49]) struggle to suppose that man can be whatever he tries to make himself become, and this is a view neither entailed by Marx's system nor ever expressed by him. Certainly, it is an important task to establish what are the biological constraints on the possible variety of human nature, and the theorists of socio-biology are making a contribution to this question even if all their positive conjectures are in error. Even a well-founded theory of man's biological limitations, however, is not social theory, or any part of it. For, if a conception of human nature is indeed indispensable to social theory, it is as its prelude and not as its foundation.

MacIntyre is on the right track, however, in denying that a conception of human nature (or a social theory embodying or presupposing a view of man) can have practical or moral authority. This is a conclusion profoundly subversive of Marxism in whatever epistemological mode its propositions are framed. For, whether metaphysical, scientific or mythopoeic in character, the central notions and theses of Marxism have always been supposed by its exponents to be capable not merely of illuminating conduct but of guiding and inspiring it.[50] The running together of theory and practice in this way has led to a disastrous confusion of categories in modern thought from which we are only lately recovering. But that is another story, and one that cannot be told here.[51]

11 Against Cohen on proletarian unfreedom[1]

In a series of important papers, G.A. Cohen has developed a forceful argument for the claim that workers are rendered unfree by capitalist institutions.[2] His argument poses a powerful challenge to those (such as myself) who think that capitalist institutions best promote freedom. Yet, formidable as it is, Cohen's argument can be shown to be flawed at several crucial points. It is not one argument, but three at least, and one of the goals of my criticism of Cohen on this question is to distinguish and assess the various separate lines of reasoning that together make up his case for the unfreedom under capitalism of workers as a class. Cohen argues of workers that they are rendered unfree by *the institution of private property* on which the capitalist system depends, that they suffer *a form of collective unfreedom under capitalism*, and that they are *forced to sell their labour power under capitalism*. Against Cohen, I will maintain that every sort of unfreedom which he shows to exist under capitalism has a direct counterpart under socialist institutions. For that reason, Cohen's arguments establish nothing about the distinctive bearings of capitalist institutions on freedom. Indeed, the upshot of Cohen's arguments is a set of conceptual truisms about individual and collective freedom and unfreedom, force and justice, which have application wherever these concepts themselves find a foothold. Within the framework of Cohen's reasoning – in which an obsolescent philosophical method of conceptual analysis is applied to the terms of conventional liberal discourse – these truisms are incontestable. At the same time, they tell us nothing of substance about the impact of capitalist and socialist institutions on the freedom of workers. Most particularly, Cohen's arguments tell us nothing about the *comparative freedom* of workers under capitalist and socialist institutions. I shall myself advance a number of arguments for supposing that workers as a class under socialism are likely to be far less free than they are under capitalism. But even if my arguments for the greater freedom of workers under capitalism are inconclusive, Cohen's argument for proletarian unfreedom demonstrably fails.

PRIVATE PROPERTY, CAPITALISM AND LIBERTY

Cohen argues first that capitalism cannot constitue or be equated with liberty (even economic liberty) because capitalist institutions rest upon, or comprehend, private property. Private property, Cohen maintains, necessarily restricts liberty. (For the purposes of my argument, I shall follow Cohen's example in treating 'liberty' and 'freedom' as synonyms. I do not intend to endorse any *general* thesis of their synonymy.) He asserts: 'free enterprise economies rest upon private property: you can sell and buy only what you respectively own and come to own. It follows that such economies pervasively restrict liberty. They are complex structures of freedom and unfreedom'.[3] Or, as Cohen put it in a later essay: 'private property pretty well *is* a particular way of distributing freedom *and unfreedom*. It is necessarily associated with the liberty of private owners to do as they wish with that they own but it no less necessarily withdraws liberty from those who do not own it. To think of capitalism as a realm of freedom is to overlook half its nature'.[4] In the latter paper Cohen spells out his point more systematically: 'For consider', he urges, 'if the State prevents me from doing something I want to do, it evidently places a constraint on my freedom. Suppose, then, that I want to perform an action which involves a legally prohibited use of your property. I want, let us say, to pitch a tent in your large back garden. . . . If I now try to do this thing I want to do, the chances are that the State will intervene on your behalf. If it does, I shall suffer a constraint on my freedom. The same goes for all unpermitted uses of a piece of private property by those who do not own it, and there are always those who do not own it, since "private ownership by one person presupposes non-ownership on the part of other persons".'[5] Cohen in his earlier piece uses a similar example to make the very same point: 'Let us suppose that I wish to take Mr Morgan's yacht, and go for a spin. If I try to, then it is probable that its owner, aided by law-enforcing others, will stop me. I cannot do this thing that I wish to do, because others will interfere. But liberty, as Narveson [has] reasonably said, is "doing what we wish without the interference of others". It follows that I lack a liberty here.'[6]

Cohen's argument, then, is that private property institutions restrict liberty, because their existence or enforcement involves interferences with some persons doing as they wish. He adopts here Jan Narveson's rough account of liberty as 'doing what we wish without the interference of others', saying that 'when a man cannot do what he wishes, because others will interfere, he is unfree'.[7] For the purpose of assessing this argument of Cohen's, I shall follow him in adopting Narveson's definition.

If this argument of Cohen's aims to show that the liberty-limiting effects of private property institutions are peculiar to or distinctive of private property, it fails. In part it trades on the truism that one person's freedom, like one person's private ownership, always entails another's restraint or unfreedom: if anyone has a freedom to do something, this means at least that others do not prevent him from doing it. But this thesis of the correlativity of freedom with unfreedom – the theory that having or exercising freedom always presupposes or entails restraint of freedom – has no special connections with the notion of property. One person's freedom to do something has as its shadow the unfreedom of other persons to prevent that person from (or interfere with that person) doing it, just as one person's owning something has its shadow in others' not owning it. These are perfectly formal truths within a certain discourse of freedom. They tell us nothing about the weight or importance of the unfreedoms generated by private property institutions.

This last remark may be stated in another way. *All* property institutions – capitalist, socialist, feudal, or whatever – impose constraints on the liberties of those who live under them. It is true of every system of property that there will be many things that persons wish to do that they will be interfered with (or prevented from) doing. This is only an entailment of the evident truth that all systems of property are embodied in legal and moral rules which create opportunities and limit the options of those who live under them, where these opportunities and options will have a significant impact on the freedoms of the various social groups affected by them. Most obviously, in so far as the moral and legal rules that go to make a system of property are enforced, those who wish and attempt to act in ways prohibited by these rules will be restrained from doing so, or at least be under threat of such restraint. Their liberty will thereby be curtailed. This is manifestly true of *any* institution of property. Only a Hobbesian state of nature, in which no one owns anything because there are no enforceable rules about property, might appear to form an exception to this truth. Even there, where there is no system of property but only the fact of possession, persons will often be prevented from doing as they wish by others' possession of things the former need in order to implement their plans. There is then a restraint of liberty, not only under any institution of property, private or collective, but in any society in which anyone possesses anything – that is to say, in virtually any imaginable condition of social life.

This exceedingly obvious truth may be illustrated with an example. Consider a society which holds its means of production in common ownership and whose citizens have only use-rights as individuals over them. Think of a coastal tribe which lives by fishing and whose means of production are canoes. The canoes are owned by the tribal community as a whole, but each individual tribesman has use-rights in them. How does such an institution of communal ownership bear on the freedom of the tribesmen who live under it? It is clear that there are many things that individual tribesmen may wish to do which they will be interfered with in or prevented from doing. They cannot use them any more frequently, or for longer time periods, than the usufructuary rules allow. No tribesman can (without threat of sanction) take a canoe for his exclusive and permanent use, or give a canoe away as a gift, or sell or rent a canoe to a non-tribesman. If a tribesman tries to do any of these things, the property rules of this system of communal ownership will be enforced against him. He may be ostracized, or punished by loss of his use-rights in the canoes. Again, if the property system in the tribe is truly communal ownership in the means of production, and not one of corporate ownership, the tribesman will have no 'share' in the means of production which he can take with him if he chooses to leave the community. The tribe might allow use-rights in canoes to be sold, but to the extent that it did, its system of communal ownership of the canoes would be attenuated. For this reason, a system of true communal ownership has clear implications of the liberty of migration from the community. Tribesmen might not be prevented from or interfered with in leaving the community, but it would be harder for them to do so, since they would leave with little or nothing. Investing in a new means of production would be similarly difficult, or impossible, for the tribesmen as individuals. These last points aside, it is transparently clear that, even as such a system of communal ownership creates and enlarges freedom in some respects, it restrains and curtails it in others. Communal ownership, one might say, pretty well *is* a distribution of freedom *and unfreedom*. Like any system of property rules, communal ownership is a complex structure of freedom and unfreedom. To think of communal ownership as a realm of freedom is to miss half its nature.

This point may be further illustrated by a consideration of Cohen's own example of communal ownership: 'Neighbors A and B own sets of household tools. Each has some tools which the other lacks. If A needs a tool of a kind which only B has, then, private property being what it is, he is not free to take B's one for a while, even if B does not need it during that while. Now imagine that the following rule is imposed, bringing the tools into partly common ownership: each may take and use a tool belonging to the other without permission provided that the other is not using it and that he returns it when he no longer needs it, or when the other needs, it, whichever comes first. *Things being what they are* (an important qualification: we are talking, as often we should, about the real world, not about remote possibilities), the communising rule would, I contend, increase tool-using freedom, on any reasonable view'.[8]

Cohen's confident judgement that communal ownership of tools enhances tool-using freedom on any reasonable view is hard to accept. He acknowledges that 'some freedoms are removed by the new rule. Neither neighbor is as assured of the same easy access as before to the tools that were wholly his. Sometimes he has to go next door to retrieve one of them. Nor can either now charge the other for use of a tool he himself does not require. But these restrictions will likely be less important than the increased range of tools available.'[9] It seems plain that other, more important freedoms will also be lost by the communizing rule. There is, first of all, the freedom to engage in long-term planning about the use of tools. Since the tools can be taken without permission at any time when they are not needed for use, neither household can effectively engage in long-term planning of their tool-use. (The inability under Cohen's scheme of households to form and implement plans for long-term tool-use may be an implication of a simpler difficulty of his scheme. The difficulty is that it says nothing about what will be done under it when households 'need', or wish to use, tools at the same time.) It is precisely this loss of freedom resulting from the inability to make long-term plans that has in many societies led to usufructuary rules of property being supplanted by ones based on individual ownership, which allow for contractual arrangements for the renting of tools and other capital assets. There is, in addition, the freedom, which each tool-user hitherto enjoyed, of determining the rate of depreciation of the tools. For, in the real world – and it is the real world we are talking about, not remote possibilities – tools are worn out by the jobs they do. Different jobs wear out tools at different rates and in different ways, as do different ways of using tools. Under the communizing property rule, no one has the freedom to decide on a rate of depreciation or to implement the policies needed to secure it. Nor – and this is a distinct point, though one that follows from the preceding one – does anyone have the freedom to decide when the tools are to be replaced, whether because they are worn out or because new tools have become available which do the job better. These are freedoms possessed and exercised under private property institutions which wither or disappear under the Communist rule. They are not unimportant freedoms for tool-users. Their loss under the Communist rule must diminish tool-using freedom in important respects not mentioned in Cohen's account of it.

It might be objected that these criticisms depend on interpreting Cohen as hypothesizing a system of full communal ownership, whereas what he sketches is one of only partial common ownership. I am unsure how partial common ownership of tools is to be understood, but, most naturally, it would seem to mean that, when the need of the owner to use the tool competes with that of his neighbour, the owner's need trumps that of the neighbour. The owner does not have an unencumbered right of liberal ownership in the tool, then, but he can always retain or retrieve the tool from his neighbour when he needs to use it. Against this interpretation of Cohen's scheme, I maintain that it does not describe any system of property rights that is workable in the real world. Who is to decide when the owner needs the tool, and who is to arbitrate disputes as to when it is needed by him? If the owner refuses to hand over the tool to the neighbour, because he believes the neighbour's use of it will depreciate the tool to the point that his own future needs for it will go unmet, is he acting within his rights under the scheme of partly communal ownership? Would he be doing so if he retained the tool on the ground that he is uncertain how long he will need it for a job in which he is currently engaged, or about to start? In the real world, it is reasonable to suppose, these questions would be answered by the scheme of partly communal ownership collapsing into full private property or full Communism in tools. The scheme of partly communal ownership is, for this reason, an unviable half-way house, and cannot be invoked to answer the criticisms I have developed earlier. I accordingly disregard this interpretation, and proceed on the assumption that, if Cohen's scheme is to be a genuine alternative to private ownership in tools, it must encompass fully communal ownership of them.

It might further be objected that the sense of freedom has shifted here from freedom as non-interference with what one wishes to do to a sense in which it designates the options available.[10] The objection is not an absurd one, but it is baseless. If each tool-user wishes to plan long-term use of the tools, determine their rate of depreciation, or implement a decision as to their replacement, he will be prevented form doing so unless all the other tool-users accede to his wishes. Just as under private property institutions an owner has a veto over non-owners as to the uses to which his property is put, so under communal ownership every participant in the communal ownership scheme has under the rules constituting the scheme a veto over the uses to which the common assets are put. In Cohen's example, any member of the communal ownership scheme can invoke the Communist rule against any of the uses I have mentioned. To be sure, there is a logical possibility that all the co-owners will come to agreement on the uses to which I have referred, so that no one will in fact be prevented from doing as he wishes. In the real world, given that persons have different purposes, values, and rates of time preference, this is a most remote possibility, but even if – granting a socialist transformation of human nature and a corres-pondingly greater conformism in values among the co-owners – it were a reality, it would be irrelevant to the issue at hand. For, as Cohen himself appears to think,[11] freedom as non-interference is curtailed not only when a person cannot in fact act as he wishes (because of interferences by others), but also, counterfactually, when it is true that he *would* be interfered with if he acted on desires he does not in fact possess. Thus, in Cohen's example, tool-users are denied freedom to determine rates of depreciation of tools, and so on, even if they never in fact wish to so determine them. They are denied that freedom because, *if* they so wish, the Communist rule could be invoked and enforced against them. They would then be prevented from doing as they wish to do. It is incontrovertible that this is a real and important set of freedoms that has thereby been lost. Moreover, these are freedoms that would be attenuated or diminished, if (in response to the problems I have adduced) the Communist rule were qualified by another rule – a majoritarian rule, say – for the adjudication of issues of capital depreciation and investment. Even if it were so qualified by majoritarian decision procedures, the Communist rule would still extinguish tool-using freedoms possessed under private property institutions. True, if all accepted the outcome of a majority decision, even where it went against the preferences of some, it could not be said that any had been coerced. The freedom of some would still have been reduced, however, since (as we have noted in the case of unanimous agreement) they would have been coerced in the counterfactual case in which they did not accept the majority decision. It is a nice question for Cohen's account, though not one I can address here, whether tool-using freedom is greater under the unqualified communist rule, or under a Communist rule qualified by majoritarian (or other) procedures. What is unambiguously clear is that important tool-using freedoms are lost in either case.

It is hard, then, to understand Cohen's confidence in asserting that, in this example, freedom for tool-users has on any reasonable view been expanded. For myself, I incline to the contrary view: on any reasonable view, freedom has been diminished for tool-users in Cohen's example. I will not press this last point, however, since I will return to the question of judgements of on-balance freedom in a later section of this chapter. Certainly, I do not deny that there are cases where it is reasonable for reasonable men and women to disagree in their judgements of on-balance freedom. Perhaps Cohen's example is such a case. It remains indisputable that private and communal property systems each generate and distribute freedoms and unfreedoms and that Cohen has said nothing which has a tendency to show that communal ownership has the advantage from the standpoint of liberty.

COHEN'S CONCEPTION OF FREEDOM: A DIGRESSION

It is worth pausing at this point to remark that the conception of freedom that Cohen deploys throughout his writings on proletarian unfreedom is not Marx's, but instead one derived from standard liberal discourse. As Cohen theorizes it, freedom is non-interference with individuals acting as they wish to act (or might wish to act). This is a conception of freedom defended forcefully by Bentham and developed with great power in our own times by Isaiah Berlin.[12] In the context of Cohen's argument, this liberal conception of freedom has several salient features. In it, freedom is sharply distinguished from other values. Freedom is freedom, not justice, welfare or whatever: it is one value among many. (Each thing is what it is, and not another thing.) In general, in fact, Cohen seems to want to work with a conception of freedom that is value-free and morally neutral, so that judgements about freedom will be empirical rather than normative claims. This is a point to which I shall return later in this chapter. Again, freedom is attributed primarily to individuals, and not to groups, collectives, or classes. This is so (or appears to be so) even when the freedom Cohen is theorizing is a form of collective freedom. Finally, freedom as Cohen conceives of it is a matter of degree. This is so, inasmuch as some persons may typically be interfered with less than others in doing what they want. In a capitalist society, for example, according to Cohen, owners of property are typically freer than non-owners. It is precisely Cohen's thesis that in capitalist society owners of property have freedoms which proletarians lack.

It is clear enough that this is a distinctively liberal conception of freedom that is being invoked by Cohen. It would not be endorsed by critics of liberalism such as Arendt or Marcuse,[13] and, if it accords with ordinary usage, it is with the ordinary usage of liberal societies. It is no less clear that the conception of freedom that Cohen employs is not Marx's. It has been argued persuasively elsewhere that Cohen's view of freedom is not only distinct from but incompatible and incommensurable with Marx's.[14] I will not rehearse these arguments here, but a few points, unavoidably brief and dogmatic in character, are worth making about the many points of contrast between Cohen's liberal notion of freedom and the conception employed by Marx. It is, to begin with, important to note that Marx's conception of freedom is on any plausible view not value-free but value-dependent: it embodies or expresses a distinctive view of the human good. Very roughly, this is the view that the good for man is found in conscious, cooperative productive activity (and not, for example, in the individual pursuit of pleasure or in contemplation). Again, freedom is not in Marx's view to be attributed primarily to individuals. It is predicated of the human species itself and of individuals only as instances of it (or, perhaps, as members of the various social classes which constitute the historic self-disclosure of the species in its pre-Communist manifestations). For this reason, it is wholly unclear that one person's freedom can in the Marxian account (as it plainly does in Cohen's liberal account) conflict with another's. In class society, the freedom of a proletarian to do something may indeed conflict with that of a capitalist, but in Communist society, as Marx sketchily conceives of it, it seems that there will be no important instances where freedoms conflict. Finally, it was not Marx's view that, whereas proletarians were rendered unfree by capitalist institutions, capitalists themselves were free (or even freer) under them. Marx's view, surely, as that *both* capitalists and proletarians are unfree under capitalism, even if (or precisely because) the freedom of a proletarian to do something is rendered nugatory by a conflicting freedom of a capitalist. For Marx, freedom is a collective good rather than an attribute of individuals, and (at any rate in Communist society) it is otiose to consider how conflicts among individual liberties are to be arbitrated or resolved. It is because Marx conceives freedom in this way that he can claim to be developing a genuine critique of bourgeois notions about liberty.

Cohen's argument, by contrast, aims to be an immanent criticism of the liberal understanding of freedom. He wishes to show that capitalist societies contain important unfreedoms by the *standard of liberal freedom itself*.[15] The principal burden of my criticism of Cohen is that his argument issues in claims of an entirely formal sort, which give no strength to a case for the specific disadvantages of capitalism in terms of freedom. Accordingly, save for the arguments of the section of this paper in which I attempt a *substantive* assessment of capitalist and socialist institutions in terms of workers' freedom, my own critique of Cohen is in turn an immanent criticism. For the purposes of my argument I accept the liberal conception of freedom. Whether it is an adequate conception is another question, which I hope to address on another occasion.

INDIVIDUAL LIBERTY AND COLLECTIVE UNFREEDOM

Cohen's second argument for proletarian unfreedom turns on the claim that any member of a group may be free to do something that every member of the group is not free to do. Thus, whereas it may be the case that any worker can become a capitalist, it does not follow that workers as a class are free so to do. (I am here following Cohen's conception of capitalism, which in turn follows Marx's. For them, a capitalist society is not simply one exhibiting private property in the means of production – since many societies, including societies of yeoman farmers, say, exhibit this feature – but one in which a propertyless majority must sell its labour to a capital-owning minority. At this stage, I will not dispute this understanding of capitalism, since I will question its adequacy later in my argument.) For Cohen, the unfreedom of workers under capitalism is in the fact that 'each is free only on condition that the others do not exercise their similarly conditional freedom',[16] so that 'though most proletarians are free to escape the proletariat, indeed even if all are, the proletariat is an imprisoned class'.[17] In other words, if the freedom of any worker to leave his class depends on the fact that most others do not also attempt to leave it, then the class of workers is unfree even if every worker has the freedom to become a capitalist.

These arguments, first stated in Cohen's paper of 1979, are developed in his paper of 1983. There he cites Marx's remark that 'in this bourgeois society every workman, if he is an exceedingly clever and shrewd fellow, and gifted with bourgeois instincts and favored by an exceptional fortune, can possibly convert himself into an *exploiteur du travail d'autrui*. But if there were no *travail* to be *exploite*, there would be no capitalist nor capitalist production'.[18] Cohen develops the thought contained in Marx's remark by way of an example:

> Ten people are placed in a room the only exit from which is a huge and heavy locked door. At various distances from each lies a single heavy key. Whoever picks this up – and each is physically able, with varying degrees of effort, to do so – and takes it to the door will find, after considerable self-application, a way to open the door and leave the room. But, if he does so, he alone will be able to leave it. Photoelectric devices installed by a jailer ensure that it will open only just enough to permit one to exit. Then it will close, and no one inside the room will be able to open it again.
>
> It follows that, whatever happens, at least nine people will remain in the room.[19]

Cohen argues from this analogy that

> Each is free to seize the key and leave. But note the conditional nature of his freedom. He is free not only *because* none of the others tries to get the key, but *on condition* that they do not. . . . Not more than one can exercise the liberties they all have. If, moreover, any one were to exercise it, then, because of the structure of the situation, all the others would lose it.
>
> Since the freedom of each is contingent on the others not exercising their similarly contingent freedom, we can say there is a great deal of unfreedom in their situation. Though each is individually free to leave, he suffers with the rest from what I shall call *collective unfreedom*.[20]

Cohen's argument here is, perhaps, a more substantive version, or a concrete application, of the thesis of the correlativity of freedom with unfreedom: the freedom of the few workers who become capitalists presupposes the collective unfreedom of the many workers who do not. Now it is worth observing that there is so far nothing very determinate in this relationship of individual liberty with collective unfreedom under capitalism. We do not know *how many* workers becoming capitalists would overturn Cohen's argument. Suppose most workers had a period as capitalists during their lives. Would this render Cohen's attribution of collective unfreedom to the proletarian class invalid? Cohen might allow that collective proletarian unfreedom no longer exists in a society in which most workers spend part of their lives as capitalists, but deny that the economic system in which this can occur is any longer clearly a capitalist system. Such a denial seems unreasonable. In our supposition of a society in which most workers are capitalists for part of their lives, the constitutive institutions of capitalism – private ownership of the means of production and market allocation of capital and income – are by hypothesis fully preserved. (That is the point of hypothesizing that most workers spend part of their lives *as capitalists*.) Admittedly, Cohen might object that capitalism necessarily presupposes a propertyless proletarian majority, and, if he did, his objection would be an authentically Marxian one. That is not a sufficient reason for accepting Cohen's objection, however, since it amounts to identifying capitalist institutions with that nineteenth-century variant of them studied by Marx and, thereby, ruling out a priori the possibility of a proletarianless capitalism. I shall return to this last point later. Against my criticism, Cohen might further argue that whether or not workers are free in a system in which they spend part of their lives as capitalists depends crucially on *how much* of their lives workers spend as capitalists. This seems to be part of the force of Cohen's assertion that 'the manifest intent of the Marxist claim is that the proletariat is forced at (time) *t* to *continue* to sell his labor power, throughout a period from *t* to *t* + *n*, for some considerable *n*'.[21] The point here is not unreasonable. If most workers had to sell their labour power for only a small part of their lives, if (in other words) they spent most of their lives as capitalists, they would no longer be proletarians. In this circumstance, indeed, the proletariat – and with it proletarian unfreedom – would have all but disappeared. In the hypothetical case I have invoked, however, the near disappearance of proletarian unfreedom comes about in virtue of the spread of capital among the workers rather than by the abolition of capitalist institutions.

It is, of course, a standard position in Marxian political economy that the kind of society I have envisaged cannot exist, or cannot exist for very long. Processes of market concentration and proletarian immiseration will prevent the diffusion of capital among workers which alone could raise them within capitalism from the status of proletarians. This is an empirical claim in economic theory which is open for us to dispute: developments such as the growth of pension funds and of labour unions with significant capital assets might be seen as giving evidence of a trend towards the sort of capitalism-without-a-proletariat to which my hypothetical example points. Cohen's model of capitalist property institutions, in which the capitalist is the sole proprietor of the means of production, is an anachronistic one, best suited to economic life in England in the early nineteenth century. It has little relevance to the late twentieth-century reality, encompassing employee shareholding, management buy-outs, and profit-related pay. It may be premature or speculative to suggest that these developments attest to a trend to a proletarianless capitalism. Nevertheless, even were my example to remain entirely hypothetical, it would demonstrate that, as a matter of its structure or logic, proletarian unfreedom as Cohen conceives of it may be overcome, abolished, or reduced in a variety of ways, of which socialism is (at best) only one.

The indeterminacies in the relation between individual liberty and collective unfreedom under capitalism have implications of another sort for Cohen's argument. Cohen allows that 'collective unfreedom comes in varying amounts, and it is greater the smaller the ratio of the maximum that could perform it to the total number in the group'.[22] (It seems to be an implication of Cohen's view that collective unfreedom is a variable magnitude that collective freedom likewise comes in varying amounts. Whether it follows from this that a circumstance of complete collective freedom is impossible, since one collective freedom entails another collective unfreedom, is a question I cannot here pursue.) If collective unfreedom is thus a matter of degree – and not, for example, a condition in which individuals simply are or are not – then it matters vitally how large, *and how variable*, are the opportunities of individual emancipation by the acquisition of capitalist status. Perhaps the more proletarians there are who seek to become capitalists, the more opportunities there will be for them to do so. The possibility certainly cannot be excluded a priori, and, as I have already argued, the empirical theory which would deny it is at the very least controversial and disputable. Cohen's argument seems to depend on the assumption that, no matter how large the number of proletarians seeking to become capitalists, the number of opportunities to do so will remain fixed, or at least will not expand significantly. He makes explicit this assumption when he discusses another example of collective unfreedom:

> Suppose, for instance, that a hotel, at which one hundred tourists are staying, lays on a coach trip for the first forty who apply, since that is the number of seats on the coach. And suppose that only thirty want to go. Then, on my account, each of the hundred is free to go, but their situation displays a collective unfreedom.[23]

Cohen goes on:

> The coach case is a rather special one. For we tend to suppose that the management lay on only one coach because they correctly anticipate that one will be enough to meet the demand. Accordingly, we also suppose that if more had wanted to go, there would have been an appropriately larger number of seats available. If all that is true, then the available amount of collective freedom non-accidentally accords with the tourists' desires, and, though there is still a collective unfreedom, it is, as it were, a purely technical one. But if we assume there is only one coach in town, *and some such assumption is required for parity with the situation of proletarians*, then the tourists' collective unfreedom is more than merely technical.[24]

Cohen's assumption of fixity in the range of opportunities for workers' escape from proletarian status, which he admits is essential to the argument for proletarian unfreedom, looks entirely arbitrary. It is defensible, if at all, only by reference to propositions in Marxian economic theory, which are nowhere argued by Cohen. These are propositions having to do with the systemic scarcity of capital under the capitalist system. It is this alleged scarcity, presumably, which explains the claim that there are so few points of access from the proletariat to the capitalist class. I do not think it can fairly be said that there is any plausible contemporary statement of Marxian economic theory which supports the claim that capital is subject to a sort of endemic scarcity under capitalism. Much empirical evidence would in any case count against such a claim. Indeed, there is evidence that suggests a conjecture directly opposed to that of Marxian theory – the conjecture that, the more workers succeed in becoming capitalists, the greater are the opportunities of the remainder to do so. This is to say that the analogy of the locked room from which only one person can escape may be wholly misleading. A better analogy might be that of a group seeking to climb a mountain, where the more members of the group who succeed in doing so, the easier it is for those left behind to be raised up by the strength of those who have gone on before. There is nothing to say that such an analogy does not fit the case of modern capitalism better than Cohen's. In any event, in the absence of a plausible theory which gives to the relation between individual liberty and collective unfreedom under capitalism the determinacy or fixity which Cohen admits to be necessary to his argument, we have no reason to think proletarian unfreedom a necessary feature of capitalism. Or, to put the matter in different terms, the indeterminacies of the relationship that Cohen postulates between individual workers and their class situation are abated only by invoking an empirical theory he gives us no reason to accept.

The most fundamental objection to this argument of Cohen's is an altogether different one. It is one that focuses on the condition of simultaneous or joint access to some opportunity, action, or status which Cohen specifies as a necessary condition of freedom in respect of it. Cohen specifies this condition, negatively and by implication, when he specifies the necessary and sufficient condition of collective unfreedom. He tells us: 'Collective unfreedom can be defined as follows: a group suffers collective unfreedom with respect to a type of action A if and only if performance of A by all members of the group is impossible'.[25] He clarifies further: 'A person shares in a collective unfreedom when, to put it roughly, he is among those who are so situated that if enough others exercise the corresponding individual freedom, then they lose their individual freedom'.[26] Cohen's definition of collective unfreedom seems radically at variance with much of our standard thought. We do not usually suppose that, unless any subscriber to a telephone system can use it at the same time as every other or most other subscribers, then the entire class of telephone users is rendered unfree by the system. Perhaps Cohen would maintain that this example, though technically a case of collective unfreedom, is not an interesting one. Let us concede the point. I do not think that that could be said of many social institutions of which his definition would yield a description in terms of collective unfreedom. Consider, in this regard, the institution (proposed by C.B. Macpherson[27] and others as a device for diminishing risks to individual liberty under socialism) of the guaranteed minimum income. The guaranteed minimum income, like many other socialist institutions, depends for its existence on its being used at any one time by only a few. The freedom of any worker to take up his guaranteed income, and to live on that alone, depends on the unfreedom of most others, whose labour sustains the guaranteed income scheme.

On Cohen's definition, all workers in the socialist society are rendered unfree by the guaranteed income scheme. Recall in this connection his statement that 'a group suffers collective unfreedom with respect to a type of action A if and only if performance of A by all members of the group is impossible'.[28] We may go further. Each socialist worker is free to live on the guaranteed income not only *because* most others do not, but *on condition* that they do not. Then *each socialist worker is free (to live on the guaranteed income) only on condition that the others do not exercise their similarly conditional freedom*. Not more than a few workers can, at any one time, exercise the liberty they have. If, moreover, more than a few were at any time to exercise it, then, because of the structure of the situation, all the others would lose even this conditional freedom. Since the freedom of each socialist worker is contingent on the others not exercising their similarly contingent freedom, we can say that there is a great deal of unfreedom in their situation. Though each is individually free to live on the guaranteed income, he suffers with the rest from a form of *collective unfreedom*.

Like the collective unfreedom suffered by proletarians under capitalism, the collective unfreedom of socialist workers in respect of the guaranteed income is suffered by them as individuals. It is not a group unfreedom. 'A person shares in a collective unfreedom when, to put it roughly, he is among those who are so situated that if enough others exercise the corresponding individual freedom, then they lose their individual freedoms'.[29] By contrast with genuine collective unfreedom, the unfreedom of the proletariat to overthrow capitalism is a group unfreedom, since 'no individual proletarian could ever be free to overthrow capitalism, even when the proletariat is free to do so'.[30] By this criterion, the unfreedom of the socialist worker in respect of the guaranteed income is a genuine one and not a group unfreedom. Structurally, it is no different from proletarian unfreedom under capitalism.

I am leaving aside here the important question of whether, when collective freedoms are lost by individuals, what is lost are individual freedoms. For Cohen's argument to go through, it must be the case that collective freedoms are not only freedoms possessed or lost by individuals, but also instances of individual freedom as he conceives of it. This is to say that collective unfreedom and freedom may be analysable in terms of interference and non-interference with individuals' opportunities to act as they wish. Yet there is in Cohen no systematic argument for the reducibility of collective freedom and unfreedom to individual freedom and its absence. (Perhaps Cohen thinks that collective and individual unfreedoms are extensionally equivalent, but not collective and individual freedoms, but he does not argue this, and it is hard to see how such an asymmetry could be sustained.) Nor is this surprising, since the two sorts of freedom seem on the face of it categorically distinct, and possibly even embody incommensurable notions of freedom. I mention this gap in Cohen's reasoning, not in order to try to demonstrate that there are indeed two notions of freedom at stake in his argument, but simply to remark that his argument founders unless one kind of freedom (or unfreedom), the collective sort, is reducible without remainder to the other, individual sort of freedom and unfreedom.

The analogy between proletarian unfreedom under capitalism and worker unfreedom under socialism (in respect of the guaranteed income), though close, is not exact. In the case of proletarian unfreedom, as Cohen conceives of it, there are a few that are free in capitalist society – the capitalists (including those proletarians who succeed in becoming such). The reference group of those suffering a collective unfreedom to become capitalists cannot encompass the capitalists themselves. In the socialist society, all are unfree with regard to the guaranteed income. (There is an asymmetry here between the collective unfreedoms at issue if, as I have earlier argued, a capitalist society might exist in which all are capitalists, and if, as seems self-evident, there can be no socialist society in which all live on the guaranteed income and nothing else.) This brings out again an important point – that collective unfreedom, no less than individual unfreedom, is for Cohen a matter of degree. Individuals, as members of societies or groups, may suffer varying degrees of collective unfreedom. In the last section of this paper, I will argue that socialist institutions may generate more collective unfreedom for workers than do capitalist institutions. This is so even if collective unfreedom is (as I have argued earlier) a pervasive feature of social institutions generally. At this point, I want to observe only that, whereas not all are unfree under capitalist institutions (to become capitalists), there is at least one collective unfreedom which all suffer under socialism – that relative to the guaranteed income. It is unclear to me whether Cohen would consider this a lesser degree of collective unfreedom than that which obtains for workers in capitalist societies.

In fact, Cohen appears to think that not all collective unfreedoms are undesirable simply on account of the unfreedom they contain. He tells us that 'some collective unfreedom, like some individual unfreedom, is not lamentable'. And, crucially, he goes on: 'It is what this particular unfreedom forces workers to do which makes it a proper object of regret and protest. They are forced to subordinate themselves to others who thereby gain control over their, the workers', productive existence'.[31] This is a crucial passage inasmuch as it aims to specify what is bad or wrong in the collective unfreedom of proletarians under capitalism. It is an extremely unsatisfactory passage, at the same time, since subordination to others and control by these others of workers' productive life is not peculiar to, or even distinctive of, capitalist institutions. Workers may, as I shall later argue, be forced to work for others in a socialist system, thereby losing control of their productive lives. What is distinctive of, or peculiar to capitalism, is that workers *sell* their labour – an option denied them under feudal and socialist institutions. Cohen has said nothing, however, to show the special evil of such selling of workers' labour. If, on the other hand, the lamentable aspect of proletarian collective unfreedom is in the fact that the option of not working at all is an undesirable one, so that workers are forced to work, then it must be observed that this is a collective unfreedom found in all societies, albeit in crucially variable degrees. Cohen here in fact comes close to conceding my argument that collective unfreedom is a pervasive property of social institutions[32] and is to be found as clearly in the institutions of a socialist society as it is in those of capitalism. Thus, nothing of importance appears to follow from Cohen's arguments about the collective unfreedom of proletarians. In the absence of further considerations, there is nothing to say whether their unfreedom is lamentable or not, or, in general, to show that it is a proper object of moral concern. He achieves the result that proletarian collective unfreedom is an interesting and lamentable unfreedom, rather than a technical or trivial one, only by invoking the altogether independent claim that workers are forced to subordinate themselves to others who thereby gain control over their productive lives. Without this further consideration, the argument that proletarians suffer a collective unfreedom, though perhaps valid, is uninteresting and indeed trivial.

This conclusion follows inexorably from the logic of Cohen's argument. Like any other sort of unfreedom, collective unfreedom is not for Cohen necessarily an evil. For, like the concept of freedom in general, the concept of collective freedom is supposed to be value-free. Accordingly, the badness, wrongness, or moral importance of a specific collective unfreedom must depend on other considerations. (Presumably, it is these other considerations that are invoked *when we make comparative judgements of collective unfreedom.*) In Cohen's account, the importance of collective proletarian unfreedom is explained by reference to the claim that workers are forced to work for capitalists. It is therefore to Cohen's arguments about force and freedom in the workers' situation that I turn for illumination.

LIBERTY, FORCE AND JUSTICE

Cohen believes, with Marx, that workers are forced to sell their labour power to capitalists, and are thereby rendered unfree. He thinks that workers under capitalism may be in some important respects freer than Marx supposed.[33] But he defines workers (under capitalism) as 'those who are forced to sell their labour-power'. He asks: 'Is the stated condition necessary and sufficient? Certainly not all who sell their labour power are proletarians, but the condition is that one be *forced* to sell it. Still, it must be admitted that plenty of salaried non-proletarians are as much forced as many workers. So the condition is not sufficient'. He goes on further to ask 'whether the condition is a necessary one: *are* proletarians forced to sell their labour power?' He informs us that 'Robert Nozick answers negatively', but that 'Nozick's objection to our condition rests on a false because moralised account of what it is to be forced to do something'.[34]

Let it be noted that Cohen has not so far given us any reason *in favour of* supposing that proletarians are forced to sell their labour power, and thereby are rendered unfree. He has adduced instead an argument *against* Nozick's claim that their having to sell their labour power fails to render them unfree – the argument that Nozick's conception of freedom is 'moralised' and so 'false'. Cohen spells out this argument against Nozick by asserting that 'to prevent someone from doing something he wants to do is to make him, in that respect, unfree: I am unfree whenever someone interferes, *justifiably or otherwise*, with my actions. But', Cohen goes on 'there is a definition which is implicit in much libertarian writing, and which entails that interference is *not* a sufficient condition of unfreedom. On that definition, which I shall call the *moralised* definition, I am unfree only when someone does or would *unjustifiably* interfere with me.'[35] He further develops his argument against Nozick in a later piece, contending that:

> Robert Nozick might grant that many workers have no acceptable alternative to selling their labour-power. . . . But he denies that having no acceptable alternative but to do A entails being forced to do A, no matter how bad A is, and no matter how much worse the alternatives are, since he thinks that to have no acceptable alternative means to be forced only when unjust actions help to explain the absence of acceptable alternatives. . . . Nozick's objection to the thesis under examination rests upon a moralised account of what it is to be forced to do something. It is a false account, because it has the absurd upshot that if a criminal's imprisonment is morally justified, then he is not forced to be in prison. We may therefore set Nozick's objection aside.[36]

Nozick's argument that workers are not forced to sell their labour power is to be rejected then, according to Cohen, because the idea of unfreedom or forcing which it deploys conflates interference with justifiable interference, which in turn has the absurd result that the justifiably imprisoned man is not forced to remain in jail.

Cohen's argument against Nozick is feeble and sloppy and fails for several reasons. To begin with, Nozick's argument is *not* that *justifiable* interferences are not interferences with liberty. It is that the domain of liberty is specified by principles of justice, so that a *justicizable* interference with liberty is an impossibility. What Nozick's view excludes as a possibility is not, then, justified restraint of liberty, but justicizable restraint of liberty – that is to say, restraint of liberty justified in terms of justice. Accordingly, *justified* violation of the liberty demanded by justice remains a violation of liberty. Nozick's account of violating side constraints which protect liberty so as to avert a moral catastrophe[37] tells us this: when we violate side constraints and thereby commit an injustice, we do indeed curtail liberty, but we justify doing so by invoking the larger morality within which justice is usually (but not in this case of potential moral catastrophe) paramount. So, whereas justice and liberty cannot compete with one another, moral considerations may in extremity justify a violation of the liberty that is demanded by justice. (I pass over the possibility that the scope of justice is bounded or limited by circumstances of moral catastrophe in such a way that rights violations are impossible in such circumstances, since this seems plainly to be a possibility which Nozick does not wish to envisage.) For these reasons, it is mistaken to hold, as Cohen does, that Nozick conflates restraint of liberty with justified restraint of liberty.

It remains true, nonetheless, that Nozick's is a normative conception of liberty. In Nozick's account, the demands of liberty are given by a theory of justice – by the theory of entitlements he sets out in his book. By contrast, Cohen wishes to use only a 'neutral' or 'non-normative' conception of freedom. Thus he tells us that 'whatever may be the correct analysis of 'X is free to do A', it is clear that X is free to do A if X would do A if he tried to do A, and that sufficient condition of freedom is all that we need here'.[38] It is this 'non-normative' account of freedom[39] that Cohen invokes against Nozick. What are we to make of it? Cohen argues that Nozick's view is 'unacceptable' because it yields the 'absurd' conclusion that 'a properly convicted murderer is not rendered unfree when he is justifiably imprisoned'.[40] The absurdity of this result is, presumably, in the fact that it conflicts with ordinary-language uses of terms such as 'force' and 'freedom'. Cohen's argument itself rests on a confusion. Consider the case of the would-be rapist who is forcibly prevented from raping his victim. On Nozick's account, it is indeed true that forcibly preventing a rapist from committing the act of rape deprives him of no freedom, since the act of rape encompasses an unjust assault on another person's body and liberty, and is therefore an act which no one is entitled to perform. I, for one, do not find this result particularly counterintuitive. It seems to me to square better with our ordinary linguistic and moral intuitions than the Benthamite view which conceives of laws against rape as restricting the liberty of rapists (if only a worthless or disvaluable liberty) for the sake of protecting the liberty of their victims. I will not press this point, however, since Cohen's confusion arises elsewhere. It is plain to all of us that justice demands the restraint of rapists. Now, on Nozick's account, there is no liberty to commit rape, and so no rapist liberty to be restrained. The rapist is forcibly prevented from committing rape, but *he is not thereby rendered unfree*. At the same time, the rapist's liberty may yet be restrained if he is imprisoned for his crime. To think otherwise is to move illegitimately from the injustice of the act of rape to the justice of the penalty of imprisonment. The mere fact that rape is an unjustice, taken by itself, has nothing to tell us as to the just punishment for rape. It does not even tell us that punishment is called for in justice. If it is, then perhaps, as in Islamic law, the just punishment of rape is not loss of liberty but, instead, loss of life. Only a full theory of retributive and corrective justice can tell us what justice demands as the legal remedy for rape. Nozick's entitlement theory of justice makes no claim to comprehend the demands of justice addressed in retributive and corrective theory: its subject matter is a different one. For this reason, it might very well be that imprisonment for the crime of rape constituted a restraint of the rapist's liberty, even if forcibly restraining him from the act of rape did not.

In Nozick's account, liberty has primacy among the demands of justice (as it does in Rawls's theory of justice as fairness). Liberty and justice are linked in Nozick's theory, inasmuch as forcibly restraining A from unjustly restraining B is not to restrain A's liberty. A may be forced to do something, or to refrain from doing something, then, and still not be rendered unfree by that forcible restraint. One must *have* a liberty before it can be restrained. One may be restrained, without it being true that it is one's *liberty* that has been restrained. This Nozickian view that forcible prevention of an unjust action is not a restraint of liberty is an entirely general thesis which in no way presupposes Nozick's own account of justice. It is a feature, also, of Rawls's theory, in which private ownership of the means of production is not among the requirements of justice. Against this view of liberty or freedom as a moral notion, Cohen invokes his 'neutral' or 'non-normative' conception, stated earlier. Cohen's conception of freedom as a value-free notion seems to me unacceptable for a number of reasons. I will not consider these here, however, since I will address them later in this section. Also, they arise from a position in philosophical method held by Cohen which I shall expound and criticize in the next part of this chapter.

What are Cohen's arguments *for* the claim that workers under capitalism are forced to sell their labour power? Cohen does not deny that they are unfree to do so, only that they are not free not to do so. Indeed, he insists that workers are free to sell their labour power inasmuch as one is in general free to do what one is forced to do. Being forced to sell their labour power *entails* that workers are free to sell it. He argues:

> before you are forced to do A, you are, at least in standard cases, free to do A and free not to do A. The force removes the second freedom, but why suppose that it removes the first? It puts no obstacle in the way of your doing A, and you therefore remain free to do it. We may conclude, not only that being free to do A is compatible with being forced to do A, but that being forced to do A entails being free to do A. Resistance to this odd-sounding but demonstrable result reflects failure to distinguish the idea of being free to do something from other ideas, such as the idea of *doing something freely*. I am free to do what I am forced to do even if, as is usually true, I do not do it freely, and even though, as is always true, I am not free with respect to whether or not I do it.[41]

Thus, workers in a capitalist society, unlike slaves in a slave society, are free to sell their labour, even though they are forced to do so (and so are unfree not to do so).

The unfreedom in workers having to sell their labour power is for Cohen in the fact that they have no acceptable alternative. They may in a pure capitalist society choose to beg, or starve, but those are not acceptable alternatives: they are accordingly forced to sell their labour power. On the other hand, Cohen allows that, objectively speaking, most proletarians could (as some immigrant groups have done) acquire sufficient capital to rise from proletarian status: 'Proletarians who have the option of class ascent are not forced to sell their labour power, just because they do have that option. Most proletarians have it as much as our counterexamples (the immigrants) did. Therefore most proletarians are not forced to sell their labour power'.[42] Cohen here allows that most proletarians are *not*, in objective fact, forced to sell their labour power. As he admits: 'One would say, speaking rather broadly, that we have found more freedom in the proletariat's situation than classical Marxism asserts'.[43] His argument that, though most proletarians are not forced to sell their labour power, they are nevertheless unfree, *is one that appeals solely to the collective proletarian unfreedom created by the conditionality of each proletarian's freedom to leave the proletariat.* This is demonstrated by the fact that, having discussed the case of the people in the locked room, Cohen concludes 'by parity of reasoning, that although most proletarians are free to escape the proletariat, and, indeed, even if every one is, the proletariat is collectively unfree, an imprisoned class'.[44] This is to make his argument circular. We saw at the end of the last section that the proletariat suffered an interesting, lamentable collective unfreedom, only if it could be shown that it is forced to sell its labour power. We find now that, since most proletarians admittedly are not forced to sell their labour power, the argument for their being unfree not to do so depends on their suffering collective unfreedom as an imprisoned class. We find, in short, that Cohen advances no argument (apart from the weak argument from collective freedom) for the thesis that workers are forced to sell their labour.

The point may be put in another way. The claim that workers are forced to labour under capitalism, because they are not free to sell their labour power, has a corresponding application to the situations of workers under socialist institutions. Under a pure capitalist system, according to Cohen, the worker has no acceptable alternative to working for the capitalist. The proletarian may choose to beg or starve, but, anciently, it is only an irony at his expense to say that he is free to do so. It is ironical to suggest that the proletarian is free to do these things, since we all know them to be undesirable (and, indeed, unacceptable) alternatives. However, note that, on Cohen's own conception of freedom as being value-free, the proletarian in truth *is* free to beg or starve, even though the statement that he has these freedoms may have an ironical flavour. The proletarian is free to beg or starve because no one in a pure capitalist system will interfere with him or prevent him from doing these things. In Cohen's account, therefore, *the proletarian is free to leave the proletariat by refusing to sell his labour to the capitalist*. He has this freedom so long as he may without interference beg or starve.

Though he is free to refuse to sell his labour power to the capitalist, the proletarian is nonetheless forced to do so, since he has no acceptable alternative. He is free to do what he is forced to do, Cohen has already told us, because being free to do something is a necessary condition of being forced to do it. The logic of Cohen's argument requires him to go further than this. It requires him to accept that the proletarian is forced to sell his labour power even though he is free to refuse to do so. This is so, at least in part, because 'force', unlike 'freedom', is for Cohen a normative concept. It embodies standards of desirability and acceptability. It is only the conjunction of the value-free notion of collective unfreedom with the value-laden notion of force that gives Cohen his conclusion that workers are non-trivially and lamentably unfree under capitalism.

His argument, then, turns on the claim that workers are forced to sell their labour power under capitalism. (Some may well think that Cohen's account *of freedom* is unacceptable because it has the absurd upshot that proletarians are free to leave the proletariat by turning to beggary or submitting to starvation. I let this pass.) But is it true that they have no acceptable alternative? It would be true if their only alternatives were beggary or starvation. As we have seen, however, Cohen admits that, objectively speaking, most proletarians are in the same position as immigrant groups – they can become capitalists by accumulating capital. Like immigrants, then, most proletarians have another exit from their proletarian status. They need not become lumpenproletarians, but may become capitalists. Having made this admission, Cohen's only argument for proletarian unfreedom is the claim that most workers cannot exercise this freedom at the same time. This is the argument from collective unfreedom I have already criticized, and it is the only argument Cohen has to offer. If workers have other, acceptable alternatives to leaving the proletariat apart from becoming beggars or starving, then the collective unfreedom which the argument establishes is only a trivial one.

Let us, though, in a spirit of charity, set these arguments aside, and allow that there is a sense that the worker is forced to sell his labour power to the capitalist. Let us proceed to compare the proletarian's situation with that of the worker in a socialist state. By hypothesis, the latter cannot acquire private capital and live off that, and, since beggary will presumably be illegal, he cannot live by begging. Unless he is disabled or ill, and so (presumably) in receipt of government benefits, his only source of regular livelihood is his income from his work. Perhaps family or friends can support him for a while, but let us suppose that, like beggary under capitalism, this is an unacceptable alternative – always supposing, contrary to the historical experience of actually existing socialist states, that it is an alternative that is not legally forbidden. Since the socialist worker has no acceptable alternative to working for the socialist state, he is *unfree* not to do so. Because he is not free not to work for the socialist state, he is *forced* to do so. This is true whether the political form of the socialist state be democratic or authoritarian, and whether the economic unit of the socialist state is a public corporation or a worker cooperative. All that is required is that state or public authorities be the sole permissible source of employment. The unfreedom of proletarians not to work for capitalists has as its mirror image the unfreedom of socialist workers not to work for the state – or, more precisely, for those who exercise power through the state. Like proletarians, socialist workers find themselves in a situation in which their productive lives are subject to control by others. It is ironical to suggest otherwise.

THEORIES, CONCEPTS AND PHILOSOPHICAL METHOD

The upshot of my argument is that every charge of unfreedom that Cohen can intelligibly make against capitalism may be made just as well against socialist institutions. If workers are rendered unfree by the system of private property on which capitalism depends, they are also rendered unfree by a communal property system. If they suffer collective unfreedoms under capitalism, they suffer other collective unfreedoms under socialism. If they are not free not to sell their labour power under capitalism, if they are *forced* to sell their labour power under capitalism, they are not free not to work under socialism. This is to say that, in every one of the three respects in which capitalism renders workers unfree, there is a clear parity with a feature of socialist institutions in virtue of which they are rendered unfree. Nor is the a reason for this parity hard to find. In so far as they establish anything, Cohen's arguments give support to a series of conceptual truisms. This is, indeed, the manifest character of Cohen's arguments, which all of them consist in an application of a method of conceptual analysis.

For several reasons, Cohen's adoption of this method in political philosophy is misconceived. In the first place, as I have already argued, it can yield only conceptual truths, if it yields anything at all. Such truths can tell us nothing substantial about the fate of freedom under rival institutional arrangements. To find out about that, we must look to a theory of the real world. As things stand, Cohen appears to suppose that, by eliciting conceptual truths, he is in fact saying something about freedom in the real world. It is hard to explain otherwise his recourse to such portentous expressions as 'complex structures of freedom and unfreedom'. It is a delusion, however, to suppose that conceptual analysis can tell us the way things are in the world.

The philosophical method which Cohen adopts is in any case super-annuated. The 'analysis' of 'concepts' would be defensible as a strategy in philosophical inquiry if it were the case, as Kant supposed, that the categories of the human understanding were invariant and universal. Otherwise, the object of analysis can only be *words*, in all the miscellaneous diversity of their usages. Among us, at any rate, there is no clear uniformity of usage in respect of the key terms of moral and political discourse. Consider, for example, Cohen's idea of liberty. The notion of freedom within which he works is not an unequivocal deliverance of ordinary language, which contains 'normative' as well as 'descriptive' uses of 'freedom' and 'liberty' and their associated expressions. As its most sophisticated exponents have long recognized,[45] a neutral or value-free definition of liberty is a term of art, a technical expression developed as part of a reconstruction by stipulation of the terms of ordinary discourse. Further, even if ordinary usage were consistent, it is wholly unclear that it would have authority for political thought. As Joseph Raz has observed, 'linguistic distinctions . . . do not follow any consistent political or moral outlook. . . . What we need is not a definition nor mere conceptual clarity. Useful as these always are they will not solve our problems. What we require are moral principles and arguments to support them.'[46] And further: 'It is . . . important to remember that that concept [the concept of political freedom] is a product of a theory or a doctrine consisting of moral principles for the guidance and evaluation of political actions and institutions. One can derive a concept from a theory but not the other way round.'[47]

Because ordinary language embodies no consistent outlook, the appeal to ordinary language cannot even begin the task of developing a theory of freedom. Even if ordinary usage did disclose a coherent conception of freedom – say, a conception of the liberal sort which Cohen deploys unreflectively and without criticism – the conceptual truths derivable from an analysis of such usage would amount only to local knowledge of our current linguistic practices. It is wholly unclear to me why Cohen supposes that local knowledge of this sort should or could be authoritative in moral and political philosophy. Many ordinary-language usages, or 'concepts', embody and express repugnant moral judgements. (Consider the rich terminology of popular racism.) Why should the deliverances of ordinary thought and practice have any claim on reason, or any weight at all in philosophical inquiry? How, in particular, are they supposed to be able to support *principles* for the assessment and regulation of acts and institutions? They might do so, if (once again with Kant) it were supposed that only one set of practical maxims would emerge from an application of the categories of our understanding. So far as I am aware this heroic supposition is not one that Cohen has endorsed, but without it, the results of the analysis of ordinary language are likely to be inconclusive or merely conservative. Finally, even if such criticisms could be countered, the archaic Rylean methodology which (at least in his work on proletarian unfreedom) Cohen practices fails to address the powerful scepticism about meaning voiced by many recent philosophers, such as Quine and Kripke.

What moral and political philosophy demands, instead of the pursuit of illusory concepts, is the construction of theories – theories which at once latch on to features of the real world and track our dominant moral concerns. Granted, such theorizing should be conducted with as much clarity as we can achieve. It should also, and crucially, help us to understand why freedom is restrained in the real world. The philosophical method which Cohen employs encompasses a disseveration of concepts from theories and theories from values in political thought. Now it may well be that there are some terms in our discourse, such as 'power',[48] which are best theorized in value-free terms, but I doubt that freedom is such a term. Everything suggests we are on firmer ground if we think of freedom as a moral notion.[49] The task of a theory of freedom is to give freedom a definite content by reference to a larger moral and political theory. Most particularly, it is to specify the liberty that is demanded by justice. The demands of justice are, further, to be explained in terms of the requirements of the well-being of individuals – which need to be spelled out in terms, not only of their basic human needs, but also by reference to their cultural traditions and historical circumstances.[50] The structure of liberties demanded by justice will vary according to these aspects of individual well-being. The task of theorizing freedom is, then, one which necessitates a close familiarity with the actual needs of human beings and with the cultural and historical contexts in which these needs are shaped. This task is not advanced by a bankrupt philosophical method in which descriptions of local linguistic behaviours masquerade as fundamental truths of moral and political life.

A theory of freedom, accordingly, will treat freedom as a moral notion. It will embed that notion in a larger theory. That larger theory will have to do, in significant part, with what human beings are like and with the way things are in the world, but it will also express our evaluation of human beings and the world. A theory of freedom should have explanatory power as well as moral force. It should help us to understand the world as much as it equips us to assess it. In particular, it should do what Cohen's account signally fails to do – help us to assess the on-balance freedom achieved by rival institutional frameworks.

CAPITALISM, SOCIALISM AND ON-BALANCE FREEDOM

How, then, are the rival institutions to be assessed? As Cohen himself acknowledges, making such an assessment is no easy matter. 'Each form of society (capitalist and socialist) is by its nature congenial and hostile to various sorts of liberty, for variously placed people. . . . Which form is better for liberty may depend on the historical circumstances'.[51] As Cohen again acknowledges, there are two distinct questions about capitalism, socialism and freedom. 'The first, or *abstract* question, is which form of society is, just as such, better for freedom, not, and this is the second, and *concrete* question, which form is better for freedom in the conditions of a particular place and time'.[52] In respect of the first, abstract question, Cohen offers 'the following intractably rough prescription':

> Consider, with respect to each form of society, the sum of liberty which remains when the liberties it withholds by its very nature are subtracted from the liberties it guarantees by its very nature. The society which is freer in the abstract is the one where that sum is larger.[53]

Cohen's prescription, as it stands, is not easy to apply. There is no mechanical way of individuating liberties, and so no mechanical way of computing which society has the greater sum of liberties. If by 'liberties' Cohen (in consistency with his general conception of liberty as non-interference) means acts which persons are not interfered with by others in doing, such liberties are very different in the importance they have to those who possess and exercise them. Even if a mechanical procedure were available whereby we could individuate and count liberties, such a procedure would for this last reason (that it could not attach weights to the liberties so specified) fail to tell us what we want to know – namely, *how much liberty* each society contains. This is only to state once again a result of recent liberal thought – that judgements of degrees of freedom on-balance cannot as a rule be made without invoking standards of importance in respect of the liberties being evaluated.[54] This is to say that, even though there are central cases where we have no difficulty in making assessments of on-balance or comparative liberty, a libertarian calculus is an impossibility.

This is not to say we are left without resources in the attempt to weigh capitalist and socialist institutions as to the comparative freedom they contain, whether in general or for workers specifically. We have in fact several methods of proceeding. One is to make the move of disaggregation or decomposition of liberty into basic liberties which John Rawls does in his *A Theory of Justice* and subsequent writings.[55] For the most part, Rawls's basic liberties are the civil liberties to which Cohen refers when he tells us that these freedoms of speech, assembly, worship, publication, political participation, and so forth are not necessary concomitants of capitalism.[56] If we accept Rawls's list of the basic liberties, we *can* assess capitalist and socialist societies in respect of them. In the real world, though it is true that capitalism is not always accompanied by the basic liberties, it is no less true that the basic liberties have never been found in the absence of capitalism. There is not a single historical example of a socialist or, in general, a non-capitalist society in which these basic liberties are respected. In the historical circumstances with which we are familiar, there is no doubt which form of society is better for liberty. And, in so far as workers value the basic liberties, there is no doubt which form of society is better for workers and their liberty.

Against the Rawlsian move, which seems entirely unambiguous in its results, Cohen may make a number of objections. He may object that, however true it is in our current historical circumstances that socialist societies fail to protect the basic liberties, the argument from the basic liberties against socialism is nevertheless inconclusive. Perhaps we ought to regard our current historical predicament as something to be rejected or overcome, rather than simply accepted, and perhaps a socialist society is achievable in which the basic liberties *are* protected. This is an objection I will not address, though there are powerful reasons in positive political theory[57] for rejecting it, since my own argumentative strategy on this question is satisfied if it is admitted that our present historical context answers the question of on-balance freedom decisively in favour of capitalist institutions.

Cohen might make another, different objection to the Rawlsian move I have made. The Rawlsian move depends on excluding entitlement to property in the means of production from the set of basic liberties. Since property rights in the means of production, individual or communal, do not figure among the basic liberties as Rawls theorizes them, the choice between capitalism and socialism cannot turn on how their respective property institutions create and sustain liberty. (The choice may be, and should be, informed by a theoretical conjecture about the causal role of capitalist and socialist property institutions in sustaining the basic liberties. That is another question.) If we bring the property system back into the assessment of on-balance liberty, it may be that the unequivocal result we earlier obtained no longer holds. A society might curb some of the basic liberties and yet, because its property institutions extended liberty in important ways, do better from the standpoint of liberty than a society in which the basic liberties are perfectly protected. This is the view of many Leninists about the Soviet Union. I do not say that that is Cohen's view of the Soviet Union, but it does give him a way of resisting the upshot of the Rawlsian move.

Such a countermove does not save Cohen's case, however. Let us forswear the idiom of the basic liberties and adopt the conception of freedom as non-interference which Cohen deploys. Let us accept the result which Cohen derives by applying that notion of freedom to capitalist institutions – the result that capitalists are freer than proletarians. They are freer in the sense that, because they have resources in the means of production, they are less often (or less significantly) interfered with in doing as they wish, and so (let us say) have more or better options at their disposal than proletarians do. Accepting Cohen's conception of freedom and the resultant inequality of liberty under capitalism, how does workers' freedom fare under socialism? There seem to be clear respects in which workers' options will be severely diminished under socialist institutions. It is an important argument against socialism that, in transferring the control of employment from a diversity of competing employers to a single public authority, it will unavoidably curtail the options of workers. The point has been well put by Hayek:

> That the freedom of the employed depends upon the existence of a great number and variety of employers is clear when we consider the situation that would exist if there were only one employer – namely, the state – and if taking employment were the only permitted means of livelihood . . . a consistent application of socialist principles, however much it might be disguised by the delegation of the power of employment to nominally independent public corporations and the like, would necessarily lead to the presence of a single employer. Whether this employer acted directly or indirectly he would clearly possess unlimited power to coerce the individual.[58]

Or, as Leon Trotsky, one of the chief architects of the Soviet system, put it pithily: 'In a country where the sole employer is the state, opposition means death by slow starvation. The old principle, who does not work shall not eat, has been replaced by a new one: who does not obey shall not eat.'[59] Cohen has told us that, under capitalism, workers 'face a structure generated by a history of market transactions in which, it is reasonable to say, they are *forced* to work for some or other person or group. Their natural rights are not matched by corresponding effective powers.'[60] It is an implication of Hayek's argument that, in a socialist economy, workers will face a structure generated by political power in which, it is reasonable to say, they are *forced* to work for the state. Their legal rights are not matched by corresponding effective powers.

Against Hayek's argument, it might be objected that it fails to take account of the possibility of a form of market socialism, in which there is a diversity of worker cooperatives and so a variety of employment opportunities for workers. It is not to be doubted that such a decentralized socialist system would likely be better for liberty than any centralist system could. Still, there will be important respects in which workers' liberty will be curtailed under market socialism. The problem is clearest when we consider workers who belong to a minority group. Communal systems of ownership of productive resources may be expected to find it hard to permit such minorities to advance, perhaps most particularly when they are operated by democratic procedures. Consider, by way of example, what would likely have been the fate of immigrants of alien cultural traditions, in Britain and the United States, if they had had to gain access to productive resources solely through a democratic political process. Whenever there is a prejudiced majority, such minorities are likely to have narrower options even under market socialism than they do under market capitalism, where a few self-interested capitalists are sufficient for them to be able to borrow or rent resources on the basis of which they can build up capital of their own.

Even when discriminating majorities are lacking, workers' options are limited by the necessity each faces of having in his cooperative to secure the agreement of his fellows for the introduction of any novel practice. As Hayek has again put it, 'action by collective agreement is limited to instances where previous efforts have already created a common view, where opinion about what is desirable has become settled, and where the problem is that of choosing between possibilities generally recognized, not that of discovering new possibilities'.[61] This point is reinforced when we realize that, because of the fusion of capital ownership with job occupation under market socialism, the dependency of the individual worker on his cooperative will be considerably greater than his dependency on his employer in a capitalist society.

As for the worker cooperative itself, it too will be in a circumstance of dependency. If market socialism is to remain a form of socialism, productive capital will have to be subject to political allocation rather than private provision. Workers will have access to capital only through the agencies of the socialist state. Because private capital is forbidden, no worker can individually acquire enough capital to live on. Even as a member of his collective, he is always dependent on the capital that is allocated him by government. Perhaps worker-cooperators will have discretion over how much of their profits they set aside for investment in the enterprise and, to that extent, a part of their capital might be self-generated. But it seems clear that start-up capital and capital needed to stave off bankruptcy, or permit large-scale expansion, will have to be politically allocated. Workers under a market socialist system will confront a situation in which sources of capital are concentrated in one, or a few, state investment banks. They will have far fewer sources of capital than existed under capitalism. It is hard to see how this fact can avoid restricting workers' options.

The general point behind these arguments is that the freedoms generated by capitalist institutions are not only those enjoyed or exercised by the owners of capital.[62] This is a point recognized by Cohen when he notes that capitalism is a liberating system by contrast with its predecessor systems, such as slavery and feudalism.[63] He omits to note that many of these freedoms, depending as they do on a multiplicity of buyers of labour and sources of capital, would be extinguished by state socialism and diminished under market socialist institutions. Capitalist institutions may, then, be defended as institutions that promote workers' freedom better than any realizable alternative. This may be so even if it be conceded that workers are less free than capitalists. For it is still arguable that they are freer than they would be under any other institutions. All forms of socialism, in particular, appear to diminish that control over the disposition of his own labour and person which the worker gained with the advent of capitalism. It remains unclear on Cohen's account what are the freedoms conferred on the worker by socialism which might compensate for this loss.

If I am right in arguing that workers, even as a class, are better off in terms of liberty under capitalist than under alternative institutions, this supports a defence of capitalism that is to be conducted strictly in terms of its liberty-promoting effects. This argument is that the inequalities in liberty which Cohen finds in capitalist institutions are those which maximize the freedom of workers. Capitalism might then be defended as an economic system which satisfies a variation on Rawls's difference principle – a variation in which it applies only to liberty (and not to the other primary goods). Unlike Cohen, I do not suppose that an argument for capitalism from freedom can or should be severed from one that invokes justice. Nor, indeed, do I imagine that the demands of justice can be specified independently of an account of the well-being of those concerned – though I have not tried to give any account of well-being myself. The considerations I have advanced suggest that capitalism may nevertheless be defended by reference to an argument of freedom alone. The result of these considerations as to substantive liberty on-balance under capitalism and socialism is that capitalism does best for liberty, even for those within capitalism who have the least liberty.

The comparative assessment in terms of freedom of socialism and capitalism may take a third form – by considering collective unfreedom under each set of institutions. Let us, in this connection, go so far as to concede that most proletarians are collectively unfree to become capitalists, thereby putting aside the possibility of a capitalism-without-a-proletariat which I mentioned earlier. If we do this, we may say (in another idiom than Cohen's) that being a capitalist is in a capitalist society a *positional good* [64] – one that cannot be possessed or enjoyed by all. It is just in virtue of its positionality that Cohen argues for the collective unfreedom of proletarians in respect of it. Now perhaps, in the real world, being a capitalist *is* a positional good, as Cohen and other Marxists suppose. A real collective unfreedom is thereby generated for workers. This tells us nothing, however, as to the *relative* or *comparative* collective unfreedom of workers under capitalist and socialist institutions. It does not even adequately explain the moral significance of the collective unfreedom of the proletariat under capitalism. It shows only that under capitalism workers suffer a collective unfreedom – the unfreedom to become a capitalist – which, it is supposed, socialism would abolish. I have argued earlier that socialism would, in effect, universalize and entrench this unfreedom. Let us accept Cohen's argument to his conclusion, though, and see how workers fare as to their collective freedom under socialism.

Under socialism, then, we shall allow, workers will be rid of the collective unfreedom to become capitalists. At the same time, it is likely that a good many other collective unfreedoms would be spawned under socialism. It is a feature of all forms of socialism that resources which are allocated by market processes under capitalism are subject to political allocation instead. This is true even under market socialist institutions, in which at least investment capital is politically allocated. In the real world, however, political power is itself a positional good. It cannot be had or exercised by all equally. The positionality of political power entails that, when resources are subject to political control and allocation, they too acquire the attributes of positionality. Thus in 'actually existing' socialist societies, education, housing and health services exhibit a degree of positionality which likely far surpasses that possessed by analogous services in Western capitalist nations. Workers in such socialist states suffer a degree of collective unfreedom in respect of the Communist élite's access to good apartments, hard-currency stores, higher education for their children, adequate medical care, and so forth, which plausibly exceeds any similar positionality in capitalist societies.[65]

Attempts to explain this fact and which rely on *ad hoc* claims about historical backwardness, illiberal traditions, or inauspicious circumstances in the societies concerned neglect systematically the role of political allocation of resources in shaping the incentives of individuals in such societies. By contrast with societies in which resources are primarily allocated by markets, individuals in socialist societies have an almost irresistible incentive to seek positions of power in the party apparatus from which they can assure benefits to themselves and their offspring. Hence the predictable transfer of command positions and their associated benefits across generations of *nomenklatura* in the socialist states. By contrast, in so far as access to goods is in capitalist societies mediated via the market, it is inherently likely to display less positionality than in socialist states. This is so because, except where they are highly monopolistic, markets tend to redistribute resources unpredictably across economic agents and, most especially, across generations.

In general, we may expect that, with the politicization of resource allocation that socialism brings, goods which hitherto had not been positional will become so. In so doing, they will generate collective unfreedoms in respect of them which had not existed before. The pattern of collective unfreedoms in society will mirror that of the possession of the supreme positional good, political power. In this situation, socialist workers will be imprisoned as a class, even if (dubiously enough) each of them is free to join the ruling élite. The collective unfreedom which they will suffer in respect of the positional good of political power will, in its turn, spawn collective unfreedom in respect of all the goods that political power allocates – that is to say, most of the goods of economic and social life. It is difficult to resist the conclusion that workers under socialist institutions will suffer a degree of collective unfreedom unknown in capitalist societies.

CONCLUDING REMARKS

The arguments Cohen adduces as to proletarian unfreedom are mostly formal. They support truisms which tell us nothing of substance about the advantages in terms of freedom of capitalist over socialist institutions. When we turn from conceptual analysis to realistic considerations, we find powerful reasons for supposing that socialist institutions will do worse than capitalist institutions from the standpoint of workers' freedom. We find that the parity of unfreedoms between the two systems that is supported by Cohen's atavistic philosophical methodology is, in fact, entirely delusive. In other words, if the goal of Cohen's argument is to demonstrate the existence of unfreedom under capitalism, it succeeds – but only because the unfreedom he discusses exists in every institution of property (and probably in every imaginable society). It seems decidedly implausible that Cohen should devote five papers, which develop a novel and implausible conception of collective unfreedom and contrive to make a host of minute distinctions in the discourse of freedom, to establish so banal and trifling a result. If, on the other hand, Cohen's goal is the more interesting one of showing that worker's freedom, or freedom in general, is greater under socialist institutions than within capitalist institutions, his argument to this result demonstrably fails. When we consider the substance of things, we have every reason to think that workers' freedoms will flourish best under capitalist institutions. Oddly enough, this supposition is amply confirmed by historical experience. And that is another argument in favour of a form of theorizing which, unlike Cohen's, seeks to explain and assess the freedom and unfreedom we find in the real world.

12 Totalitarianism, reform and civil society

What must be true for post-totalitarianism to be a possibility? This question – a question as to the conditions under which totalitarian political orders may mutate, or successfully transform themselves, into orders, authoritarian, liberal or otherwise, in which the constitutive features of totalitarianism have been transcended or suppressed – presupposes a conception of totalitarianism itself. The history of the idea of totalitarianism, however, is a history of controversy. Presented initially by theorists and practitioners of Italian fascism as a positive notion,[1] the idea of totalitarianism acquired in post-War literature[2] an unequivocally pejorative connotation, being used to capture the common features of National Socialism and Soviet Communism in their worst and most terroristic periods. It was later subject to criticism and attack, both by Marxists and by others,[3] who sought to deny its theoretical coherence and utility and who tried to represent it as an ideological construct of liberalism and conservatism which was deployed for the purposes associated with (or attributed to) the Western powers during the period of the Cold War. My inquiry is based on the rejection of this latter view and on a commitment to the validity and usefulness of totalitarianism as a central category in contemporary social and political theory. This does not mean that I endorse the conventional conception of totalitarianism, as developed in the post-War Anglo–American literature. Legitimate as it may be, this conventional usage obscures a number of interesting questions. Is totalitarianism necessarily or inherently terroristic, or is terror a developmental phase which some totalitarian orders pass through? This is a question with obvious relevance to the possibility of post-totalitarianism, since it allows that a totalitarian regime may sustain and reproduce itself by means other than the threat of violence. Can the institutions of democratic capitalism be characterized as encompassing a totalitarian order, as Marcuse and others[4] have alleged? Is totalitarianism a uniquely modern phenomenon, or are there instances of it in ancient times?

Can post-totalitarian orders in which civil societies have clearly emerged, be subject to successful retotalitarianization? Or is the move from totalitarianism typically irreversible?

What of the cultural roots of totalitarianism: is it alien to the Western tradition, an aberration within it, or a development of elements of the most central, ancient and fundamental Western traditions? I shall approach these and related questions by way of a critique of the received notion of totalitarianism and of its standard applications to the Soviet case. The standard conception of totalitarianism equates it with such phenomena as mass terror and a charismatic leader with a cult of personality. It suggests that, in the absence of clear evidence of these phenomena, we have a post-totalitarian regime. By contrast, the conception of totalitarianism I shall advance enables us to recognize as neo-totalitarian the forms of social and political control that have emerged recently in the Soviet Union, and to distinguish such a neo-totalitarian regime from the genuine post-totalitarianism that exists in Poland, Hungary, and, more precariously, in the Baltic states.

The danger of the conventional conception is that it may blind us to the varieties of totalitarianism. This is not to say that totalitarianism is a sort of cluster-concept, with the variety of totalitarian regimes being unified only by a pattern of family resemblances. For I shall maintain that the totalitarian project is constituted by a single objective – that of merging state and society in a new order from which the conflicts of interest, purpose and value which are found in all historic societies have been extirpated. This definitively totalitarian objective may be stated with greater precision. *The totalitarian project is the project of suppressing civil society – that sphere of autonomous institutions, protected by a rule of law, within which individuals and communities possessing divergent values and beliefs may coexist in peace.* Implementing this project involves another, and even more stupendous project: that of remaking the identities of those who have come within the sphere of totalitarian power. A number of theorists, such as Heller,[5] have seen in this project of making over human nature on a new model the most essential, definitive feature of totalitarianism. I shall argue that, whereas the totalitarian project has in many instances succeeded in destroying civil society, it has nowhere forged a new humanity. I shall take the destruction of civil society to be the chief historical result of totalitarianism. Indeed, on the view I shall defend, the suppression of civil society is not so much a consequence, or a side-effect, of totalitarianism, as its very essence.

It is for this reason, again, that I shall affirm the radical modernity of the totalitarian phenomenon. Totalitarianism is uniquely modern, not only because it presupposes a contemporary technology of repression, but chiefly because it expresses a revulsion against the distinctively modern institutions of civil society. It did so even in China, where Communism sought to legitimate itself as a project of modernization. I shall affirm the radical modernity of totalitarianism as a political order, even though I will maintain that its cultural origins are in elements of the most ancient and central Western values and ideas (and not, for example, in the traditional cultures of Russia and China.)

In particular, interpretations of the Soviet Union in terms of the antique categories of tyranny or empire miss the mark by invoking concepts to capture realities of which Montesquieu or Aristotle could have had no conception. When Pipes argues that 'the techniques of police rule, introduced piecemeal by the Russian imperial regime, were first utilized to their fullest potential by their one-time victims, the revolutionaries',[6] he neglects the very radical discontinuities (which I shall later spell out in detail) between the magnitude of repression between the Tsarist and Bolshevik regimes, and, above all, he passes over the fact that the Tsarist secret police was never employed to liquidate entire social groups.

Equally far from the mark is the claim that totalitarianism existed in ancient times. When Barrington Moore cites the adoption in ancient China of 'the famous pao-chia system of mutual surveillance, which resembles and long antedates modern totalitarian procedures' he confuses totalitarianism with a technique which has been adopted by a variety of types of government. When he goes on to refer to 'the hsiang-yueh system of periodically lecturing the population on Confucian ethics' as another 'revealing precursor of modern totalitarian practices . . . they demonstrate conclusively that the key features of the totalitarian complex existed in the premodern world',[7] he neglects the revolutionary character of totalitarian ideological indoctrination.

Totalitarian ideologies are instruments of social transformation and seek to displace traditional systems of belief. That is why the academic *canard*, that Communism is a modern secular or political religion, is true only in the sense in which occultism and theosophy are religions – the sense in which all are modernist projects of supplanting the mysteries and tragedies of inherited faiths with gnostic techniques of liberation, represented as applications of scientific method. There is an inherent paradox in totalitarianism in that it deploys modern ideology in the service of an anti-modernist project. Because it embodies a revolt against modernity, totalitarianism can only be its shadow. If totalitarian orders are to be reformed, accordingly, such reform can be achieved only by way of a rediscovery of the most distinctive institutions of the modern world – the institutions of civil society.

The question of the possibility of post-totalitarianism, accordingly, is the question whether totalitarian regimes may so alter their nature as to allow the re-emergence or re-invention of those institutions of civil life to whose destruction they were committed. Indeed, since the emergence of civil society encompasses a mutation in the very nature of totalitarianism, a question inevitably arises whether totalitarian orders are capable of reform, and, if they are not, how are current developments to be understood?

It is enmity to civil society, with its constitive institutions of private property and the rule of law, rather than opposition to liberal democracy, which is most nearly definitive of totalitarianism. 'Civil society' here refers to the domain of voluntary associations, market exchanges and private institutions within and through which individuals having urgent conceptions and diverse and often competitive purposes may coexist in peace. It is this conception, I believe, that is held in common by such otherwise very different theorists as Locke and Hegel. In both, civil society is distinguished sharply from the state. But each recognizes that the institutions of civil society need definition and protection by law, and so cannot flourish without the shelter of government. There are many types of government, however, under which a civil society may exist – as many varieties of authoritarianism, for example, as there are of democracy. Only the unlimited government of totalitarianism is incompatible with civil society. For this reason, non-totalitarian, and indeed post-totalitarian regimes may come in a variety of forms, of which liberal democracy is only one. In all of its varieties, however, post-totalitarianism represents the inversion of the totalitarian order, not a terminal phase in its development. For a totalitarian regime to cease to be such, it must be able to recall the civil life it has lost, or else to fashion anew the institutions of civil society. My purpose in this paper is to speculate about the conditions under which actually existing totalitarian regimes might successfully negotiate this transformation and so resurrect, or adopt, a civil society.

In fact, my project here will be the more limited one of conjecturing as to the prospects of such a metamorphosis in Soviet-bloc regimes. I pass over as not centrally germane to my purpose the example of Nazi Germany, in which a totalitarian regime perished through military defeat, and all of the Fascist states, none of which was genuinely totalitarian (even where, as in Italy, it claimed to be). I pass over these other potential instances to totalitarianism, primarily because the Soviet example constitutes the paradigm case. In terms of chronology, the Soviet Union was the modern world's first totalitarian state. Further, its example animated every subsequent totalitarian (or would-be totalitarian) state. As Schapiro has said:

> The originator of the technique of mass manipulation, in modern times, was Lenin; not only Stalin, but Mussolini certainly and Hitler (through the German Communists) indirectly, learned it from him. . . . Lenin never became (or ever wanted to become) a Leader such as Hitler or

Stalin; but in the course of building up his technique of mass manipulation as part of the process of ensuring victory for his party he provided a model for these very different men.[8]

Lenin initiated not only totalitarian techniques of mass manipulation, but also most of the other distinctive institutions of totalitarianism – such as the concentration camp and the extra-legal powers of the secret police. As Nolte has argued,[9] there is also a case for ascribing to the Bolsheviks the responsibility for pioneering the techniques of mass extermination which the Nazis later emulated in their genocides. For these reasons, then, I feel justified in focusing on Soviet-type instances as paradigm cases of totalitarianism. For a different reason, lack of space, I do not discuss in any systematic fashion the potentially very important case of Communist China other than by brief comments on the contrasts between traditional forms of despotism in China and Chinese Communist totalitarianism and a short comparison of the prospects of economic reform in China and the Soviet Union. I restrict the scope of my inquiries to the topical, but also globally decisively important question: Can the reform movements within the Soviet bloc – such as *perestroika* in the Soviet Union, Solidarity in Poland, and the various experiments in multiparty pluralism in Hungary and in the toleration of oppositional movements in the Baltic states – succeed to the extent of re-establishing civil societies, or something akin to them? My project here is not the hazardous one of prediction, though I will speculate as to the likely failure of *perestroika*, but that of theorizing the conditions of, and constraints upon, the emergence of post-totalitarian regimes within the Soviet bloc. Pursuing this theoretical goal involves me in making significant distinctions between circumstances and prospects in different countries, particularly as to the causal origins of the various reform movements. It also implicates me in the business of attempting to specify those features of Soviet totalitarianism which give it its essential character and which are most relevant to the possibilities of post-totalitarianism.

Here I shall make little use of the famous five-point syndrome of totalitarian regimes proposed by Carl Freidrich in 1954,[10] since it conflates historically contingent aspects of Soviet-style totalitarianism with its constitutive features. I shall focus instead on what I shall maintain are the three key features of totalitarianism – its suppression of the institutions of civil society, and especially of the rule of law, the central planning of the economy and the character of the totalitarian regime as a *weltanschauung*-state. And, to anticipate my conclusions, I shall submit that current movements for reform, such as *perestroika* in the Soviet Union, are responses to the ruinous failure of the command economies – a failure that has left even the servile *nomenklatura* of these regimes underrewarded. The tactical objective of the Soviet reform process is the refinancing of the system by Western credit. The strategic objective is the stabilization of the Soviet totalitarian order – which incorporates the goals of engineering a shift in the distribution of military power in Europe and the forging of subsidy relationships between the EEC and the Comecon countries. In all important respects the Soviet *perestroika* embodies an authentically Leninist strategy which includes a significant component of strategic disinformation. The crucial question – which I shall address towards the end of this paper – is whether the new Leninist strategy of the Soviet leadership risks unleashing uncontrollable forces in the Soviet bloc, and in the Soviet Union itself, which threaten the system's very existence, or whether, despite its colossal failures, the Soviet system can again renew itself through a combination of selective repression and Western aid. There is also the question whether, even granted massive doses of Western capital and technology, the Soviet system can do anything more than stave off for a while the prospect of a catastrophic economic collapse, with all the unpredictable political consequences that would have. In any case, we need to ask what are the implications for the prospects of post-totalitarianism in Poland, Hungary, the Baltic states and elsewhere in the Soviet bloc. Before we can even approach these questions, however, we need to consider what are the constitutive features and decisive episodes in Soviet totalitarianism.

THEORIZING SOVIET TOTALITARIANISM: THE CONVENTIONAL METHODOLOGY

We may begin by making some cautionary remarks on the methodology of conventional Soviet studies. The conventional wisdom among Sovietologists is that the Soviet state is a state like any other, whose distinctive features are derived from Russian political and cultural traditions. According to this dominant view,[11] the Soviet state is a tyranny, in whose formation Muscovite traditions of authoritarian rule are at least as significant as Marxist-Leninist ideology. If this is so, then the methods appropriate to the study of the Soviet state are no different from those used with any other state – the methods of standard political science, such as theories about political culture, the study of interest groups, of the modernization of institutions, and so on. It is no exaggeration to assert that this methodology has been thoroughly unproductive and indeed counterproductive in its impact on Western perceptions of the Soviet Union. It is radically defective for a number of reasons. In the first place, this conventional methodology is bound to exaggerate grossly the importance of cultural factors in explaining Soviet totalitarianism. That this is so is demonstrated by the profound similarities between Soviet-type regimes having very different cultural traditions. Despite their diverse political traditions, the East European states exhibited during the Stalinist period structural affinities – such as the campaign against religion and the attempt to impose a single *weltan-schauung*, the attack on the peasantry, show trials, a terroristic secret police and the regimentation of intellectual life – which are explicable only by reference to their being modelled on the Soviet totalitarian state. Again, the structural affinities between the periods of socialist construction in the Soviet Union and in Communist China – the reliance on slave labour in a vast Gulag, the catastrophic waste and malinvestment generated by a command economy which promoted rapid industrialization at the expense of the ruin of agriculture, and repression of minority peoples – overwhelm any divergences between the two regimes which their different cultures may account for. Yet again, Communist regimes remote from the Soviet Union, and acting on radically different cultures, have emulated Stalinist policies aimed at the destruction of peasant life – as in Ethiopia, where the Communist government goes so far as to call its policy for the forcible resettlement of the peasantry by the term, 'systematization', used for the same policy in today's Stalinist Romania. Other examples, from Cuba, Mozambique and Angola, for instance, could easily be used.

Finally, whatever their cultural contexts, all Communist regimes display at present some decisive common features – the existence of an extensive parallel economy, the allocation of such goods as education and housing by a corrupt and exploitative *nomenklatura* and a consequent pattern of extreme social stratification – which dominate their respective cultural inheritances. This may be affirmed, even if it be readily allowed that there are distinctive cultural factors – in Russia, Poland and Bohemia, for example – which have modified somewhat the development of the totalitarian regimes there.

My strategy of argument will be to subject the conventional methodology of Soviet studies to an historical critique, in the first instance, by confronting it with six aspects of Soviet totalitarianism that it systematically neglects or underestimates:

- the economic, political and cultural achievements of late Tsarism;
- the dependency of the Soviet economy on Western capital and technology;
- the central role of Marxist-Leninist ideology in Soviet development;
- the specifically Leninist origins of Soviet totalitarianism;
- the economic functions of the forced labour camps in the period of socialist construction and the genocidal character of the policy of agricultural collectivization; and
- the use by the Soviet leadership of techniques of strategic disinformation.

Having illustrated the poverty of the conventional methodology of Soviet studies by these examples, I shall proceed to attempt to theorize Soviet totalitarianism, more positively, by reference to the three characteristics that distinguish it most radically from a civil society – its lack of the institutions of market exchange and of their indispensable matrix, the rule of law, and the continuing identification and legitimation of the Soviet state by reference to the ideology of Marxism-Leninism. Soviet totalitarianism is *not* a despotism or a tyranny, but an economic chaos contained in a political state of nature. Only by so understanding it can we grasp its ruinous poverty together with its awesome capacity for self-reproduction. We understand it adequately, finally, when we see the necessity to the Soviet regime of its third feature -- its legitimation by a Marxist-Leninist ideology that at once animates the present policy of *perestroika* and pro- hibits the only real reform – the recreation of civil society.

The alternative methodology I shall adopt in this chapter is distinguished by its taking seriously the role of Marxist-Leninist ideology in accounting for Soviet policy. It postulates that the Soviet state has no legitimacy, and (aside from the KGB) barely an existence, apart from that system of ideas. It focuses on the features that distinguish the Soviet system from authoritarian states – in particular its control of information and its involvement of its subjects in the processes and practices whereby it reproduces itself. In seeking a better understanding of the Soviet system than that found in the conventional methodology, I shall make use of two bodies of theory whose salience to the Soviet phenomenon is persistently neglected in the conventional wisdom – Austrian economic theory and Virginia Public Choice Theory. Applying these bodies of theory to the Soviet system generates an alternative perspective on it in which its most distinctive features are captured and rendered intelligible. This alternative methodology does not deny that there exist within the Soviet system the phenomena studied in the standard approaches – it acknowledges that there are competing interest groups, just as it emphasizes that there are markets, and it does not deny that native Russian traditions are to be found within the Soviet system – but it affirms that these phenomena tend to reinforce the stability of the Soviet totalitarian order (often by being manipulated by it) rather than to weaken it. By its virtual elimination of the private sphere within which such phenomena arise and flourish in pluralist and in authoritarian states, Soviet totalitarianism drastically modifies their typical effects. It creates an altogether novel political order – a lawless Leviathan whose subjects are victims of a recurrent Prisoner's Dilemma in which they are constrained to reproduce the system that enslaves them.

THE ACHIEVEMENTS OF LATE TSARISM

The dominant methodology involves a massive distortion of Russian history. It neglects the emergence, during the last half-century of the Tsarist regime, of a strong and resilient (if never wholly dominant) tradition of liberal legal and political philosophy, whose development has been definitively analysed by Walicki,[12] and which made an important contribution to the constitutional reforms of the regime's last two decades. It grossly exaggerates the character of late Tsarism as a police state (as Norman Stone and others have shown)[13] and underestimates the many characteristics it had in common with other authoritarian states in Europe, such as Prussia. And the conventional wisdom which represents the Soviet Union as the continuation of Tsarist traditions disregards evidence of the extraordinary economic, cultural and social progress which occurred during the last decades of Tsarism. Let us be specific. In a book published six months before the outbreak of the First World War, the French economist Edmond Thery notes that in the five-year period from 1908–12, coal production increased by 79.3 per cent over the preceding five years; iron by 24.8 per cent; steel and metal products by 45.9 per cent. Even allowing for inflation, the output of heavy industry increased by 74.1 per cent from 1900 to 1913. Again, between 1890 and 1915, the rail network almost tripled.[14] As to the magnitude of foreign investment in Russia – frequently, if often inconsistently, cited as evidence of Russian backwardness – Norman Stone has noted that on the eve of the First World War foreign investment in Russia had declined as a proportion of total investment by from one-half in 1900 to a fifth in 1914. By 1909 Russia had already become the world's fourth industrial power.[15]

Nor was progress confined to industry. Thery reports that, in agriculture, wheat production between 1908–12 rose by 37.5 per cent over the preceding five years; rye by 24 per cent; barley by 62.2 per cent; oats by 20.9 per cent; and corn by 44.8 per cent. With good harvests, as in 1909 and 1910, Russian wheat exports made up 40 per cent of world wheat exports, and even in bad years they amounted to 11.5 per cent. In social policy, spending on education doubled in the decade between 1902–12, and, by 1915, over half of all children between eight and eleven years of age were in school, and 68 per cent of all military conscripts were literate. Welfare legislation in Russia followed a Bismarckian pattern, although in Siberia conditions approximated more closely to *laissez-faire*. As in Bismarck's Prussia, various schemes of workers' insurance were introduced, and late Tsarist Russia followed Prussia in pioneering the rudiments of the twentieth-century welfare state.[16] As Dominic Lieven has noted, Russia followed Prussia, also, in having a civil service that in the last decades of the nineteenth century 'approached the Weberian ideal type'.[17] Although development was in many areas uneven, Tsarist Russia in its last half-century was not the autocratic, Asiatic despotism that is the caricature in conventional theturography, but instead a dynamic, progressive European state.

During its last half-century, Russia experienced an explosion of cultural energies, achieving a flowering in the arts – in literature, painting, dance and religious thought, for example – which has rarely been matched in European cultural history. The last decades of Tsarism saw much policy that was clumsy, ill-conceived, or repressive – particularly in the policies of Russification of the national minorities and discrimination and persecution against Jews. The rapid progress achieved in the economy, in cultural life and in some aspects of policy (but not, alas, in constitutional affairs, where policy was lagging and faltering) is nevertheless especially impressive, given the demographic explosion and consequent urban problems which government confronted. As Heller and Nekrich observe[18], the statistics for these years are revealing – and when the October Revolution occurred, it was a direct result of the First World War.

Perhaps the most striking discontinuity is in the area where the conventional methodology finds most similarity between the late Tsarist and the early Bolshevik regimes – that is, the discontinuity between the repressive activities of the Okhrana and the Cheka – GPU – OGPU. The demonstratable discontinuities, detailed below, are most obviously in the magnitude, scale and intensity of repression. A crucial discontinuity is also in the *quality* of repression: the Okhrana, unlike any of the Bolshevik security services, did not act extra-legally, but within a rule of law, and it did not seek to liquidate whole social categories. It is against this background that the quantitative comparisons made by Dziak19 are to be assessed:

LATE-TSARIST PERIOD (1826–1917)

Executions
1826–1906: 894
1866–1917: 14,000 approx.
1866–1900: 48; 94
1906 (six months of the Stolypin military field tribunals): 950
1907: 1,139
1908: 1,340
1908–12: 6,000
'Following the 1905–7 Revolution': 11,000
'Eighty years that preceded the Revolution in Russia': 17/year (average)

Deaths from executions, pogrom murders, and deaths in prison
1867–1917:   25,000

Convicts at hard labour
1913:   32,000 (year largest numbers were reached)

Political exile without confinement
1907:   17,000 (year largest numbers were reached)

Maximum number imprisoned (criminals and politicals)
1912:   183,949

EARLY SOVIET PERIOD (1917–24)

Executions by Cheka and tribunals
1917–23   200,000
1918 and 1st half of 1919:   8,389
1917–20:   12,733
'Civil War':   50,000
1918–19:   1,700,000
1918–23:   2,500,000 per annum

Deaths caused by Cheka
1917–22:   250,000–300,000

Deaths from the suppression of 'rebellions' and from prison and camp treatment
1917–24:   300,000

Executions in the Crimea following General Wrangel's defeat and evacuation
1920–21:   50,000–150,000

Hostages and prisoners in camps and prisons (1917–23)
1918:   42,254 hostages/prisoners in camps and prisons
1919 (to July):   44,639 hostages/prisoners in camps and prisons
1918:   47,348 hostages/prisoners in camps and prisons
1919:   80,662 hostages/prisoners in camps and prisons
1920 (late):   25,336 camp inmates plus 24,400 Civil War prisoners;
      48,112 prisoners in RFSFR NKYU prisons; 60,000 NKYU
      prisoners according to commissar of justice
1921 (Jan.):   51,158

1921 (Sep.):   60,457
1921 (Dec.):   40,913; 73,000 prisoners in NKYU prisons
1922 (Oct.):   60,000
1923 (Oct.):   68,297

It is unequivocally and undeniably clear from these figures that, in addition to the arbitrary and extra-legal character of the Bolshevik terror, the quantitative increases in the various kinds of repression in the Bolshevik regime, as compared with those of late Tsarism, are so enormous as to amount themselves to a qualitative transformation in the nature of the regime – from authoritarian to totalitarian.

It is not only that, as Dziak has put it, 'an unbroken patrimony between Tsarist repression and Soviet terms cannot be claimed'. It is not even that, as he also observes,

> Even at the height of its repression against revolutionaries, Tsarist courts offset Okhrana and Gendarme actions, thereby exercising a restraining hand. In Lenin's system the courts were either ignored, or became creatures of the Cheka.[20]

The crucial point is that the extra-judicial coercion and terror of the Cheka were directed against whole social groups, and primarily against the peasantry and workers. According to Soviet statistics used by Dziak, of the forty thousand NKVD inmates for December 1921, almost 80 per cent were illiterate or nearly so, and so from peasant or worker stock. As Dziak concludes, decisively:

> It simply was not Tsarist policy or practice to exterminate whole categories of people. . . . The Cheka's class war certainly was an 'aristicide' of the leading sectors of tsarist society, but its more numerous victims were the very classes it claimed to represent and serve.[21]

There is, finally, the evidence of the *size* of the two security services, with Richard Pipes noting that in 1895 the Okhrana had only 161 full-time personnel, supported by a Corp of Gendarmes amounting to less than 10,000 men, while by mid-1921, the Cheka accounted for approximately 262,400 men, *not counting* Red Army, NKVD and militiamen.

The external counter-intelligence activities of the Tsarist police were restricted, as Piper notes, virtually to a single institution, the Russian Embassy in Paris, which employed a handful of people to keep surveillance on politically active Russian émigrés.[22] A comparison of the Tsarist external counterintelligence commitment with that of the Soviet KGB is impossible, but also unnecessary, given the vast magnitudes of difference in scale that everything we know suggests. The Western conventional wisdom, so deep-rooted in academic folklore as to be probably unshakable, that Bolshevik terror was but a continuation of a Tsarist police-state, is controverted by all available evidence. On the contrary, all the evidence supports the view of late-Tsarist Russia as a civil society on the European model, which it was the historic role of the Bolsheviks (animated, ironically, by a European ideology) to destroy. Before it was destroyed by the Bolsheviks, the late-Tsarist regime was one that compares favourably with the great majority of governments that exist today. It is highly probable, in fact, that were the Soviet Union now what it was in 1913, it would come within the twenty states that are most liberal and least oppressive in today's world.

SOVIET DEPENDENCY ON THE WEST

In truth the conventional image of late Tsarism better fits the early decades of the Soviet Union in certain important respects. Throughout its history, the Soviet Union has been crucially dependent on Western capital and technology. Indeed, Western aid may well have secured the survival of the regime during its periods of worst crisis. As Besancon has said

> international society has on several occasions saved the Soviet regime in moments of crisis. I need only mention Herbert Hoover's American Relief Administration mission, which saved between five and six million peasants starving to death during the famine of 1921, and American aid in World War 2. Even during the most desperate War Communism – the War Communism of the first Five Year Plans – the West sent the Soviet Union considerable sums of money, technology and engineers.[23]

Western aid was, however, no less important in the construction of Soviet power than in preserving it from collapse. The Treaty of Rapallo, signed between Germany and Soviet Russia in April 1922, was decisively important in promoting both the economic and the military power of the Soviet state. It provided for the establishment of joint Soviet–German industrial and commercial firms, with more than two thousand German technicians arriving in the Soviet Union in the wake of the treaty being signed. The Treaty of Rapallo also initiated an important period of Soviet–German military cooperation, enabling the Germans to circumvent the Treaty of Versailles and rebuild the German army with state-of-the-art weapons manufactured and tested in the Soviet Union in return for the provision of training facilities for Red Army officers in Germany. The intimacy of this connection may be gauged from the fact that German and Russian chemists collaborated in the production of experimental poison gases.

This period of Soviet–German cooperation came to an end in 1927 with the Shakhty trial[24] of German engineers, after which the Soviet Union turned to the United States for assistance. Heller and Nekrich report that, whereas in mid-1929 the Soviet Union had technical agreements with twenty-seven German firms and fifteen American firms, by the end of 1929 forty American firms were cooperating with the Soviet Union. They go on:

> The five-year plan could not have been implemented without foreign assistance. In 1928 a group of Soviet engineers arrived in Detroit and requested that Albert Kahn and Company, an eminent firm of industrial architects in the United States, design plans for industrial buildings worth 2 billion dollars. . . . According to an agreement with the Supreme Economic Council of the USSR, the American firm agreed to design all aspects of Soviet industry, heavy and light. Foreign designers, technicians, engineers, and skilled workers built the industrial units of the first five-year plan. Primarily they were Americans, who pushed the Germans out of first place in 1928; after them came the Germans, British, Italians and French. The dam on the Dnieper was built by the firm of Colonel Hugh Cooper, a prominent American hydraulic engineer; the majority of the largest Soviet power plants were equipped by the British firm Metropolitan–Vickers; Western companies designed, built, and equipped Magnitogorsk and Kuznetsk, the Urals Machinery Works, the Kaganovich Ball Bearing Plant in Yaroslav, among others
>
> The full extent of Western economic and technological aid to the Soviet Union will not be known until the Soviet archives are opened up. The Western firms that collaborated with Moscow have concealed the information almost as carefully as their Soviet partners. Nevertheless, the American historian Anthony Sutton has come to the conclusion, on the basis of German and English archives, that 95 percent of Soviet industrial enterprises received Western aid in the form of machines, technology, and direct technical aid.[25]

Such direct Western aid to the Soviet power is a recurrent, almost a continuous feature in its development. In recent times, it has included economic and military assistance to Soviet satellite powers, as in the case of British commercial and governmental aid to Marxist Mozambique. Side by side with direct aid, there has been the explosive growth in recent decades of Western bank lending to the Soviet bloc, with Western credits amounting to 50 billion dollars by 1978. By the 1980s, the Soviet Union was financing Western development of its resources with Western credit. West European capital financed the construction of the gas pipeline from the USSR to Western Europe, assuring an annual profit of 5–8 billion to the Soviet Union, and in 1981 the Deutsche Bank and the Mannesman A. G.

steel corporation entered a contract worth 16.5 billion with the Soviet government to develop its Siberian energy resources.[26] By the end of 1988, Soviet foreign debt was estimated at about 43 billion dollars, much of it loaned to the Soviet Union by Western banks at lower interest rates than those offered to blue-chip multinational corporations such as IBM or Shell.[27] It is difficult to resist the conclusion that the Soviet Union, in its demonstrated dependency on Western capital, technology and (let us not forget) food imports, resembles the conventional caricature of Tsarist Russia as an underdeveloped, backward power far more closely than did the reality of late Tsarism.

THE CENTRALITY OF MARXIST-LENINIST IDEOLOGY IN THE DEVELOPMENT OF THE SOVIET UNION

The dominant methodology of conventional Western Soviet studies demonstrably exaggerates the continuities in political culture between late Tsarism and the Soviet state and has passed over or suppressed the many evidences of the dependency of the Soviet Union throughout its history on Western aid. In its attempts to apply the categories and techniques of Western political science to Soviet political life, the conventional discipline of Sovietology has systematically neglected, or tried to interpret away, the decisive role of Marxist-Leninist ideology in explaining the strategies and tactics of Soviet leaders, and has consigned to an Orwellian memory hole the formative impact of ideology in constituting and reproducing the most distinctive institutions of the Soviet state.

Perhaps the most fundamental of the blind spots of the conventional methodology concern the experiment in War Communism, the origins of the Gulag and the functions of the Gulag in the period of socialist construction, in each of which ideology played a decisive part. War Communism was the project Lenin initiated in the Spring of 1918 of realizing the utopian fantasies of his *State and Revolution*, written just before the October Revolution. The conventional view, whose dominance was secured by the work of Maurice Dobb and E. H. Carr,[28] is that War Communism was forced on the Bolsheviks by the exigencies of civil war. More recent studies by Paul Craig Roberts, Thomas Remington and Silvana Malle[29] have demonstrated that War Communism was not an emergency measure, but a policy having the conscious goal of abolishing market institutions. This policy, like many other aspects of Leninist totalitarianism (including the institution of forced labour), has a direct ancestry in the thought of Marx himself, for whom socialism and Communism were, first and last, the abolition of commodity-production and market exchange. In accordance with this Marxist project, a great leap forward was attempted, in which money was suppressed, private trade was banned, compulsory labour service introduced and grain requisitioned from the peasants at fixed prices. The results of this experiment were catastrophic. Famine broke out in the cities, industrial production collapsed and in 1921–2 famine followed the collapse of food production in the countryside. But the most significant collapse during the experiment in War Communism between 1918–22 was that in population itself. According to Soviet sources, in excess of five million lives were lost as a result of the famine of 1921–2. In addition, at least ten million lives were lost in the course of the Civil War. Whereas it may be questionable to attribute the resultant total entirely to the experiment in War Communism, the human cost in terms of lives of this period of social revolution and revolutionary war is fully comparable to that of the later period of Stalinism – and perhaps serves as a better illustration of the practical consequences of Communism in the full rigour of its doctrinal purity.

War Communism exemplifies a decisive characteristic of the Soviet state from its inception in the Bolshevik dictatorship – its character as a *weltanschauung*-state. Tsarist Russia was a monarchy in which the head of state was also head of the Church – as in the case of the United Kingdom to this day. It was never a state dedicated to the revolutionary transformation of its subjects's beliefs and the inculcation of a new orthodoxy. Nor were its policies, foreign or domestic, governed, primarily or consistently, by an ideology. The Bolsheviks, by contrast, were guided by ideology, and that primarily, from the start. As Dziak has observed in regard to the terror of these years of War Communism: 'The Cheka operated under an all-embracing plan, simple though it was: the bourgeoisie were to be exterminated. That this mass extermination was premeditated, and not merely, as Soviets claim, a response to White reaction and foreign intervention, is seen by its continuance well after the defeat of the Whites and the withdrawal of foreign forces, that is, well into the 1920s.'[30]

The War Communism period exemplifies the totalitarian origins of Soviet Communism in all three respects – in the institution of a *weltanschauung* state, in the destruction of the rule of law by an extra-judicial secret police, and in the attempt to eradicate the institution of market exchange. These are features of the Soviet state that it has exhibited throughout its history, and which persist to the present day.

THE LENINIST ORIGINS OF SOVIET TOTALITARIANISM

Another distinctive feature of the Soviet state, ignored by the dominant methodology, is the origin of the terroristic secret police, and of the concentration-camp system, in Leninist theory and practice. This was a development fraught with significance for the future, since it heralded the emergence of one of the constitutive features of Soviet totalitarianism – the omnipresence of extra-legal coercion and the creation at the political level of a lawless state of nature. Credit for first use of the term concentration camp goes to Trotsky, but the idea of establishing forced labour camps as part of a project of socialist re-education originates with Marx and the institution was established by Lenin. Shortly before the October 1917 coup, Lenin declared that he would adopt the institution of compulsory labour, which would be more potent that the guillotine, which merely terrorized and broke active resistance, while forced labour would break passive resistance, particularly among proletarians.[31]

Mass terror was characteristic of the Soviet state from its inception, with Dzerzhinsky giving unlimited 'extra-judicial' powers – including powers of execution – to all regional Chekas in September 1918. In January of 1918, Lenin had agreed that the Cheka might appropriately be renamed 'The Commissariat for Soviet Extermination', but judged it impolitic to do so.[32] In 1921 the Cheka assumed responsibility for the problem of the millions of homeless children in Russia, taking direct control of the camps and homes where many of them were sent. In 1922 the GPU, the Cheka's successor, acquired further extra-judicial prerogatives, which were once more expanded in 1926. The GPU inherited from the Cheka, also, the notorious Solovetsky concentration camps, whose existence and character were revealed to an indifferent public opinion in the West by survivors in the 1920s. The institutional framework of Soviet totalitarianism was constructed by Lenin – a fact which has been studiously ignored under *glasnost*. The suppression of the patrimony of Stalinist totalitarianism in that of Lenin under the Soviet *glasnost* to the present time is, in all probability, inevitable, since acknowledging this unbroken historical continuity would be a death-blow to the legitimacy of the Soviet system. One may state the same point in other words, by affirming that the acid test of Soviet *glasnost* will come when it proceeds to demystify Lenin and Leninism and recognizes in these the origins of the current pathology of the Soviet state.

THE FUNCTIONS OF FORCED LABOUR CAMPS IN THE SOVIET ECONOMY

A further blind spot of the dominant methodology is the economic role of the Gulag, which is evaded or distorted in conventional Soviet studies. It is represented as peripheral in importance, or else as an aberration of socialist planning, rather than as an indispensable instrument of Soviet power during the period of the Five-Year Plans. A classic example of this interpretation is found in Nove's *Economic History of the USSR*. In this book of over three hundred pages there are only a few scattered remarks on the subject of the camps. We are told, for example, that

> in this period (the period of the Great Leap Forward) prisoners and deportees, especially the latter, emerged as a significant factor in the life of the country. For example, only a small portion of the inhabitants of the new town of Karaganda went there of their own volition.[33]

Later, Nove refers to the human cost of the period of socialist construction 'in the diversion to camps of unknown millions, of whom a high proportion were above average in intelligence, energy and technical knowledge'. And he admits that 'Especially after 1936, officials of the NKVD . . . exercised important supervisory functions through the economy, and they also ran a big economic empire using forced labor, until the break-up of this empire after Stalin's death'.[34] Nove comments on the human cost of collectivization – in terms of deaths caused by famine and deportation – that

> The Soviet population in 1926 was 142 millions, and for 1932 it was officially estimated at 165.7, since it had been increasing at the rate of about 3 millions a year. In 1939, seven years later, it was only about 170 million. Somewhere along the way well over 10 million people had demographically disappeared. [Some, of course, were never born.][35]

Nove concludes, judiciously:

> Perhaps it is Russia's tragedy . . . and a measure of her achievement that, despite all that happened, so much has been built, and not a few cultural values preserved and handed on to a vastly more literate population.[36]

An incomparably more accurate account of the economic significance of the Gulag, and of the human costs of collectivization, is given by Nekrich and Heller. As they put it:[37]

> As early as 1929 all the camps had been placed under the direction of the OGPU, which for years had directed the archetypal camp at Solovki. The OGPU became the country's largest construction company. With a virtually limitless supply of unskilled labor at its disposal, the OGPU conducted massive arrests of engineers and technicians to manage the unskilled laborers. A new, purely Soviet institution arose, the *sharashka*: a prison in which engineers, scholars, and researchers worked in their fields of specialisation for the interests of the state. At the large-scale building sites, in the super-factories, the specialists were monitored by armed guards. The largest construction site of the First Five-Year Plan, the Baltic-White Sea Canal, was built by prisoners under the leadership

of 'engineer-wreckers'. Trotsky's dream of 'militarised labor' became a reality under Stalin in the form of the 'penalisation of labor'. The gates of the camps were adorned with Stalin's words; 'In the Soviet Union labor is a matter of honor, power and heroism'.

The reliance on slave labour has continued to be a stable feature of the Soviet system, as is demonstrated by the use of North Vietnamese conscripted labour in the construction of the Siberian gas pipeline over the past decade or so.

On the genocidal character of agricultural collectivism, Nekrich and Heller write:

> The full story of this first socialist genocide has yet to be written. Chronologically, the first genocide of the twentieth century was that of the Armenians by the Turks. The massacre of Don Cossacks by the Bolsheviks during the civil war likewise approached genocidal proportions. The Turks destroyed a population of a different faith and nationality; the Cossacks suffered during a fratricidal civil war.
>
> The genocide against the peasants in the Soviet Union was unique not only for its monstrous scale; it was directed against an indigenous population by a government of the same nationality, and in time of peace.
>
> In 1945, after the defeat of Nazi Germany and the public disclosure of all its crimes, jurists, sociologists, psychologists, historians, and journalists began the inevitable controversy over whether the German people had known about the Nazi crimes or not. There is no question that the Soviet city people knew about the massacre in the countryside. In fact, no one tried to conceal it. Stalin spoke openly about the 'liquidation of the kulaks as a class', and all his lieutenants echoed him. At the railroad stations, city dwellers could see the thousands of women and children who had fled from the villages and were dying of hunger. Kulaks, 'dekulakised persons', and 'kulak henchmen' died alike. They were not considered human. Society spat them out, just as the 'disenfranchised persons' and 'has-beens' were after October 1917, just as the Jews were in Nazi Germany.[38]

Again, it must be observed that the political creation of an artificial terror – famine with genocidal results is not a phenomenon restricted to the historical context of Russia and the Ukraine in the 1930s, but is a feature of Communist policy to this day, as evidenced in the 1960s in Tibet, and now in Ethiopia. The socialist genocide of small, 'primitive' peoples, such as the Kalmucks[39] and many others, has been a recurrent element in policies at several stages in the development of Soviet and Chinese totalitarianism.

Once again, Communist policy in this respect faithfully reproduces classical Marxism, which had an explicit and pronounced contempt for small, backward and reactionary peoples – no less than for the peasantry as a class and a form of social life. And the reliance on forced labour camps, like agricultural collectivization, was an inexorable consequence of the Marxist-Leninist project of eradicating one of the constitutive institutions of civil society, market exchange, together with its legal matrix in the institution of private property.

SOVIET TOTALITARIANISM AND STRATEGIC DISINFORMATION

The conventional methodology neglects or suppresses the economic role of the Gulag in the period of socialist construction and it is silent as to the genocidal character of the policy of collectivization. This is so, in part at least, because of the high degree of control over information achieved under Soviet totalitarianism, and also because Western observers have often been reluctant to publicize information in their possession about the worst failings of the Soviet system. Thus the famine in the USSR in the early 1930s was little reported in the Western media, and Eugene Lyons writes in Chapter 15 of his autobiography, *Assignment in Utopia*,[40] 'The Press Corp Conceals a Famine', of his own participation in the suppression of what was then known of the millions of deaths the famine was causing. The collaboration of the Western media with the Soviet authorities in concealing their worst atrocities is further exhibited in the silence which reigned in Western media for about a quarter of a century as to the forcible repatriation and subsequent fate of over two million people claimed by the Soviet Union after the Second World War.[41] It is likely that Soviet responsibility for the Polish Katyn massacre will be admitted, under *glasnost*, by the Soviets themselves, before it is admitted by the British Foreign Office, which continues to adhere to the fiction of Nazi responsibility for that atrocity. The history of Vlasov's Russian Liberation Army (ROA), its role in the liberation of Prague and its statement of enmity to Nazism and Stalinism in the Prague Manifesto, have only recently been given an accurate historical statement.[42] Western authorities have colluded with Soviet authorities in concealing nuclear disaster and the existence of the nuclear Gulag.[43] It is only as a result of the Soviet *glasnost* that the almost apocalyptic ecological catastrophes in such areas as that surrounding Lake Aral have been publicized in the West. One of the many ironies of the present Soviet policy of *glasnost* is that, in focusing on aspects of Soviet history which in the West have been discussed only in rare, obscure and neglected émigré journals, it has served to reveal the scope and limits of Western *glasnost*.

The dominant Western methodology goes most seriously astray in its neglect of the Soviet use of strategic disinformation. This blind spot in Western perception and theorizing is particularly disquieting given the similarities evident between the current *glasnost* strategy and the highly successful disinformation exercise conducted during the period of the New-Economic Policy (NEP). Under the NEP, market relationships were partially restored in the economy, with peasants in particular being freed to charge market prices for their products, and so to enrich themselves. (When the NEP was ended by Stalin, the peasants found their new wealth liable to confiscation – a fact with direct relevance to present Soviet experiments with cooperatives.)

This disinformation exercise was inaugurated along with the NEP in 1921 by the formation by the OGPU inside the USSR of a false anti-Bolshevik organization, the Monarchist Alliance of Central Russia, otherwise known as the Trust, and operating under the cover title of the Moscow Municipal Credit Association, which replaced an earlier and genuine group destroyed by the OGPU in 1920. Unimportant in themselves, the historical details of the Trust are illuminating in revealing the mechanism of what Dziak has called 'the prototypical deception and protective operation in the Soviet repertoire'.[44] The Trust operation had been proceeded by an earlier deceptive operation, usually known as Sindikat 1, in which the OGPU attempted to penetrate the organization of Boris Savinkov, former War Minister in the Kerensky government and friend of Polish leader Pilsudski and of Winston Churchill. A second operation, Sindikat 2, ran concurrently with the Trust, and successfully lured Savinkov back into the Soviet Union. Perhaps the first of the Soviet deception operations was that against the British agent, R.H. Bruce Lockhart, in the Summer of 1918. It is possible that, at the same time, the British agent Sydney Reilly was 'turned'. In any case, Reilly claimed later to be convinced of the authenticity of the Trust, and, like Savinkov, was persuaded to return to the Soviet Union, where he probably perished.[45]

The primary objective of the Trust was to weaken, divide and neutralize the powerful anti-Soviet émigré movement that had arisen in Europe in the wake of the great Russian diaspora after the Civil War. Numbering over a million, of whom a quarter were White officers or men, the anti-Bolshevik émigrés constituted a threat the Soviet government could not afford to ignore. A secondary goal of the Trust was to persuade the governments and intelligence services of the Western powers that the revolutionary socialist government of the Bolsheviks was on the brink of a metamorphosis, of which the NEP was only an intimation, into a traditional Russian regime which could safely and easily be integrated into the international community.

The formation of the Trust was accompanied by the capture by the OGPU of two important émigré movements, the 'Changing Landmarks' movement and the 'Eurasian' movement. Apparently originating as early as 1918 among the old intelligentsia in Russia, the movement found expression in several voices in 1920. In the Summer of that year a former Cadet leader and lawyer, Professor Gredeskul, undertook with the approval of the authorities a speaking tour of the Soviet Union. *Slavic Dawn*, a Prague émigré newspaper, in a statement characteristic of the movement, affirmed that the Bolsheviks were now defenders of the Russian national interest. In the autumn of 1920 there appeared in Harbin, Manchuria, a seminal statement of 'changing landmarks' ideology, a collection of articles entitled *The Struggle for Russia* by Nikolai V. Ustryalov, a former Kadet and supporter of Admiral Kolchak. Written by six members of the émigré community, of which Ustrayalov was most prominent, the collection appeared subsequently in Prague, under the title *Smena Vekh*, in 1921. The theme of the collection, which was taken up by sympathizers within the conservative intelligentsia such as Shulgin, Efimovsky, and Klyuchnikov, was that the Bolshevik government was in process of mutating into a nationalist dictatorship on lines theorized in the writings of reactionary thinkers such as Konstantin Leontiev and Joseph de Maistre.

The movement received substantial unofficial support from the Soviet government, which facilitated the publication in Prague and Paris of a weekly magazine, *The Change of Signposts*, and in Berlin a journal called *On the Eve* (Nakanune). In 1922 the Soviet government allowed the movement to publish journals *New Russia* and *Russia* in Leningrad and Moscow. *Smena Vekh* journals also appeared in Riga, Helsinki, Sofia and Harbin. Nakanune survived with Soviet subsidies until it was closed in June 1924. A year and a half later, the 'changing landmarks' movement was suppressed in the USSR. As Dziak comments:

> *Nakanune* faithfully reflected the Soviet party line and was of immense value to Moscow as an émigré instrument of conversion in the Soviet cause . . . like the Trust, it (the Changing Landmarks movement), when it had served its purpose, was eliminated.[46]

The Eurasian movement followed a similar pattern of evolution. In 1921 an anthology was published in Sofia entitled *Iskhod k Vostoku (Exodus to the East)* advocating Russian nationalism, the idea that the political culture of Russia was as Asiatic as it was European and speculating that the Bolshevik regime might be a proto-version of an appropriate authoritarian system for Russia. *Exodus to the East* was followed by a further seven volumes, the last appearing in 1931. A *Eurasian Chronicle* appeared in twelve volumes between 1925 and 1937. The Eurasian movement flourished until 1928, when it split and began to decline, but its importance continued well into the 1930s, when it was influential in gaining the collaboration of sympathetic émigrés with the Soviet government.

Between 1921 and 1927 the Trust organization achieved major successes in its campaign of disinformation. Leading émigré leaders such as Boris Savinkov and Generals Wrangel and Kutepov were contacted by Trust agents and convinced of its authenticity. The émigré leaders in turn were decisive in convincing Western intelligence services of the genuineness of the Trust. By the mid-1920s, it seems that no less than eleven Western intelligence services were heavily dependent on the Trust for information about developments in the Soviet Union.[47] For Western governments, the policy implication of the Trust was clear – the dissident forces within the Soviet state were to be aided by diplomatic recognition, the expansion of trade and a curb on destabilizing anti-Soviet activism. Everything should be done that might ensure the success of the NEP. As Dziak has summarized this strategy:

> the disinformation fostered through the Trust reinforced the initiatives of the NEP, which was also overseen by Dzerzhinsky in his dual capacity as chief of state security and chief of the Supreme Council of National Economy. From this perspective, the NEP itself served a deception purpose in that it helped to refinance Soviet industry at Western political and economic expense.[48]

From the standpoint of the Soviet leadership, the NEP and its associated disinformation exercises were indeed successes. Some ten per cent or more of the Russian émigré community returned to the Soviet Union, including several of its leaders such as Savinkov and Kutepov. The émigré movement was never again a significant threat to the Soviet regime. Western powers assisted in the reconstruction of the Soviet economy, above all Germany, which also built up the Soviet war machine. The NEP period was also a period of political consolidation for the Soviet regime. Vestiges of the old political parties in the Soviet Union were eliminated. Religious activity was brought firmly under political control in the pro-regime 'living churches'. Powerful nationalist movements in Georgia, the Ukraine, Armenia and the Asian republics were suppressed and these nations subjected to full annexation. Mongolia became the first Soviet satellite state. Twelve new communist parties joined the Comintern. By the time Stalin closed down the NEP and wound up the Trust, it had substantially achieved its goals 'to prevent internal revolt, expand foreign trade, attract foreign capital and expertise, gain diplomatic recognition from non-Communist countries, prevent major conflict with the Western powers, help to exploit the contradictions in and between the capitalist countries, neutralise the émigré movement, and help to promote world revolution through the Communist movement'.[49]

There are ominous parallels between the disinformation exercises of the NEP period and current policies of *glasnost*. The objective of financing the reconstruction of the ruined Soviet economy with Western capital and technology is the same. Now, as then, Germany is likely to play a crucial role in supplying capital. An activist diplomacy is gaining major concessions from the Western powers, as a result of which the USSR can proceed with its programme of modernizing its military forces while appearing to reduce its offensive capability. Side by side with a diplomacy which divides NATO, diminishing almost to vanishing point the Western perception of Soviet enmity and so promoting the psychological disarmament of the West, the USSR has increased the activities of its intelligence services, particularly in Germany and Britain, with the objectives of expediting technology transfer and manipulating opinion. (The reorganization of 1987 of key departments within the KGB and GRU is likely to prove one of the more enduring achievements of *perestroika*.) Such are the clear parallels between current developments and the NEP period. They suggest that *perestroika* is best interpreted as a reversion to a Leninist strategy of disinformation and activist diplomacy (the latter encompassing exercises in tactical retreat, as in Afghanistan) and the abandonment of the clumsy, costly neo-Stalinist strategies of the Brezhnev period. They suggest that we are now witnessing the 'sixth *glasnost*', the boldest yet, designed to destroy the Western perception of Soviet enmity and permit the Western refinancing of the Soviet system. As Epstein has put it:

> By 1989, at virtually no cost to Soviet power, the sixth *glasnost* had provided the Soviet leadership with not only the tens of billions of dollars in credits it required to further expand its industrial (and military) capacity, but . . . was perceived as less of a threat to Western Europe than the United States.[50]

Granted these parallels, how are present developments to be understood as responses to the contemporary situation in the Soviet Union? I have specified as the chief defects of the conventional methodology of Soviet studies its reliance on standard techniques of analysis in political science and, in particular, its deployment of inchoate notions of political culture. This methodology neglects the structural affinities displayed by all Communist regimes. In the present sections, I have argued that the conventional methodology neglects the potential for strategic disinformation possessed and exercised by the Soviet regime (not only in the Trust episode, but in later episodes such as the WIN operation in 1947–51.[51]) The alternative line of analysis and theorizing developed here is that of the Soviet Union as a system constituted, from its inception, by Leninist ideology and a terroristic security service. We may even go so far as to concur with Dziak, and refer to the Soviet Union as 'a counter-intelligence state'.[52] On this view, the Soviet Union is a totalitarian order whose character as such is guaranteed by the KGB, whose role in representing the Soviet Union to the external world ought never to be underestimated. Current policies of *perestroika* and *glasnost*, on this alternative analysis, are authentically Leninist exercises in strategic deception.

The parallels between the present period and that of NEP, suggested by the alternative methodology I have advanced, are real enough. Nevertheless, they do not of themselves account for the crucial differences in the historical contexts of the two episodes. By comparison with the NEP period, the USSR now confronts far graver problems of ethnic conflict, nationalist and separatist tendencies, religious and fundamentalist movements and environmental degradation. For reasons I shall try to specify in a later section of this paper, it is far from clear that the economic renaissance of the NEP period, brief and partial as it was, can be repeated. Nor is it obvious, or even plausible, that infusions of Western credit can facilitate the resurrection of the USSR's senile industries. The financial burdens of the Soviet state, including an estimated 14 billion dollar per annum commitment to non-military support of the East European Communist regimes and analogous commitments to Cuba, are incomparably greater than those of the fledgling Soviet state. Even if it was conceived as a grand deception, the policy of *glasnost* is extraordinarily risky for the Soviet leadership. Indeed, however it was conceived – and a Leninist interpretation of its inception seems by far the most plausible – the current Soviet policy confronts difficulties and hazards far greater than any that the Soviet regime has ever faced in peace time. So as to theorize these phenomena, we need to abandon the blinkered perspective of Kremlinology, which has dominated Soviet studies for lack of any disciplined theoretical alternative. We need to ask: what are the real-world constraints that govern and constrain the Leninist strategy and tactics of the Soviet rulers? In order to answer this question, we must attempt, more directly and systematically, to theorize the constitutive features of Soviet totalitarianism.

SOVIET TOTALITARIANISM: CALCULATIONAL CHAOS IN A POLITICAL STATE OF NATURE

Central in the Soviet totalitarian order are the failure of central planning and the political consequences of that failure. The War Communism episode shows that the Bolsheviks took seriously the Marxian commitment to the abolition of the institutions of market exchange. As Roberts and

Stephenson have said: 'Public ownership of property is not the defining characteristic of Marxian socialism; central planning is. In Marxian socialism, there is no exchange; therefore, there is no private property (rights to exchange)'.[53] The suppression of private property follows from the abolition of commodity production, not vice versa. The project of replacing the institutions of market pricing with institutions of central planning confronts massive and insuperable difficulties, well theorized in the work of the Austrian economists Mises and Hayek.[54] The argument of Mises is that economic calculation presupposes market pricing: the information required for rational resource-allocation – information about relative scarcities and consumer preferences, for example – is so complex that no central planning authority could possibly collect it. The number of transactions in a modern economy, again, is so enormous that the planner will face an insuperable problem of calculation if he attempts to simulate market processes in a mathematical model. Hayek's argument focuses on the epistemological impossibilities of central planning rather than its practical difficulties: it is a problem of knowledge, not merely a problem of calculation, which is fatal to the socialist project of supplanting market institutions. The knowledge which the planner requires is dispersed knowledge, scattered about society, and it is often local knowledge of circumstances that are in their nature ephemeral. Most importantly, the knowledge possessed by economic agents is often practical knowledge, embodied in skills or dispositions, and only slightly theorized by the agent. Indeed, the tacit knowledge on which we all rely in our economic dealing may be only partly theorizable: it may contain elements, such as entrepreneurial perceptions or traditional practices, which cannot be given any full theoretical statement. Because much of it has this tacit or practical character, economic knowledge cannot be retrieved and collected by the planner. This last argument was developed independently by Michael Polanyi,[55] who saw that it imposed an insuperable limit on the planning both of science and the economy. In economic life, as in science, the planner is defeated by the fact that we always are making use of knowledge of parts of which we are bound to remain ignorant, and we always know more than we can ever say.

In this Hayekian and Polanyian account, the role of market institutions is that of discovery procedures which allow for the disclosure and utilization of dispersed knowledge. This is a very different model from that of classical economic theory, in which the market is a device for relating scarce resources with competing ends. In the Hayekian–Polanyian model, no one has knowledge of the available resources: if the market exists to economize on anything, it is on knowledge, the most irremediably scarce resource of all.

The implications for economic policy and institutions of the Austrian calculation argument are radical. There is, first, the implication that in the absence of market pricing of most factors of production there will be calculational chaos. This is a result which puts paid, not only to the discredited Lange–Lerner model[56] of competitive socialism through the medium of market simulating devices, but also to the anachronistically fashionable idea of a market socialism of competing worker-cooperatives.[57] It demolishes the latter since, if the calculation argument applies at all, it has its clearest application to capital: it suggests that only market institutions can deploy the dispersed knowledge required if capital is to be subject to an efficient allocation. This carries with it a second result for policy – that most factors of production, including most capital, be held in decentralized private ownership, or in other words, that there is no viable middle way between the institutions of market capitalism and those of central planning.

The radical implication for current policy is that no programme of *perestroika*, or economic reform, can hope to succeed which does not encompass dismantling the socialist system of ownership and dispersing its productive assets as private property. Such a policy of privatization is feasible, however, only on condition that the dispersed assets may be securely held and exchanged. This is in turn possible only under a rule of law in which private property is protected from arbitrary seizure by government. (It is the absence of the rule of law, and all that entails, that accounts for the lack of economic progress in non-totalitarian states such as the dictatorships of Latin America and Africa.) It is obvious that the institution of a rule of law would amount to the suppression of one of the key structural features of Soviet-style totalitarianism, since it would impose important constraints on the hitherto unlimited discretionary power of the state. We must ask ourselves, why might the ruling élites of a totalitarian state accept such a constraint on government? Answering this question requires examining the political environment of the Soviet economic chaos, and the constraints imposed on feasible reform that it imposes.

THE INCENTIVE STRUCTURES OF SOVIET CENTRAL PLANNING: A PUBLIC CHOICE APPROACH

The argument so far has been entirely epistemic. It has been the argument that, whatever its goals or the motives of the ruling élites that control it, central planning cannot achieve a rational allocation of resources. This is not to say that it cannot succeed in achieving specific and limited goals: the examples of the Soviet space program, and even more of the build-up of the Soviet war machine, show that it can so succeed. Plausibly, however, it has done so only with the aid of Western technology, and only at the cost of displacing scarce resources from civilian uses and thereby further impoverishing Soviet society, including elements of its privileged *nomenklatura*. The epistemic argument – the argument that central economic planning is an epistemological impossibility – is important precisely because it is insensitive to the incentive structures that govern the planners. Its result is that the planners will fail in most of their objectives, whatever they are – whether or not they recognize consumer preferences, for example, aim primarily to reward the *nomenklatura*, or simply to modernize the war machine. As James Sherr has put it in his authoritative study, *Soviet Power: The Continuing Challenge*,

> Whatever its ostensible purpose, the elimination of the market and the creation of a command economy has one clear consequence: the who, what, and how of economic relations is determined by planners, not by those who produce and consume. It is the structure of the system that demands this, not the unimaginativeness or selfishness of those involved. An enterprise director cannot do what he considers best for society since, without the market's signals, he cannot know what this is. He may know the difference between a tractor that works and one which does not, but he cannot know how many tractors are required, what sort of tractors to build, and where they are most needed.[58]

One large part of the rationale of *perestroika* is indeed to achieve the three objectives specified above more effectively than is possible under central planning. The result of the calculation argument, however, is that economic reform is bound to fail, and these objectives will be unachievable, without the reconstruction of a regime of private property under the rule of law. Failing that, the objectives of *perestroika* can be achieved, if at all, only by a massive Western refinancing of the Soviet system.

The predictive content of the calculation argument is that a centrally planned economy cannot exist. What exists under central planning institutions is a complex structure of parallel markets, relying on historic, capitalist or black market prices, subject to recurrent episodes of authoritarian intervention. This theoretical result, worked out in Polanyian terms in Paul Craig Robert's *Alienation and the Soviet Economy*[59] is amply corroborated by such excellent empirical studies as Peter Rutland's *The Myth of the Plan*. Rutland concludes:

> it turns out that the structure of the command economy is not what one might naively expect to find – it is messy, overlapping and subject to endless and obscure organisational mutation.[60]

At the present time, what exists in the Soviet Union is exactly that which is predicted in the calculation argument – a chaos which reproduces itself by covert reliance on parallel markets and by continuous mutations in the planning structures themselves.

We must consider the environment of incentives within which the planners operate, independently of the problems of knowledge which they confront, and the larger structure of incentives which surrounds those who inhabit the Soviet state. For the planners, it is clear, all the incentives of the soviet system point to conservatism and risk-avoidance rather than initiative or constructive investment. As Sherr has said,

> Virtually extinct in the Soviet Union after sixty years of socialism is the linchpin of capitalism, the entrepreneur. (To the extent that he survives, he is apt to make the illegal second economy his habitat.)[61]

Planners are bound to be risk-averse in their investment policies, and, since no error-elimination mechanism for inefficient investments exists under central planning institutions, they have an incentive to conceal malinvestments by diverting further resources into them. Even aside from these insuperable epistemic problems, the command economy contains an incentive structure that is biassed against efficiency. The very existence of the massive planning bureaucracies creates a powerful interest against the liberalization of economic life. As Sherr again puts it,

> Replacement of plan by market is in itself a surrender of power, since it means the elimination of planners. At present, Soviet agriculture, and therefore the day-to-day lives of Soviet peasants, are regulated by hundreds of thousands of officials and thirty-three ministries. If production and exchange were henceforth to be determined by those who produce and consume, what functions would their former controllers then perform? What powers would the state still posses over those thus emancipated?

The economic interests of the planning bureaucracies only reinforce one of the defining features of Soviet totalitarianism, which is the obliteration of the economy as an element of an autonomous civil society. As Sherr concludes:

> It is not the KGB, 'indomitable' as it is, which makes the Soviet Union a totalitarian society, nor even the CPSU's monopoly of political power, but the fusion of political and economic power. Monopoly of power – Stalin's first justification of the planning system – will probably be its last defence.[62]

The same incentive structure that guarantees the economic inefficiency of the command economy also confers on it a powerful political stability.

The analysis we have developed so far has followed the Public Choice School in attributing to planners the same motives we attribute to actors in the market-place – it theorizes the bureaucrat as *Homo economicus*. Another tool of the Public Choice School, game theory, may help to illuminate the structure of Soviet totalitarianism as a generalized Prisoner's Dilemma and so to explain its phenomenal stability.

SOVIET TOTALITARIANISM AS A POLITICAL STATE OF NATURE AND THE NEW HOBBESIAN DILEMMA OF ITS SUBJECTS

Soviet totalitarianism, like that in Communist China, differs from any kind of traditional despotism in virtue of its near obliteration of civil life. This has a momentous consequence – that for all of its subjects daily life must be conducted within the institutions of the Soviet state. It is the state, or one of its arms, that determines the job a person holds, the apartment he lives in, the education available to his children and all of the other crucial dimensions of his life-chances. In the Soviet Union, to a far greater extent than in any Western country, housing, education and employment are positional goods in that access to them is achieved primarily through position or influence in the Party or its subordinate hierarchies. It is of vital importance to understand that this is true, not only of the exploitative *nomenklatura*, but of virtually everybody in the Soviet system, and gives to everyday life there an aspect of mutual predation lacking in societies where most goods are allocated by markets. It means that, in the Soviet Union, exchange is often a zero-sum transaction – what one gains another loses. It means that, however estranged they may be from it, subjects of the Soviet state must daily renew its institutions, and thereby perpetuate it in existence. This is so, even when they turn to the ubiquitous parallel economy for sustenance, since the illegal economic networks which enable it to reproduce itself exist only on its sufferance. For this reason, no subject of the Soviet system can escape contamination by its practices.

The characteristics of the Soviet totalitarian order as a political state of nature encompass a paradox, since in Hobbes and other contractarian thinkers the state of nature is (by definition) pre-political. Like all true paradoxes, however, this one contains an important truth. Soviet totalitarianism has in common with the Hobbesian state of nature, first and last, *lawlessness*. Without legal order, there are no protected domains of independence within which individuals may frame and enact their plans. Worse, since there is no law, anything may be judged to be illegal: every Soviet subject must live in a permanent legal twilight in which any act of his may be arbitrarily criminalized. Given that the necessities of daily life demand constant breaches of rules and regulations, every Soviet subject is permanently vulnerable for their infractions – but he would be so, even if by a miracle he had not breached any known rule, since the security organs still retain extra-judicial powers. Further, some laws – such as that against anti-Soviet activity – are susceptible to any interpretation. This condition of lawlessness brings into being an environment of *uncertainty* which also resembles that of the Hobbesian state of nature. For in it no one can be bound to keep agreements with others, save by extra-legal means, and there is an incentive for everyone to use all available resources of power to protect his interests against possible attack by others. Power is vested in the Party and its organs. Thereby arises that process of constraint *mutual predation*, so characteristic of Soviet life, in which Soviet subjects use the power of the Party to prey upon one another. Finally, even though it is far from being pre-political (indeed everything in it is politicized), the Soviet totalitarian order is akin to the state of nature in that lacks the institutions of civil society. To say that it is a political state of nature, then, is to say that it is a lawless polity, in which the war of all against all is conducted through the medium of the Party and its auxiliary institutions.

It is the genius of the system that it constrains its victims to renew it. The great majority of its subjects, including most of the *nomenklatura*, would undoubtedly be better off without it, but they are compelled to recreate it daily. Their exchanges are often not zero-sum so much as negative-sum – they leave each worse off. In this the captives of the Soviet state resemble the denizens of Hobbes's state of nature, condemned by their insecurity to a war of all against all that none may escape. This is the Prisoner's Dilemma in a classic form: rational prudence as engaged in by each produces insecurity and impoverishment for all. The Soviet state is a phenomenon which even Hobbes's dark vision could not have foreseen – a Leviathan in which lawless power and a predatory state of nature are inextricably intertwined.

The darkest side of Communist totalitarianism – its ability to implicate its victims in its worst atrocities – has been well expressed by Simon Leys:

> If totalitarianism were merely the persecution of an innocent nation by a small group of tyrants, overthrowing it would still be a relatively easy matter. Actually, the extraordinary resilience of the system resides precisely in its ability to associate the victims themselves with the all-pervasive organisation and management of terror; to turn them into active collaborators and accomplices. In this way the victims acquire a personal stake in the defense and preservation of the very regime that is torturing and crushing them.[63]

As he acknowledges, Leys's observation parallels many made by Alexander Zinoviev. We need not take literally Zinoviev's assertion[64] that Stalin's power was the ultimate expression of the power of the people to accept the insight it contains – that one of the chief sources of the stability of totalitarianism is its ability to implicate its victims in the terror and repression to which they and their fellows are subject.

One explanation of the stability of totalitarian orders, then, is in the morally compromised condition of their subjects. The endemic scarcity of the necessities of life, and their control by the Party and its subordinate organizations, condemns the Soviet subject to compete with his fellows in collaborating with the system that oppresses him. The impact of this daily necessity to lie, cheat, and distrust one's fellows, and thereby to renew the system by which all are held captive, is not illuminated by standard Arendtian notions[65] of the atomization of social life in totalitarian orders. Such atomization is real, but (as such observers as Havel[66] have noted) the impact of totalitarianism on personality is yet more destructive. It tends to the very fragmentation of personality, to a pervasive demoralization, anomie and disintegration of the person that perhaps only Orwell foresaw. This is not to accept Alexander Zinoviev's extreme thesis that totalitarianism has indeed created a new man, *Homo sovieticus*,[67] whose personality has been entirely collectivized. The evidence is that, though he exists, *Homo sovieticus* is rare – most Soviet subjects retain their pre-Soviet ethnic, religious and moral identities. Though they have thus survived intact, for the most part, the identities of the subjects of totalitarian orders have been injured in ways that further compound the difficulties of moving toward a stable post-totalitarianism – a post-totalitarianism that is not anarchy or chaos.

THE PROSPECTS FOR *PERESTROIKA*

How might the Soviet political state of nature be transcended? Only, it seems, by the emergence of an Hobbesian sovereign. On the most benign interpretation to which it is subject, *perestroika* may be seen as the project of just such a sovereign – on the model, perhaps, of Peter the Great – aiming to construct in the Soviet Union a framework of law within which enterprise and civil society might shelter. In support of this interpretation might be cited Gorbachev's anti-corruption campaign and his frequent invocations of socialist legality.

In fact, the available evidence supports the opposite interpretation – that *perestroika* is in substance the project of suppressing the nascent forms of civil society that had begun to emerge during the Brezhnevite era of stagnation. During those two decades, there had occurred throughout the Soviet Union, but especially in parts of Soviet Asia, the growth on a large scale of illegal businesses, controlled and indeed owned by Party bosses enjoying considerable autonomy. The forms of civil life represented and expressed in this 'mafia' were thoroughly distorted by the totalitarian environment which they inhabited and on the basis of which their initial power rested. Nevertheless, the extensive network of parallel institutions which this mafia operated sustained the manifest prosperity of the provinces in which it operated, most particularly Uzbekistan and Kazakhstan, and it enabled a section of Soviet society to create a space within which quasi-autonomous institutions could exist and in which resources could be diverted from the control of the state to private ends.

In many parts of the Soviet Union, the so-called 'era of stagnation' was in fact a period of illegal boom. It is precisely this prosperity which is being threatened or destroyed by *perestroika*, with its campaigns against corruption. Here we reach an insoluble contradiction in the policy: its objective of reasserting central Party control over local and regional satrapies is in irreconcilable conflict with the objective of economic renewal. Free markets and contractual exchange barely existed during the era of stagnation, but simulacra of them flourished on a grand scale in the parallel institutions of the illegal economy. Like black markets everywhere, those of the Soviet era of stagnation were inefficient, inequitable and unworkable in enterprises requiring large injections of long-term capital; but they mitigated the catastrophes of the central planning institutions, putting to productive work resources that would otherwise have been wasted and thereby generating a standard of living higher than any achievable by planning.

From the standpoint of the totalitarian party, however, a flourishing parallel economy means a diversion of resources into a sphere that is not controlled by the state: a key objective of *perestroika* is therefore to reclaim these 'privatized' resources for the state sector. In economic terms, the results of this policy have been, and can only be disastrous. It entails disrupting and often destroying the principal efficient institutions of production and exchange in the Soviet economy. In political terms, *perestroika* expresses the project of renewing totalitarianism, of reincorporating within the totalitarian order the quasi-autonomous social forms that characterized the Brezhnev period. As Francois Thom has succinctly observed:

> The Law against Unearned Income has signalled the start of an offensive against civil society in the purest Communist tradition.[68]

The economic aspect of *perestroika* will almost certainly fail. It must fail, not just because it tends to destroy the parallel institutions that have hitherto partly supplanted the planning institutions, but also because it deprives the planning institutions of signals from the parallel economy by which they have long been guided. A real shift to a market economy – the only way in which economic renewal can be achieved[69] – is excluded because it would entail the reconstitution of a civil society and the end of the totalitarian fusion of the economy with the polity. It is in any case doubtful whether the motives and dispositions needed to run a Western-style economy persist in the Soviet Union – particularly when everyone knows that the profits of enterprises established under *perestroika* are liable to NEP-style confiscation whenever the policy is reversed. After two generations of civil war against civil society, a market economy, along with other elements of civil life, can probably only exist in the interstices of the totalitarian state. The economic objectives of *perestroika* can be achieved, if at all, only in enclaves of the Soviet economy where Western capital is under Western management, and does not disappear into the abyss of the central planning institutions.

THE FUTURE OF THE SOVIET UNION: OTTOMANIZATION?

If the Soviet case is treated as a paradigm, it has a clear implication: post-totalitarianism, the dissolution of totalitarian institutions and the reconstitution of civil society, is achievable by a process of internal evolution only in states where some civil institutions have remained intact. This result is corroborated by the Polish example, where the Church was never substantially incorporated into totalitarian administration, and by the Baltic states, where a flourishing parallel economy, together with a strong sense of nationhood, combined to limit the effectiveness of the post-War reconstruction on the Soviet totalitarian model. In these states, a reversion to totalitarianism could probably not be accomplished even by recourse to military repression, which (as in Poland in the early 1980s) would instead achieve merely an authoritarian despotism. In the Soviet Union, a reversal of the policy of *glasnost* in the wake of economic collapse is, by contrast, bound to shatter the present precarious neo-totalitarian equilibrium and precipitate a return to totalitarianism. It is profitless to speculate on the forms that Soviet totalitarianism will assume in the period after the likely termination of the present policies. A recurrence to Brezhnevite 'stagnation', and the 'Ottomanization'[70] of the Soviet Union, with the provinces and the republics regaining a measure of *de facto* independence, seems the most benign outcome at present imaginable, but even that does not look very likely. The economic situation in the Soviet Union probably prohibits any such reoccurrence, with a catastrophic collapse, and consequent widespread famine, being predicted by Soviet economists in mid-1989 as real possibilities in the USSR two or three years hence.[71] A policy of military repression on the model of that applied in China in mid-1989, inaugurated in response to nationalist and religious disturbances themselves manipulated by local Party bosses, is well within the bounds of possibility. In the medium to longer term, a policy of exploiting Russian nativist sentiment – already evident in the leeway permitted to the Pamyat organization – may develop as a means of buttressing the totalitarian regime with populist support. Whatever the specific form it might take, a reversion to classical totalitarianism in the aftermath of economic collapse need not mean that the present policy has altogether failed. If it yields diplomatic victories and an influx of capital – with the current German–Soviet negotiations producing something akin to a second Treaty of Rapallo – the policy of *perestroika* might be assessed as having succeeded despite its economic failure, since it will have secured for Soviet totalitarianism yet another lease on life.

There is, however, another side to this scenario. Even if totalitarianism were to be re-imposed in the Baltic states, say, and the neo-totalitarianism project of *perestroika* reversed (along with *glasnost*) in the Soviet Union in the wake of economic collapse, the prospects for classical totalitarianism in the USSR over the longer term of a decade or more are poor. For, even if the Soviet Union were to emulate the Chinese model, it would not return to wholesale Stalinist terror, which the majority within the Party would resist. It would instead rely solely on military force, together with selective police repression. In such circumstances, the maintenance of ideological conformity – the reproduction of the *weltanschauung*-state – is likely to be an increasingly low priority. In other words, if there is a reversion to classical totalitarianism in the USSR, it is likely to be relatively brief, being followed by worsening economic crisis and a slow shift to an 'Ottomanized' authoritarianism, held together (as in the era of stagnation) by military force, but against a background of worsening economic decline and increasing popular discontent. *Retotalitarianization*, if it occurs in the Soviet Union, will not last long – almost certainly, less than a generation. If, as Walicki has argued[72], the days of totalitarianism are numbered, once the *nomenklatura* comes to be concerned solely with self-reproduction, and is no longer animated by a project of retotalitarianization, it bodes ill for the repressive policies of the current neo-Stalinist leadership in China.

It may even be the case that the Soviet Union is itself on the verge of launching into a transitional period of post-totalitarianism. The dramatic collapse of the Communist monopoly of power in the GDR, following on the dismantling of the Berlin Wall and the no-less-sudden blossoming of popular opposition in Czechoslovakia, may be interpreted (if the analysis developed earlier has any plausibility) as tactical moves in a Soviet strategy of 'reverse Findlandization', modelled on the authentically Leninist paradigm of the Treaty of Brest-Litovsk (which in 1918 ceded large parts of Russia, including the whole of the Ukraine, to Germany). The aim of this strategy is to secure the rapid decoupling of the United States and Western Europe (which American economic weakness in any case renders inevitable in the medium term) and the neutralization of most of Western Europe at the cost of Soviet withdrawal from Eastern Europe. Even if, as is likely, this strategy is successful, it is an extraordinarily dangerous one for the Soviet Union to adopt. It risks strengthening secessionist movements within the Soviet Union and triggering new movements for independence in areas (such as Soviet Central Asia) which have, until now, been quiescent. If such a scenario of internal disintegration were to begin to unfold in the USSR, the most likely outcome would *not* be a project of retotalitarianization, but instead recourse to classical authoritarian measures of martial law and police repression. In that eventuality, however, the Soviet Union would have become irreversibly post-totalitarian.

The prospects of the experiments in controlled democracy in Hungary and Poland will depend mainly on the degree of success each achieves in its policy of economic reform. Even in these comparatively favourable cases, the shift to a market economy will involve dislocations and costs that may destabilize the fragile political settlements achieved there. In Poland, the economic programme of Solidarity is not wholly coherent, but even a consistent policy of full marketization carries with it the risk of dividing Solidarity in the country from Solidarity in the city (and for that reason finds little favour outside the Party). In Hungary, which has passed from a non-terroristic totalitarianism sustained chiefly (as was long the case in Czechoslovakia) by economic sanctions to a controlled democracy without any significant intervening phase of post-totalitarianism, the political settlement may appear even more precarious. Recourse to repression in Hungary may, however, be rendered less likely by the role that Hungary may play in Gorbachev's European diplomacy. Here Hungary and Poland are very different: though they have in common an economic crisis, including an unsustainable foreign debt, they are to be distinguished in that developments in Poland have arisen endogenously, whereas in Hungary they occur at least in part in response to exogenous pressures from within the Party and, perhaps, the Soviet Union. For this reason, repression could be achieved more easily in Hungary than in Poland should policy undergo a major reversal in the Soviet Union and its European diplomacy be dislocated, or the domestic Hungarian political process be destabilized by economic collapse.

In both Poland and Hungary, the danger exists of a recourse to a post-Communist dictatorship as the necessary political mechanism for the transition to a market economy. Such a 'Pinochet solution' to the transition problems of dismantling the centralized economy is unlikely to occur in Czechoslovakia or Eastern Germany, with the former returning to the strong social-democratic traditions of the post-War years and the latter eventually being integrated into West German democratic institutions as part and parcel of the inexorable process of reunification. In the rest of Eastern europe, classical Communist totalitarianism is already showing signs of weakness (as in Bulgaria), and even Romania may not prove immune to change or collapse. In these parts of Eastern Europe, however, the project is of *re-Balkanization* rather than of transition to civil society. The model for such a prospect, in these parts of Eastern Europe (and, indeed, in the Soviet Union), may be contemporary Yugoslavia, with its intractable ethnic conflicts, profound economic problems, weak populist governments, and chronic tendencies toward disintegration. In all these areas, post-totalitarianism may mean political authoritarianism superimposed on social and economic chaos.

The answer to the question with which we began – what must be true for post-totalitarianism to be a possibility? – has proved to be that important elements of civil society must remain intact if the transition to a full civil society is to be achieved. Where, as in the Soviet Union, these are lacking, totalitarianism appears (at any rate for the medium term) to be a one-way street. Even in Poland, where civil society was never fully suppressed, the conflicts of interest generated by a policy of marketization could produce considerable political instability, and endanger the otherwise well-conceived policy of buying off the apparatchik class. The possibility suggests itself, in the light of these considerations, that the task of reforming a Communist economy confronts problems that are insoluble. Like the Soviet Union itself, most of the states of the Soviet bloc (even where a return to classical totalitarianism is not a realistic prospect) cannot be expected to fulfil the first condition of a stable post-totalitarianism, which is a stable market economy. They must expect, not the reconstitution of civil society, but Ottomanization – the process of decline, corruption and the waxing of the institutions of the parallel economy that characterized the era of stagnation in the Soviet Union, but in a context of worsening economic conditions for the entire bloc.

Except perhaps in Poland and Hungary, Czechoslavakia and East Germany, the waning of totalitarianism, as it seems likely to occur over the medium term, primarily for economic reasons but accelerated by ethnic and nationalist conflicts, is unlikely to be accompanied by the waxing of a civil society. For the foreseeable future, chaos and instability, contained only by the recurrent threat and exercise of military force, seems the most likely outcome for the USSR. The reform policy of *perestroika* founders, in the end, on the overwhelming likelihood that the transition from totalitarianism cannot, save in exceptional circumstances, be conducted in an orderly fashion. Instead, it is to be seen as the prelude to a process of repression, decline and instability that resembles the beginnings of revolution more than it does any kind of reform.

THE CULTURAL ORIGINS OF SOVIET TOTALITARIANISM

On the account I have tried to develop, the Soviet totalitarian regime owes its stability primarily to internal factors – to the public choice problems generated by any move to a civil society and to the new Hobbesian dilemma that constrains its subjects. I have also argued that Western aid has been decisive in enabling the regime to recover from crisis and to expand. The upshot of my account has been to confirm the soundness of Lenin's insight into the nature of Western capitalist states – which, Lenin prophetically observed, were bound to compete with each other in forming the Soviet state. This competition, like the Prisoner's Dilemma that sustains the Soviet totalitarian order internally, is doubtless statable in game-theoretic terms. It goes far to explain the lack of effective Western strategy in regard to the Soviets, and the strategic advantage the Soviets have in formulating long-range policy in regard to the West.

The question arises as to why Western opinion has systematically mis-understood the nature of the Soviet regime, and in particular why Western opinion lacks any perception of the enmity of the Soviet Union to Western civil societies. I submit that a major part of the explanation for this blind-ness is in the fact that Soviet Communism has its roots in elements of the most ancient, central and fundamental Western traditions – and not, as the conventional wisdom supposes, in Russian political or religious culture.

What are the cultural origins of Soviet Communism? In order to answer this question we must ask another: What are the intellectual antecedents of Marxism? Kolakowski[73] has located one source of Marxism in the Greek, and especially the neo-Platonic preoccupation with the contingency of human existence, which was transmitted to Marx via Hegel. In this account, Marxism is a secularized version of the mystical soteriology of Greek Platonism in which a return to the unalienated human essence replaces reabsorption in the Absolute as the form of salvation and release from contingency. Kolakowski's analysis neglects or underestimates the contri-bution of Judeo–Christian traditions to the intellectual and moral formation of Marxism. For it was Christianity, with its conception of human history as a moral drama, which allowed the Platonistic soteriology to be trans-formed into an historical theodicy. This is the insight captured by Voegelin in his interpretation of modern political religions as gnostic immanent-izations of Christian eschatology. As Voegelin puts the point:

> The characterisation of modern political mass movements are neopagan, which has a certain vogue, is misleading because it sacrifices the his-torically unique nature of modern movements to a superficial resemb-lance. Modern redivinisation has its origins rather in Christianity itself,

deriving from components that were suppressed as heretical by the universal church.[74]

The same point is made by Michael Polanyi:

> Had the whole of Europe been at the time of the same mind as Italy, Renaissance Humanism might have established freedom of thought everywhere, simply by default of opposition. Europe might have returned to – or if you like relapsed into – a liberalism resembling that of pre-Christian antiquity. Whatever may have followed after that, our present disasters would not have occurred.[75]

On this interpretation, Marxism is a Christian-historicist gloss on a Greek-rationalist doctrine of salvation. It should be noted here, however, that contrary to the conventional academic wisdom, Western Christianity is far more implicated in the generation of Marxism than Eastern Christianity. For Western Christianity imbibed the elements of Aristotelian rationalism as transmitted via Acquinas into the medieval world, together with the humanist values of the Renaissance and the secularizing impact of the Reformation, that had little impact on Russian Orthodoxy. For Orthodoxy, with the exception of a few iconoclastic thinkers (such as the early Berdyaev[76]), Marxism represented the incursion of a Western ideology into Russian Christianity – and one which, furthermore, had emerged in the West partly because of the decadence of Western Christianity. This is not to deny that, as Besancon has shown,[77] Soviet Communism has some sources in an alienated Russian intelligentsia – a point emphasized by Solzhenitzyn[78] and prophetically made by Dostoyevsky.[79] It is to question the common Western belief that Soviet Communism was ever sustained by elements in Russian religious life – against which it has waged a perpetual war.

It is from its expression of the central tenets of the European Enlightenment, however, that Marxism, and its embodiment in Soviet Communism, derives its essential appeal to Western intellectual opinion. It is here that the Jacobin lineage of Leninism, and the character of the French Revolution as the first precursor of twentieth-century experiments in social engineering via the mass liquidation of entire social groups need to be noted. The recent revisionist historiography[80] of the French Revolution has noted its terrorist nature, in particular the fact that, whereas at the time the Bastille was stormed, it contained fewer than ten inmates, by the time the Terror had run its course around half a million Frenchmen were incarcerated for political reasons, many of whom would perish in jail. We know that Lenin was himself much influenced by the Jacobism precedent as an early experiment in what Talmon has well called 'totalitarian democracy'.[81] There seems to be good reason, then, to see a clear historical linkage between the two revolutions, both as to their goals, their strategies and the types of institutions they produced.

It is in the common origins in the secular faith of the Enlightenment that the affinity of the two revolutions is most plainly seen. The ideas of a self-consciously planned society and of a universal civilization grounded in scientific knowledge are central elements of that religion of humanity that is expressed in both Marxism and liberalism. They express, in a distinctively modernist fashion, values and beliefs – rationalistic and optimistic – derived both from the Greco–Roman classical tradition and the Judeo–Christian traditions that are coeval with Western civilization. It is in this truth that the central paradoxes of totalitarianism are to be found: the paradoxes of its enmity to the civilization that gave it birth and the paradox that, though Marxism-Leninism is a modernist ideology, Soviet totalitarianism is at war with the most fundamental institutions of the modern world as it has thus far developed. We may justly judge that von Laue exaggerates greatly, when he avows that 'it was the West which, by the model of its superior power, has shaped the Soviet dictatorship. Soviet totalitarianism has basically no more than the caricature echo of Western state and society, the best copy feasible under Russian conditions.'[82] Von Laue's extreme overstatement, like the claim that Western societies have totalitarian aspects, nevertheless expresses a grain of truth – the truth in the claim that totalitarian ideology has its roots in Western tradition, and totalitarian regimes are episodes in the global process of Westernization, aberrant and distorted not by the traditional societies which they destroy but by elements within the Western tradition itself.

Western opinion's blind spot in regard to the nature of Soviet communism is congenital and incorrigible. It expresses an integral part of the Western world-view. One may even say, without too much exaggeration, that (just as totalitarianism is only the shadow of modern civil society) so Soviet Communism is only the shadow cast by the European Enlightenment. A realistic perception of Soviet enmity to Western civil societies presupposes an insight into the defects or limitations of Western traditions of which the animating ideology of the Soviet regime is an authentic development. Nothing supports the hope that Western opinion is capable of the self-criticism such an insight requires. If it comes to pass, the fall of Soviet totalitarianism is most likely to occur as an incident in the decline of the occidental cultures that gave it birth, as they are shaken by the Malthusian, ethnic and fundamentalist conflicts which – far more than any European ideology – seem set to dominate the coming century.[83]

October, 1989

13 Western Marxism: a fictionalist deconstruction

The visits that Wittgenstein made to the Soviet Union in the late 1930s must be among the least researched episodes in his life. Most of his biographers mention the visit he made in 1935, and a few refer to a later visit in 1939. None tells us anything of substance about what he did there, and, in particular, none of them gives any clue as to how his experiences in the USSR might have influenced Wittgenstein's philosophical development. We learn that during his first visit Wittgenstein was offered a Chair in Philosophy at the University of Kazan (where Tolstoy had studied) and that for a while he considered seriously the possibility of settling in the Soviet Union. We learn nothing, or little, of Wittgenstein's intellectual contacts in the Soviet Union. It is only very recently, in fact, that we have come to know of the most formative of Wittgenstein's intellectual encounters in the Soviet Union, which occurred in his conversations in 1935 and 1939 with the neglected Hungarian Marxist thinker, L. Revai.[1]

Since Revai's life and work remain little known in the West, it is worth sketching their main outlines. Born in Budapest in 1881, the first son of a well-established banking family, Revai made a minor mark on Central European intellectual life in the first decade of this century as a literary theorist. His work at that time (now virtually unobtainable and nearly forgotten) was derivative and unoriginal, being an eclectic weaving together of a variety of currently fashionable themes. It reveals nothing of the intellectual radicalism which distinguishes his mature theorizing and amounts to a highly conventional application of Kantian and Schopenhauerian conceptions to familiar questions in the theory of culture. In the 1920s Revai published hardly at all. He had joined the Communist Party shortly after its foundation in 1918, abandoning the romantic syndicalism of his youth for a Leninism he was never to renounce, and seems to have occupied himself for a decade or more in political and organizational work. Little is known, even now, of Revai's thought during this period. We know that in 1933 Revai left Hungary for the USSR, and stayed there until 1945. From the present volume we learn, for the first time, that in 1936 Revai was incarcerated in a labour camp, from which (as one of the very few to have returned from internment at that time) he was released in 1938. It is only with the present volume, above all, that we learn that on several occasions in 1935 and 1939 Revai met Wittgenstein, and engaged with him in conversations which left a lasting mark on the philosopher's later thinking.

Revai's life after the War was uneventful. He pursued his oblique and elusive career in Hungary as a translator and occasional anonymous contributor to Budapest cultural reviews. Scarcely known in his own country or elsewhere, seeming to have acquired few, if any, disciples or followers, Revai published nothing under his own name (except for a brief statement of neutrality during the disturbances of 1956). He died in 1973. Throughout nearly thirty years of obscurity in his native land, ignored by the authorities and without even the dubious privileges of a dissident intellectual, Revai worked patiently and indefatigably on his master-project – the development of a Marxist theory of language.

Revai's life-work was never completed. The six essays collected in *The Word as Deed: Studies in the Labour Theory of Meaning* are only fragments, embodying all that remains of a massive project, and constituting the literary remains of a thinker whose input on the development of Western thought has thus far been entirely esoteric. It is, indeed, only owing to the resourcefulness of the collection's two editors that Revai's work has been rescued from oblivion and its bearing on Wittgenstein's philosophy revealed. In an extended biographical foreword to the collection, Olsen and Kahn piece together an account of Revai's life and thought from the evidences of the papers recovered (through the intervention of his sole disciple) from his modest apartment in Budapest. They are able to tell for the first time how Revai, having by them emerged from a stay in the Gulag, spoke with Wittgenstein about the conception of language as an incident in human labour which he had begun developing in the 1920s in Hungary, and which his experiences in the camps had crystallized into a more definite doctrine. In the camps, Revai told Wittgenstein, the complex grammar of civil society was dissipated, and speech returned to its more primordial function as an integrating mechanism in the human transformation of physical energy. It was in the camps, where the forces of production were developed in transparent social relations without the mediation of mystifying ideological structures, that the adverbial labyrinth of language was deconstructed into the aboriginal rudiments of imperatival speech. Revai's discovery in the camps was of an *Ursprache*, made up of speech-acts whose sense was exhausted in their uses in the ongoing *praxis* of labour. It was this discovery which Wittgenstein exploited, when in the *Investigations*[2] he experimented with the possibilities of a language consisting only of words connected with a single activity.

> The philosophical concept of meaning has its place in a primitive idea of the way language functions. But one can also say that it is the idea of a language more primitive than ours. Let us imagine a language. . . . The language is meant to serve for communication between a builder A and assistant B. A is building with building-stones: there are blocks pillars, slabs and beams. B has to pass the stones, and in the order in which A needs them. For this purpose they use a language consisting of the words 'block', 'pillar', 'slab', 'beam'. A calls them out; B brings the stone which he has learnt to bring at such-and-such a call. Conceive this as a complete primitive language.

In Wittgenstein's work, the manifest political content of Revai's discovery is lost, sublated and recuperated in a reactionary and unhistorical reification of ordinary usage. For Revai, by contrast, the *Ursprache* of the camps was the problematic from which he was to develop his first formulations of a materialist theory of meaning. And the discourse of the camps had in Revai's thought another significance, elaborated fully by him only much later, as a dialectical pre-figuration of the speech community of communist society, in which words are only shadows cast reflexively by the self-consciousness of deeds.

In part, no doubt, because the exercise of dating Revai's writings remains speculative and conjectural, the collection is organized in conceptual rather than chronological fashion. It is in the first three essays that we find Revai's chief theses on meaning, use and labour set out in programmatic terms. His most radical thesis concerns the place of the most primitive unit of meaning, the *ergoneme*, in the constitution of the act of labour. Revai's insight here – an insight that he probably communicated to his colleagues at the Marx–Engels Institute in Moscow, and which may have been a factor in his subsequent incarceration – was that the decisive step to the human species from its animal forbears cannot consist, as Engels supposed, in the development of tools. If man is a tool-using animal, he is defined (and defines himself) by the exercise of the most distinctively human tool of all, that of language. What is only *work* in animals – the expenditure of energy through the manipulation of matter – becomes *labour* in humans, since it is from the first saturated with a semantic superstructure. This is the dialectical counterpoint of Goethe's bourgeois-humanist dictum, *Im Anfang war die Tat*. Revai insisted that, whereas speech is a moment in the constitution of the act of labour (and language itself the shadow of speech) labour itself is the most primitive of all speech-acts. Without the *ergoneme*, which is the reflexive self-recognition of deeds, we have, not labour, but only work. But the most primitive unit of meaning is not theorized, for Revai, after the fashion of bourgeois-semantic atomism as an element from which complex structures of meaning are constituted piecemeal. Rather, the *ergoneme* is found only in the holistic semantic structures which arise along with the social relations of labour. It is, for this and other reasons, a radical error to model language-use on the reified metaphor of *the speaker*. To do so is to consecrate the fetish, central to the *bourgeois-Robinsonnade* of Western linguistic theory, of the auto-nomous language-user, and to suppress recognition of speakers as social ensembles of *ergonemes*. It may be said that Revai's entire project was a project of transcending the subjectivist-idealist problematic of *the speaker*. As he puts it himself, magisterially: 'It is not speakers who labour, but labour that speaks'.

For Revai, accordingly, the primitive unit of meaning, the *ergoneme*, is a necessary constituent of the act of labour itself. Further – and it is in the collection's second essay that Revai develops his critique of the ideological construction of *the speaker* – units of meanings are always distributed over complex semantic structures, which themselves mirror constellations of labour power. It is within these structures that we must situate the activity of speech. If we do this, we find, once again, not the speaker, but the speech-community – the historically specific construction of labour powers. It is here that Revai makes one of his boldest moves, and identifies speech-communities with classes. The radical intent of such a move in the USSR in the late 1930s should be obvious, and stands in need of no elaboration. The third and fourth essays treat of the political economy of meaning. Among the topics addressed are the unity of speech and act in pre-class societies, the primitive accumulation of meaning, surplus mean-ing and the expropriation of meaning, the sequestration and enclosure of meaning in early industrial capitalism, the estrangement of word from meaning in advanced capitalist orders, and related topics.

In the last two essays, Revai brings his theorizing to bear on theoretical controversies being conducted in the USSR from the late 1930s onwards. We learn from the editors that Revai's thoughts were stirred in the late 1940s and early 1950s by the debates surrounding the contributions made by N. Y. Marr to linguistic theory. Stalin, we recall, had criticized Marr not only because of his attempts to develop a theory of the class-specificity of languages, but also because, in separating language from thought, Marr had lapsed into Idealism. Revai's paper bears the marks of his earlier thought, but it appears to have been occasioned by Stalin's response to the contri-butions of D. Belkin and S. Furer to the debate on Marr's linguistics. Stalin criticizes Belkin and Furer for failing to appreciate the distinctively human character of language-use, and so for neglecting to distinguish language-use from the signs and gestures of animals. Observing that

> linguistics treats of normal people possessing a language, and not of anomalous deaf mutes who lack a language, [Stalin asks:] How do matters stand with the deaf mutes? Does their thought function, do ideas originate? Yes, their thought functions, ideas do originate. It is clear that since the deaf mutes lack a language, their ideas cannot originate on the basis of language material.... The ideas of deaf mutes originate and can exist only on the basis of the images, perceptions and conceptions formed in practice about the objects of the exterior world and their relations among themselves, thanks to the senses of sight, touch, taste and smell. Outside of these images, perceptions and conceptions, thought is empty, devoid of any content whatever, i.e. it does not exist.[3]

Revai's commentary on this debate, never published in his lifetime, has as its problematic the thesis of the semantic constitution of the labour-act and (as its dialectical counterpart) the thesis of the construction of meaning by labour power. From this problematic Revai derives his further thesis that the question of the place of language in the 'superstructure' or 'base' of social relations is, and cannot avoid being, wrongly posed – a position he shared with Stalin. Much of the fifth essay is addressed to this question. It is in the last of the essays, however, that Revai reveals his political intent, when he comments, cryptically and suggestively, on *the epoch of silence*. The society of deaf mutes, he argues, is the society of Western capitalism in its final stages, in which language has been replaced by gestures, and labour evacuated of its meaning-content. The 'empty chatter' of capitalist verbosity, in so far as it expresses at no point the semantic content of labour, embodies *the silence of the proletariat* as its dialectical condition. The silence of the period of socialist construction, by contrast, is fecund with labour content. Revai does not try to suppress reflection on the organization by administrative measures of speech and language in the Stalin period, nor does he aim to pass judgement on it, after the fashion of bourgeois moralists. He sees the Stalin period, instead, as one in which the necessary publicity of meaning was, for the first time, given concrete historical realization. The fiction of the speaker, together with the Idealist shibboleths of subjectivity and private language-use, were during this period subjected to a decisive critique on the terrain of *praxis*. The socialist administration of language-use, then, is an historically necessary phase in the elimination of the problematic of the subject. In theorizing it in this fashion, Revai gestures in his last essay to the practice of speech in Communist society. There, he maintains, the interiority of thought is transcended, and speech utters itself in a dialogic context in which it is realized as the semantic form of the community of labourers. It is superfluous to comment on the remarkable affinities between Revai's conception of Communist discourse and that developed later by Habermas.

In addition to an extended biographical foreword, the collection is distinguished by a long analytical postscript, in which the editors consider how Revai's theorizing is to be assessed and developed. It must be said at once that their own perspective is very different from Revai's, whose classical labour theory of meaning they repudiate explicitly. Nor should this be surprising, since one of them, G. Olsen, had already in his important *Sense and Reference in Marxian Semantics* [4] abandoned many of the central tenets of an orthodox Marxian account of meaning. By contrast with Revai, Kahn and Olsen are methodological nominalists, whose project is that of generating the complex semantic structures of Marxian linguistic theory from individual speech-acts. They invoke here work by another linguistic theorist of their school, P. Reimer,[5] who aims to reconstruct classical Marxian meaning theory, without postulating the *ergoneme*, solely on the basis on constellations of speech-acts. Most innovatively, drawing heavily on work of Kahn's, they advance a reformulation of the orthodox Marxian theory of surplus meaning, in which the exploitative extraction of meaning from workers is analysed and explained in terms of the thesis that the meaning-content of each labour-act is retained by the labourer only on condition that that of every other be subject to expropriation. 'Each may speak, but all are silent' – so Kahn summarizes a long chain of subtle reasonings whereby the silence of the proletariat is reaffirmed in the new Marxist theorizing. In the final section of the analytical postscript, Kahn and Olsen present competing accounts of the relations between labour power and semantic structure, with Olsen arguing against Kahn that the attribution to semantic structure of an inherent development tendency is an illicit global generalization from the historically specific semantic structures of the capitalist mode of production. In so developing rival theoretical paradigms within a shared problematic, Olsen and Kahn give further evidence, if such were needed, of the progressive character of the research programme on which they are engaged.

In Kahn and Olsen's postscript to this invaluable collection, the central insights of Marxist thought are preserved by the appropriation of the most powerful techniques of bourgeois thought. Until now, Revai's work had only an occult impact on Western thought by way of its influence on the greatest of twentieth-century philosophers. Given the creative development to which Revai's thought is subject in Olsen and Kahns' postscript to this volume, it will be extraordinary if Revai's work does not come to exercise a commanding authority over the most advanced sections of the Western academic class.

14 Post-totalitarianism, civil society and limits of the Western model

INTRODUCTION

The sudden collapse of Communist power in Eastern Europe, and its weakening in the Soviet Union, have been interpreted by many in the West as evidences of the global triumph of democratic capitalism. At its most extreme, this interpretation has been extended by Francis Fukuyama into the thesis that history, conceived as the history of conflict between rival ideologies and systems of institutions, is over, and liberal democracy has been revealed as the final form of human government.[1] The manifest bankruptcy of Communist institutions has been interpreted as conclusive evidence in support of the universal appeal of Western institutions and values and the expectation has been engendered that it can only be a matter of time before civil societies on the Western model come to exist in all the post-Communist countries.

My aim in this paper is to contest this received view, or, more precisely, to try to sift in it what is true from what is false. My conclusion will be threefold. First, I shall hold that it is true that Communist totalitarianism is in the throes of a terminal crisis, such that attempts to reproduce it (as in China) are bound in the medium term to fail. Second, I shall argue that, whereas the viable post-totalitarian regimes which emerge in the wake of Communist totalitarianism must have the character of civil societies, they need not (and often will not) resemble Western liberal democracies in other important respects. Finally, I shall maintain that, although all talk of a 'third way' between capitalism and Communism is an exercise in unreality, contemporary Western democracies are in several respects defective models for the emergent post-Communist states.

It is important to begin by specifying the central, constitutive features of totalitarian political orders. As I have argued elsewhere,[2] the single most important feature of totalitarian orders is their suppression (partial or complete) of the institutions of civil society – the autonomous institutions of private property and contractual freedom under the rule of law, which allow people of divergent values and world-views to live in peaceful co-existence. Because they politicize economic life and repress voluntary associations, and because they are *weltanschauung*-states seeking to impose a single world-view on all, totalitarian regimes are constituted by the project of destroying the key institutions of civil society. Their success in this project varies from case to case, with civil society being much more comprehensively desolated in Romania and the Soviet Union, for example, than in Poland or Czechoslovakia. Whatever its degree of success or completeness, totalitarianism is to be defined by its opposition to civil society, not by contrast with liberal democracy. This point may be put in another way. Civil societies may exist and flourish under a variety of political regimes, of which liberal democracy is only one. The authoritarian civil societies of East Asia – Taiwan, South Korea, Singapore and Hong Kong – are instances in which economic and personal liberties are sub-stantially protected, but political or democratic freedoms curtailed. Indeed, historically, civil societies have been more commonly associated with authoritarian regimes or limited democracies than with liberal democratic institutions: consider the examples of Bismarckian Prussia, or Whig England (where democratic participatory freedoms were extremely res-tricted). It is a central thesis of my argument that civil society and liberal democracy need not and often do not go together, and the most decisive phenomenon in the collapse of Communism is not the adoption of demo-cratic governance but rather the emergence of civil life.

It is important, also, not to conflate the re-emergence of civil society with 'the triumph of the Western idea' (in Fukuyama's banal terminology).[3] A flourishing, dynamic and progressive civil society existed in Russia in the late-Tsarist period, which it was the mission of the Bolsheviks (acting in the service of a European ideology) to destroy.[4] Again, the fundamental elements of civil society were built up in Japan, not in the wake of defeat in the Second World War, but in the Meiji period, two generations earlier. Further, in Japan as elsewhere in East Asia, the adoption of the institutions of civil society was *not* accompanied by acceptance of Western indivi-dualist values or the abandonment of Eastern cultural traditions. Accord-ingly, although the first examples of civil society appeared in Western Europe in the aftermath of feudalism, it is a fundamental mistake to equate the emergence of civil society with Westernization, or with the spread of democratic capitalism.

Given this understanding of totalitarianism, how do things stand in the post-Communist societies? We need to distinguish different regimes at this point, so as to be clear which of them are genuinely post-totalitarian. Romania and Bulgaria, though in the medium term they are likely to become so, are not yet genuinely post-totalitarian since they are ruled by neo-Bolshevik cliques which have not permitted the re-emergence or re-construction of the institutions necessary for civil life. Czechoslovakia, Hungary and Poland all appear authentically post-totalitarian, and are prob-ably irreversibly so. The most intriguing case is that of the Soviet Union itself. It cannot be affirmed that a civil society has emerged, full-blown, anywhere in the Soviet Union. Nowhere have economic reforms re-introduced the essential preconditions of a market economy – a law of property and contract, private investment capital or an autonomous banking system. The most essential elements of civil society, private property and the rule of law, have yet to be instituted. Nevertheless, the Soviet Union no longer resembles anything akin to classical totalitarianism, and it is very doubtful whether a reversion to totalitarianism in the Soviet Union is realistically feasible. This is so for two main reasons. First, there are now in the Soviet Union powerful oppositional movements, having a large measure of autonomy from the state apparatus, which could be brought back within Communist control only by recourse to large-scale military and political repression. Most important among these autonomous movements are the independence movements in the Baltic States, Georgia, the Ukraine, and elsewhere in the Soviet Union. So deep are the popular and nationalist roots of these movements, that only repression on a massive scale could defuse them. In the case of Georgia, paramilitary repression has done little more than slow down the movement for independence. If the independence movements were to be crushed, or driven underground, a policy of repres-sion would be required that spanned the Soviet Union as a whole and radically reversed the impetus of *glasnost*.

Nothing in Soviet history, or in the present circumstances of the Soviet leadership, allows us to rule out such a recourse to repression as the only effective measure for preventing the disintegration of the Soviet state. Even if such a policy of large-scale repression were adopted, however, it could not hope to restore classical totalitarianism. *Glasnost* itself has done irre-parable damage to whatever ideological legitimacy Soviet power may otherwise have retained. It has revealed (both to Western observers and to the Soviet public) the catastrophic inheritance of over seventy years of socialist central planning – an inheritance encompassing almost apo-calyptic environmental degradation, Third World infant mortality rates, woefully inadequate housing and medical care, and industrial plant and techniques that are twenty or even fifty years out of date. The result of the revelations of *glasnost* has been to exhaust whatever ideological capital the Soviet regime may still have possessed. The Soviet Union is not now, and is most unlikely ever to become again, a *weltanschauung*-state on the classical totalitarian model. If the policy of *glasnost* is reversed, the upshot will not be retotalitarianization, but rather an authoritarian regime, shorn of the trappings of ideology in all but name, which sustains itself by a combination of selective repression, tactical concessions and Western aid.

If this is the likely scenario for the Soviet Union, how are we to interpret developments in China? There can be little doubt that in China a project of *retotalitarianization* is being attempted – in the aftermath of an experiment in market reform in which Marxist-Leninist ideology was even more comprehensively abandoned than has been the case in the USSR. We do not at present know enough to do more than speculate as to current policy and its likely upshot in China. In the short run, the policy of repression, and of reinstituting a totalitarian regime, is likely to appear to be more successful in China than any analogous policy could hope to be in the USSR. China's difficulties with her national minorities, though real, are as nothing compared with those in the USSR. Equally as important is the fact that popular disaffection does not seem to have progressed as deeply in the peasant masses in China as it has in the USSR's industrial workers. As far as we can tell, China's peasant majority remained quiescent during the events leading up to the Tiananmen Square massacre, and (so far as we know) there has been nothing in China that resembles the strike of the Siberian miners. Finally, there is little evidence that there exists in China the extensive network of underground institutions which may exist in the Soviet Union now, and which certainly existed in Poland after the declaration of martial law in 1980. For the immediately foreseeable future then, the forces of emergent civil society have been effectively paralysed in China.

The prospects for totalitarianism in China over the medium term are nevertheless poor. All available evidence suggests that genuine Marxist-Leninist ideological conviction is dead in China, and that it is being used currently primarily as in instrument of repression and of political discipline. In the absence of ideological conviction, China may resume many of the practices of a totalitarian regime, but the reality will be that of an aged *nomenklatura* clinging on to the perquisites and privileges of power. Further, the economic consequences of Tiananmen Square are not to be underestimated. Doubtless the Chinese leadership was correct in believing that foreign economic aid would not long be withheld. At the same time, it will face massive difficulties in motivating the Chinese people to resume productive work. A plausible scenario is that, over five or ten years or so, economic reform will be resumed, against the background of yet worse economic conditions. It is also plausible to suppose that, in different provinces, differing degrees and mixtures of repression and liberalization in political life will develop. Over a generation, it is difficult to envisage the successive Chinese leaderships having the capacity to resist the devolution of power within China, and the economic imperatives which will impel it in the direction of civil society. If the Soviet Union is irreversibly post-totalitarian at present, China is likely to have reached the same stage of development in a generation at most. In both cases, however, the waning of totalitarianism will not have been accompanied by the waxing of a stable civil society, but instead by a far more uneven, complex and unstable diversity of circumstances and political conflicts and settlements.

In most of the emergent post-Communist countries, it is inherently unlikely that the reconstruction of civil society can be conducted under the auspices of a democratic regime on the Western model. This is so, in part, because few of these countries have democratic traditions that are long and deep, even when they had centuries of civil life before Communist institutions were imposed upon them. Of the post-Communist states, only Czechoslovakia can claim a real democratic inheritance: all of the rest existed for all of their recent history under one or another variety of authoritarianism. Contrary to received opinion in the West, however, this is not the fundamental reason why the transition to civil society is unlikely to occur within democratic institutions. As I have argued elsewhere,[5] Western opinion has gone astray in systematically overestimating the importance of political culture in Communist regimes, and underestimating the role of Communist ideology and institutions. For all their diverse cultural inheritances, the Communist regimes of Cuba, China, Bulgaria and Eastern Germany, for example, exhibit structural affinities that can only be explained by reference to the Communist institutions and ideologies they have in common. Equally, the likely incompatibility between the necessities of the transition from totalitarianism to civil society and the preconditions of liberal democracy arises, not principally from the cultural inheritances of the various post-Communist states, but instead from the massive human and economic costs of liquidating the bankrupt economies which the post-Communist regimes inherit.

These can scarcely be exaggerated. In Eastern Germany, for example, which is in many ways in the most favourable circumstances, it is estimated that between a third and a half of the workforce will unavoidably be dislocated in the transition to a market economy, with the cost of marketization running into tens of billions of dollars over the next five to ten years. If this is the case for Eastern Germany, which is the uniquely fortunate beneficiary of a peaceful *Anschluss* with one of the world's greatest economic powers, what will be the lot of Poland, where the costs will be far greater and available capital incomparably less? The danger is that the dislocations and costs of the transition period will destabilize the fragile political settlement achieved by the Solidarity-led government. Thus far, the immense reserves of legitimacy of that government has enabled it to implement extremely painful and unpopular measures, which lowered inflation from its peak of over 1,000 per cent a year to a fraction of that. The painful adjustments inseparable from marketization have, however, only just begun, with the prospect of massive lay-offs looming ahead – without the insurance of a welfare safety-net for workers who are displaced. In such circumstances, one may not unreasonably fear syndicalist resistance to market reform, perhaps organized by ex-Communist trade unions. In that event, however, a second period of dictatorship could well ensue, with market reform being implemented via a Polish version of 'the Pinochet solution' – economic liberalization pursued under the auspices of political authoritarianism.

Such an outcome is far from being inevitable in Poland. It is still less so in Hungary and Czechoslovakia, where the economic inheritance of central planning is less ruinous than in Poland. Even in the Soviet Union, it is plausible to envisage the Baltic states surmounting the economic difficulties of the transition period through the medium of democratic institutions, given the social and political solidarity generated by the strong sense of nationhood in Lithuania and the political maturity of the Baltic peoples as a whole. Even there, however, we can discern factors which may bring about a divergence between the necessities of the transition period and democratic institutions. Ethnic conflicts that are relatively mild in Latvia foreshadow ones that are already murderous in the Caucasus. Ancient nationalist rivalries, compounded by the Stalinist legacy of mass deportations and relocation, make the prospect of a stable civil society being introduced via the process of democratization delusive in many parts of the Soviet Union. In Soviet Central Asia, democratic mass mobilization risks awakening Islamic peoples from their long quiescence and exposing them to the appeal of fundamentalism. It need hardly be stressed that Islamic fundamentalism, with its denial of any legitimate realm of purely secular activity, is incompatible not only with liberal democracy, but also with civil society in any of its many varieties.

In order to understand the colossal difficulties that are bound to be confronted in the period of transition, we need to look not only at history, but also to bodies of theory which explain totalitarianism and its current crisis. The economic failure of Soviet-style central planning is best theorized by the Austrian and Polanyian analyses of Hayek and Roberts,[6] who focus on the epistemic role of market institutions and processes as generators and transmitters of dispersed and often tacit knowledge. The Austrian and Polanyian perspectives require supplementation by the insights of the Virginia School of Public Choice,[7] which theorizes the incentive structures created by institutions of central planning, and explains how the insuperable epistemic limitations of central planning are compounded by the perverse interests planners have in concealing malinvestments. The fundamental problem of the centrally planned economy, by contrast with any market economy, is that it lacks an *error-elimination mechanism* for misconceived projects. For anything resembling an efficient coordination of economic activity to be possible, it is essential that enterprises be allowed to fail, and for the costs of these failures to be borne by those responsible for the failure. The policy implication of this Public Choice insight is the radical one that economic efficiency presupposes not only market pricing but also private property in (most of, at least) the assets and resources that are produced and exchanged.

The perspective of Public Choice illuminates not only the theoretical explanation for the failures of central planning but also the dilemmas of the transition period. The chief contribution to theorizing the phenomenon of post-totalitarianism made by the Public Choice perspective in its recognition that many interests will be injured in the transition period, which (if the theory is sound) may be expected to organize collusively to resist and thwart market reform. In a democratic environment (or in a non-democratic one, such as contemporary Romania) we may expect elements of the exploitative *nomenklatura* to forge tactical alliances with groups of workers who expect to lose out in the early phases of market reform. The dilemma of the transition period is the classic dilemma theorized in Public Choice – that collusive interests may successfully prevent changes that would benefit nearly all, including themselves.

No model exists for the successful conduct of the transition period. The model of Erhardt's sudden deregulation of the post-War German economy is largely inappropriate, for a variety of reasons. Post-Nazi Germany, unlike most of the post-Communist states, possessed largely intact much of the institutional infrastructure of a civil society – a law of property and contract, the remnants of a banking system, and so forth. Insulted and injured as these institutions had been under the Nazi regime, they had not been comprehensively destroyed, as had been the case in much of the Soviet bloc. Further, defeat in war had the unforeseen and highly desirable consequence that collusive interest groups were destroyed or dissolved in post-War Germany. This is to say that post-Nazi Germany did not have a massive *nomenklatura*, inherited from the earlier totalitarian regime. Paradoxical as it may sound, then, the situation of post-War Germany was immeasurably more favourable (from the standpoint of the re-emergence of civil society) than that of most of the post-Communist societies.

Post-War Germany had another decisive advantage in the legitimacy of its government and in the fact that the Germans could be confident that, under the rule of law, any assets acquired by them through their productive labour would not later be subject to arbitrary confiscation. By contrast, in the Soviet Union the memory of the New Economic Policy remains vivid,[8] and even where genuinely free markets are opened up the fear of subsequent sequestration of assets and profits destroys or weakens the incentive to productive work. Only the institution of a real rule of law – which means a genuinely independent judiciary and an end to extra-judicial coercion of all sorts – could so alter the incentive structure of the Soviet peoples so as to release their protective energies. We may confidently predict the imminent ruin of the economic reforms of *perestroika*, if only because no such rule of law has yet been instituted. If anything, the opposite policy has prevailed, with cooperatives being subject to arbitrary regulation and confiscatory taxation. The lesson of the Public Choice perspective, then, is that market reform will fail, when the legal infrastructure of the market economy is weak or absent. This is a lesson that applies not only to post-totalitarian societies, but also to authoritarian dictatorships, in Africa or Latin America, for example, where local kleptocracies are unrestrained by law. In both cases, economic reform has no chance of success unless it is preceded by a reform of the law. This is to say that, if (as all historical evidence and theorizing suggests) a modern society cannot reproduce itself without the institutions of a civil society, including a market economy, those institutions themselves presuppose, as their ultimate guarantor, the rule of law.

The implications of this result for the Soviet Union are radical and pessimistic. A civil society will come to exist in the USSR, only if the Communist party is denied control over the judiciary and the law enforcement agencies. It will prevail, only if the organs of state security, above all the KGB, are brought within the compass of law, at least to the degree that their Western counterparts are subject to such control. Nothing at present supports the hope that this is about to occur. Indeed, the Soviet authorities can with some truth argue that in parts of the Soviet Union, such as the Caucasus, only the unfettered discretionary authority of the military and security forces keeps at bay the Hobbesian spectre of anarchy. In such circumstances, the implementation of a rule of law is an almost impossibly daunting task.

Within the Soviet Union, the prospects for civil society vary enormously. In the Caucasus, they are slight, with the best prospect being that of a Hobbesian peace maintained by military force. (I do not mean to deny that ethnic conflicts may have been exploited by the Communist authorities for their own purposes of 'divide and rule', but only to affirm that such conflicts are real enough and in some instances amount to intractable obstacles to a stable civil society.) In the Baltic states, the prospects are much brighter, provided only that political and economic independence of Moscow can be made a reality. It is as to Russia, and analogously Georgia and the Ukraine, that it is hardest to wager any conjectures. We do not know if the Soviet state in its present form will withstand the pressures for disintegration. The official Leninist policy of establishing a genuine confederation among the existing component states of the USSR seems bound to flounder, even if it is seriously meant, given the popularity and radicalism of the various independence movements. There may well be a measure of disinformation, moreover, in the more alarmist reports that the Soviet Union is on the brink of disintegration and even of nuclear civil war. What is clear enough is that the present situation in the Soviet Union is desperately unstable. Further, as the anonymous Z has well written,[9] Western *bien-pensant* opinion goes badly astray in supposing that Western policy can (via further massive transfusion of credit, for example) stabilize the situation. In all probability, the Soviet Union a decade or so hence will resemble Yugoslavia now – a state on the edge of disintegration, with pockets of relative affluence and peace and vast areas of desolation and ethnic conflict. The chief difference from Yugoslavia, and so the principal limitation of the analogy, is that on present trends (which exhibit no real reductions in defence expenditures) the Russian component of the USSR will remain a massively armed military superpower. This is the scenario that, on current evidence, seems the most likely.

The result of the inquiry so far is that, except in a few limiting cases, the transition to civil society cannot be negotiated via the medium of democratic institutions on the Western model. What then is to be done? We cannot be content with a model that offers no hope of release from tyranny for the peoples of the post-Communist world. We can find reason for a measure of hope, I shall argue, if we abandon the model of contemporary Western mass democracy, and return to earlier conceptions of civil society, the rule of law and limited government. This requires of us an exercise in self-criticism which the Western academic *nomenklatura* shows few signs of engaging in. For the most part, Western liberal academia has responded to the collapse of Communist totalitarianism by proposing market reforms that stop well short of the necessary precondition of a viable civil society, namely, private property in most productive assets. The commonest prescription is market socialism of one sort or another. The unrealism of this conception, its instability and its utopian character, have been so often demonstrated[10] that it would be tedious to rehearse here in detail the arguments which support this result.[11] In brief, however, everything suggests that, if market socialism could be instituted at all, it would exhibit (as it has in Yugoslavia) massive malinvestment, sluggish growth and technological backwardness, structural unemployment and probably hyperinflation. Even this is to give market socialism the benefit of a doubt it does not deserve, since its adoption on a large scale would entail sacrificing massive economies of scale, and resisting or reversing the most powerful economic trend of our age – that is, it would entail the destruction in the West of the transnational corporation. In the post-Communist world, a move towards market socialism could only entrench syndicalist power and delay the integration of the post-Communist economies into the global economy. For these reasons, market socialism is a non-starter, whose only real func- tion is to serve as a fig-leaf for the naked reality of the bankruptcy of socialism in our age.

Market socialism is not among the viable options for the post-Communist societies. For them, as for us, the real options span a range from libertarian capitalism to egalitarian social democracy, all of which pre-suppose acceptance of the core institutions of market capitalism. For the post-Communist societies, at least for a generation, the libertarian capitalist model is likely to be most salient and the Swedish egalitarian model completely irrelevant. For Sweden has maintained its egalitarian welfare state, only because it has the patrimony of over a century of capitalist wealth accumulation (assisted by neutrality in two world wars). None of the impoverished economies of the post-Communist world (with the exception of Eastern Germany, and the possible and partial exception of Bohemia) has analogous wealth at its disposal, or will have such wealth for decades to come. Egalitarian social democracy simply is not a viable option for most of the post-Communist societies.

This is not to say that the best prospect for the post-Communist societies is in merely replicating Western capitalist institutions in their present forms. Although acceptance of the core institutions of market capitalism is an inescapable necessity for all of the post-Communist societies, the forms these presently assume in the West are an historic accident, contingencies in the development of these institutions rather than essential, constitutive features of them. The different post-Communist societies may reconstruct the core institution of private property in a diversity of ways, each appro-priate to their environmental, cultural and economic circumstances. Further, the degree to which they operate a mixed economy will vary significantly – though they are likely, if they are prudent, to opt for a state or public sector smaller than that in most Western countries, including the United States.

For the post-Communist societies, then, their future does not lie in slavishly replicating the mass democracies of the West. These are flawed models in several respects. In the first place, despite recent exercises in privatization, all of the Western countries are burdened with an over-extended and omnicompetent state, with political life being dominated by competition for the resources that the state commands. This has created in Western States what I have elsewhere called *the new Hobbesian dilemma*[12] – which is that, if only as a means of preserving their own assets, citizens are constrained to organize collusively so as to capture governmental power, to extract economic privileges from government and thereby to pre-empt resources. In its worst, this new dilemma generates *a political war of all against all*, with the power of the state being the chief weapon in that war. One consequence of this dilemma is that, except where policy has been made by institutions partially insulated from democratic political competition – institutions such as the Bundesbank in Germany, the Federal Reserve Bank in America, and the MITI in Japan – economic life has been dislocated by governments aiming to achieve an artificial alignment of the economic and the electoral cycles. Even in the Western states, then, civil society has been weakened and the economy substantially politicized, yielding a mild version of totalitarian democracy.

Civil society has been weakened in another way in the Western democracies. Policies of affirmative action and positive discrimination have generated a new class of group rights, politically created and allocated, which is dubiously compatible with the underlying institutions of civil society. Especially in the United States, where policies of affirmative action have been implemented to the point of absurdity, voluntary association has been restricted and the rule of law compromised by policies which confer unequal privileges on favoured minorities within the population. The inflation of the discourse of fundamental rights has, in effect, politicized judicial interpretation of the law and substantially undermined the independence of the judiciary. As a side-effect, it has rendered intractable issues (such as abortion) which in political cultures less imbued with legalism have been resolved by legislative compromise. In short, the revisionist liberalism which dominates the mass democracies of the West – the new liberalism,[13] emanating from some of the works of J.S. Mill and theorized by contemporary writers such as Ackerman and Dworkin, which has equality and general welfare rather than individual liberty as its central constitutive values – has produced weak and inordinate governments, whose constant and arbitrary interventions have seriously weakened the autonomous institutions of civil society.

The post-Communist states will rapidly reach a dead end if they seek merely to copy the institutions and practices of the Western democracies, since their economic circumstances make unlimited democracy and its excesses far more costly to them. They will be well-advised if, on the whole, they look back to earlier traditions and conceptions of civil society and limited government rather than at the practice of contemporary Western states. Here I refer to the conceptions adumbrated in the writings of the classical economists of the Scottish School, for example, in the French classical liberal school of Torqueville and Constant, and in contemporary thinkers such as F.A. Hayek and James Buchanan.[14] The insight contained in all of these writers is that democracy must be limited if civil society is to be preserved, and liberty and prosperity ensured.

What does this fundamental insight imply for the institutions and policies of the post-Communist states? In part, no doubt, it simply endorses the policy of privatizing state assets now under way in many of the East European states, since such privatization, if pursued consistently, will bring about a transfer of initiative from government to society that is virtually irreversible. For this to be so, however, there needs to be constructed a body of property and contract law in which ownership and the terms of voluntary exchange are clearly defined. Contrary to Hayekian theorists of spontaneous order and institutional Darwinism,[15] such law will not evolve of itself in the post-Communist societies; it must be deliberately constructed. Further, it must be interpreted and enforced by a judiciary that is genuinely and thoroughly independent of any government or party. It is the independence of the judiciary which guarantees the rule of law, far more than the niceties of any constitution. Achieving such independence, and guaranteeing it for the future, should be the first priority of the post-Communist states, with the framing of democratic-institutions being regarded as a task which waits upon the successful achievement of a real rule of law. Nor should the post-Communist states follow Western models in according democracy unlimited competence. They will be wise if they follow the example of those Western democracies that remove certain areas of policy – above all, monetary policy – from democratic politics. Setting up an independent central bank, preferably (as in New Zealand) constrained by rules, is a measure that would bring immense benefits to all the post-Communist states, since (as the Polish experience has shown) monetary reform is a necessary prelude to any successful market reform of the inheritance of central planning. In general, the post-Communist states should aim to build institutions that constrain democracy rather than to exalt it.

The institutions whereby the post-Communist states constrain democracy and shelter civil society will inevitably vary. In at least one, Romania, the restoration of monarchy may be the only way in which legitimacy can be regained by government. In many others, only authoritarian governments are likely to be able to reconstruct the institutions of civil life. Within the Soviet Union, in particular, there will surely be instances in which, paradoxically, the task of building up the rule of law will be one that history gives to a post-Communist dictatorship. In all of the post-Communist states, priority should be given to re-inventing civil society and limiting govern- ment by the rule of law, and the temptation resisted to ape the declining mass democracies of the West.

CONCLUSION

The upshot of our inquiry has been that current Western practice and theory is, in general, a defective model for the post-Communist states. An older tradition of civil association[16] and limited government is better suited to their needs and circumstances, which stresses the rule of law as the most vital precondition of civil society. Western opinion has missed the mark in focusing on democracy as the litmus-test of genuine post-totalitarianism. Democratic political life can (as in Romania, Bulgaria and probably the Soviet Union) be manipulated or faked in the interests of the ruling *nomenklatura* caste. Perhaps democracy could have prevented some of the most catastrophic episodes in recent Soviet policy, such as the destruction of nature (and the consequent massive ruination of human health) in the area around Lake Aral. Even there, it is the devolution of power, rather than its democratic governance, that is most essential. Once again, democracy on the Western model is likely to prove at once impracticable and even defective as an ideal for many of the emergent post-Communist regimes.

All this suggests the irrelevance to the post-Communist countries of that now-dominant Western tradition of republican-democratic thinking typified in our time by the thoughts of Hannah Arendt.[17] This is an insight, grasped rarely in Western circles, that even some Communist theorists (such as Lagowski in Poland[18]) have absorbed. On the positive side, our inquiry has suggested that it is an older tradition of conservative and classical liberal thought that has most to offer the citizens of the post-Communist regimes. It is a central feature of this older liberal tradition that, by contrast with the revisionist liberalism of Rawls,[19] for example, it is personal and economic liberties that are prioritized, not political liberties. This is only to put in other terms the classical liberal insight that individual liberty and democracy need not go together, and often do not. This is a lesson that most of the emergent post-Communist states have yet to learn.

Among contemporary thinkers, it may well be that the leaders of the post-Communist states have most to learn from James Buchanan's thought. To Hayek must go the credit for predicting, and for explaining, the collapse of the socialist economies. Nothing in Hayek's thought gives guidance, however, to those seeking to walk the long road back from socialist serfdom. It is in the metaphor of a new constitutional contract, powerfully explored in Buchanan's writings,[20] that the reality of the post-Communist regimes is best captured. For the task of those emerging from the darkness of totalitarianism is to forge a new social contract among themselves, in virtue of which both totalitarian enslavement and the servile state of the contemporary Western democracies are transcended. In forging this new conflict, the leaders and peoples of the post-Communist states must avoid both the lawless legality of the Communist past and the politicized legalism of the Western present. With all of its varieties, post-totalitarianism will be a reality that is stable and irreversible, only when the autonomy of its contrary, civil society, is defined and protected by the rule of law.

August, 1991

15 Political power, social theory and essential contestability

The starting-point of my enquiry is an observation. In recent years social theorists have been much occupied in controversy about power. Theorists have argued as to whether power is to be attributed to social actors or to social structures, about how the possession of power may be distinguished from a disposition to exercise power on specified occasions, and so on. I begin my enquiry with the commonplace observation that these controversies in the theory of power express divergencies in the philosophy of the social studies. Often, these controversies are interpreted as expressing divergent views about the merits of positivism as a stance in the philosophy of social science. Differences between positivists and the critics of positivism are posed differently in different traditions, but here 'positivism' seems to stand for the claim that in its methods and goals the study of society ought to replicate a received model of the study of nature. The practice of natural science is understood to be insulated from the value-commitments and from the philosophical bias of its practitioners and (at least in its normal periods) to display agreement on rules of method and convergence on a common body of theory. For positivists, there can be no reason why the dispassionate study of society should not in due course yield a like body of common theory, or why such theory should not serve as a common resource for partisans of opposed policies and competing interests. According to positivism's critics, the subject-matter of the social studies disqualifies any natural-scientific model for their investigation. The observational basis of the social studies (they insist) is not neutrally accessible to rival theoretical frameworks, it is captured differently by each of them. Social theories in turn are not dissociable from the moral and political commitments of their exponents. Often, critics of positivism maintain that the theory-dependency of social facts along with the value-dependency of social theories introduces a dimension of relativity or contestability into social thought. It is in virtue of this character of relativity that social theory can never replicate natural science. Social theory remains an area of intractable and inherent controversy for these critics of positivism, primarily because it is unavoidably informed by value-commitments between which reason cannot arbitrate.

This common story about controversy in the philosophy of social science may be illustrated by reference to controversy in the theory of power. Here the writings of Steven Lukes and W. E Connolly[1] are particularly illuminating for, despite several differences of emphasis in their writings, they share three beliefs which go far to support the conventional view of controversy in this area as expressive of debate for and against positivism. First, they hold that the concept of power, along with many other concepts in social theory, is essentially contestable. This is to say that its proper range of uses is inherently a matter of irresolvable dispute. For Lukes and Connolly, the essential contestability of the concept of power derives from the fact that rival applications of it embody conflicting value-commitments. So, inasmuch as it cannot help invoking some notion of power, social theory (in Lukes's and Connolly's account of it) cannot avoid being a normative exercise. Second, Lukes and Connolly agree that the point of locating power in society is to fix responsibility. They insist that responsibility, like power, is an essentially contested concept, and they acknowledge that fixing responsibility involves making a moral appraisal. Further, they wish to contrast exercises of power with the structural determination of social happenings: they assert that, though opportunities for action are structurally constrained, the subject-matter of the theory of power is human agency rather than the workings of social or historical necessity. Power is an interstitial phenomenon, arising in gaps in the structural determination of social events. Understanding the exercise of power inescapably involves the application of moral notions connected with responsibility and with the nature of persons. Third, Lukes and Connolly argue for the dependency of rival views of power on competing conceptions of human interests. These are normative notions inasmuch as they have ratifying and validating as well as descriptive and explanatory uses, but Lukes and Connolly insist that judgements about interests remain none the less partly empirical in content. They are to be spelled out in terms of the preferences that are displayed by autonomous agents who have a clear apprehension of the relevant alternatives open to them. For Lukes and Connolly, then, power is an essentially contestable concept depending on opposed conceptions of human interests, where it is the preferences of an autonomous man or woman that finally determine his or her real interests.

At the meta-theoretical level, the central thesis advanced by Lukes and Connolly is that, in virtue of the essential contestability of its constitutive concepts, any kind of social theory is a form of moral and political practice.

I shall have much to say in criticism of the nuts and bolts of their accounts, but at this point I want to observe only that there seem to be two entirely distinct theses in their writings about power. One is the thesis that the theory of power, like the rest of social theory, is beset by an ineradicable conceptual relativism such that no account of power can compel rational assent. The other is the thesis that social theorizing cannot avoid being a normative activity, that theory-making about the social world is informed by the theorist's values, so that making such theory is (whether self-consciously or not) an aspect of its practitioner's moral and political life. My comment here is that, whereas Lukes and Connolly cite the latter thesis in support of the former, the supportive connection between the two remains unspecified. Nothing that Lukes and Connolly argue about power goes any distance towards linking the theory-dependence of social facts with the value-dependence of social theories. The upshot of my argument at this meta-theoretical level will be that relativism or scepticism in social theory may have sources other than the claim that social theories are value-laden. One reason that arguments about the value-neutrality of social theories have been run together promiscuously with arguments about the theory-neutrality of social facts is to be found in the recent vogue for a jargon of essential contestability. I shall argue that, whereas claims about essential contestability may once have had utility in a campaign against certain obsolete positivisms in social science, the idiom of essential contestability constitutes an impediment to further advance in social theory. Talk of essential contestability conflates a range of distinct problems and insights in social theory whose careful disaggregation is a condition of progress in understanding its prospects and limitations.

My programmatic conclusion will be that there are many reasons for scepticism and humility in social theory, but none of them imply or pre-suppose that theorizing about society is necessarily informed (or corrupted) by the theorist's values. Before I can reach this conclusion, I must consider in detail the account given by Lukes and Connolly of the relations between power, human interests, and autonomy and their claim that judgements about the exercise of power embrace judgements about responsibility. I shall argue that there are not the logical links between the concepts of power, interests, and autonomy postulated by these writers and that they are mistaken in their belief that discourse about the distribution of power in society need be connected with the moral assessment of responsibility. A further result of my examination will be the claim that in both Luke's account and that of Connolly, liberal and socialist positions in political theory and sceptical and realist positions in moral theory coexist and compete with each other. The account of power offered by these writers is a theory divided against itself at more than one point, and I shall in conclusion suggest how this self-division may best be resolved.

POWER, AUTONOMY AND INTERESTS

According to Lukes, the common core of all conceptions of power is found in the notion of one agent affecting another. Further, when the notion of power is invoked to capture the import of a social exchange, it always comprehends the idea of significant, non-trivial affecting. Using John Rawls's distinction[2] between a generic concept and the many specific conceptions a concept may spawn, Lukes goes on to distinguish three views of power as

> alternative interpretations and applications of one and the same underlying concept of power, according to which A exercises power over B when A affects B in a manner contrary to B's interests.[3]

Each of these three views of power emerges from and operates within a definite moral and political perspective and carries with it a definite conception of human interests. The first, 'one-dimensional' or 'pluralist' view, defended by such writers as Dahl, Polsby, Wolfinger, and Merelman, for whom power is exercised in observable conflict over policy issues, presupposes a 'liberal' understanding of interests in terms of policy preferences expressed in political participation. The second, 'two-dimensional' view, expounded by Bachrach and Baratz, holds that power is exercised, not only when there is victory in a conflict over policies, but also when potential issues are organized out of the political arena, and this second view embodies a 'reformist' conception of interests which allows that they may be submerged or concealed, distorted or deflected from full expression by a series of non-decisions. According to the 'three-dimensional' view which (like Connolly) Lukes himself defends, each of the conceptions of interest presupposed by the first two views is defective. Power may be exercised over men and women even when their wants have been fully satisfied, and, in Lukes's 'radical' conception of power and interests, people's real interests are not in what they happen to want, but in whatever it is that they would want if they were to become fully autonomous agents.

As far as Lukes and Connolly are concerned, a power relation exists whenever one agent affects another significantly and does so detrimentally to the latter's interests. Before I try to probe the links they postulate between power, interests, and autonomy, it may be worth making a few preliminary observations about the conceptual analysis of power contained in Lukes's and Connolly's writings. To start with, it is not clear to me why significant affecting should be placed at the core of the concept of power. Significant affecting is a feature of many sorts of social interaction – it characterizes love and trade, among many other involvements – and it is not plausibly represented as especially or distinctively characteristic of power relations. Again, it is wholly unclear why the exercise of power should always involve a significant impact on human interests, or, most crucially, why power relations are defined as social relations involving conflicts of interest. It seems clear – and this is a point to which I will return – that power relations may involve a conflict of goals or of preferences without thereby turning on a conflict of interests. As a corollary of this last point, I cannot see why the attribute of power should be restricted to social interactions where one agent affects *detrimentally* the interests of another. No such restriction is found in ordinary thought and language, and imposing one by stipulation has counter-intuitive results.

The conceptual analysis of power advanced by Lukes and Connolly is unduly restrictive in focusing attention on the significant affecting of interests and in insisting that power has to do, only or centrally, with conflicts of interest. It introduces into the concept of power the requirement that the exercise of power occurs always in a circumstance of (manifest of latent) social conflict. This is to sanction a conflictual conception of power of the sort repudiated by those theorists (Arendt and Parsons are examples[4]) who conceive of it as a collective resource, possessed in greater or lesser magnitudes by different societies. Further, it writes into the notion of power a presumption of its maleficence, a presumption commonly made in liberal and socialist intellectual traditions, but one that is hard to sustain for all that. The concentration on 'power over' to the exclusion of 'power to' cannot be justified by the claim that such power is especially salient to political contexts, since the claim already carries with it the indefensibly restrictive (and distinctively liberal) conception of political life as somehow inherently a domain of conflicts.

It is not hard to show that the requirement of any exercise of power that injures the interests of the agent over whom it is exercised yields counter-intuitive results. At a microsocial level, I may apply force or coercion to another individual, not in order to protect or promote any interest of mine, but with the aim of benefitting him. If I succeed in attaining my aim, the exchange between us may be neutral, adverse, or favourable to my interests while it benefits those of the other. At a macrosocial level, Stalinist policies in which working-class liberties and current living standards are repressed have been defended, coherently if not at all plausibly, by invoking the long-term and on-balance interests of the working class itself. What reason could there by for denying the character of power to these relationships?

In citing these examples, I do not seek to rebut the contention that a man always loses something when power is exercised over him, but only to remark on its triviality. Presumably, everyone has an interest in acting on their current wants, even where so acting prejudices their interests taken on balance. Presumably, also, the interest that is damaged when anyone is prevented by another from acting on his current wants is the interest in autonomy. Still, it remains a commonplace that we all have interests other than the interests we have in our autonomy: no one can plausibly deny that these other interests might be promoted at the expense of our interest in autonomy. This is only to utter the truism that the damage done to an agent's interest in autonomy may well be compensated for by gains to the agent's other interests and by an improvement in these interests as a whole. All this begs a natural question about how someone's interest in autonomy is to be weighted against his other interests when their claims compete, but nothing important hinges here on this omission. A competition between the interest in autonomy and a person's other interests can be circumvented altogether only by the fraudulent expedient of attaching an infinite weight to the human interest in autonomy (relative to other human interests). I take it that, whatever the interest in autonomy comprehends, no one could sensibly allow it to overwhelm or engross all other human interests. This point is not met by the response that, when someone's interest in their autonomy conflicts with other interests, it is up to that person to trade them off against each other. Even making the heroic assumption that the person decides always to promote his or her interest in autonomy against all other interests, the possibility remains that weakness of will or poor calculation on his part will thwart this policy. This possibility opens up the prospect of an *autonomy-maximizing paternalism* in which an agent's autonomy in one area is restricted so as to promote the agent's chances of autonomy on balance. In the case I am considering, the hypothesis is that this paternalist intervention promotes the agent's interests. Whether or not it does so, I cannot see why an intervention of this sort should be refused the character of an exercise of power.

So far in my discussion, the term 'autonomy' has been used almost as a cipher. Its content has gone unspecified. We may take it for granted that its provenance is in Kantian ideas about moral personality, though as my argument proceeds it will become clear that, in Lukes's and Connolly's use of the notion, matters are not so simple. At this point I want to observe that, however the ideal of autonomy is in the end filled out, it must on any account of it be a complex achievement, having a variety of elements and capable of being realized in differing degrees. If this is so, and (as both Lukes and Connolly are at pains to insist) autonomy should be regarded as a variable magnitude rather than a threshold phenomenon, then it should be obvious that autonomy may be promoted (and even maximized) by an intervention that restricts it. A policy of restricting an agent's autonomy might, then, be licensed solely by reference to the value of autonomy. It might be so justified if, as in the case of autonomy-regarding paternalism to which I alluded earlier, the autonomy promoted is that of the agent whose autonomy is restricted. Alternatively, it might be justified in this way if an intervention reducing someone's autonomy on balance at the same time increases the autonomy of all the others affected by it and maximizes the value of autonomy in the circumstances under consideration. There are, admittedly, questions that go unanswered in the sketch I have offered of such a policy and its justification. We do not know how weighty is the interest each man has in his own autonomy: is it weighty enough to support a side-constraint against policies which promote autonomy (now or in the long term) at the expense of his (current of lifetime) prospects of autonomy? Nor do we know how, when once it is acknowledged that autonomy is a complex achievement having various elements, we are to weight these elements when a policy having regard only to the value of autonomy promotes its constitutive elements in differing degrees: we have no guidance as to how we are to make on-balance judgements even of one agent's autonomy. But neither of these questions is answered in Lukes's or Connolly's accounts, and I do not see that they impeach the drift of my argument at all.

The observations I have made so far have all been about the conceptual analysis of power held in common by Lukes and Connolly. I have questioned its special connection with significant affecting and argued that the general link with interests is undefended. More controversially, I have maintained that the requirement that exercises of power be always in circumstances of social conflict, latent or manifest, disqualifies conceptions of power as a collective resource. One general point illustrated by these observations is that Lukes's and Connolly's account of the generic concept of power is itself non-neutral in its implications for debate about the appropriate conception of power. It establishes boundaries for any bona fide conception of power, and such boundaries are certain to be highly controversial. It is hard to see how matters could be otherwise, if power is indeed an essentially contestable concept. There is no more reason to expect agreement on the formal features or conceptual analysis of power than there is to expect it on the merits of its various conceptions. The fact that neither Lukes nor Connolly has anywhere satisfactorily defended their conceptual analysis has led one commentator to observe that Lukes's argument makes sense only if it is seen as reposing on a real definition of power.[5] Given the conventionalist and relativist aspects of essential contestability theses, this is an ironical and paradoxical result.

A crucial claim made in both the accounts I am considering is that judgements about an agent's real interests, and so about the agent's power situation, retain an empirical dimension inasmuch as they are spelled out in terms of the preferences of an autonomous agent. This is a crucial claim, for on it depends the belief that the view of power it supports is a part of empirical social theory and not merely an ideological assertion. If a power relation always involves a conflict of interests, and if these interests may be latent rather than manifest, then whether a judgement about a power relation is true will depend wholly on claims about the (hypothetical and counterfactual) preferences of an autonomous agent. Everything then turns on whether the conception of autonomy at work here can be satisfactorily elucidated, defended, and given operational value.

An initial uncertainty concerns the nature of the link postulated in Lukes and Connolly between the preferences or choices of an autonomous man and his real interests. It is obvious that an agent's preferences when the agent is (relatively highly) autonomous cannot be *identified* with his or her interests for there can be no presumption that an autonomous agent will have prudence as his or her dominant motive: such an agent may, after all, choose autonomously to sacrifice his or her interests to some ideal he or she cherishes. The link must be between an agent's real interests and the agent's autonomous judgement of these interests, not between his or her real interests and whatever it is that he or she prefers when they are autonomous. This has the important implication that there may be occasions for conflict among highly autonomous men and women, even if (implausibly) the *interests* of such agents cannot conflict. There seems no reason why the social conflicts engendered among autonomous men and women whose interests harmonize but whose goals or ideals do not, should not express themselves in power relations.

A deeper uncertainty concerns the nature of the link postulated in Lukes's and Connolly's accounts between interests and autonomous choice. What an agent chooses autonomously as to his or her own welfare might merely be useful *evidence* as to where the agent's interests lie, or else it might serve as the criterion of these interests: in the latter case, an agent's interests are necessarily constituted by his or her autonomous preferences about his or her own welfare. In general, though in both writers there are occasional equivocations, Lukes and Connolly go for the view that autonomous choice is the criterion of interests, not just good evidence about them.

But, if the necessary link is not between autonomous choice or preference and real interests, but between what an autonomous agent takes his or her interests to be and what they are, it begins to look again as if human interests constitute a subject-matter independent of anyone's choices or preferences. On the one hand, if the link between autonomy and interests is criterial, then anyone's judgement of their interests will be ideally incorrigible, while on the other hand there must be room for the notion of a mistake being possible in this kind of judgement if indeed it is a judgement with an independent subject-matter. How is this difficulty to be resolved? It might be suggested that this is not a deep problem. The distinction needed might simply be that between a person's preferences for their own welfare and those they have for the welfare of others: their interests are constituted by the former. Whereas some such commonsensical distinction is in place and will be presupposed by much of what I myself later argue, it does not seem to me to meet the difficulty I have in mind. This is that there seem to be two views of the relations between autonomy and interests at issue here. One view is that an agent's preferences about his or her own prospects just are his or her interests: an agent's only reason for action is that he or she has goals, and the agent's interests are those of the goals or preferences that concern the agent. The other view is that an agent's interests are a matter of fact for the agent: they give the agent reasons for action whether or not he or she knows about or assents to them.

At this point in their theory of interests Lukes and Connolly confront an unavoidable parting of the ways between subjectivist and objectivist accounts. In one perspective, argued for by Brian Barry,[6] the concept of having an interest may be analysed wholly in terms of opportunities for the satisfaction of wants. In this view, the only relevant authority to which appeal may be made to settle questions about an agent's interests is the judgement of the agent. To be sure, inasmuch as legal or financial expertise enters into anyone's deliberations about their interests, others may advise them as to where their interests lie and even, in special circumstances, act as guardians of their interests. Except in cases of this latter sort, where someone's judgement is rendered corrigible by their lack of special knowledge, the fact that anyone's wants are their own entails that their own assessments of their interests, spelled out in terms of their basic preferences for their own welfare, are indefeasible. Apart from cases where technical expertise or suchlike is involved, this view of interests implies that, whenever anyone's basic preferences about their own welfare change, their interests change too: an agent's basic preferences cannot be the subject of a criticism in terms of his or her interests. It is true enough that an agent's current wants and interests are never the same thing even on a subjectivist view; an agent's interests even on that view of them must encompass all the wants he or she is reasonably likely to conceive in a lifetime. Indeed, if (as I have assumed) it is an agent's preferences and not the agent's mental states which go to make up his or her interests, then such interests may be protected or damaged even after he or she is dead. In this subjectivist view, then, an agent's current preferences may be overridden so as to protect his or her prospects of satisfying all his or her preferences, taken over a lifetime, and the person's interests may thereby be promoted; but it cannot be the case that such wants or preferences, when they are taken as a whole, could be thwarted for the sake of the agent's interests. In an objective view, on the contrary, the criterial link between wants and interests is severed, and a person's interests are explicated in terms of some notion of the conditions appropriate to this person's flourishing. On this objectivist view, a person may well be in error as to what his or her interests are, for though the agent's wants remain his or her own, these wants no longer decide his or her interests.

How does this, admittedly rather crude, distinction bear on the arguments of Lukes and Connolly? I think it impales them on a fork. Lukes, at any rate, cannot endorse the objectivist view of interests without abandoning the value-relativism he has elsewhere avowed[7] and without elaborating upon the theory of moral knowledge and the philosophical anthropology which links interests with conditions of human flourishing. Again, adopting an objectivist view of interests creates problems for the claim that judgements about a person's interests are liable to a straightforward empirical and behavioural test – a claim to which Lukes wishes to hold.[8] If a subjectivist view is adopted, on the other hand, problems about testability of a different sort surface. Discussing Crenson's analysis of air pollution in American cities, Lukes tells us that it is impressive because

> there is good reason to expect that, other things being equal, people would rather not be poisoned (assuming, in particular, that pollution control does not necessarily mean unemployment) – even where they may not even articulate this preference.[9]

On a subjective view, this 'good reason' of which Lukes speaks can only be an inductive wager grounded in exception-ridden generalizations about human behaviour. Where other things are *not* equal, where people must make trade-offs and the influence on their choices of culture, circumstance and temperament cannot be discounted, such inductive wagers are fraught with uncertainty. Where an inductive wager of this kind is invoked counterfactually to explain a historical development, it is hard to see how it can be the subject of any sort of test.

Underlying this disjunction between objective and subjective views of interests lies a divergence in the concept of autonomy itself. On one view, which has perhaps a genuine Kantian ancestry, autonomy is primarily a formal, procedural and open concept: it desiderates the general conditions of any respectworthy choice. Such a choice, if it is to be autonomous, must be rational – it must, let us say, satisfy criteria of means-end efficiency, embody a precept to which the agent can give a relevantly universal assent, and so on. If autonomy is construed in this way as an open notion, then it should be evident to us (even if it was not clear to Kant) that it will not specify any very determinate range of ways of life as being in conformity with human interests. It will in fact be pretty destitute of prescriptive content. If autonomy is construed in a more Aristotelian (or Spinozistic) way as a relatively closed concept, autonomous choice will be compatible only with a fairly narrowly defined range of ways of life. In this conception, the relation between autonomous choices and real interests intimated in Lukes's account will actually have been reversed: the conditions of human flourishing will now serve as providing *criteria for the identification of autonomous choice itself.* It should be clear that, whatever else it might be, this is an account in which the requirement that identification of real interests have an 'empirical basis' has been abandoned.

In Connolly's more extended treatment[10] of the concept of autonomy, an attempt is made to resist criticisms of this sort. He believes that:

> The idea of real interests is bounded by a set of core ideas we share, if often imperfectly and to a large extent tacitly, about those characteristics particularly distinctive of persons.[11]

This reference to certain defining features of persons acts as a restriction on the use of the choice criterion. Notwithstanding this restriction, Connolly's account of real interests remains within the subjectivist view; it differs from the standard 'liberal' account only by virtue of the stringent conditions it comprehends for the specification of the privileged choice situation in which the relevant preferences (which express a man's real interests) are to be displayed. Specifically, Connolly's account goes beyond the liberal account, and deviates from the standards of ordinary thought and practice, in allowing for the possibility of internal constraints on action. Like David Riesman, Connolly suggests that an agent fails to be autonomous if he or she is swayed by peer-group pressure or social convention or guided by imprintings of socialization which he or she has not critically sifted.

Connolly's account fails to meet the criticisms I have advanced and breaks down in much the same way that Mill's theory of the higher pleasures does: it underestimates the variety of human nature. This is to say that reference to the powers of deliberation and capacities for emotional involvement which make persons what they are will not allow agents' preferences to be overridden in the name of their interests in a variety of dilemmas of the sort that concern Connolly. The contented lifelong heroin addict, and the person who lives and dies in willing slavery,[12] will sometimes be able plausibly to defend their lifestyles as most efficacious in the promotion of their interests. Certainly, invoking in an aprioristic fashion the idea of the person cannot defeat this possibility. There is nothing to support the presumption that an autonomous agent cannot autonomously and reasonably act to abridge his future prospects of autonomy.

The variety of human nature creates difficulties for the supposition, entertained by both Lukes and Connolly,[13] that there may be a power-free mode of consensual authority resting on autonomous choices and involving a harmony of real interests. Given the variety of human nature, and the fact that autonomous choice is a necessary ingredient of some but not of all ideals of life and is incompatible with some valuable involvements and ways of living, we have no reason to suppose that the choices of autonomous persons will converge on any single way of life, or even that they will converge on an extended family of lifestyles, all of whose members have autonomy as a necessary ingredient. It may be that Lukes and Connolly, like Mill, imagine that, whereas there is no one way of life which all autonomous persons will elect to live, yet there is for each autonomous agent one sort of life that is appropriate to that agent. Here the idea of a real interest or real will is affirmed but predicated in Romantic (or late-Scholastic) fashion of the essence of the individual rather than of the individual's species. Apart from the point that the choice criterion has fallen away, this construal of real interests abandons the assumption that they cannot conflict with one another. Once this assumption has been abandoned or relaxed, however, we have no reason to suppose that a community of autonomous agents will lack power relations, or even that these latter will be less prominent that they would be if agents were more heteronomous. Nor can the idea of a power-free community be saved by arguing that judgements about interests cannot have a purely subjective character.[14] It might well be the case that people's judgements about their interests always appeal to shared standards of a worthwhile life, and it is sometimes the case that the want-regarding and the ideal-regarding elements in interest-judgements are inseparable. This norm-dependency of judgements about interests does not support the possibility of a general will, if only because of the manifest diversity of moral practices in the societies with which Connolly is concerned. That there are some common elements in all judgements about interests, which go some way to make them publicly defeasible, in no sense supports a Marxian (or classical liberal) thesis of the universality or non-conflictability of real interests. And finally, as I have already intimated, power relations might emerge from conflicts of goals, even in a society of autonomous persons whose interests harmonized.

Two comments emerge from this critical survey of Lukes and Connolly on power, interests and autonomy. There is in the first place a deep

obscurity in the concept of autonomy itself. Different conceptions of autonomy and of human interests seem to be embedded in different views of
human nature whose status is only partly empirical. If the choice between
rival views of human nature is not empirically severely constrained, the
possibility arises that autonomy may itself be an essentially contestable
concept. If it is, then so will be the concept of power, but the empirical
usefulness of Lukes's theory of power will be impeached. If autonomy is
not an essentially contestable concept, and rationally consensual judgements about autonomy and interests are feasible, then it is hard (on the other
hand) to see how power can be characterized as essentially contestable. The
possibility arises that the conception of autonomy implicit in Lukes's and
Connolly's accounts may even be incoherent. Both Lukes and Connolly
hold to a view of the self as a social construct: human individuality is not
for them a natural datum but a cultural achievement. Further, Lukes explicitly and Connolly tacitly endorse a value-relative stance in which the
possibility of cross-cultural, pan-human standards of flourishing is
excluded. It seems at least plausible that a substantive ideal of autonomy
can be combined with the view of the self as socially constructed only if a
strong conception of human flourishing together with a tough realism in
ethics is incorporated into the theory of autonomy; but this is a move neither
writer seems willing to make.

My second comment is in the nature of a summary of the foregoing
examination. Neither in Lukes's nor in Connolly's accounts are the criterial
links between the concepts of power, autonomy and interests postulated in
their theory satisfactorily upheld. There seems no reason to regard conflicts
of interest as especially salient to power relations, or to treat interests as
analysable into the preferences of autonomous agents for their own welfare.
The natural relation to be expected between autonomy and interests is
rather the reverse: different construals of autonomous choice are likely to
be embedded in different conceptions of human interests. In part, the
differences between rival conceptions of power will be found to derive
from the different views of human nature by which they are sponsored. It is
most unlikely that any purely empirical test will enable us to select one
from among the available range of such conceptions of human nature. I will
turn to the question of how such conceptions of human nature, which lie at
the root of different conceptions of power, may yet be criticizable in the
third and last section of this essay.

POWER, RESPONSIBILITY AND SOCIAL STRUCTURE

Against the one-dimensional view, Lukes insists[15] that power may be
exercised by institutions, collectivities and social forces as well as by

natural persons. He preserves the link between attributions of power and the ascription of responsibility by making the claim that power is definitionally exercised by agents, whose omissions as well as actions may figure as exercises of power. He goes so far as to claim that structuralist social theory, in excluding all possibility of ascribing responsibility for social events, actually eliminates the concept of power from social theory. It is hard to see how this latter claim can be maintained. A structuralist perspective in which the exercise of power loses its connection with agency and so its interstitial character and instead is identified with the operation of social structures is a perspective in which the primitive notion of power singled out by Lukes – that of significant affecting – is preserved. In Marxist structuralist theory, the requirement that exercises of power occur in a social situation of conflict of interests is also preserved. What we have in structuralist social theory is unfairly characterized as the elimination of the concept of power.

The nub of the three-dimensional conception advocated by Lukes and shared with Connolly is in the thesis that the exercise of power includes the determination of preferences by socialization. Note that this is a far stronger claim than the claim that, because overwhelming power pre-empts any challenge to it, overt conflict cannot be a precondition of the exercise of power or of the existence of power relations. Rather, it is the claim that power relations may be most pervasive and most efficacious when they are invisible to their victims. This is a claim easily recognizable in theories of ideology for which the propagation of beliefs, the maintenance of social norms and so on may all count as exercises of power. A difficulty here is that the production of ideology is rarely effective when it is a matter of conscious fabrication. If experience is any guide, moreover, those who are recognized as exercising power in ordinary thought and practice are typically no more autonomous than those over whom it is exercised: typically, that is to say, the exercisers of power are imbued with values that they have absorbed from *their* early social environment and which they have never submitted to a critical assessment. Since those who exercise power, no less than those upon whom power is exercised, have their preferences determined by the culture in which they are immersed and the institutions by which they are surrounded, how can it be justified to impute responsibility to the former but not to the latter? I take it that the latter are excused responsibility for their actions and for their omissions because manipulation and socialization may be represented as the application of force to people's minds and as constituting an excusing condition. It should be obvious, though, that those we ordinarily think of as exercising power (or as being in the upper levels of a power structure) are invariably also at the receiving end of a three-dimensional power relationship. So invariably is this the case that the analogy of a chain of command, which is irresistibly suggested by Lukes's insistence that the conditions of responsibility are coterminous with those of the exercise of power, tends to break down. In the real social world, what we tend to find are feedback loops rather than causal chains which begin in a determinate agent. If this is so, what reason can there be for insisting that judgements about power always involve fixing responsibility? This insistence seems part of a vestigially individualist, residually voluntarist aspect of the theory for which no real justification has been given.

I have pointed out already that, since the primitive notion of power is retained in structuralist social theory, it cannot be a conceptual truth within Lukes's argument that power has no place in structuralist thought. Further, I have observed that Lukes's combination of the claim that power may be exercised by collectivities and social forces as well as by individuals with the claim that its exercise always presupposes a responsible agent comes under great pressure when we recognize the ubiquitousness of heteronomy. I want now to suggest some positive reasons for dissociating the notions of power and responsibility.[16] Such an association yields highly counterintuitive results. Consider the mad dictator, who throws his weight about, does great damage to others' interests, but is not responsible (morally or in law) for his actions. Are we to deny that power is being exercised in a case of this sort? This example illuminates important areas of obscurity in the accounts of Lukes and Connolly. It is not wholly clear whether the responsibility always presupposed by the exercise of power is merely causal or properly moral. Again, are we to accept that power waxes and wanes as the conditions of responsibility are more or less satisfied?

Above all, treating power as an interstitial phenomenon always manifested by responsible agents imposes an arbitrary terminus in the regress of explanation. In a structuralist approach, by contrast, a circumstance of social change is incompletely understood unless the deliberations of the agents it includes are incorporated (at a higher level of abstraction) into a theoretical framework in which are elucidated the mechanisms of ideological production whereby social systems renew themselves. In this structuralist account, revolutions occur not because people unaccountably take advantage of opportunities history offers them, but in virtue of crises within the mechanisms of ideological reproduction which are in principle fully intelligible and whose necessity might conceivably be demonstrated. The voluntarist perspective intimated in Lukes and Connolly has as much difficulty in accommodating the idea of a systemic social contradiction as it does that of a power structure.[17]

The rigorous determinism of the structuralist approach may usefully be contrasted with the uncompromising voluntarism or actionism espoused by ethnomethodologists and by writers in the tradition of Schutz. For these theorists, social structures can never be more than the precipitates or crystallizations of the actions of individuals. This is a stance that is also displayed in Popperian writings and in the theories of interactionist sociologists for whom agents' identities are themselves superventient upon their social activities. In this perspective, the terminal explanatory level in any social theory is provided by the intentions, beliefs, decisions and activities of individuals. I do not want here to comment on the large issues of methodological individualism and determinism suggested by the contrast I have sketched, except to say that the explanatory frameworks yielded by the two approaches may not easily be subject to comparative critical assessment. Indeed, the explanatory terminus imposed within Lukes's and Connolly's account by the requirement that power relations be initiated by responsible agents seems arbitrary given the fact that power exercisers are ordinarily themselves the recipients of three-dimensional power.

If these are truly incommensurable frameworks of explanation, the attempt made explicitly by Lukes to adopt a commonsensical or dialectical middle way between them approaches the brink of incoherence. For the structuralist, after all, the realm of agency – of teleological and inter-subjective modes of understanding and explanation – must finally disappear into a system of objective social coordinates. Any methodology which retains a decisive explanatory role for people's hopes, regrets, intentions and decisions remains wedded to an obscure, moralistic and reactionary humanist anthropology. For the actionist, on the other hand, it amounts to an error of reification, a mystifying and animistic superstition, to regard social structures as more than the residues of the practical and intellectual activities of human subjects. It is acknowledged in the actionist account that social situations may acquire a logic (though not a necessity) of their own, but this is always accounted for by reference to the unintended consequences of human actions.

Thus, whereas structuralists seek to subsume discussions about human agency into an explanatory framework in which it is altogether replaced by reference to objective social coordinates, actionists try to account for the constraints operative upon human agents in terms which always make decisive reference to the acts of agents. Whereas structuralists want to eliminate discourse about agency from the discursive practices of social science, actionists aim to collapse social structures into the momentarily uncontested products of the practice of individual subjects. Whereas the actionist perspective incorporates a strong conception of the autonomy of the individual subject, for the structuralists 'autonomy' refers rather to modes of theoretical discourse or of social practice whose independence must, in the last analysis, be undermined in a comprehensive social theory.

We can now see, then, that since judgements about power and structure are theory-dependent operations, actionists and structuralists will approach their common subject-matter – what goes on in society – using divergent paradigms in such a fashion that incompatible explanations (and descriptions) will be produced. This much is indisputable: but are we to go one step further, and say that each of these divergent perspectives generates its own corroborating evidence? If we adopt this relativist position, then we will be committed to the view that we have here incommensurable views of man and society between which a rational choice is impossible. This radically relativist position depends on the claim that as between such views of man and society what we have is meaning-variance rather than theory-incompatibility. Is what we have here, then, an instance of competition between incommensurable paradigms? And, if so, must we accept that the choice between them is rationally unconstrained? Are we here at last in an area of genuine essential contestability?

SOCIAL THEORY, ESSENTIAL CONTESTABILITY AND COMPETING PARADIGMS OF POWER

Before I try to answer this question, it may be worth looking briefly at the history of the idiom of essential contestability. The epithet 'essentially contestable' was coined and first applied to concepts by W. B. Gallie in a paper presented to the Aristotelian Society in 1956,[18] but a closely similar idiom was adopted by Stuart Hampshire when in his *Thought and Action* (1959) he referred to 'essentially questionable and corrigible concepts'.[19] As a crude approximation, it may be hazarded that, however these writers conceived the *sources* of a concept's essential contestability, its contestability *consisted* in its being somehow inherently liable to rival interpretations. Nor could this simply be passed off as a matter of the open texture of many or most, perhaps all, of our concepts: what distinguished essential contestability from ordinary open texture was precisely that rivalry and dispute tended to break out, not at the edges of a consensus of agreed uses, but in what each side regarded as the heart of the concept's subject-matter.[20] Naturally, these claims tended to spawn a considerable interpretive literature, which does not seem to have done much to clear up their many obscurities. One very obvious area of obscurity is expressed in the question whether the disputes mentioned by these early writers – disputes about art, Christianity, democracy and morality, for example – are really disputes about concepts at all. Might they not be just quarrels about the uses of words? How, in any case, was an essentially contestable concept to be distinguished from those that are essentially corrigible? (Might not the identification of essentially contestable concepts as such take us into areas of essential contestability?) Further, if some concepts or terms are inherently liable to generate intractable dispute while others are merely ambiguous or confused or just happen contingently to be matters of dispute, what is it that accounts for this difference?

It is this last question that is particularly germane to my inquiry. It has already been suggested that there are no very forceful reasons for tracing the disputability of the terms of social thought back to their uses in promoting rival moral and political commitments. The result of my analysis of the Lukes–Connolly perspective on power, however, has been that two incommensurable perspectives on power are left in the field, each (the voluntarist and the structuralist) carrying with it a specific framework of explanation. Given that it seems extremely implausible that any purely empirical deliberation might settle the issue between these two perspectives, what kind of considerations could be decisive? The situation seems even worse on further reflection. If these perspectives really are incommensurable, it seems odd to say that they have any common subject-matter: perhaps what we have is indeed meaning-variance rather than competition in the use of a shared vocabulary. Perhaps, it has been suggested,[21] an incoherence in the idea of essential contestability reveals itself at this point. For, apart from the fact that realist discourse about essences seems at variance with the conventionalist presuppositions and implications of essential contestability, there seems to be a radical fault in the very notion of a contest which cannot by its nature be won or lost. If the essential contestability of a concept or of a term flows inexorably from some aspects of its subject-matter, how can useful argument proceed about the use of the term in contention that is on balance to be adopted?

I do not see any of *these* obscurities as erecting insuperable obstacles to criticizing the two perspective on power, or as detracting from what the writers on power I have discussed call the essential contestability of ideas and judgements about power. Whether these disputes are semantic or conceptual in character, they involve a pragmatic competition in which conflicting demands are made on ordinary thought and practice and on the disposition of resources for research. Further, the point at which my analysis of the Lukes–Connolly approach was broken off itself suggests how commitments standing at a terminal level of justification within the theory of power may yet be criticizable at another level. Each of the perspectives I have distinguished intimates a philosophical anthropology – a moral psychology and a philosophy of mind and action – in terms of which it may be criticized. Social theories invariably repose on some such philosophical standpoints, and it is this dependency which accounts for one aspect of their permanent vulnerability to contestation and openness to questioning.

Consider in this connection one variant of the structuralist approach to power – that elaborated in structural-Marxist writings. The central area of difficulty in all such accounts has been indicated obliquely by Hindess and Hirst in the comment that

> there is as yet no systematically elaborated theory of the political level to compare with the Marxist analysis of the economic level of the capitalist mode of production.[22]

The difficulty hinted at here is that, in developing a systematic account of ideology and of superstructural phenomena such as the capitalist state, the structuralist cannot avoid invoking some of the assumptions of a 'humanist' anthropology which the terms of his account of social structure compel him or her to reject. These anthropological assumptions, officially suppressed by structuralist thought but presupposed by some of its main theses, are to do chiefly with the complex capacities and attitudes necessarily possessed by role-bearers in post-traditional (and, perhaps, also in traditional) societies. A worker who enters into a wage contract, for example, must be capable of understanding a whole set of internally complex background notions, the possession of which gives him or her the capacity to form alternative concepts and beliefs about his or her circumstance in society. If a worker understands his or her situation well enough to discharge the roles assigned to him or her in a capitalist (or a socialist) society, then the worker has the capacity to imagine himself or herself situated in a very different social landscape.[23]

It will immediately be objected that it is precisely the function of ideology so to constrain the political reflection of workers (and others) that it remains at the level of ideology and false consciousness. To say this, however, is entirely to miss the point. For it is precisely the human capacity of critically transcending one's immediate social circumstances that generates the necessity – which, according to Althusser, will remain a feature even of Communist society – for ideological beliefs which restrict the scope of such reflection. What I am claiming is that the myopically deterministic account of human reflection encapsulated in structural-Marxist thought disables its advocates from developing any remotely plausible theory of social consciousness. Nor do I forget the self-criticisms of Althusser's more recent writings, or the revisions made to structural Marxism by his disciples Etienne Balibar and Jacques Ranciére. None of these saves the structuralist-Marxist project from failure. To acknowledge that human thought and social relations are reflexive, that is to say, that reflection on the conditions of our thought changes those conditions in that it modifies the beliefs and attitudes by which they are constituted, imposes upon us the task of elaborating a philosophical anthropology in which these distinctively human powers are explored. The metaphysical reasonings by which such an anthropology will be supported are bound to have an inherently controversial character, but this is not to say that criticism is altogether out of place here. In this instance, it is to note the latent positivism of those Marxists in the structuralist tradition who are committed to the self-defeating project of elaborating a rationalist science of society which is supposed to be able to do without a metaphysic of human nature.

My argument is that structural-Marxist theory about power and social structure incorporates a philosophical anthropology at odds with official structuralist commitments. These later commitments, in turn, I suspect, could be shown to be at odds with the anthropological postulates of our ordinary thought and practice. At no point is my argument intended to be conclusive or demonstrative. It is taken for granted that in discussing questions in the philosophy of mind and action we are in an area of metaphysical uncertainty where what are at stake are only more or less well-defended statements of opinion. As Stuart Hampshire has put it:

> No critical philosopher can not believe that an inquiry into the concept of man, and therefore into that which constitutes a good man, is the search for an immutable essence. He will rather think of any definition or elucidation of the concept as a reasoned proposal that different types of appraisal should be distinguished from each other in accordance with disputable principles derived from a disputable philosophy of mind. He will admit that this is the domain of philosophical opinion, and not of demonstration.[24]

One major source of intractable dispute in social theory (and in moral theory) is its connection with areas of metaphysical uncertainty explored in questions in the philosophy of mind and action. Dispute is interminable in social theory, in part because it slides irresistibly into dispute in philosophy, and there we have the defence of opinion and not demonstration. At any moment in discussion, one stand in social theory may well be better supported, better defended than others in the field: others (such as the structural-Marxist view I have criticized) may do badly. This characterization of criticism in social theory shows that acknowledging the inherently controversial aspects of social concepts may be combined with affirming the criticizability of social theories.

I have not suggested that intractable dispute in social theory is always an expression of conflicts in philosophy. It has another source in the underdetermination of social theory by evidence. That this is so ought to be clear from my discussion of the methodological difficulties faced by the Lukes–Connolly account. The decision procedure proposed for the identification of power relations is not just counterfactual in method, but doubly so:

power relations exist if people's interests would conflict under certain circumstances, and their interests are a subclass of the preferences they would display in a condition of relative autonomy. This approach commits Lukes and Connolly to an extraordinarily arduous testing procedure. Apart from all the difficulties involved in assessing degrees of autonomy where this is regarded as a complex achievement having distinct and diverse elements, the method seems to have an aspect of circularity: we test for power by hypothesizing what an autonomous agent would do, but we know that an agent is autonomous only if we first know the agent's power situation. Lukes's suggestion[25] that we study circumstances of social breakdown and disorder for evidence of people's latent interests is no help here: such social conditions, typically conditions where demagogy and crowd psychology are important factors, seem peculiarly ill-suited for the purpose. The Lukes–Connolly approach seems wanting if its empirical usefulness and testability are seen as including its capacity to yield falsifiable predictions and retrodictions.

These difficulties are plainly only one instance of a greater problem in any project for a science of society. Many of the evidences going into any such science will be matters of historical interpretation, and large-scale social experiments will rarely, if ever, be conclusive, owing to the impossibility of isolating distorting variables. Most crucially, however, a science of society comes up against a problem having to do with its public character. Evidence tends to elude the social-scientific investigator, if only because the latter's subjects tend to react to the categorial framework of interpretation which the investigations impose on their activities. There is this contrast of social science with natural science, that its subject-matter is people's notions and beliefs and these are worked over reflexively, both by the investigator and by the subjects in response to the investigator. I am far from attempting to dismiss in aprioristic Winchian fashion any project for a scientific study of society: at microsocial level, as Milgram's study of authority and obedience and Laing's studies of the family suggest,[26] studies satisfying fairly rigorous standards may be deeply instructive. But the reflexive relations between social-scientific investigation, human beliefs and the objects of the social world should confine the prospects of such study within very narrow limits. In the natural sciences, as in the social studies, available evidence may be compatible with a range of theories whose implications are themselves incompatible; but the social studies have the extra disability that crucial experiments are rarely, if ever, practically feasible.

It may be time to try and tie together the loose ends of my inquiry and to assess the bearing of its results on the prospects of social theory. I began by making the observation that disputes in the theory of power have been widely and not unreasonably interpreted as expressive of deeper differences over the merits of a positivist philosophy of social science. We can now see that this interpretation has validity only with important qualifications. If the ideal of value-freedom in social thought is one test of positivism, our conclusion must be that nothing in Lukes's or Connolly's writings on power impeaches this tenet of positivism: so far as we have been able to discern, this Weberian standard of scientific rigour in the social studies remains uncompromised. Persisting relativity in social science has two sources in the underdetermination of theory by evidence and the dependency of theory on metaphysical commitment. These aspects of the limitation of social thought should incline us to a Pyrrhonian humility about our own social theorizing and encourage us in scepticism about any large claims for social thought. I cannot see that these insights into the limitation of social thought warrant description in the inflated idiom of essential contestability.

The writings of Lukes and Connolly retain great heuristic (and pedagogic) interest in disclosing two radically divergent paths of development for social thought. One, associated with an open conception of autonomy, a non-cognitivist moral epistemology and a fallibilist and conventionalist methodology, supports a recognizably Weberian conception of social theory. It has no direct bearing on conduct, but in its commendation of impartiality as an intellectual virtue and its frank recognition of the diversity and internal conflicts of human values it may have some affinity with a tradition of justifying argument in liberalism. The other, bound up with a closed view of autonomy, a form of moral objectivism and a method of real definition, is familiar from Marxist projects for a social science. Here the scientific study of society, because it is supposed to reveal necessary laws of social development, has a directly practical motive. It is such a conception which is supported by the constant emphasis in both Lukes and Connolly on the supposed fraudulence of the distinction between fact and value in social theory and by their attribution to social theory of an ineradicable political dimension. Nothing in recent writing *justifies* the attribution to social theory of this political or practical character, and even the thesis of the essential contestability of social concepts may be impoverished by it.

The current of writings on power and related concepts in which theses about essential contestability or conceptual relativism are deployed has had the virtue of strengthening the sceptical spirit in social thought and of undermining dogmatic and absolutist claims. But, if social thought is not to be lost in a no man's land of political controversy, its practical character needs to be denied and its direct links with moral and political life severed. We need to be able once again to assert with confidence that, however meagre its result in increased insight, social theory has no warrant for existence save in the pursuit of understanding.

16 An epitaph for liberalism

If there is a single characteristic that typifies liberal political philosophy in the United States over the past quarter century, it is its domination by a jurisprudential paradigm. Complex questions about restraint of liberty – such questions as the control of pornography, and the termination of life in abortion and euthanasia – that in other countries, and other traditions of liberal discourse, are treated as issues in legislative policy, involving a balance of interests and sometimes a compromise of ideals, have come to be treated in the United States, primarily or exclusively, as questions of fundamental rights. The model of reasoning presupposed in this turn to legalism in recent American theory is that of the judicial interpretation of constitutional rights rather than of the formulation of public policy in political discourse. In its subtler articulations, such as the later works of John Rawls, the juristic model for liberal theorizing has been substantially qualified by the recognition that it is applicable only to a subclass of constitutional democracies (perhaps comprising only the United States), and still cannot decide all vital issues in political controversy about the legal restraint of liberty. Yet, even the Rawlsian project of specifying a set of fixed and determinate liberties exemplifies the legalist illusion that animates recent liberal thought in America.

The legalist turn in recent American liberal thought has had predictably deleterious consequences – ones that would not have surprised the authors of the *Federalist Papers*. In political contexts, it has generated a series of intractable conflicts, which portend deepening division, growing ungovernability and even a sort of chronic, low-intensity civil war in the United States. Of these conflicts the abortion question is only the most obvious, but it serves well enough to illustrate the fateful implication for political practice of the hegemony of the paradigm of a rights-based jurisprudence that has been inflated by the inordinate claims of liberal theorizing – that, since conflicts of fundamental rights cannot be moderated, their judicial interpretation can mean only unconditional victory or complete surrender for the protagonists to the dispute. This is not a recipe for civic peace, or for a stable liberal civil society.

In intellectual contexts, the dominance of legalism within liberal thought has debauched standards of argument. Taken by themselves, neither the terms of fundamental rights theory, such as they are, nor the provisions of the American Constitution give any definite answer to current questions about abortion, pornography or similar issues. In recent American liberal theory on the legalist model, the vacuities of rights theory and the indeterminacy of the Constitution have been remedied by the adoption of a conventionalist stratagem in which the ephemeral banalities of liberal academic culture – affirmative action, or the arcana of antisexism – are read into the constitution, and then elevated to the status of universal verities. It is probably an inevitable upshot of liberal legalism of this sort that it should represent the local (or parochial) knowledge of its practitioners – shifting and hardly very determinate as it is in the work of Ronald Dworkin and Bruce Ackerman, for example – as a repository of universal truths.

Joel Feinberg's four-volume study *The Moral Limits of the Criminal Law*[1] breaks with this legalism in order to revert to an older, saner, if in the end radically flawed tradition – that of John Stuart Mill. It is not an extended exercise on the jurisprudential model, but instead a study of the moral constraints on law-making, addressed to a hypothetical ideal legislator. The first thing that must be said of Feinberg's work is that it is the exemplary statement of Millian liberalism as it applies to the legal limitation of liberty: it is comprehensive, systematic, argued with a rigour and scrupulousness unmatched, let alone surpassed, in any comparable study.

These exemplary standards were set in Feinberg's first volume, *Harm to Others*.[2] There, he distinguished between a non-normative conception of harm as setback to interest, and a normative conception of harm as wrongful conduct in which a person's rights are violated; and went on to make a host of important and useful distinctions in which moral harm, vicarious harm, posthumous and prenatal harm, and other harm cases were analysed and their content specified. Feinberg's minute and illuminating taxonomy of the notions of harm and interests aims to give Mill's famous 'one very simple principle' – the principle that no one's liberty may be restrained, except to prevent harm to others – a definite sense sufficient at least for its use in contexts of legal policy-making, but it is far from clear that it resolves successfully the chief problems confronted by anyone who seeks to make practical use of Mill's principle in legislation.

Feinberg interprets the harm principle as forbidding restraint of liberty, save where there is harm to others' interests, and these latter are interests that constitute a valid claim to a moral right. In this he is faithful to Mill himself, and to Mill's best twentieth-century interpreters, such as J. C. Rees. No more than Mill or Rees, however, does Feinberg give any clear or compelling account of the relations between having an interest, making a valid claim, and possessing a moral right. He tells us that any interest may generate a valid claim, and so a moral right, except vicious and wicked interests, 'if such there can be'. Aside from the question how we are to determine the wickedness of interests, it is clear that the world of moral rights will be a densely populated and quarrelling one, since the multitude of interests, often making competing claims on action, which each of us has, will spawn a host of conflicting rights. Whereas Feinberg recognizes this to be a difficulty in the application of Mill's principle as he interprets it, he seems to underestimate greatly the extent to which it diminishes the utility of the harm principle as a guide to legislation. In Mill, the difficulty is resolved, at least in theory, inasmuch as the deficiencies of the harm principle as a guide to action are remedied by appeal to the demands of the Principle of Utility itself. For, in both Mill and Feinberg, the harm principle specifies only a necessary condition of justified liberty-limitation: it tells us, not what we ought to do, but what we *may* do in restraining liberty.

Feinberg's case is, in truth, worse than Mill's, inasmuch as he lacks even the fall-back position of appealing to the requirements of welfarist conse-quentialism as a guide to action once the harm principle has been satisfied. He avoids the illiberal possibilities of Mill's position, in which large and inequitable restraints on the liberty of minorities could be sanctioned by the prevention of small but widespread harms to large numbers of people, but only at the price of leaving us with no way of weighing competing interests or arbitrating the conflicting rights that they yield. Feinberg's account is not saddled with the burden of a wholesale maximizing consequentialism, with all the illiberal implications that creates in the application of the harm principle. For that very reason, however, and because Feinberg deliberately refrains from embedding the harm principle in a more comprehensive moral theory, his attempt to give a content to the principle in terms of the redundant jargon of moral rights is thoroughly unpersuasive.

The larger project pursued in volumes two to four is that of defending the Liberal Position, which is that 'The harm and offence principles, duly clarified and qualified, between them exhaust the class of good reasons for criminal prohibitions'.[3] The Liberal Position then states an exclusionary principle, ruling out (as good reasons for legal coercion) such other prin-ciples as legal paternalism, legal moralism, and perfectionism. Like *Harm to Others*, *Offence to Others* argues that there are both normative and non-normative uses of 'offence', with only the former, wrongful offence being intended in the offence principle, which lays down that

It is always a good reason in support of a proposed criminal prohibition that it is necessary to prevent serious offence to persons other than the actor and would be an effective means to that end if enacted.[4]

Feinberg develops a powerful argument to the conclusion that offences that are harmless may nevertheless sometimes be subject to legal prohibition, making extensive use of the model of nuisance law, but recognizing the inadequacy of that model for what he calls 'profound offences', in which the offended person experiences offence, not only or primarily to his own feelings, but to values that are conceived to be independent of his feelings.

In the course of his analytical survey, Feinberg investigates the role of consent in relation to offensive subjects, the place of the *Volenti* standard ('one cannot be wronged by that to which one consents') and the character of pornography and obscenity. *Harm to Self* addresses the principle of legal paternalism – that

It is always a good and relevant (though not necessarily decisive) reason in support of a criminal prohibition that it will prevent harm (physical, psychological or economic) to the actor himself.[5]

Feinberg defends this antipaternalist injunction by reference to the personal sovereignty and right to autonomy of the individual – considerations at once impeccably Millian in pedigree and at the same time eminently questionable. He distinguishes between 'soft' and 'hard' paternalism, defending the former, which mandates coercive state intervention with dangerous self-regarding behaviour only when that behaviour is substantially non-voluntary, or when temporary intervention is necessary to establish whether it is voluntary or not, as 'properly speaking, no kind of paternalism at all'.

As well as this liberal argument for soft paternalism, *Harm to Self* incorporates penetrating analyses of various riddles of voluntariness, such as reasonable assumption of risk, failures of consent (as in coercive pressures and offers), defective belief and incapacity. The final volume, *Harmless Wrongdoing*, treats issues of legal moralism, moral conservatism, the relations of autonomy and community, and legal perfectionism (legal coercion for the promotion of excellence or virtue). Feinberg again tries to argue for the Liberal Position that harm and offence to others are the only considerations that are always good reasons for criminalization of behaviour, while maintaining that the damage to tradition, community or virtue flowing from adherence to this position has been exaggerated by critics of liberalism, or is a cost that must be borne for the sake of preserving personal autonomy and sovereignty.

With admirable candour, Feinberg acknowledges that the theory that emerged from his investigations is not at all the 'one very simple principle' which Mill advanced in *On Liberty*, but 'a much more complicated construction'. He goes so far, indeed as to admit in the conclusion to the final volume that 'As things now stand, liberalism as strictly defined in this work is not only not plausible, it is quite clearly not true'.[6] At this point, Feinberg is inclined to fall back on a view of liberalism as simply a presumption in favour of liberty, from which it follows that 'Liberalism, however it is further specified, is a matter of degree, depending on how great a surcharge the liberal would impose on the reasons that can outweigh liberty.'[7]

In this last formulation, Feinberg allows to the Liberal Position an indeterminacy he seeks to attenuate by the assertion that personal sovereignty has an absolute weight, trumping any interest that might support legal coercion with the self-regarding domain. It is this stand on anti-paternalism, as upon a last redoubt, that qualifies his definitive judgement that, contrary to the original intent of his study, 'the most plausible liberalism' allows that

> All of the major coercion-legitimising principles (the harm and offence principles, legal paternalism, legal moralism) and subprinciples (e.g. moral conservatism, strict moralism, the exploitation principle, legal perfectionism) state reasons that are at least sometimes relevant (to the justification of restraint of liberty). I would now go so far as to say that they all state reasons that are *always* relevant, though usually of very slight weight.[8]

It is evident from these statements that, in the course of writing this superb series of volumes, Feinberg's intellectual virtues of rigour and honesty have compelled him to abandon the Liberal Position with which he began. His final position is worse than that. There is nothing in the final volume against legal moralism, conservatism and perfectionism, that justifies the infinite or absolute weight Feinberg assigns to personal sovereignty. After all, on any view that accepts a diversity of ultimate values, or which accepts that the human interest in sovereignty or autonomy will be only one interest among many, personal sovereignty will *not* always trump all the rest. The only argument Feinberg offers for the absolutist status of personal sovereignty is that

> without this supplementary feature liberalism will be fatally vulnerable, that it will condone illiberal claims on ultimately liberal grounds.[9]

This argument is not only weak because it will appeal only to already committed liberals or because it is dubiously consistent with Feinberg's looser definition of liberalism in terms of a generally defeasible presumption in favour of liberty. It weakens his position by suggesting that, once liberal thought has reached the degree of sophistication it has in his elaboration of the Millian paradigm, it has a self-defeating effect.

The self-effacement of liberalism that is evident in the closing chapters of Feinberg's work, and which follows upon the ruin of his original project, results from the pluralist insight – profoundly developed in the thought of Isaiah Berlin – that a wide diversity of considerations is relevant to questions about the restraint of liberty, none of them always trumping the rest. This pluralist standpoint is strengthened when it as acknowledged that the promotion of personal autonomy, for example, may depend on the existence of a public or common culture, which presents to the agent an array of worthwhile options. The preservation of such a culture may, however, commit the law to moralist and perfectionist policies of sorts which Feinberg is bound to oppose. They will be not just non-coercive policies of subsidy or education, which are beyond the scope of Feinberg's argument, but (sometimes, at least) policies of legal prohibition. (Where they can be made effective, and are not too costly in other terms, policies of criminalization of extremely addictive drugs probably come into this category.) Again, concern for the autonomy of the agent may well justify measures of this kind, independently of their contribution to the preservation of common culture within which worthwhile choices can be made. A pluralist will accept, with a doctrinal liberal even à la Feinberg must resist, that promotion of liberal values such as autonomy sometimes encompasses adoption of policies that are illiberal in that they curb personal sovereignty. Like any other ingredient in human well-being, autonomy is an interest that is sometimes best enhanced when it is limited – and which has as its matrix conditions that constrain it.

The self-effacement of liberalism, manifest in Feinberg's study, is peculiar to the Millian tradition his book exemplifies. It is apparent in Joseph Raz's great book *The Morality of Freedom*,[10] in which the salience to restraint of liberty of paternalist and perfectionist principles, the indispensable contribution to personal autonomy made by a public culture, and the impossibility of State neutrality in respect of the promotion of virtue and the positive realization of human capacities are given a demonstrative statement. In Raz's case, liberalism effaces itself by way of an immanent critique in which liberal society emerges in the end as only one among a variety of orders in which human beings may flourish. In both thinkers, whose works together constitute the high-water mark of recent liberal theorizing, the project of giving liberalism a universally compelling foundation has been abandoned, and the attempt to formulate definitive and uniquely determinate liberty-limiting principles given up or severely qualified. Foundationless and virtually contentless, liberalism has then the aspect of the Cheshire Cat, becoming the vanishing spectre of a once-living doctrine.

It is a tribute to Feinberg's study that, by contrast with those who seek in the empty slogans of equality or fundamental rights to give liberalism a content derived solely from the trivia of recent academic debate, he should have returned liberal theory to a judicious and dispassionate consideration of substantive issues. If his study should prove to be an epitaph on Millian liberalism or yet another example of liberalism's self-effacement, it remains a colossal achievement, definitive and magisterial, a book which makes a permanent contribution to legal and political philosophy.

17 The end of history – or of liberalism?

It is a truism that socialism is dead, and an irony that it survives most robustly as a doctrine not in Paris, where it has suffered a fate worse than falsification by becoming thoroughly unfashionable, nor in London, where it has been abandoned by the Labour Party, but in the universities of capitalist America, as the ideology of the American academic *nomenklatura*. But socialism is most obviously, and most irreversibly, defunct as an ideology in the Communist bloc. There, *glasnost* has surpassed the wildest hopes of Western anti-Communists in discrediting the institutions of central planning and brilliantly illuminating the intractable problems of the Soviet system.

But what does the collapse of socialism as a political faith portend for the future of political life and thought? In a provocative and well-received article, 'The End of History',[1] Francis Fukuyama announces in a quietly apocalyptic voice that the failure of socialism means

> an unabashed victory of economic and political liberalism [and he promises] the end point of mankind's ideological evolution and the universalization of Western liberal democracy as the final form of human government.

The prophecy that human history is about to end and a new historical epoch about to begin is of course a recurrent one in the history of Western thought. It is probably an unintended irony that Fukuyama's article should stand as a contribution to the project of a secular theodicy first undertaken by the *philosophes* of the French Enlightenment, but most notably and energetically pursued in the Marxian system of thought which Fukuyama correctly perceives to be now in a terminal decline. But it is in any case difficult to understand the basis for Fukuyama's confidence about the historic role of liberal democracy in bringing history to a successful close. His confidence cannot be a reflection of the state of liberal political philosophy, since that is manifestly parlous. In my recent book, *Liberalisms:*

Essays in Political Philosophy,[2] and particularly in its Postscript, 'After Liberalism', I have argued that despite its overwhelming dominance in Anglo–American philosophy, liberalism has never succeeded in showing that liberal democratic institutions are uniquely necessary to justice and the human good. In all its varieties – utilitarian, contractarian, or as a theory of rights – liberal political philosophy has failed to establish its fundamental thesis: that liberal democracy is the only form of human government that can be sanctioned by reason and morality. It therefore fails to give rational support to the political religion of the contemporary intelligentsia, which combines the sentimental cult of humanity with a sectarian passion for political reform.

The consequent debacle of liberal political philosophy is not something we have any reason to lament. For liberals are committed to the heroic enterprise of denying a very obvious truth – the truth that there is a legitimate variety of forms of government under which human beings have flourished and may still hope to prosper. Who can doubt that human beings flourished under the feudal institutions of medieval Christendom? Or under the monarchical government of Elizabethan England? It is in virtue of its repression of this evident truth that liberal discourse has acquired its stridency and intolerance – indeed, its almost obsessional character. In seeking to construct a liberal ideology, liberal theorists are attempting what even they must sometimes see to be impossible. They are struggling to confer the imprimatur of universal authority on the local practices they have inherited. The absurdity of this project has, indeed, been tacitly recognized by one of this century's subtler liberal thinkers, John Rawls, when in his later work he revealed that he aims only to give a coherent philosophical statement of the character and premises of a particular historical tradition – the (American?) tradition of constitutional democracy.

If Fukuyama's confident expectation of the End cannot be explained by the state of liberal philosophy, from what does it derive? It is the expression, most likely, not of a political philosophy, but of a philosophy of history, one dominated by the notion that liberal democracy is history's *telos*, other modes of government being recognized only as progressions toward, or aberrations from, that end.

The grain of truth in this interpretation of history is that it is only through the development of civil society – a society in which most institutions, though protected by law, are independent of the state – that a modern civilization can reproduce itself. Without those institutions – for example, private property and contractual liberty under the rule of law – modern societies invariably undergo a descent into poverty and barbarism. Civil society is the matrix of the market economy, which both history and theory show to be the precondition of prosperity and liberty in the modern world.

This is a truth that even the Soviet leadership may now be learning, after having waged for over seventy years an incessant war on all the civil societies that have come within its sphere of domination. It is one that the Iranian fundamentalists are beginning to accept, however grudgingly, as they retreat from the position that a modern state can be governed exclusively through the precepts of the Islamic *sharyah*. And it is a truth that will become painfully clear to the aged Stalinists of Communist China, when they are forced by circumstances to perceive the economic ruin that flows from trying to confine an emergent civil society in a newly re-sewn totalitarian straitjacket.

To say that no modern state can renew itself with a decent degree of prosperity unless it contains the institutions of a civil society is, however, very far from allowing that liberal democracy is 'the final form of human government'. Civil societies come in many shapes and forms and thrive under a variety of regimes. The authoritarian civil societies of East Asia – South Korea, Taiwan, and Singapore – have combined an extraordinary record of economic success with the protection of most individual liberties under the rule of law without adopting all the elements of liberal democracy.

Or consider the case of Japan, which Fukuyama's mentor, the Hegelian scholar Alexandre Kojève, rightly recognized as the key exception to the trend of global homogenization. To be sure, Japan has become a consumerist culture, and its political institutions are liberal democratic. Yet the crucial decades of modernization in Japan occurred in the late nineteenth and early twentieth centuries; modernization was generated internally and was not imposed from outside; and, uniquely, the Japanese succeeded in grafting on to the unbroken stem of a traditional culture the institutions of a modern civil society. As a result, Japan has in the last two decades emerged as a global economic superpower, and must willy-nilly (whether it wishes to do so or not) become a superpower *tout court* in the coming century. This has been achieved without any deep commitment to the constitution imposed upon Japan at the end of the Second World War, and certainly without the support of the ideas and values that are supposed to undergird market institutions in the West, such as individualism, universalism, natural rights, Judeo–Christianity, or the idea of progress.

The East Asian examples show that Western achievements can be reproduced, and for that matter surpassed, without any acceptance of 'the Western idea' of which Fukuyama speaks when he refers to 'the triumph of the West'. The ongoing disintegration of Communism on the Soviet model gives Fukuyama's argument no better support. The avowed aim of the twin Soviet reform policies of *perestroika* and *glasnost* is to break the totalitarian mold and reconstitute a civil society. Even if it is successful, however, the Soviet reform policy is unlikely to result in a triumph of Western liberalism. To attempt to foretell the future cost of Gorbachev's reform policy is idle. Already, however, *glasnost* has to its credit a considerable achievement. It has revealed for all time the ruins of the totalitarian project initiated by Lenin in 1917. This is the project, intimated in Lenin's horrible saying, 'We must be engineers of souls', of destroying the traditional identities of the human beings within its power and reconstructing them as specimens of the new socialist humanity. Prosecuted relentlessly and without mercy for over two generations in an incessant war against religion, the family and nationality, this totalitarian project has been shown by *glasnost* to have been a stupendous failure. As they emerge from the shadows of totalitarianism, the peoples of the Soviet Union reveal themselves, not as specimens of socialist (or liberal) humanity, but as Ukrainians or Balts, Catholics or Muslims, bearing traditional identities in no way compromised by decades of totalitarian indoctrination. The forms of national and religious life that are reasserting themselves in the Soviet Union give the lie to the totalitarian idea (echoed by innumerable Western liberals) that human beings can be remodelled according to the dictates of rationalist ideology. If anything, the traditional identities of the peoples of the Soviet Union may be healthier than those in many Western nations, where subtler forms of indoctrination have had a more corrosive effect in rendering traditional forms of life decadent.

It is precisely because the revelations of *glasnost* give the lie to the totalitarian project of reshaping human nature that they also confound Fukuyama's account. If the newly self-assertive peoples of the Soviet bloc are not specimens of *Homo sovieticus*, neither do their political beliefs have anything in common with the rationalist and egalitarian liberalism which has dominated American life for fifty years. They are defined, and define themselves, not primarily as buyers and sellers in markets, nor as abstract bearers of rights and entitlements, but in terms of their membership in a nation or a church. They may share a common longing for emancipation from the Soviet system, but that is all they share. Each of the subject peoples in the Soviet bloc harbours particular claims, territorial or otherwise in character, which sets it in conflict with the rest. It is for this reason that the waning of the Soviet system is bound to be accompanied by a waxing of ethnic and nationalist conflicts – just the sort of stuff history has always been made of. These conflicts are, in part, undoubtedly a legacy of Stalinism, since it was Stalin who ruthlessly dislocated entire peoples and relocated them without regard to their history or traditions. But these conflicts also embody age-old enmities and loyalties, which are now coming back to the surface after decades totalitarian suppression. What we are witnessing in the Soviet Union is not, then, the end of history, but instead its resumption – and on decidedly traditional lines.

All the evidence suggests that we are now moving back into an epoch that is classically historical, and not forward into the empty, hallucinatory post-historical era projected in Fukuyama's article. Ours is an era in which political ideology, liberal as much as Marxist, has a rapidly dwindling leverage on events, and more ancient, more primordial forces, nationalist and religious, fundamentalist and soon, perhaps, Malthusian, are contesting with each other. In retrospect, it may well appear that it was the static, polarized period of ideology, the period between the end of the First World War and the present, that was the aberration.

If the Soviet Union does indeed fall apart, that beneficent catastrophe will not inaugurate a new era of post-historical harmony, but instead a return to the classical terrain of history, a terrain of great-power rivalries, secret diplomacies, and irredentist claims and wars. The vision of perpetual peace among liberal states, which has haunted Western thought at least since it was given systematic formulation by Immanuel Kant, will soon be seen for what it always was – a mirage that serves only to distract us from the real business of statesmanship in a permanently intractable and anarchic world.

Fukuyama's brilliant and thoughtful argument is a symptom of the hegemonic power of liberalism in American thought. So ubiquitously pervasive are liberal ideas and assumptions in American intellectual life, and such is their constraining power over public discourse, that it sometimes seems barely possible to formulate a thought that is not liberal, let alone to express it freely. The domination of the American mind by liberal ideology has fostered blind spots in American perception of the real world that have been immensely disabling for policy.

The fetish of open government, as symbolized in the Freedom of Information Act, congressional oversight, and the respectability given to leaking, prevents the United States from ever again engaging in any major covert operation. The domination of public life by the power of the invasive media calls into serious question the capacity of the United States to wage any war larger, more protracted, or with significantly heavier casualties, than the invasion of Grenada. Liberal egalitarianism in education, coupled with absurd and counterproductive affirmative-action programmes, has resulted in a de-skilling of America that is awesome in magnitude. (Consider that, whereas at age six Japanese and American children have roughly similar mathematical abilities, at age 18 the average Japanese child has the mathematical competence of the top 1 per cent of American children.)

In many other areas, liberal ideology has in America proved itself to be the enemy rather than the friend of civil society. In its expression in radical feminism and in affirmative-action policy liberalism has sanctioned the invasion of privacy, the curtailment of freedom of association and the erosion of contractual liberty. Because of the ravages wreaked on civil society by liberal ideology America already has a more bureaucratized and regulated, less tolerant, more divided, and more statist society than virtually any other modern democracy, squandering the historical patrimony of civil society on which American pre-eminence in the world rested. Liberal ideology guarantees blindness to the dangers that liberalism has itself brought about. In sum, the danger for America is that, confronted with comparative and soon, perhaps, absolute economic decline, an uncontrollable crime epidemic, and weak or paralysed political institutions, it will drift further and further into isolation and disorder. At the worst, America faces a metamorphosis into a sort of proto-Brazil, with the status of an ineffectual regional power rather than a global superpower.

In general, all speculations about the future are riddled with hazards. Michael Oakeshott, the English conservative philosopher, has written that we know as much about where history is leading us as we do about future fashions in hats. There are, perhaps, only two things of which one may be reasonably sure. The first is that the days of liberalism are numbered. Especially as it governs policy in the United States, liberalism is ill-equipped to deal with the new dilemmas of a world in which ancient allegiances and enmities are reviving on a large scale.

We know this much at least: history will not end with the passing of liberalism, any more than with the collapse of Communism. The second thing we know for sure is that we have no reason whatever to expect that our future will be markedly different from our past. As we have known it, human history is a succession of contingencies, catastrophes and occasional lapses into peace and civilization. If this is the case, there is at least one misfortune that we will surely be spared – the melancholy and boredom that is evoked by the prospect of the end of history.

October, 1989

Part III
Questions

18 The politics of cultural diversity

In 1946, the subtle and neglected Hungarian philosopher Aurel Kolnai wrote of the Habsburg Empire:

> Imperial Austria, like Switzerland, notwithstanding the numerical disproportion of their different nationalities, did not have 'minorities' because they had no ruling nation'.[1]

I begin my reflections with this thought, since it seems to me to embody a possible solution to a problem which besets much contemporary political thought and practice. The problem I have in mind may be defined, provisionally at least, by a question: What are the political forms best suited to a condition of society marked by substantial cultural diversity? This question ought to arise naturally, when we consider the novelty of our condition.

Almost all of us live in societies which are not unified by any single cultural tradition, but which contain a variety of traditions and ways of life. Our great cities shelter vast enclaves of traditional life, often introduced by recent immigrants, at the same time as they nurture liberal bohemian milieux where conduct is governed by taste and preference rather than by any set of established mores. Within most modern states, we find forms of family life based on romantic love and on arranged marriage. We meet, each of us in his daily life, those for whom religious faith pervades their sense of life, and those for whom it is a barely intelligible irrelevance. Our societies encompass a kaleidoscopic diversity of attitudes to sexuality and gender, death and the human condition, even as they harbour a prodigious diversity of ethnic inheritances and styles of life. It is this condition, in which society intimates a diversity of possibly incommensurable values and world-views, which is often characterized as cultural pluralism, which I believe ought to be at the top of the political agenda of modern states. Yet, though the fact of cultural diversity is noted often enough, its political implications are rarely explored. We find the reason for this strange neglect, I believe, in a doctrine that is held in common by most modern political thought. It is this modern doctrine, or heresy – the heresy that political orders ought to embody or express the cultural identity of homogeneous moral communities – which I seek to attack and undermine in the course of developing these reflections.

At the most abstract and fundamental level, the question I am addressing has to do with how the human subject is to be conceived, and what are the implications for political order of a well-founded conception of the subject. On the negative or critical side, my concern is to expose and overturn a presupposition about the human subject which is held in common by the political theories which dominate the contemporary scene. It is an assumption about human identity or subjecthood which animates all the dominant forms of liberalism, conservatism and socialism, which I wish to stigmatize as erroneous in theory and pernicious in practice. This assumption – the assumption that the varieties of human identity, if they are not altogether constructions of political practice, ought nevertheless to be mirrored or imprinted in the central institutions of political order – is made in varying ways in the different political perspectives in which it is found.

In some perspectives, the role of political institutions is to shore up tottering identities, to heal the scars inflicted on established traditions by cultural change, whereas in others the project is that of constituting new identities by the use of political power. The project of constituting new forms of human identity through political practice is, indeed, the pre-eminent contemporary form of this modern heresy, and it is found in many current varieties of liberalism. It finds its starkest and crudest form in Marxism, however, and, above all, in the species of Marxism contrived with opportunistic genius by Lenin. For Marx, as for Lenin and all of Marx's followers, the historical forms of human identity, as they are expressed in inherited cultures' traditions and folkways, are in no way to be taken as authentic expressions of human nature and creativity. Instead, all the forms of life in which human beings have hitherto found their identities are condemned as contingencies, shadows cast by underlying structures of production. In this reductionist perspective, all the varied cultural achievements of mankind are epiphenomena, transitory reflections of changes in the economic base of human society. With this much (or little) we are all familiar. But the positive, and mythological aspect of Marxian historical materialism,[2] is less obvious, and less commonly commented upon. It is the Marxian conception of true or essential human nature as being hidden and submerged, thwarted and mutilated by all the historic forms in which human beings have ever lived.

Now in the real world of human history, men are not abstract instances of the human species, but articulators of definite ways of life that reflect their circumstances and at once express and confer on them a distinctive identity. Marxian Communism, by contrast, seeks to expunge the cultural inheritances of mankind, and thereby also to roll back the most powerful achievements of the modern world in the interests of a mythic entity – that of universal humanity. That this myth – the myth of a human essence shorn of religion, family, locality and all the accidents of time, purged of conflict and released from contingency – is a gnostic rather than a Christian or a Jewish myth is unimportant here, save to illuminate the fact that the character of Marxism-Leninism as a religion, remarked upon in a thousand academic clichés, is extremely disputable. The peculiarity of Marxism, in both its primitive form and its more developed Soviet version, is its fusion of gnostic ambition with scientific pretension. If Marxism is a religion, it is only in the sense that occultism and theosophy – modern forms of magical thought which seek an abatement of tragedy and mystery through a sort of rationalistic gnosis – are religions.

Marxian philosophical anthropology is committed to the view that all the forms of human identity which have achieved concrete historic realization are aberrations, unavoidable episodes (perhaps) in the growth of human productive powers, but nevertheless episodes which conceal rather than disclose the human essence. Men and women are not, as they suppose themselves to be, Poles, Spaniards, Englishmen or Scots, Catholics, Jews or Muslims. They are only men and women, instances of the human species which have acquired an ersatz cultural identity through the accident of belonging to a particular class in a given historical epoch. It follows from this essentialist anthropology that, except in so far as they are instrumental in promoting the expansion of production and so in building up the necessary economic conditions of Communist society, all the historic realizations of human identity – in religion, art and cultural tradition – are alien and inimical to the realization of the human essence.

It must not be supposed for a moment that this Marxian philosophical anthropology has been unimplicated in Communist practice. It is a central element of Marxism-Leninism that, when it comes to pass, Communist humanity will be unlike any that history has known. All the cultural attachments which have granted real men their identities will have been effaced, and only quintessential humanity will remain. It is one of my chief arguments that, contrary to Marxism, the quintessential humanity which is to appear on the historical stage has no existence and, in fact, designates nothing. For this reason, the practical result of Communist policy has not been to liberate men from ersatz and oppressive cultural identities, but instead to make war on the only identities their subjects possess.

It is, perhaps, worth noting that the practical nullity of Marxian conceptions of socialist man is evinced in the bizarre phenomenon of displaced patriotism which may be observed in generations of the Western leftist intelligentsia. These groups adopted the Soviet Union, and later China, as a focus for the needs for allegiance which they denied in themselves by their repudiation of their own inherited loyalties. The result was an ersatz patriotism in which allegiance was transferred to a remote and largely imaginary society and state. It is only by reference to this displaced or ersatz patriotism, I believe, that we can begin to comprehend the many absurdities in Western intellectual perceptions of the Soviet system. The grotesque representations of the Soviet system evident in the work of Shaw and the Webbs, Aragon and Sartre, are at least partly explicable in terms of the demands of a repressed need for patriotic allegiance and collective identification. Nor is this phenomenon only of historical interest. We need to remind ourselves that it is probably only the relative brevity of the Pol Pot regime, and its defeat by Vietnamese occupying forces backed by the Soviet Union, that explains the fact that it is not now routinely described by the Western academic class in terms of iconoclasm and innovation in urban planning.

At this point, we may undertake a brief survey of Communist policy, beginning by looking back at a neglected aspect of Marx's system – its antimodernist impulse. Marx inherited from Hegel a self-image of consummate modernity, but in Marx's case this was only a self-deception. Unlike Hegel, who accepted as an historical fate the complexity of contemporary society and its domination by a spirit of individuality, Marx cherished an ideal – the ideal of Communism – whose content is given by the denial of the most distinctive features of modern culture. Thus the very things that best define a modern society – an extensive division of labour, a complicated system of status stratification and a diversity of cultural traditions – are all set to disappear in Communism, along with the institutions of money and market-pricing without which industrial society cannot (in fact) reproduce itself. Most fundamentally, the central character of the modern period – the autonomous individual with access to a variety of forms of life and modes of thought – will vanish in a Communist society which has suppressed the experience of moral conflict and intellectual suffering. For, as we recall from the speculations of *The German Ideology* (written by Marx with Engels in 1846 and first published in 1932), both art and philosophy – the central activities in which modern men explore the ironies of their condition and seek to plot its limits – will be redundant by virtue of the dissolution of their historical locus, the human individual, and the absorption of that individual in to a new communal life.

Marxist theory has always been committed, then, to the elimination of the modern expression of human identity as individuality. But it – and therefore also Communist practice – has always aimed to destroy those surviving forms of cultural identity which conserve a pre-modern sense of selfhood. When the Bolsheviks came to power, they declared a war on the native traditions of Russia that to this day has lost none of its urgency. Their aim was to effect a radical rupture with the past, so as to force the emergence of a new order in which national identity, along with other forms of cultural identity that had existed in the old world, played no part. It is this aim which probably best explains the economically counterproductive war on the Russian and Ukrainian peasantries in the 1930s, and which accounts in significant part for the Communist genocides of such peoples as the Kalmucks.

It is vitally important to recognize the enmity of Soviet Communism to Russian traditions, because this is what gives the lie to the dominant Western (and East European nationalist) interpretation of the Soviet system as a continuation of Muscovite traditions of despotism under a new flag. It is this interpretation – according to which political cultures may be grouped into pairs, civic and despotic, democratic and tyrannous, with that of Russia being classified as a quasi-oriental despotism – that is invoked when there is talk of 'the last empire' or 'the New Tsars'. This typology of regimes, with its antique echoes of Aristotle and Montesquieu, wholly occludes our vision of the Soviet system, which (like National Socialist Germany) is by no means a traditional tyranny any more than it is an oriental despotism.

The conventional wisdom among Western scholars, in seeking to explain away the horrors of the Soviet system as inheritances from a barbarous Russian political tradition, neglects the role of Marxian theory in constituting and reproducing the Soviet system[3] and the relentless hostility of both to the traditions and achievements of the Russian people. The so-called Russian empire of our time has, in truth, few points of similarity with the empires of nineteenth-century Europe. It benefits neither the Russian people, who remain among the poorest nations in the Soviet system, nor even the Soviet élite, whose most cherished privilege is the opportunity to defect. In projecting into Soviet reality the concepts and images of the past, Western observers fail to grasp the radical modernity of the Soviet totalitarian system. At the same time, and paradoxically, the Bolsheviks in laying waste the inherited traditions of Russian life failed to lay down a solid foundation for genuinely modern development. In obliterating the civic culture that had prevailed during the last decades of Tsarism, the Bolsheviks pushed Russia off the trajectory of real modernity on to a bizarre and surreal path whereby some of the most distinctive aspects of the modern world were realized in an uncompromising and terrible form.

From the perspective of Marx and Lenin, the Soviet Union is a double failure. It has not realized the antimodernist fantasy of a form of communal life from which individuality has disappeared, but has rather brought about a savage rebirth of a character from the early modern period, the Hobbesian individual for whom every social relationship is an act of exchange. It is this Hobbesian character who is the true *Homo Sovieticus*. At the same time, the real social life which survives in the Soviet Union today is one in which the broken traditions of the old world – traditions of religious devotion, cultural piety and romantic love – are asserted against the immovable power of the Soviet state. As for Soviet man himself, he is uniquely a creature of Soviet power and has no existence outside it.[4] So it is that, even in his Hobbesian reality, Soviet man is a lie – a vulgar forgery of the desperate but not ignoble character depicted by the author of *Leviathan*. Yet he is the only result of the project announced with Lenin's hideous boast that the Bolsheviks would become engineers of souls – a result squalid and pitiable enough to warrant Kolakowski's acid remark that 'thus Prometheus awakens from his dream of power, as ignominiously as Gregor Samsa in Kafka's *Metamorphosis*'.[5]

What do the catastrophic results of the Marxian project of constituting a universal human identity, shorn of local and historical attachments, tell us about the nature of human selfhood? In the simplest terms, the history of Communist practice can be seen as the practical self-refutation of Marxian philosophical anthropology. Seventy years after the Bolshevik Revolution, most subjects of the Soviet system still define their identities in religious and national, rather than class or political terms. They are, and remain, Poles, Ukrainians, Muslims and Christians. The self-defeating effect of Communist practice should lead us to jettison all theorizing about human society which treats the historic cultural identities it contains as spurious or merely contingent variations on the theme of generic humanity.

To a very considerable extent, human beings are self-defining animals: they differ from the other animal species precisely in their ability partly to constitute for themselves their own identities. This is to say that, for humans, personal identity is not a natural fact but a cultural artifact. We are what we are, not because nature has made us this way, but because we (and 'we' here includes our ancestors) have made us what we are. It is neglect or suppression of this truth that goes far to account for the pernicious absurdities of racist thought and practice. If the identities of persons are artifactual and not natural, if they vary within the broad constraints imposed by our biological endowment and exhibit a rich variety of kinds and forms, then any essentialist or naturalistic conception of the human species is to be rejected as false if not incoherent. We are left with human beings in all the miscellaneous diversity with which they present themselves to each other.

This conception of human beings as partly self-defining creatures has a critical leverage on contemporary theorizing which far extends from its impact on Marxism. For it cuts against at least the dominant forms of Western liberalism, which all turn on the philosophical fiction of abstract individuality. All of them, that is to say, found their theorizings on a conception of the human subject in which its identity and moral powers are conferred on it, not by a moral inheritance or a cultural tradition, but by the attributes of universal humanity. But the idea of a universal human individuality, which is a feature of the currently dominant liberalisms, misrepresents a distillation of our own experience as a universal truth. By contrast with other and earlier societies, ours is one in which status hierarchies are permeable, roles complex and often conflicting and social monitoring of personal behaviour intermittent and weak. These features of our culture are, indeed, ones we take a pride in, and which (in so far as they are conditions of the values of personal independence and privacy that we cherish) are parts of our freedom. The complexity of the social networks in which each of us moves, and the fact that none of them, or their associated moral communities, ever claims the entirety of our life or loyalty, is the source in common experience of the liberal idea of the autonomous individual.

Among us, and in some measure in every society touched by modernity, the liberal individual is an historical reality, a cultural achievement perhaps more precious than any other bequeathed to us by European civilization. To deny the historical reality of liberal individuality is then absurd, but to turn it into a universal theory – or, after the fashion of the Enlightenment, to appoint it the *telos* of history – is to traffic in illusions. To acknowledge liberal individuality as a distillation of modern experience, and thereby to recognize the historicity of liberalism itself, is to relinquish the pretensions of doctrinaire liberalism to universal validity. In coming to understand liberal individuality as an appropriate rendition of our experience as moderns, however, we abandon the distinctively modern (or Enlightenment) project of grounding liberalism on the universal maxims of autonomous reason. That in so recognizing the time-bound modernity of the liberal individual we do not (in the jargon or recent thought) deconstruct the individual, but rather initiate a form of post-modern individualism that is fully conscious of its own historical particularity, is a paradox to which I shall shortly return.

It is in its insistence on recalling to us the local character of our experience of individuality that the strength of conservative philosophy lies. It dispels the hallucinatory perspective of abstract humanity, and draws us back to the narrower, but more substantial standpoints of real human beings, in all their quiddities and miscellaneity. Conservative thought has inestimable value in correcting the illusion that we are, or can ever be, dispossessed or unencumbered selves, free-floating sovereign subjects, distanced from all social convention and heirs to no tradition. Conservative philosophy contains, then, an incisive critique, not only of the stupendous delusions of Marxism, but also of the lesser, but no less mistaken errors of the dominant liberalism. From conservative thought, we can glean a devastating criticism of the liberalism of J. S. Mill's *On Liberty*, where uncriticized and flawed conceptions of autonomy and individuality combine with an obsessional enmity to tradition and convention to yield a liberalism in which rationalist hubris, antinomian individualism and a sentimental religion of humanity reinforce and strengthen each other.

The liberalism of *On Liberty* hinges on the neglect of cultural tradition as the matrix of human individuality and its issues in the absurd proposal that autonomy be theorized (and practised) as an independence of tradition rather than as variations on particular traditions. The liberalism of *On Liberty* – which may not be the only, and, as I have argued elsewhere,[6] is certainly not the most defensible liberalism to be found in Mill's writings – distracts us from the truth that autonomy and individuality wax, not in a post-traditional society, but rather in a society encompassing many traditions, among which individuals may move freely, but with each of them exercising a constraint of opinion over its practitioners.

The form of society celebrated by Millian liberalism – the liberalism from which all the dominant liberalisms of the present day are derived – is not, in truth, any sort of pluralist society. It is instead a society ruled by an élite of opinion-formers – Mill's secular version of Coleridge's clerisy – which relentlessly propagates a narrow, partisan ideal of rationalistic individualism and progressivism. In this blinkered view, traditions are encumbrances and obstacles to individuality, rather than the media in which it alone exists and finds expression, and the inherited variety of folkways and lifestyles is a garden of weeds to be winnowed and levelled rather than explored and enjoyed. We see this clearly in J. S. Mill himself, who writes sneeringly that 'Nobody can suppose that it is not more beneficial to a Breton, or a Basque . . . to be (French) than to sulk on his rocks, the half-savage relic of past times, revolving in his own little mental orbit', thereby giving expression to that contempt for small peoples and cultural minorities which he held in common with Marx.

In theory as well as in practice, Millian liberalism is a force for cultural homogeneity and against diversity, a political tendency for which progress is more important than liberty. And by progress is here meant, not the uncalculated exfoliation of human energies, but the imposition of a plan of life in which the prejudices and anxieties of the late nineteenth-century European intelligentsia are made mandatory for all. In its political manifestations in our times, Millian liberalism has been a programme for cultural conformity, with much of the inherited diversity of our society being treated as an aberration from the cramped and suffocating norms of Hamp- stead and Bloomsbury. The ambition of Millian liberalism – a social world without Gypsies or Hasids, in which immigrant cultures are speedily assi- milated to the mores of a bourgeoisie from which the redeeming virtues of entrepreneurship and self-reliance have all but disappeared – is a sort of universal bohemia whose practical realization, mercifully, is probably impossible.

The impossibility of the goal does not, however, make its pursuit less harmful. By a dialectical twist in its own inner logic, the dominant liberal-ism of our time has responded to the threat of cultural homogeneity which is the nemesis of its efforts by adopting another form of cultural imperial-ism, in which the remnants of overwhelmed traditions are preserved as spectacles for public consumption in subsidized ghettoes. It is in this way, I suspect, that we should understand the liberal enthusiasm for policies of positive discrimination – as a belated and unwitting recognition of the desolation which liberal policies of social engineering have wreaked on our societies. (Examples that come to mind are the destruction of working-class communities in Britain by municipal housing policies, and of black com-munities by urban renewal programmes in the United States.) It is this un-conscious recognition of the levelling and conformist effect of modern liberalism which also partly explains the bizarre excesses of multi-culturalism – that fashionable form of paternalism which aims to embalm the dead or dying vestiges of submerged or occluded traditions and preserve their remains as public spectacles. I shall argue later that this multicultural mania is in truth the negation of respect for cultural diversity. Here I wish to assert that the disasters of recent liberal policy are evils which flow inexorably from any liberalism, such as that of John Stuart Mill, which seeks to achieve the political domination of the liberal individual instead of aiming for a political order which can be shared by a variety of forms of life, including that of the liberal individual.

It is in undermining the excesses of liberal individuality, in insisting that our identities are constituted and not encumbered by the forms of life that we inherit, that the virtue and success of conservative thought lies. At the same time, the conservative critique of the abstract individualism of liberal theory often, if not typically, issues in a conception of the human self, and a prescription for political order, which can be shown to be radically flawed. The conservative theorist, like the communitarian critic of liberal-ism from the Left, moves unreflectively from the truth that we are none of us encumbered or disembodied selves to the very different, and indeed manifestly false proposition that we are, or ought to be radically situated selves – that is to say (I am here explicating the idiom of recent com-munitarian theory[7]) selves whose identity is contoured by membership in a single moral community and mirrored in the institutions of a single political order. This is the belief, shared by Leftist communitarian theorists such as

Sandel and by Hegelian conservatives such as Scruton,[8] that moral life flourishes only when personal identities are constituted wholly by embeddedness in a single moral community, and, further, that such moral communities demand and are entitled to the protection of a political order with which they are or ought to be coextensive. It is to this belief that I referred when I spoke of a modern heresy as the target of my thoughts. In its simplest form, this belief is expressed in modern thought as *nationalism*, which has been characterized with unsurpassable clarity by Isaiah Berlin as the claim that

> the essential human unit in which man's nature is fully realised is not the individual, or a voluntary association which can be dissolved or altered or abandoned at will, but the nation; that it is to the creation and maintenance of the nation that the lives of subordinate units, the family, the tribe, the clan, the province must be due, for their nature and purpose, what is often called their meaning, is derived from its nature and purposes; and that these are revealed not by rational analysis, but by a special awareness, which need not be fully conscious, of the unique relationship that binds individual human beings into the indissoluble and unanalysable organic whole which Burke identified with society, Rousseau with the people, Hegel with the state.[9]

The belief that political order presupposes deep moral solidarity, and its further presupposition, that the identities of persons are or ought to be defined by membership of a single moral community, else they be deformed or estranged, is not restricted to nationalist theorizing. Rather, it animates most modern thought, and it is especially prominent in contemporary criticism of liberalism.

I have acknowledged an important truth in the conservative and communitarian critique of liberalism which fastens on weaknesses in the dominant liberal conception of the human subject. Against the presently dominant kinds of conservatism, however, I wish to argue that they exhibit a remoteness from historical reality which is peculiarly damaging in a form of thought which rightly seeks to elevate the particulars of concrete practice over the delusive universals of abstract theorizing. For the communitarian-conservative conception of the radically situated self can be shown to have no application to modern experience and to model what is, at best, a limiting case. We can see this, to begin with, when we reflect on our own experience. We are none of us defined by membership in a single community or form of moral life. We are 'suckled on the milk of many nurses', as Fulke Greville put it, heirs of many distinct, sometimes conflicting, intellectual and moral traditions. Further, the traditions to which we are heirs are not windowless monads, self-sufficient and fully individuated entities which (like pebbles) may coexist without interacting. They are rather prisms, each of which refracts the light cast by the other traditions which environ it, and which together throw into each of us a shifting pattern of colours. The complexity and contradictions of our cultural inheritance give to our identities an aspect of complexity and even of plurality which is not accidental, but (if we may use such a term) essential to them. For us, at any rate, the power to conceive of ourselves in different ways, to harbour dissonant projects and perspectives, to inform our thoughts and lives with divergent categories and concepts, is integral to our identity as reflective beings.

This same point can be put in other terms: the experience of *marginality* is familiar to all of us as a dimension of our identity which is integral to it. Because it is our condition to belong to many different, and often discrepant networks and communities, we belong wholly to none of them. The power of distancing ourselves from any relationship or attachment, of imagining ourselves to have severed or altered any one of the many involvements which enter into our identities, is itself a central element in our identity. Even as we are constituted by our attachments, *we* (perhaps not all men and women) are constituted by the knowledge that we can alter or dissolve any of them. To wish this to be otherwise, to seek to suppress the experience of marginality, is to seek to alter our nature.

To wish to alter our nature, however, is also to seek to expunge our history. For the condition of moral complexity to which I have alluded is not a novelty of modern decadence, but instead a phenomenon that manifests itself in European life at least since the late-medieval period. We find an accurate reading of European history, I believe, in Michael Oakeshott's observation that

> The urge to impose upon a state the character of a *solidarite commune* is certainly a notable disposition, but, so far from being the dominant disposition of the modern European political imagination, it is easily recognised as a relic of servility of which it is proper for European peoples to be profoundly ashamed . . . no European alive to his inheritance of moral understanding has ever found it possible to deny the superior desirability of civil association without a profound feeling of guilt.[10]

That Oakeshott's reading of European history is superior to any advanced by communitarian conservatives is confirmed by even a cursory glance at the rudiments of the history of the modern European state. It is a plain fact that few, if any, modern European states coincide with any national community. The sovereign state of the United Kingdom is precisely that, a kingdom encompassing four nations, and not a nation-state. Again, what is Spain but an artifact of monarchy? And, lest we neglect an apparent counter-example, let us recall that as late as 1870, a survey of French school children reported that the majority of them were unable to name the nation in which they lived, but instead named their province or region.[11] The belief that national consciousness is a long-established feature of European peoples is, in fact, profoundly unhistorical, and for that reason deeply unconservative. It is a chimera produced by a mistaken theory which understands political order in a quasi-naturalistic fashion as an expression of a pre-existent community, when it is properly understood as a matter of strictly political allegiance to the artifact of sovereign authority. As Kolnai again puts it well:

> human society is not composed of nations . . . in the same clearcut way in which it is composed of individuals, or, for that matter, of sovereign states. The spectrum of nationalities is full of interpretations, ambiguities, twilight zones. It follows that the conceptions of nationalism (as a universal principle), the conception of a 'just' or 'natural' order of nation-states is – in fact and in theory – pure utopia. There can be neither an order of states nor of frontiers in which there does not enter to a large extent the factor of arbitrariness, contingency and historical accident. Pretending to 'purify' the body of mankind – like other enterprises of a naturalist pseudo-rationalist sort, purporting to lay down 'evident principles' which generally prove illusory – means to push arbitrariness to its extreme limit.[12]

I have ascribed to conservative thought deep insights into human identity which much liberalism neglects. It is a conservative insight that the Whig (and Marxian) idea of historical folkways and concrete forms of life as aberrations – as veils behind which is to be found (in Stuart Hampshire's words)

> an abstract universal man dressed in neo-classical drapery, as in some Reynolds paintings, to indicate that he belongs to no particular place or time, (framed in) the unearthly light of the ideal, classical and timeless scene (wherein) reason cannot tell him how he should be married or how he should speak to his children . . . or give one local loyalty precedence over another[13]

– that this idea is a mirage.

I have found in conservatism, that is to say, the important truth that liberal and Marxian conceptions of universal humanity are false or incoherent and harmful in practice. I want now to develop further a criticism of the dominant forms of contemporary conservatism, which are communitarian and often nationalist in temper, by trying to delineate more positively the sort of political order which does *not* depend on a pre-existent moral solidarity. My submission is that, in the subtle mosaic of traditions which is modern society, government is ill-fitted to act as guardian or protector of any of the traditions it shelters. It cannot claim to express any deep, undergirding moral community in the society, since no such community exists. In this circumstance, the task of the state is to keep in good repair what Oakeshott calls civil association – that structure of law in which, having no purpose in common, practitioners of different traditions may coexist in peace. Modern states are peculiarly apt to be distracted from this vital task by the reflex of governmental hyperactivism which they all exhibit. Every problem or evil, from drug abuse to family breakdown, is perceived as a dire threat to an established order which it is the duty of government to protect. Against this modern prejudice, I would cite Wittgenstein's remark that trying by deliberate contrivance to shore up an ailing tradition is like trying to repair a broken spider's web with bare hands. There is a special absurdity in invoking the authority of government to intervene in problems to which government has no solution. None of the manifestations of contemporary decadence about which conventional conservative opinion is so alarmed are threats to the survival of society, and a true conservative policy would rather be one that in most things left society to look after itself. The resources of renewal and self-repair in society are surely far greater than any that can be mobilized by the ramshackle action of government.

The implication of this perspective for the character of the modern state is that (contrary to the conventional wisdom, socialist and conservative) modern government must be limited government. Where deep moral solidarity is lacking, where (as in all modern societies) there is cultural diversity rather than seamless community, the role of government is first and last that of preserving liberty in civil association under the rule of law. The liberty that is preserved is that of the liberal individual, but it is a liberty that thereby guarantees cultural freedom – the condition in which individuals may opt to explore an inherited form of life, or migrate across traditions to a chosen lifestyle, if they so wish. Cultural diversity is protected, in this perspective, by a political order which protects the old liberal freedoms of conscience, occupation, contract and enterprise. The form of government distinctive of such a political order is not the minimum state of recent libertarian theory, but it is akin to the limited state of classical liberalism. It is a form of government in which each person, and therefore also each cultural tradition which the society contains, possesses an equal freedom to develop themselves, compatibly with the equal freedom of the others to do likewise.

Two points of clarification are worth making about this conception of government in a society characterized by substantial cultural diversity. The first is that, according to the view I am developing, the place of government is to respect diversity in cultural traditions, and so allow for the emergence of rival and perhaps incommensurable forms of human flourishing, but not to attempt to institutionalize traditions or ways of life in state-subsidized ghettoes. The political order which I am commending is accordingly at the farthest extreme from that promoted by contemporary agitators for multi-culturalism. For these latter, animated by a moral hatred of the dominant traditions and a voyeuristic fascination with submerged, overwhelmed or oppositional cultures, seek to entrench minority traditions in protected institutions and to confer on them arbitrary privileges.

This multiculturalism is bogus and pernicious, because it expresses a racist conviction that minority cultures can never maintain themselves without paternalistic support and because it seeks to replace one form of cultural imperialism by another. (That minority cultures do not always need political protection is shown by the history of the Indian immigrant population in Britain and of the Chinese and Japanese in the United States, where in each case governmental institutions have proved a hindrance rather than an aid to minority advancement.) Further, as the tragic history of the American black population shows, such paternalistic and welfarist measures typically serve only to complete the devastation of traditional family and cultural life, already damaged by social prejudice and economic hardship. The final result of contemporary multiculturalism, if it could be achieved, would in fact be a mirror image of the system of privilege and separatism favoured by authoritarian conservatives – in short, the institu-tionalization of a cultural apartheid.

That government should wash its hands of contemporary multiculturalist manias does not mean that it should become a nightwatchman state. Government may properly act to supply underproduced public goods and to assist the needy in their struggles toward opportunity and independence. In general, however, government should refrain from itself producing the goods it seeks to generate in society. In the vital area of education, for example, there is much to suggest that we would be better off with a system of tax deductions and vouchers whereby families could provide for them-selves privately, than we are with the bureaucratic monolith of state school-ing. It has been too little noted by proponents of state schooling that public provision of education generates intractable problems where, as with us, society contains divergent ways of life with discrepant conceptions of the family and of personal fulfilment. The inner-city British Moslem does not take the same view of the role of schooling as does the secular humanist in Kensington, and it is unavoidable that an educational system provided by the state will become an arena for political struggle in which weak or ill-organized minorities will lose out and educators will be distracted from their central tasks.

That state provision of education is a recipe for social conflict and the politicization of life in a multicultural society is an instance of the general truth that governmental provision of social services is bound to yield a pressure for cultural homogeneity which only the cost of protracted political conflict curbs. The policy implication of this truth is that both social stability and individual liberty are best served if government withdraws from such activities and confines its intervention to funding voluntary choice in education and elsewhere for families and individuals with slight means. It is in such a direction that wise policy should move, and this is a point especially relevant to conservatives, who are conspicuous for their neglect of the fact that the subversive effects of the invasive state on liberty and tradition are integral to its very existence and are not significantly diminished when the state machine is captured for a while by parties with a conservative temper.

It is a consequence of the view I have been developing that, if government is to shelter the variety of traditions which our society contains, then it should favour none of them particularly. This, in turn, implies that there is no guarantee that long-established traditions and forms of life will succeed in reproducing themselves. It may well be, in fact, that the withdrawal of government to limited and definite functions would actually quicken the pace of cultural change in some areas of social life. In particular, the form of life of the liberal individual will in the liberal political order I am outlining be only one way of life among many, and nothing (except its own resources of vitality) guarantees that it will retain primacy among the cultural traditions which have found a home among us. We do not need to see every social change as an improvement to accept this as an inevitable result of the proper limitation of governmental power. Traditions and ways of life that require for the successful reproduction more from government than protection from the rule of law and the provision of opportunity for those with few resources probably do not deserve to survive.

It is not the office of government to buttress failing identities, to confer identities on persons afflicted with anomie, or, in general, to make the world safe for cultural traditions endangered by the freedom that is protected by civil association. Nor is it the task of government to protect waning traditions by confining their practitioners to tax-funded institutional reservations. This has been the increasing tendency of governments in their policy toward minorities in many Western states. But it is this protectionist policy in respect of social movements and ways of life, I believe, that John Anderson was criticizing when he wrote his remarkable essay on the Servile State.

The argument I have developed goes against the grain of most contemporary thought – socialist, liberal and conservative – in that it denies to government the task of conserving (or, in the case of all Communist and many liberal states, destroying) cultural identity. Against Marxian socialism I have urged the catastrophic consequences of the attempt to construct a new human identity by the political engineering of souls. Against communitarian and authoritarian conservatism, I have argued that the long-standing complexity of European traditions disqualifies any project of using political power to create or conserve a radically situated subject whose horizons are those of a single moral community. This reactionary conservatism, I have argued, neglects the fluidity and elusiveness of traditions in general, and, more particularly, it ignores the modern reality, in which traditions constantly individuate themselves anew, transforming each other as they do.

I have criticized, also, that form of liberalism (the dominant contemporary form) which seeks through government to impose upon all the form of life of an alienated fragment of the Western bourgeoisie. My argument is nevertheless consonant with a liberal tradition, sounder and truer than that which has been dominant since John Stuart Mill, which sees government not as the pacemaker for any specific conception of progress, but instead as providing the framework within which different ways of life and styles of thought may compete in peaceful coexistence. It is this conception which animates the Scottish Enlightenment and the writings of Tocqueville and Constant and which inspires much in *The Federalist Papers*. It is this conception of limited government, with its origins in classical liberalism, which I believe to be most appropriate to our condition as persons living in a society which is not unified by any single tradition. It is a conception which should be studied with special care, I believe, by reflective conservatives and by liberals who have not lost the skill in self-criticism on which they pride themselves.

The conception I wish to commend here confronts serious difficulties, all of which arise from the fact that it appears to go against the spirit of the age. In the first place, it is not clear what are the institutional forms appropriate to a state which respects cultural diversity and does not seek to bolster or embody any specific form of cultural identity. The example of the Habsburg Monarchy, with which I began and which certainly did shelter a myriad of nationalities and traditions, is not an encouraging one for us. Contemporary sentiment is relentlessly inimical to imperial institutions, despite the evident historical fact that their desuetude or destruction has mostly been attended by dictatorship or tribalism. Further, the instance of Switzerland, which Kolnai cites as evidence of the possibility of several linguistic and religious communities being integrated within a single political order based on extensive decentralization and localization of governmental functions, does not seem easily exportable. Such success in harbouring diverse communities within a single political order depends in Switzerland on political traditions which are centuries old and which have very distinctive historical origins. Moreover, the record of local or federal schemes of governmental devolution and decentralization is not elsewhere particularly impressive.

In Britain, local government has proved more vulnerable to capture by extremists than has national government, and has been the scene of many conflicts between ethnic and cultural majorities and minorities. Again, in the United States the massive apparatus of federalism, separation of powers and judicial review has not prevented (and may well have facilitated) the extensive politicization of social life via the exploitation of litigation and the invocation of constitutional rights, whose content is often not liable to strict construction. There is, finally, a danger in all schemes of con-sociational or confederal devolution of government powers, that (save in exceptional circumstances, as in Switzerland) they leave the association of states open to conquest or subversion by external aggressors. For these reasons, we go up a blind alley if we suppose that we can forge the political institutions appropriate to a circumstance of cultural diversity by recourse to traditional devices of devolution and localization which have nearly everywhere failed.

There is a deeper difficulty in the view I have been developing of the relations between political order and cultural identity, and that is a dilemma of allegiance. Political orders which have successfully transcended the need for moral solidarity or community have, historically, either been empires (as with the Romans and the Habsburgs), religious institutions (such as those of medieval Christendom and Islam in their periods of greatest toleration) or else monarchies, as in the splendidly anachronistic case of the United Kingdom. None of these sources of allegiance is available on any large scale today. There are no true empires left, few monarchies, and the exemplars of religious political order with which we are, alas, becoming increasingly familiar are examples of a rabid and barbarous funda-mentalism, as in Iran. We may go yet further. Allegiance to liberal orders, where it has not had its roots in religious faith, has typically been imposed by secular myths which few of us any longer take seriously. Thus liberalism in France and America was sustained by the historical theodicy of the Enlightenment, with its mythologies of natural rights and global progress. These are the myths which suffuse modernity and ground the modern project of giving moral and political life a rational foundation. When we cease to subscribe to them, we acquire the paradoxical character of post-moderns, heirs to all the achievements of modernity, but not to its seminal myths. From the perspective of my problem here, the question naturally arises, what might sustain a political order that encompasses many traditions and varieties of human identity, if both the traditional and the modern sources of allegiance to such an order are unmistakably on the wane?

I address this question in the hope that the dilemma it marks is not of the Polish variety – insoluble, but not serious – which it is the fate of those subject to Communist domination to suffer. I hazard the guess that we may go some way to resolving it by looking back to the early modern period, when many of our current dilemmas were perceived with a drastic clarity which we have lost. It is perhaps in the works of Hobbes, who wrote for an age of religious wars and barbarous movements much like ours, that we glimpse the outlines of a form of government suited to our circumstances. It is a form of government devoted to securing the peace, and that first of all, thereby leaving the largest space for liberty of thought and action. It is a unitary form of government, without complicated devices for devolution, in which all or most of the activities not essential to the primary peace-keeping task of the state are left to private initiative. It is in this notion of a form of government having such strictly limited functions that we may, possibly, find a clue to our present dilemma. What it suggests is the salience to our condition of a state that is strong but small, in which the little that is not privatized is centralized, and in which practitioners of diverse traditions are left at liberty, so long as they do not disturb the common peace, to refine and develop their forms of life. This is a form of government devoted not to truth, or to abstract rights, and still less to any conception of progress or general welfare, but instead one which by securing a non-instrumental peace creates the possibility of civil association.

It is in this possibility, and perhaps in this alone, that we may hope for a resolution of the perplexity with which I began my reflections. It may still be doubted, all the same, if the kind of state I have envisaged could command allegiance when it lacks the support of an inspiring mythology. Here I would like to suggest the possibility that, in recognizing that we lack the moral solidarity sought by socialists and most conservatives, we may yet be able to draw on the resource of another kind of solidarity – that of civilized men and women, practitioners of different traditions, who nevertheless have in common a perception of enmity in regard to the totalitarian states and rebarbarizing movements of our time. We – the heirs of European traditions who have enjoyed the freedoms of civil association, or who have come within its sphere by forced or chosen migration – are few, feeble and not mankind. We know that (as Hume observed of liberty in England) our freedom is a singularity, not the upshot of any inevitable source of events, and that it has no future that is guaranteed. We do not pretend that our identities express the essence of the species; we recognize them to be products as much of chance as of choice. In short, we take ourselves as we are, and we are not ashamed of our identities. It is this sensibility which I defend here and which, despite its clumsiness, I am tempted to call post-modern liberal conservatism.[14]

The name we give to this sensibility is unimportant. What is important is the possibility of a form of political solidarity that does not depend on shared moral community, but only on the mutual recognition of civilized men and women. Such solidarity may be, as Spinoza says of wisdom, 'as rare as it is precious'; and the freedom that it expresses and engenders may well prove to be an exception in the life of the species. Yet, so long as we can learn the skill of defending with inflexible resolution an order we know to be underwritten neither by nature or history, we have reason to hope that the idea of a society of many distinct but interpenetrating traditions, a society in which men and women come to respect and cherish their differences and are ready to act together to protect them, is more than an idle dream.[15]

19 Conservatism, individualism and the political thought of the New Right

Perhaps the most remarkable and among the least anticipated developments in political thought and practice, throughout the Western world in the 1980s, was the conquest of conservatism by the ideas and doctrines of the New Right. This conquest was nowhere total, and it was not by any means universal. It can be justly termed hegemonic, nevertheless, in precisely the Gramscian sense, in that conservative parties, governments and intellectual journals came to be dominated by a discourse and an agenda of policy that emanated from thinkers of the New Right and embodied a searching and often harsh critique of conservative thought and practice during the thirty years or so that followed the Second World War. Indeed, the hegemonic character of the political thought of the New Right – a hegemony that may prove to have been fragile and ephemeral, but which at present shows only few and small signs of strain – was attested by the fact that during the 1980s the parties of the Left felt constrained to adopt much of the discourse, and many of the policies, that conservative governments had imbibed from the theorists of the New Right. In one case, that of New Zealand, it was the Labour Party that implemented the most radical and far-reaching programme of economic reform (on lines suggested by New Right thinkers) that has been attempted in any Western democratic state – a reform programme that, despite its upheavals and difficulties, has compelled the conservative National Party in New Zealand to adopt a rhetoric of economic liberty and market competition that is very different from the Keynesian and protectionist rhetoric and policy that are its historical inheritances. It would be rash to essay the judgement that the policy achievements of governments animated by the ideas of the New Right are irreversible. It is reasonable, at the same time, to affirm that a sea change has occurred in political life in the Western democracies, and more particularly in conservative thought and practice in the English-speaking nations, that has many of the marks of irreversibility.

The hegemony of the New Right within conservatism emerged in a very definite historical context. Even if, as I have intimated, it will probably have some consequences for both conservative and socialist policy and rhetoric that are irreversible, it is sensible to suppose that the hegemony of the political thought of the New Right, both within and outside conservatism, will be limited by the historical contingencies that brought it into being. This is so, most particularly, in regard to its domination of conservative thinking. For, though the relations of the New Right with the received tradition of conservative thought and practice are highly complex and controversial, there can be no doubt that the novel orthodoxy of New Right thought within conservatism has initiated as much rupture with recent practice as it has (on some accounts) restored conformity with an earlier and supposedly a purer conservatism. My object in this exploration will be to attempt to define the content, limits and varieties of doctrine on the New Right, and to specify the affinities and tensions that have arisen between the New Right and the received inheritance of conservative practice. Except by way of an occasional comparison with conditions in the United States, I shall confine myself to the British experience. And I shall focus my inquiries around the central and fundamental question of the place and character of individualism within conservative doctrine – a question that has been answered very differently both by thinkers of the New Right and by their conservative critics.

A rehearsal, not of my arguments, but of my conclusions, may be apposite. I shall conclude that, whereas the New Right correctly perceived that a generation of conservative practice had led modern Western democratic states into a dead end of corporatist stagnation in which a ratchet-effect operated that moved the political centre steadily leftwards, its theorists consistently neglected the cultural inheritance which is the matrix of a stable capitalist order. In part because of their debts to the rationalist tradition of classical liberalism, the principal theorists of the New Right failed to perceive the dependency of individualist civil society on a dwindling but real patrimony of common ideas, beliefs and values. In some cases, they subscribed to the unrealizable and dangerous utopian project of a minimal or neutral state enforcing a regime of common rules that is not underwritten by a fund of common culture. In no case did the thinkers of the New Right undertake the historical researches necessary in order to illuminate the sources of the stability of the capitalist order in Britain or the United States. The political thought of the New Right, even in its subtlest expressions (as in Hayek), transmitted to conservatism an abstract rationalism and legalism that occludes serious theorizing of the conditions under which market capitalist institutions have for centuries enjoyed an almost unchallenged hegemony in Britain and the United States. In other words, the New Right has in its theorizing failed to grasp the historical and cultural presuppositions and limits of the kind of civil society they seek to maintain, restore or enhance. And this theoretical neglect has disabled the policies of governments animated by the thinking of the New Right, in that policy (as distinct from rhetoric) has been concerned almost solely with securing the legal and economic conditions of market competition and thereby of general prosperity, and has only rarely and inadequately addressed the cultural conditions that undergird and sustain a stable market order. In so far as the New Right ever nurtured a hegemonic project, this has been compromised in political practice by the blind-spot it has contained regarding the importance of the culture of individualism of which a market economy is only the visible part.

It is to this culture of individualism, ancient in England and resilient if insulted and injured, even in our own times, that theoretical inquiry and historical research should now turn. Here the argument I develop diverges from that of conservative critics of the neo-liberal New Right, such as Roger Scruton, who have perceptively and powerfully criticized the neglect within neo-liberalism of the common culture that founds Western civil society and enables it to reproduce itself across the generations. My argument diverges from this conservative critique, in as much as it maintains at once that our common cultural inheritance is individualist, and that its political embodiment cannot always, or even as a rule, coincide with that of the modern nation-state. The character of this individualist inheritance, as we receive it at present, and the forms in which it may enjoy a political embodiment, are very difficult issues, about which I can here only offer inconclusive speculations. The upshot of my reflections, however, is that, since individualism as a form of life pre-dates liberalism as a political doctrine by centuries, it is reasonable to expect (and to hope) that individualist culture will survive the demise of liberalism. And, since individualism and liberalism are not to be confused, it is a mistake on the part of conservative critics of the New Right to suppose that civil society can do without its individualist inheritance, or find a surrogate for that inheritance in the modernist project of integral nationhood.

What, then, was the New Right?[1] At the level of policy, it is not difficult to identify the salient themes of New Right thought. Policy animated by the ideas of the New Right sought to dismantle the corporatist institutions built up in Britain in the post-War period, to limit government and at the same time to restrain the power of inordinate organized interests such as the trade unions, to achieve a stable currency and abandon deficit financing and, in general, to engineer a transfer of initiative and resources from government to civil society that was massive and politically irreversible. In practical terms, such a policy orientation expressed itself in measures for the privatization of state-owned industries, in the Medium Term Financial Strategy, tax reduction, a curb on public expenditure, and a variety of supply-side measures deregulating prices, wages, rents and some planning controls. It is not such detailed policy measures that will interest the historian of the New Right, however, but rather their philosophical and theoretical inspiration. The intellectual perspective which infused these policies was not that which had dominated post-War British conservatism; it came from outside the Conservative Party, from the works of F. A. Hayek and Milton Friedman, and from the free market think-tanks, above all, from the Institute of Economic Affairs.[2] The pedigree of this perspective on policy and society was classical liberal, not conservative. This is to say that it was strongly and sometimes stridently individualist, it sought to reduce government to an indispensable minimum, and (except, to some extent, in the work of Hayek[3]) it concerned itself very little with the cultural or social conditions of a stable restoration of market institutions. In economic policy, the impact of classical liberal thought, especially as developed and applied (during decades of neglect by the mainstream of academic life) by the IEA, was crucial and indispensable. The classical liberal inheritance, consistently and judiciously implemented in the early years of the Thatcher period, enabled government to act to dismantle, probably for good, a significant portion of the detritus of corporatist institutions left by a generation of passive and reactive conservative government and policy-making.

As it was embodied in the early years of Thatcherism, the classical liberal orientation of much policy could also legitimately claim a genuine conservative pedigree. The allegation of the Tory 'wets',[4] that Thatcherism represented a rupture in an otherwise unbroken tradition of conservative thought and practice, does not survive historical scrutiny. Nineteenth-century conservative government, whether that of Disraeli or of Salisbury, conceived itself as superintending the institutions of civil society, and occasionally supplementing them, but not as being in the business of managing the economy. This is to say that, at least until the 1930s, British conservatives conceived government as the guardian of civil association (in Oakeshott's terminology[5]). The idea of government as an enterprise association – as a sponsor or pacemaker of economic growth, say – is in fact quite alien to the British conservative tradition. In this respect, then, Thatcherism can make a genuine claim to have revived or restored an earlier tradition of conservative government.

There is another, and more fundamental reason in support of the thesis that Thatcherism embodies a genuine British, or more precisely English tradition, and is not an incursion into British political life of an alien liberal or conservative doctrine. This is in the historical fact, profoundly explored by Alan Macfarlane[6] that English life, contrary to the conventional historiography of Polanyi[7] and of Marx, has had an individualist character at least since the thirteenth century. The idea that there was, in the seventeenth century or earlier, a Great Transformation of English life from communal to individualist forms, an idea that has entered political thought from the work of C. B. Macpherson,[8] does not accord with demonstrable facts about English history – facts to do with personal mobility, land use and the pattern of family life. If, as MacFarlane has persuasively argued, England was an individualist society immemorially, then the project that animated Thatcherism – the project of limiting government and reviving civil association – is one that seeks to reassert the most ancient and fundamental English traditions.

Neo-liberalism and Thatcherite conservatism are, then, seeking to restore and reproduce an English individualist culture that is our historical inheritance. Where they appear to differ is in their recognition, or neglect, of the historical conditions and inheritance which allowed this culture to sustain itself for so long. As Jonathan Clark has argued[9] English individualism – the culture that grounded English civil society – was not liberal but instead authoritarian individualism. This is to say that it depended on a nexus of beliefs, practices and inhibitions which conferred legitimacy on it and constrained the corrosive tendencies about which the Scottish writers and particularly Ferguson, were concerned in their theorizing about the potentially self-destructive effects of the anonymity and moral laxity that were latent in individualist life. These tendencies were inhibited in English authoritarian individualism by the strength in England of a common moral culture and, more particularly, by the authority of the Anglican church (and, later, by the moral discipline imposed by non-conformist Christianity). Similar religious traditions in the United States for a century or more constrained the tendencies toward anomie and hedonism which (as Tocqueville perceived) were otherwise present in the individualism of a culture lacking in the hierarchies that had structured individualism in England.

Thatcherite conservatism has distinguished itself from neo-liberalism, and has established its affinities with American neo-conservatism, by its reiterated emphasis on the familiar and religious values that legitimated capitalist institutions in their Victorian heyday. Thatcherite conservatism has the advantage over neo-liberalism, for this reason, in that it explicitly addresses the character of the cultural matrix of individualist civil society. It is far from clear, however, that the invocation of Victorian values – religious and familial – can do the job of legitimating market institutions that is required of such values by the Thatcher project. This is so for several reasons. In the first place, England is in the late-twentieth century a massively secularized society. In this it resembles most closely the Scandinavian countries and Japan, and differs sharply form the United States (which in turn accounts for the non-existence in England of anything resembling the American phenomenon of the Moral Majority). It is wholly anachronistic to expect that Christianity, and more particularly the Church of England, will ever have the political significance in England that it possessed throughout the seventeenth, eighteenth and nineteenth centuries. Indeed, in so far as the Anglican church has had influence on political life in England, it has been to further the tendencies whereby market institutions and individualist civil society are delegitimated, since the dominant part of Anglican social theology has for decades been infused with the anti-capitalist mentality that pervades intellectual life in England more generally.

The second reason why the Thatcherite appeal to the common cultural inheritance of individualism cannot work is the substantial enhancement of various sorts of pluralism within English society. The mass immigration of the 1960s has contributed to English life an ethnic and a religious pluralism that is unalterable and irreversible in any foreseeable future. Given the self-assertion of British Islam, and its demands for separate state-funded schooling, it is likely that this pluralism will increase, rather than diminish, over the coming decades. A similar, though more diffuse and less politically visible pluralism is widespread in English society in attitudes to marriage, sexuality and other belief-dependent institutions and practices. If the English common culture was ever a seamless garment, it is no longer so. It is questionable whether a strong and resilient common culture any longer prevails in England. It is beyond reasonable doubt that its content has been attenuated, and its significance in performing a legitimating role in respect of civil society in England weakened. Nor is there any reason to suppose that Thatcherite rhetoric has had any transforming impact on the diverse and indeed fragmented culture which now exists in England.

What might supplement the dwindling common culture as the legitimating force that sustains a capitalist regime in Britain? In practice, both Thatcherites and neo-conservatives in the United States have relied – thus far successfully – on economic growth, and the manifest failure of both post-War macroeconomic management and of socialist command economies, to sustain the electoral support needed for neo-liberal economic policies. Unless the most optimistic among the American supply-siders[10] are right, and the business cycle has been abolished, it seems imprudent and complacent to suppose that the hegemony of market institutions can rest forever on increasing prosperity. (Environmental concerns may in any case constrain the pursuit of constant economic growth.) In the context of the mass democracies of contemporary Britain and the United States, there is every reason to suppose that a period of protracted economic difficulty would swing the political pendulum back to interventionist, and in the

United States protectionist, economic policies, and could well end the long tenure in power of the Conservatives and the Republicans. This is not to say that we need fear in England a return to full-blooded socialism. The intellectual hegemony of the New Right in economic theory, and the collapse of socialism as a doctrine in both Eastern and Western Europe, rule out any doctrinal survival of socialism. Again, many of the policies implemented under the incisive Thatcher government are politically irreversible. (Most privatizations fall into this category.) What is to be feared in the wake of protracted economic difficulty is not socialism, but a return to corporatist and interventionist policies that not only injure the autonomous institutions of civil society but also compound the economic difficulties that evoked them. In the United States, more than in Britain, the end of the long boom may well see a serious crisis in financial institutions weakened (as much of corporate America is) by inordinate debt, and a policy response which reinvigorates the American tradition of combining isolationism with protectionism. In the British case, where fiscal prudence has been maintained, we are likely to see a return to 'stop-go' economic management, against a background of high inflation, high interest rates and revived union power.

Exclusive or primary reliance on economic growth as the legitimating condition of market capitalist institutions in the context of mass democracy is unwise and will predictably fail. An alternative, suggested by High Tory critics of the neo-liberal components in Thatcherism such as Roger Scruton, is little more promising. Scruton argues that it is nationhood that provides the indispensable foundation of liberal civil society in our time. Scruton's argument has considerable merit in exposing the insufficiency, and the inconsistency, of those such as Parekh[11] who have maintained that a multicultural society can be supported (as supposedly in America) solely by liberal legalism and constitutionalism. Scruton's positive endorsement of nationhood as the condition of a stable civil society is nevertheless unpersuasive. In historical terms, what has sustained the most successful civil societies has not been nationhood but monarchy (as in the British case) or empire (as in the Hapsburg Empire which Scruton discusses.) If civil society has a future in contemporary Spain, again, it is in virtue of monarchy, since Spain as it now exists is little more than a composite state which itself is an artefact of monarchy. Scruton also underestimates the modernity of nationhood. As late as the 1870s, a majority of French school children identified themselves by their provinces, and not as French. In Europe, nationhood is in most countries the construction of political élites, not the expression of the solidarity of peoples. Ironically, the modern European nation-state is mostly the creation of nineteenth-century classical liberalism, which was an agency for centralization and against localism.[12] Examples such as Poland and Japan, where nationhood and statehood coincide, are in fact highly exceptional, and not at all the rule.

Minogue and Kedourie[13] are closer to the mark than Scruton, when they observe that nationalism is a modernist project inspired by romantic doctrine. In the post-colonial world, it has acted as a destroyer of traditional forms of life and as a pace-maker for Communism. Where it has expressed a genuine, pre-political or social popular solidarity, it has typically been one that was once embodied in statehood, and is preserved as such in popular memory – as in the Baltic states. (Only the Kurds come to mind as a possible exception to this generalization.) Finally, when nationalism has arisen within a civil society governed by a rule of law, as in the Sikh phenomenon in India, it has acted as a threat to civil society. In all these respects, the modernist cult of nationalism is akin to the no less modernist phenomenon of fundamentalism. With rare exceptions, such as Poland and the Baltic states, it is characterized by enmity to civil society and not by support for it.

Neither neo-liberalism nor its conservative critics, if my reasonings are sound, recognize the cultural foundations and historical limits of individualist civil society. In this they may be influenced by a conflation of individualism with civil society that is valid in the English and American contexts but not in a world context. The English and European theorists of civil society – Hobbes, Locke, Hegel, Touqueville and others – represented as an inherent and universal truth the connexion between individualist culture and a civil society encompassing market institutions. The experience of the last decade or so, however, in which powerful and stable market economies have emerged in the non-individualist cultures of Japan and Korea, for example, suggests that the connection between individualism and civil society is contingent and not necessary. This recent experience supports the Scottish and neo-conservative fear that, in slowly consuming its pre-individualist foundations, Western civil society may (as Schumpeter speculated[14]) be a self-limiting historical episode.

For the present, no doubt, such fears are exaggerated – although it remains to be seen how American culture responds to the novel experience of continuing, and probably inexorable, economic decline. The concerns I have explored suggest, however, that there are no easy answers to the question, what is now the content of the common culture that supports and legitimates market capitalism? And this in turn suggests that the policy agenda of post-Thatcherism will need to be judicious and balanced when it comes, as it inevitably must, to seek to retard or reverse the further erosion of the moral capital on which market institutions must rely. The crusade for Victorian values is, as has already been intimated, an exercise in anachronism. This is not to say that there cannot be serious policies aiming at strengthening what remains of the common individualist culture in

England. In education, in social and welfare policy, there are desirable reforms, well within the limits of what is politically possible, which could well strengthen the family and reinforce the popular sense of individual responsibility. Enforcing the obligations of the delinquent parent in one-parent families, wherever this is feasible, is only one rather obvious sample. In education, a Natural Curriculum which enforces literacy in English, which promotes an understanding of British history, and which perhaps incorporates a civic education, could do something to restore the fabric of the common culture.

No government can create a culture where it is absent, or engineer the renewal of a culture where it is moribund. As Wittgenstein put it, deliberately continuing to renew damaged or weak traditions is as hopeless as trying to repair a broken spiders web with one's bare hands. Government has, nevertheless, and contrary to neo-liberalism, a vital role in regard to the culture of individualism. Negatively, it can refrain from damaging it, by abandoning policies which create dependency, overturn traditional disciplines and encourage irresponsibility.[15] Positively, it can provide a framework of policy and institutions within which individualist culture is protected and nurtured. In so doing, it is tending the pre-individualist forms of life – family and local life, for example – that are the soil on which individuality grows and thrives. It is only by addressing these cultural pre-conditions of individualism, and framing sensible policy in respect of them, that the current hegemony of market institutions can be preserved, and a secure future for civil society achieved.

The philosophical insight which such desirable reforms embody is that, even where (as in England) individualist culture is immemorial, it is not primordial, but depends on a background of beliefs, values and institutions which both form and constrain individuality. It is this cultural patrimony of individualism that neo-liberal thought ignores, and which Thatcherite policy has insufficiently addressed. Individuality, as we know it, is not a natural fact, but a cultural achievement. The persons who inhabit and reproduce a liberal civil society are not biological organisms but historical artefacts, products of a long and often arduous struggle to build up and maintain specific sorts of institutions and practices. With us, at any rate, individualism and civil society have always gone together, and civil society has no future apart from the culture of individualism. Ironically, it is this culture that is being threatened, especially in the United States, by a left-liberalism which regards the undergirding institutions of liberal civil society – marriage, private property and so forth – as constraints upon, and not as conditions of individual freedom. The irony in intellectual history is that it is liberalism, at least since Mill,[16] that has transmitted the enmity to civil society and to the moral traditions that support it that has long been evident in modern Europe in the antinomian character of the anti-individual (in Oakeshott's expression[17]) – the dislocated, anomic character, typified by Rousseau, who seeks a release from the burdens of freedom in the recreation of a form of communal solidarity that, in England at any rate, was always largely imaginary.

Individualism in England is not – as it is in Turkey, say – an imposition from above, generated by legality and military force. It is our common cultural inheritance. But, as I have argued throughout, the renewal across the generation of this individualist tradition cannot safely be left to chance. Government has a vital role in preserving, or repairing, the framework of practices and replenishing the fund of values, on which individualism depends for its successful reproduction. If Thatcherism was ever an hegemonic project – and that is how is should rightly have been conceived – it condemned itself to failure by its faulty grasp of the cultural preconditions of market liberalism. It may be that, despite its continuing economic success, Western civil society is in an irreversible decline, which government can retard but not reverse. Even in this worst case, it remains the intellectual responsibility of conservatives in the era of post-Thatcherism to theorize the conditions under which civil society in England may retain its vitality. In this task they are distracted by neo-liberal and holistic High Tory doctrine which fails to attend to the minute particulars of our individualist inheritance and which does not illuminate the deeper tradition that it expresses. Civil society – which is to say a society that, under a rule of law, allows the great majority of transactions to be conducted in autonomous institutions, and in which the bulk of economic life is realized in market exchanges among legally recognized owners of private property – is the only form of life in which civilization has been enjoyed by modern Europeans. Oakeshott has characterized civil society in the English form with unsurpassable clarity:

What, then, are the characteristics of our society in respect of which we consider ourselves to enjoy freedom and in default of which we would not be free in our sense of the word? But first, it must be observed that the freedom we enjoy is not composed of a number of independent characteristics of our society which in aggregate make up our liberty. Liberties, it is true, may be distinguished, and some may be more general or more settled and mature than others, but the freedom which the English libertarian knows and values lies in a coherence of mutually supporting liberties, each of which amplifies the whole and none of which stands alone. It springs neither from the separation of church and state, nor from the rule of law, nor from private property, nor from parliamentary government, nor from the writ of *habeas corpus*, nor from the independence of the judiciary, nor from any one of the thousand other devices and arrangements characteristic of our society, but from what each signifies and represents, namely, the absence from our society of overwhelming concentration of power.

Similarly, the conduct of government in our society involves a sharing of power, not only between the recognised organs of government, but also between the Administration and the Opposition. In short, we consider ourselves to be free because no one in our society is allowed unlimited power – no leader, faction, party or 'class', no majority, no government, church, corporation, trade or professional association or trade union. The secret of its freedom is that it is composed of a multitude of organisations in the constitution of the best of which is reproduced that diffusion of power which is characteristic of the whole.[18]

If conservatives are serious in the commitment to the project of achieving a political hegemony for this form of life, they must return their theorizing to history. For, in returning us to a self-understanding hitherto clouded by defective history – liberal, Marxist or High Tory-holist – they will thereby strengthen the intellectual hegemony which the thought of the New Right has achieved in economic theory and policy. And, in so doing, they will make a small, but vital contribution to the success of the political project of securing hegemony for civil society – by creating a discourse in which its most central institutions can be theorized as historical achievements.

20 What is dead and what is living in liberalism?

This book is written for those who are in sympathy with the spirit in which it is written. This is not, I believe, the spirit of the main current of European and American civilisation. The spirit of this civilisation makes itself manifest in the industry, architecture and music of our time, in its fascism and socialism, and it is alien and uncongenial to the author. This is not a value judgement. It is not, it is true, as though he accepted what nowadays passes for architecture as architecture or did not approach what is called modern music with the greatest suspicion (though without understanding its language), but still, the disappearance of the arts does not justify judging disparagingly the human beings who make up this civilisation. For in times like these, genuine strong characters simply leave the arts aside and turn to other things and somehow the worth of the individual person finds expression. Not, to be sure, in the way it would at a time of high culture. A culture is like a big organisation which assigns each of its members a place where he can work in the spirit of the whole; and it is perfectly fair for his power to be measured by the contribution he succeeds in making to the whole enterprise. In an age without culture, on the other hand, forces become fragmented and the power of an individual man is used up in overcoming friction. But energy is still energy and even if the spectacle which our age affords us is not the formation of a great cultural work, with the best men contributing to the same great end, so much as the unimpressive spectacle of a crowd whose best members work for purely private ends, still we must not forget that the spectacle is not what matters.

I realise then that the disappearance of a culture does not signify the disappearance of human value, but simply of certain means of expressing this value, yet the fact remains that I have no sympathy for the current of European civilisation and do not understand its goals, if it has any. So I am really writing for friends who are scattered throughout the corners of the globe.

L. Wittgenstein[1]

INTRODUCTION

In this chapter of eight sections, I will consider what are the most essential or fundamental constitutive elements of liberalism. In the first four sections of the chapter, I will consider how these fare when subjected to the force of radical value-pluralism. I conclude that none of the four constitutive elements of doctrinal liberalism – universalism, individualism, egalitarianism and meliorism – survives the ordeal by value-pluralism, and that liberalism, as a political philosophy, is therefore dead. In the last four sections of the paper, I argue that what is living in liberalism is the historic inheritance, now re-emerging in parts of the world in which it was suppressed, of a civil society whose institutions protect liberty and permit civil peace. Arguing that, over the long run of human history, civil societies are not the only legitimate societies, I conclude nevertheless that a liberal civil social society is the best one for cultures, such as all or virtually all contemporary cultures, which harbour a diversity of incommensurable conceptions of the good.

The position defended here is post-liberal in that it rejects the foundationalist claims of fundamentalist liberalism. This is to say that it denies that liberal regimes are uniquely legitimate for all human beings. Human beings have flourished in regimes that do not shelter a liberal civil society, and there are forms of human flourishing that are driven out in liberal regimes. Liberal orders have, then, no universal or apodictic authority, contrary to liberal political philosophy. At the same time, it will be my argument that the four constitutive features of liberalism can be given a rational defence when they are contextualized and historicized as features of late modern (or early post-modern) societies and polities. Though there will not be (and need not be) any convergence on a single form of government, nevertheless all, or nearly all forms of government that allow for commodious living will in the foreseeable future be ones that shelter the institutions of civil society. These institutions, in their turn, will be animated by the practice of liberty that is our historical inheritance. Our task as theorists of our historic inheritance of civil society is, on this view, to seek for a better understanding of the practice and culture of liberty that is our patrimony, and which is now exfoliating in many varieties in several parts of the world. If the argument of this paper is sound, the death of foundationalist liberal political philosophy should not concern us greatly, since it enables us to return to its historic source in the practice of liberty.

DOES LIBERALISM HAVE A HISTORY?

What was liberalism? In order to answer this question, we need to ask another: Does liberalism have a history? This latter question is not as absurd as it seems, since it is the result of recent work, by Pocock and others, to controvert the standard liberal self-interpretation. On this conventional liberal view, memorably expressed by J. S. Mill,[2] modern liberalism is merely the contemporary expression of a tradition of free-thinking and antinomianism that is virtually immemorial, but extends back at least as far as Socrates. The upshot of recent scholarship has been to deconstruct this liberal self-interpretation, and to theorize 'liberalism' as a much more discrete episode in the history of thought. On the Pocockian view,[3] at any rate, it is an error to view Locke, Kant, Smith and Mill, say, as expositors of a single tradition of ideas, if only because the Scottish thinkers, for example, who are often regarded as the prototypical classical liberals – Smith and Ferguson, say – were themselves deeply influenced by traditions of civic humanism and classical republicanism whose relations with 'liberalism' are, at best, ambivalent. On this view, if 'liberalism' has a history, it begins sometime early in the nineteenth century, when the word 'liberal' acquired its contemporary meaning. For exponents of this view, it is a sort of whiggish illusion that is fostered in respect of liberalism, when it is theorized as existing before the French Revolution, and as having a genealogy extending back to the ancient world.

It is, fortunately, unnecessary to attempt to settle the historical controversy which this view has generated. For, on this view and also on the standard liberal self-interpretation, modern liberalism received its paradigmatic statement as a comprehensive ideology in the writings of J. S. Mill. To be sure, other, earlier writers are on both views clearly identifiable as expositors of a liberal intellectual tradition – Constant and Tocqueville, for example, and other disillusionist liberals who wrote in the wake of the French Revolution. It is in J. S. Mill, however, that (on all views) we find *the liberal syndrome* of ideas most explicitly and recognizably articulated. With Mill, one is in the same company as later, and latter-day liberals – a company that includes Dworkin and Rawls, among others.

To affirm the identity of a liberal intellectual tradition spanning Mill and Rawls is *not* to deny that it is a very complex tradition, containing recessive and dialectical moments. It is not to pass over, or to seek to suppress, the new liberalism of the late nineteenth-century English Hegelians, such as Bosanquet and Green, or the somewhat holistic, even communitarian liberalism of such as Hobhouse. Nor is it to endorse the mistaken view, earlier exposed in my own writings,[4] that liberalism can be easily and uncontroversially divided into classical and revisionist varieties, with the classical liberals being devoted primarily to negative liberty, and the revisionists being a species of welfarist or egalitarian liberal. One result of Pocock's work will stand, even if his substantive claims are rejected or qualified: a methodological scepticism about intellectual historiography

which commends suspicion about history that is written in terms of enduring concepts, after the fashion of Lovejoy. This scepticism should caution
us against seeking too much continuity or coherence, even in a liberal
intellectual tradition that starts with Mill.

This methodological preamble aside, we can still identify a matrix of
ideas, recognizable by all or most liberals, and by their critics, as constituting the liberal syndrome. Following earlier work of mine,[5] I shall
specify four key ideas, found in J. S. Mill, and echoed in virtually all
subsequent liberal writers. First, there is the idea of *moral or normative
individualism* – the idea that, since nothing has ultimate value except states
of mind or feeling, or aspects of the lives of human individuals, therefore
the claims of individuals will always defeat those of collectivities, institutions or forms of life. This claim, as Raz has noted,[6] is a variant on the thesis
of *humanism* – the modernist belief, which has nevertheless deep roots in
Judaeo–Christianity, that only human beings and their forms of life have
ultimate value. A second element in the liberal syndrome is *universalism* –
the idea that there are weighty duties and/or rights that are owed to all
human beings, regardless of their cultural inheritances or historical circumstances, just in virtue of their standing as human beings. This strong
anti-relativist claim is, in my view, essential to any liberal view that is
constitutively liberal – any view, such as Kant's, Mill's, or that of the early
Rawls, that regards a liberal regime as, at least potentially, the best and
uniquely right one for all mankind, even if in many contexts approxi-
mations of it are all that can be achieved. In other words, without denying
that other regimes may be necessary stages on the path to a liberal regime,
and perhaps even going so far as to recognize that, for some peoples, a
liberal regime will never be fully or stably achieved, constitutive, fundamentalist or doctrinal liberalism must still affirm that all political institutions are to be assessed on the single scale that measures their
approximation to a liberal regime. This second idea leads one, naturally
enough, to the third element in the liberal syndrome, namely *meliorism*. By
this is meant the view that, even if human institutions are imperfectible,
they are nonetheless open to indefinite improvement by the judicious use of
critical reason. To say this is to say that, though no contemporary liberalism
can credibly presuppose historical laws guaranteeing inevitable human
improvement, equally, no contemporary liberalism can do without some
idea of *progress*, however attenuated. The fourth and final element of the
liberal syndrome issues intelligibly from the first three – liberal *egalitarianism*. By this is meant the denial of any natural moral or political
hierarchy among human beings, such as was theorized by Aristotle in
respect of slavery and by Filmer of absolute monarchy. For any liberal, in
other words, the human species is a single-status moral community, and

monarchy, hierarchy and subordination are practices that stand in need of an ethical defence. The implications of this position for ideas of consent as the basis of political obligation, and of democracy as an institution devised to meet requirements of public justification of the use of political coercion, are clear enough.

The claim made here is that, even if it be true that not all liberals subscribe to every one of these theses, together they add up to a system of ideas that most contemporary liberals would find difficulty in rejecting. All four ideas are clearly present in the thought of J.S. Mill, who for the purposes of my argument I will treat as the paradigmatic liberal. It should be noted, finally, that I have not included in the four ideas constitutive of the liberal syndrome any specific prescriptive *principle* – say, a principle prioritizing liberty or equality. I have not done so, precisely in order to advance a conception of liberalism that is sufficiently copious, catholic and eclectic as to be tolerant of the entire extended family of views that have and do legitimately call themselves 'liberal'. It is an implication of this last point, again, that I have not identified liberalism with any foundational political morality – a rights-based morality, say, or a contractarian morality. This too secures for the discussion of liberalism a methodological tolerance of its many legitimate varieties, and aims to guarantee that whatever critical judgements the argument yields regarding liberalism will be true for all its instances.

INCOMMENSURABILITY AMONG VALUES AND THE ILLUSIONS OF PROGRESS

How far do the ideas I have specified – ideas shared, I would say, by Paine, Condorcet, Kant, Mill, Dworkin and the early Rawls – stand up to criticism? Are they viable elements in a currently defensible theoretical outlook? I have in earlier work exploited recent inquiry into indeterminacy and incommensurability in fundamental values to argue that a doctrinal liberalism aiming to specify a unique set of basic principles having universal prescriptive authority cannot be achieved. I want now to examine the four elements of the liberal syndrome in order to see what, if anything, of them survives an analogous critique. So as to anticipate my conclusion, it is that none of them can withstand the force of strong indeterminacy and radical incommensurability among values. Considered as a position in political philosophy, accordingly, liberalism is a failed project. Nothing can be done, according to the argument here developed, to rescue it: as a philosophical perspective, it is dead. What then is living in liberalism? The aspect of liberalism that remains alive for us, I shall argue, is the conception and the historic reality of civil society that has been bequeathed to us. This conception and set of practices embodies or exemplifies, in historically contextualized form, the four constitutive features of doctrinal liberalism. The argument will be that, though it is not the case that a liberal civil society possessing these features is the only, or necessarily the best society from the standpoint of human flourishing, nevertheless it is the only sort of regime in which *we* – in our historical circumstance as late moderns – can live well. There is an historical argument for liberalism, in other words, which maintains that a civil society constitutes the only sort of society through which a modern civilization can reproduce itself. (It is not denied on this view that there may be exceptions to the generalization just stated – Saudi Arabia may be one – but it is asserted that they will be few, and perhaps short-lived.) On this view, although it is true that there have been great civilizations that did not encompass anything resembling a civil society, it is nevertheless true that civil society, and therefore the liberal inheritance it carries with it, is for us an historical fate. The worth of civil society for us as moderns (or post-moderns) is that it permits the peaceful coexistence in a *modus vivendi* of incommensurable values and perspectives on the world. For this reason, I shall conclude, the only forms of liberal theorizing that command a claim on our allegiance in our historical circumstance are the Oakeshottian account of civil association and the Berlinian liberalism which is itself founded on radical value-pluralism.

In Berlin's theorizing, the pretensions of philosophy are radically humbled, in that it is denied that philosophical inquiry (or indeed practical reasoning) can arbitrate deep conflicts among ultimate values, issue in a prescription for the good life for all men, or found any specific way of life. Further, in Berlin's theorizing, the current liberal project, most transparently pursued in the work of Rawls, of aiming to state and derive a unique set of principles about liberty, is explicitly rejected by reference to the thesis that conflicts among liberties, no less than conflicts among other values, may be (and often are) conflicts among incommensurables that are insusceptible to rational arbitration. In Berlin's liberal perspective, the hubristic ambitions of liberal political philosophy are chastened, and a humbler and more realistic mode of theorizing adopted.

In Oakeshott's theorizing, which several commentators have perceived to have important affinities with liberal thought,[7] the task of philosophy is restricted to that of illuminating our inheritance of practice and specifying its postulates. More particularly, Oakeshott seeks to gather from the miscellaneity of practice the most essential features of *civil association* – that form of human association, by no means natural or universal among human beings, but rather a distinctive historical achievement, in which human beings are united not in any common purpose (as they may be in war, for example) but instead by their subscription to an authoritative body of non-instrumental rules. For Oakeshott, as for Berlin, despite their profound differences in many other areas of thought, philosophy may elucidate practice; it can never aspire (as perhaps it did among the Greeks) to govern it. It is this form of inquiry, in which we aim for a better grasp of practice in order then to return to it in all its vicissitudes, that I shall defend against the foundationalist illusions of liberal philosophy.

This is to anticipate the upshot of a complex and at every point contestable argument. Let us begin by considering the impact for the liberal idea of *progress* of the thesis of fundamental value-incommensurability. Here an analogy from the arts may be helpful, in the first instance, to overcome intuitive resistance to the very idea of incommensurability. Consider the drama of Sophocles and of Shakespeare, or, closer to us and to each other, the drama of Shakespeare on the one hand and of the French classicists, Corneille and Racine, on the other. In what sense are the plays of Shakespeare, say, better or worse than those of Sophocles or Racine? It is true that these art objects belong to the same recognizable genre – that of drama; yet it seems thoroughly absurd to try to rank them on any single scale of excellence. Despite their membership of a common genre, they are simply too different in style and theme to allow of any such assessment. Within any such subgenre, no doubt, assessments of better and worse are feasible and even commonplace, and we may sensibly talk of improvement or decline in the tradition which is expressed in Greek tragedy or in French classicism. Again, within any culture we may be able to distinguish great art from art that is mediocre or worthless. Accordingly, though it makes no sense to rank the poetry of Donne and Gerald Manley Hopkins on a single scale, we can clearly discern the superiority of these incommensurables over the doggerel of e. e. cummings, say. Further, there may be cross-cultural considerations which enable us to distinguish the art objects of a higher culture from those of a lower: this is a point I cannot pursue here, but which it is important be made, since the perspective of incommensurability that is being opened up here is confused, almost infallibly, with that of cultural relativism.

These misunderstandings aside, the argument is that, in general, there cannot be progress in the arts, if by that is meant improvement throughout human history. There may be progress or decline even across traditions, as when a tradition of high and great art – art in which the powers of human imagination and creativity are maximally employed – is succeeded by a tradition that is shallow or feeble. The theme of incommensurability among artistic goods affirms, nevertheless, that there is no one form of great art that is best, since there is no overarching standard whereby such a judgement could be made. Examples of this can be found, both within our own cultural history, and by comparison with other great civilizations. Even within a context as culture-specific as that of Christian churches, it is difficult to see how the excellences of a Baroque cathedral could be put in the balance against those of a Gothic. It is even harder to imagine what overarching standards could be invoked to weigh the merits of the Parthenon against those of Notre Dame, or of either against the Shinto Shrine at Isee.

The idea of global progress in the arts is incoherent. It is incoherent, if only because the arts are not in the business of representation and of measuring, with ever greater accuracy, a wholly independent subject matter. Instead, we understand the arts rightly, if we see them as historic creations of a highly inventive species, embedded in and emerging from specific forms of social life with definite and diverse cultural and historical inheritances. The analogy in ethics and politics should be plain. As Isaiah Berlin has put the case for incommensurability in ethics and politics, with a clarity and power upon which I cannot hope to improve:

> There are many objective ends, ultimate values, some incompatible with others, pursued by different societies at different times, or by different groups in the same society, by entire classes or churches or races, or by particular individuals within them, any one of which may find itself subject to conflicting claims of uncombinable, yet equally ultimate and objective, ends.[8]

Speaking of Vico and Herder, Berlin observes that:

> For them, values are many; some of the most fascinating come to light in the course of voyages, both in time and space; some among them cannot, in principle, be harmonised with one another. This leads to the conclusion, not explicitly formulated by either thinker, that the ancient ideal, common to many cultures and especially to that of the Enlighten-ment, of a perfect society in which all true ends are reconciled, is conceptually incoherent. But this is not relativism. . . . At the heart of the best-known type of modern historical relativism lies the conception of men wholly bound by tradition or culture or class or generation to particular attitudes or scales of value which cause other outlooks or ideals to seem strange and, at times, even unintelligible; if the existence of such outlooks is recognized, this inevitably leads to scepticism about objective standards, since it becomes meaningless to ask which of them is correct. This is not at all Vico's position, nor . . . is it in general that of Herder either.[9]

The pluralism which asserts a fundamental incommensurability of ultimate values is not, then, any species of relativism, nor does it belong to any of the many varieties of modern subjectivism or scepticism about values. It is instead a realist or objectivist view. *Objective pluralism* of this sort affirms that ultimate values are knowable, that they are many, that they often conflict and are uncombinable, and that in many of such conflicts there is no overarching standard whereby their claims are rationally arbitrable: there are conflicts among the incommensurables. The diversity of ultimate values, great as it is, is not infinite; it is bounded by the limits of human nature. 'Incompatible these ends may be; but their variety cannot be unlimited, for the nature of men, however various and subject to change, must possess some generic character if it is to be called human at all'.[10] This pluralism, bounded as it is, may come in several varieties, and may operate at several levels. Within the moral code of a particular culture, there may be lacunae that generate dilemmas which neither the code itself, nor the practical reasonings of the individual, can resolve. Hence are generated the radical or tragic choices among competing evils or rival excellences, in which whatever is chosen entails some great loss or involves some irreparable wrong, of which Berlin has often written. Also, there is the variety of pluralism which illuminates value-conflict, not within cultures or individuals, but between cultures or whole forms of life having incommensurable values as constitutive elements. These varieties of pluralism may interpenetrate one another, especially when (as in the late modern world) cultures and forms of life have come to interact deeply with one another, are no longer easily individuated, so that many individuals find themselves (in Fulke Greville's phrase) 'suckled on the milk of many nurses', formed by many distinct cultural traditions.

Objective pluralism carries with it the implication that there is a radical moral scarcity which it is our fate as humans to endure. In the form in which it is most subversive of the classical foundations of Western civilization, this species of pluralism denies the coherence of the Form of the Good, as theorized by Plato, and rejects the thesis of the unity of the virtues, as advanced by Aristotle. In this pluralist view, not only are all genuine goods not necessarily harmonious, but goods may depend for their existence upon evils, virtues on vices. In *this* aspect, pluralism is a variation on the theme of the imperfectibility of human life, traceable back to Jewish and Christian sources. In its deepest implication, however, pluralism does *not* mark the imperfection inherent in the nature of things: it destroys the very idea of perfection. It thereby strikes a death-blow at the classical foundation of our culture, expressed not only in Plato and Aristotle, but in the Stoic idea of the *logos* and in Aquinas's conception of a world order that was rational and moral in its essence, even as it was the creation of the Deity, one of the central attributes of which was perfection.

Objective pluralism, because it destroys the idea of a perfect human life, is fatal to this Greco–Roman, rationalist dimension of our cultural inheritance. It also undermines a no less foundational element in our civilization, derived from the Judeao–Christian tradition, which is the notion of the *meaningfullness of human history*, conceived in the moral terms of redemption or of improvement. For it is evident that, if we lack overarching standards whereby to assess history as a whole, then, as Herder perceived, 'general, progressive amelioration of the world' is 'a fiction'. True, there may be improvement within any particular culture, as judged by its own standards; and there may, as limiting cases, be a few instances, in which we can judge that, granted all relevant incommensurabilities, there has been a betterment or a worsening in goods and evils that are not culture-specific, but generically human. This latter limiting case gives no support, however, to the whiggish conception of history as a narrative of progress, as a moral drama with *ourselves* as its *telos*, which is one of the many illegitimate offspring of Judaeo–Christianity that inform the sentimental and absurd religion of humanity which is the secular faith of the Western intelligentsia. On the pluralist view, human history as a whole has, and can have, no meaning;[11] it is, at best, a series of adventures in civilization, each singular and discrete, leading nowhere, and at no point disclosing or approximating the features of 'man *qua* man'.

Objective pluralism, then, has radically subversive implications for the two traditions that form the twin pillars of Western civilization – the Greco–Roman and the Judaeo–Christian. It is also subversive of central elements of other cultural traditions. In China, for example, there is a Confucian tradition of historiography in which history is written in terms of moral advance and decline, which is subverted by pluralism, if such history is supposed to have more than a local authority. And in India there is a tradition of moralizing and rationalistic Buddhism, disallowing contradictions in the nature of things, which is also threatened by incommensurability.

Objective pluralism of the radical sort advanced here recognizes incommensurabilities among generic human goods and evils as well as incommensurabilities between (and within) specific cultures or forms of life. As to generic human goods, it may be that there are virtues or excellences that, however various their expressions in different forms of life, are not culture-specific. It may be that courage is a human virtue *tout court*, though its varieties may be immense, and we are sometimes unsure whether we have rightly identified it. So, also, with justice and mercy. But – as many works of literature, such as Melville's *Billy Budd*, show us – the practical demands of these generic human virtues may be conflicting, and such conflicts may be among incommensurables. Again, contrary to the thesis of the unity of the virtues advanced by Socrates and Aristotle, it may be (according to the objective pluralist view) that some are uncombinable in a single person. This is a thesis in moral psychology and anthropology to which I shall return later. There may be uncombinabilities and incommensurabilities among other generic human goods – between a life devoted to intense physical pleasure, and a life devoted to long-term projects, or the life of a family man who wishes to live long enough to see his grandchildren grow. And, not least importantly, there may be conflicts among incommensurables, where there are generic human evils. Between pain and death, violence and subtle coercion, and many other impediments to human flourishing, there may on the objective pluralist view be radical and tragic choices to be made in respect of which reason leaves us in the lurch. (It is at this point that radical value-pluralism undermines traditional conceptions of natural law.) None of these incommensurabilities among universal or generic human goods and evils in any way supports unrestricted cultural relativism about values, or endorses any of the modern varieties of ethical subjectivism and scepticism.

Objective pluralism recognizes that many goods are specific to, and dependent upon, particular forms of life. The life of a late medieval troubadour could not be lived in ancient Egypt any more than the life of a temple courtesan could be lived in medieval Christendom. (The term 'form of life' is here being used with deliberate indeterminacy, so as to encompass whole cultures as well as styles of life within specific cultures. At no point does the argument presuppose that forms of life are easily or uncontroversially individuated.) On the pluralist view, it will sometimes be the case that goods or excellences that are specific to definite and uncombinable forms of life are also incommensurables. Different forms of life may embody virtues and excellences which, though they are each of them recognizably great, cannot rationally be ranked or weighed against each other. As between the life of a bushido warrior and a Renaissance scientist, say, there is on the pluralist account no measuring rod whereby they could be assessed, no scales whereby they could be put in the balance. Conflicts among incommensurables will also occur within specific forms of life. Within the form of life constituted by Catholic Christianity, the virtues of a nun are not combinable with those of a mother; and it may be that this incompatibility expresses an incommensurability, resolved in practice only by the non-rational call of vocation. On the pluralist account, then, conflicts among incommensurables, thought hardly ubiquitous, are pervasive in human life. This is a result that goes very much against received intellectual tradition and against much commonsense intuition.

Pluralism goes against the grain of our cultural inheritance by also offending the banal pieties of liberal humanism, and by being offensive to the common stock of ordinary intuitions. How, then, is it to be defended? What sort of theory of knowledge could support these claims about the incommensurability of ultimate values? It has already been noted that a value-pluralist ethical theory cannot avoid being a realist theory. But of what species of realism are we speaking? And what are its epistemological credentials?

We can approach the latter question, first, by observing that objective pluralism is bound to be anti-intuitionist in its account of our knowledge of ultimate values. In this we follow J. S. Mill, who saw that intuitionism has an inherently conservative tendency in that it treats as finally authoritative the pre-reflective judgements of persons in their local cultural environments. If, as with most academic moral philosophers in our time, these are meagre, conformist and impoverished cultural environments (the environments of most contemporary universities), and if the lives and experiences of those whose intuitions are consulted and considered authoritative are also therefore shallow and narrow, then the moral judgements and theories they eventuate in will likewise be shallow and narrow. Intuitionism in ethics is to be rejected, then, because it sanctifies the deliverances of local knowledge, however restrictive or distorted they may be. (In our day, the local knowledge that is so sanctified is not that of ordinary folk, but instead that of an inexperienced and culturally illiterate lumpenintelligentsia.) The most plausible alternative to intuitionism is the position sketched by Mill, in which value judgements are always tested at the bar of experience, but in which they are exposed to all the evidences of anthropology, history, literature, social science and of experiments in living. As Skorupsky well puts the nub of Mill's methodological naturalism in the epistemology of ethics:

> Any political philosophy which supposes that some forms of life are objectively better in that they offer truer forms of happiness or more emancipated modes of existence – and which does not ground that claim in something transcendental or revealed – must defend itself by appeal to naturally shared human dispositions.... Certain dispositions of feeling must be shared by humans in such a way as to define normal responses. Not necessarily statistically normal; but one to which the organism, when not impeded from its natural path, or suffering from some internal capacity or disease, tends, and in which it finds a resting point from which it does not wish to escape, which it reflectively prefers. Then to fail in the response is to suffer from an incapacity which deprives one of access to a mode of experience which, for human beings, is intrinsically worthwhile. By the same token, it must be possible to distinguish between external conditions which impede or distort the natural flowering of a human being's dispositions, and those which facilitate it. A human being achieves fullest satisfaction, the life of greatest well-being, when those natural dispositions are fully expressed.

It achieves a stable eudaemonic equilibrium – a mode of life it would reflectively prefer even with an imaginative grasp of options.[12]

The epistemology that Skorupski identifies as Mill's is a naturalistic one with important affinities with the less metaphysical aspects of Aristotelian ethics. It specifies as the subject matter of ethics human well-being or flourishing, and it treats the content of well-being and flourishing, not as consisting merely or mainly in subjective preferences or desires, but as a matter that is at least partly objective, encompassing the use of human capacities in a life that is, or may be, reflectively judged to be worthwhile. This neo-Aristotelian epistemology denies what Raz has perceptively called 'the transparency of values'[13] – the error that the content of our well-being is clear to each of us. Though I cannot here develop the point, but will return briefly to it later, this Millian epistemology is akin to Aristotle's in representing human emotions as nearer to perceptions than to sensations – in other words, in attributing to emotions a rationality (or irrationality) they are denied on any purely or crudely Humean account of them.

An epistemology of value that acknowledges objective pluralism and value-incommensurability will nevertheless differ from Aristotle's in crucial and fundamental respects. It will be non-hierarchical, in that incommensurability precludes objective rankings or weightings of ultimate values. It will therefore refrain from prioritizing or privileging any one form of life – say, the life of rational inquiry, of contemplation or wealth-creation, of prayer or selfless devotion to others – as the best for the human species. Unlike the Millian moral epistemology, it will not suppose that moral inquiry will eventuate in a Peircean ideal convergence. Rather, as a species of objective pluralism in ethics, it will expect inquiry to issue in an ultimate divergence of ethical perspectives – a point to which I shall later return. As has already been observed, it will deny the unity of the virtues, emphasizing instead conflicts among human excellences, some of which will be incommensurables. It will, for that reason, deny that the good life is for most people necessarily a mixed life: for, if the ingredients of a mixed life are incommensurables, there will be no uniquely rational combination of them, and rough equality will be no more rational than any other mixture. (From a standpoint that acknowledges incommensurabilities among ultimate values, the Aristotelian doctrines of the unity of the virtues and of the mean may seem like little more than a prescription for mediocrity.) And finally, since a pluralist will not take for granted the local context of the *polis* that seemed natural to Aristotle, but will recognize with Aristotle the dependency of central human individual excellences on various forms of communal life, an objective pluralist will have good reason to favour a variety of regimes, communal and political, in which a diversity of uncombinable excellences may flourish. It will be seen later that this last point has radical and subversive implications for liberalisms of a doctrinal or fundamentalist sort.

Objective pluralist epistemologies of value may be characterized as a species of *plural realism* in value theory. They are comparable with, perhaps even applications of, the species of plural realism (or, as it might also be called, *perspectivism*) in general epistemology that Dreyfus has discovered in Heidegger's later thought. As Dreyfus convincingly argues, Heidegger is not (contrary to common interpretations) a pragmatist, an instrumentalist or a relativist, any more than he is an idealist, a physicalist or a materialist. Instead

> Where ultimate reality is concerned, later Heidegger could be called a *plural realist*. For a plural realist there is no point of view from which one can ask and answer the metaphysical questions concerning the one true nature of ultimate reality. Given the dependence of the intelligibility of all ways of being on Dasein's being, and the dependence of what counts as elements of reality on our purposes, the question makes no sense. Indeed, since reality is relative to finite *Dasein*, there can be many true answers to the question, 'What is real'? Heidegger looks like an idealist or a relativist only if one thinks that only one system of description could correspond to the way things really are. But for Heidegger, different understandings of being reveal different sorts of entities, and since no one way of revealing is exclusively true, accepting one does not commit us to rejecting the others. There is a deep similarity between Heidegger and Donald Davidson on this point. Both would agree that we can make reality intelligible using various descriptions and that what our claims are true of under a given description has whatever properties it has even if these descriptions are not reducible to a single description, and whether we describers and our ways of describing exist or not.[14]

Dreyfus notes the affinities of the later Heidegger's plural realism with aspects of the thought of the later Wittgenstein.[15] He further specifies what he means by plural realism when he says:

> once we see that Newton's laws are true, we see that nature was already the way they reveal it to be even at the time of Aristotle. Conversely, if Aristotle's terms successfully picked out natural finds (relative to final causes), his account is still true today. Again, instead of relativism, we get plural realism . . . there can be many systems of practices that support assertions that point our many different and incompatible realities . . . even if a system does succeed in pointing out things as they are, that does not show that the kinds it discovers are the ultimate basis

of reality. Reality can be revealed in many ways, and none is meta-physically basic. . . . For Heidegger . . . as finite beings capable of dis-closing, we work out many perspectives – many lexicons – and reveal things as they are from many perspectives. And just because we can get things right from many perspectives, no single perspective is the right one.[16]

Plural realism *in ethics* is the view that, whereas there are definite limits on the varieties of human flourishing, there are many forms of life, often exhibiting divergent and uncombinable goods, in which human beings may flourish, and none of them is the one right way of life for man. The epistemology which supports plural realism in ethics is what Brouwer has called *dispositional* ethical realism[17] – the view, attributed to Mill by Skorupski, that values (like secondary properties) are discovered by us when we find our responses coming to equilibrium under appropriate circumstances of experience and reflection. Such realism is a form of *internal* realism, in that it conceives of values or reasons for action, not as external Platonistic entities of some sort, but as truths about our natures and practices. It is distinguished from any sort of subjectivism or scepticism by its affirmation that we may be mistaken about our well-being, which is never constituted, wholly or simply, by our wants or preferences. Where plural realism in ethics differs from many other realist positions in ethics – say, Aristotle's – is in its denial that there is one best form of life for the human species that is rationally discoverable. On the contrary, plural realism recognizes that, just as it is natural for our species to speak a vast diversity of languages, so it is natural for it to flourish in a great variety of ways. To put the point in Heideggerian terms: plural realism recognizes that, since the nature of human beings is a question for them, since it is only partly determinate and is therefore partly self-defined, no single conception of the good life can be founded on a conception of human nature. This follows inexorably from the recognition that human beings, unlike other animal species, transform their needs and are part self-creators, over time and in history. For this reason, on the plural realist view, no form of the good life can be final, any more than any can be said to be uniquely rational or natural.

In this version of internal realism, it is acknowledged that our forms of life are underdetermined by our natures. Unlike other animal species, human beings can flourish in an immense variety of worlds, each of their own making. The objectivity that is claimed for values in this view derives in part from their roots in common human nature and in part from the public, but diverse and sometimes incommensurable, practices that human beings have invented for themselves. Whereas these different practices or forms of life may be mutually intelligible, and so, in one sense, comparable with one another, they are not for that reason necessarily commensurable by reference to our common human nature. Limiting cases aside, very different forms of life may be equally legitimate forms of human self-creation, each carrying within it its own norms. The point of this variant of realism is that, though at the margin some forms of life may be injurious to human well-being, there are many, diverse and incompatible, forms of life in which human well-being may be realized. We can recognize as genuine forms of human flourishing a whole variety of forms of life, while at the same time recognizing that none of them is the best form towards which all others approximate.

In other words, in this neo-Aristotelian version of objective pluralism I have borrowed (with radical revisions) from J. S. Mill,[18] the variety of incommensurable forms of human flourishing disclosed to us in history and ordinary experience, though creations of an inventive species, are radically underdetermined by the generic powers and capacities of human beings. They are possibilities realized by us, not demands imposed upon us by our nature. Though it will readily be acknowledged that here are forms of social life in which the human good is thoroughly compromised, so that the variety of incommensurable human flourishings is bounded, it is not for that reason determinate. In particular, it is not confined to forms of flourishings that can be accommodated within a liberal regime.

What does plural realism portend for the liberal conception of progress? Its implications are highly destructive. The empty pieties of a liberal humanism that seek to theorize human history as a whole in terms of a notion of progress have been effectively subverted by Hampshire, when he observes:

Hegelianism, positivism, Marxism, constructed in the shadow of Christianity with a view to its replacement, purported to give an account of the development of mankind as a whole, an account of the destiny of the species: this included an alienation or fall, followed by a political and social redemption, leading to a final salvation of humanity. From the standpoint of a naturalistic philosophy, looking only at the so far known facts of human history, the gross implausibility of these accounts comes from the false speciation and the false humanism. 'Humanity' is either the name of a distinct animal species, with impressively distinct powers of mind and with an uncertain future, or it is the name of a class of being constituted as distinct by the intention of its Creator; and of course the name may sometimes be used with both meanings in mind. If the supernatural claims about the Creator's intentions are dismissed, there remains no sufficient empirical reason to believe that there is such a thing as the historical development of mankind as a whole, unless the natural history of the evolution of the species is intended. What we see in history is the ebb and flow of different populations at different stages of social development, interacting with each other and exhibiting no common pattern of development. Using older historical categories, we can reasonably speak of the various populations flourishing and becoming powerful at some stage and then falling into decadence and becoming comparatively weak; and historians can reasonably look for some general causes of these rises and falls. Even if some such general causes can be found, they will not by themselves point to a destiny, and to an order of development, for mankind as a whole.[19]

The upshot of these reasonings is that liberal meliorism – the position which ranks societies or regimes as they approximate to a liberal order, and which treats them as corrigible by that standard – is indefensible. It is felled by a pluralism that denies the coherence of the idea of perfection, even as it is rendered implausible by the risibility of the Enlightenment fantasy of the evanescence of imperfection.[20] How do the other elements of the liberal syndrome fare when subjected to the impact of objective pluralism?

OBJECTIVE PLURALISM, UNIVERSALISM AND LIBERAL EQUALITY

According to the *universalist* component of the liberal syndrome, there is a set of principles conferring on all human beings weighty claims in justice or rights. These may be contextualized somewhat in their content, or they may be grounded in an ethical theory (such as Millian utilitarianism) that is not itself deontic. It is definitive of liberalism, nevertheless, that it should confer upon all human beings certain basic equalities. For this reason, the *universalist* and the *egalitarian* elements of liberalism are complementary and mutually supportive, rather than competitive. How does value-incommensurability affect this pair of liberal values? It is evident, in the first place, that there are many forms of human flourishing that cannot coexist with liberal equality. All excellences that depend upon inherited hierarchy or involuntary subordination, that presuppose the embeddedness of persons in roles and statuses that are constitutive of their identities and from which they are unfree to exit, are bound to be crowded out from any regime that is at all liberal, or else to exist within it in peripheral, marginal or *ersatz* forms. This is, in part, only to restate a point already made here, that the Aristotelian account of human flourishing is excessively, if not obsessionally, monistic. As Stuart Hampshire has wisely observed:[21]

The claim that many well-known assertions about human potentialities are mistaken and not reasonably defensible does not entail that we can hope to show that one, and only one, such claim is defensible and not mistaken. At this point I leave Aristotle because he believed that the essential human potentialities are fixed, once and for all. . . . Any conception of human potentialities has to represent a target which is not only always moving, but is also moving in several dimensions. Any simple conception is either too abstract and too general, too lacking in complexity, to count as a representation useful for ethics; or the representation, faithful to the changing and moving target, is too evidently open-ended, and admittedly provisional, for any final truth to be claimed.

He goes on to ask:[22]

Why did Aristotle, writing about the distinctive features of human beings, not mention the Babel of natural languages, the proliferation of religions with their exclusive customs and prohibitions, the attachment of populations to their separate and peculiar histories, the manifold frontiers and barriers, with the aid of which social groups and populations try to maintain their separate identity? Why did he not see this species-wide divisiveness, the drive to separateness and conflicting identities, as at least one distinctive feature of human beings among all the animal species?

Aristotle's extraordinary selective blindness to the universal truth that it is one of the most distinctive dispositions of generic humanity to constitute for itself a myriad of local identities is a species of cognitive dissonance that has been transmitted to modern liberalism, with its denatured fiction of generic personhood. It also supports, within any culture, the modernist resistance to any division of roles or statuses, any unchosen division of labour, whereby virtues and excellences that could not coexist in a single person may flourish in a single society. As Hampshire again puts it:

So great has been the influence within contemporary moral philosophy of Hume, Kant and the Utilitarians that it has been possible to forget that for centuries the warrior and the priest, the landowner and the peasant, the merchant and the craftsman, the bishop and the monk, the musician or poet who lives by his performances, have coexisted in society with sharply distinct dispositions and virtues. . . . Varied social roles and functions, each with its typical virtues and its peculiar obligations, have been the normal situation in most societies throughout history.[23]

The impact of value-pluralism for the egalitarian component of the liberal syndrome is that a richer diversity of human goods, excellences and forms of flourishing may be, or at least has been, achieved in societies that are highly stratified and differentiated, than may be achieved in ones that are highly mobile and in which roles and statuses are easily interchangeable. In the latter sort of society, there will be an unavoidable depletion, and eventual extinction, of all those virtues and excellences that depend for their existence on hierarchy and deference and on men and women knowing their station and its duties. It is important to note that the uncombinabilities Hampshire here invokes are what Raz has usefully termed *constitutive incommensurabilites*[24] – they are conflicts of values occasioned, not by contingencies such as the shortness of human lives or the scarcity of resources, but by the very natures of the goods that are uncombinable. A priest cannot, compatibly with his avocation, adopt the virtues of a soldier, or a nun the excellences of a courtesan. A friend, as we understand one, cannot demand payment for his conversation. A lover, among us, cannot remain such, while charging a fee for his or her company. These are incommensurabilities constitutive of the identities at stake in such relationships. It is important to note here, briefly and parenthetically, a point I shall develop more systematically when discussing Berlin's argument from value-pluralism to liberalism – the point that, whereas the most radical form of value-conflict is found among constitutive incommensables, incommensurability and uncombinability are nevertheless distinct moral phenomena. Goods may be uncombinable, and yet readily subject to scalar evaluation: we may have good, even sufficient reason to make a ranking of them. At the same time, incommensurable goods may be combinable: we may each of us embody in our lives a chosen mixture of incommensurable goods, such as professional advancement and family life, strenuous activity and leisurely contemplation, and so on. It is when uncombinability and incommensurability come together, as in Raz's account of goods whose very constitution or nature precludes ranking or commingling, that we have the deepest sort of conflict among values.

Constitutive incommensurabilities of these sorts are akin to those conjectured in moral psychology, when we reject Aristotle's thesis of the unity of the virtues. A person with the virtues of courage, resolve, resourcefulness, intrepidity and indomitability is unlikely to possess the virtues of modesty and humility. One may go further. A man who has the Machiavellian Renaissance excellences of *virtu* and *superbia* cannot possess the Christian virtues of humility, any more than can Aristotle's great-souled man. Both between and within different forms of moral life, these constitutive incommensurabilities among the virtues shatter the complacency of Aristotelian moral psychology. Consider again the salience of value-pluralism for the Aristotelian account of the rationality of the emotions. A person whose orientation towards his life is tranquil and hopeful is likely to be incapable of despair. By despair is meant here, not the depression or sadness by which one may be struck, in bereavement or in tragedy, but instead the emotion which persons may have when they judge that their prospects of ever flourishing have been finally extinguished. Such an emotion expresses a rational belief, not an ephemeral mood; and, for that reason, a person incapable of it, in the appropriate circumstances, stands convicted of irrationality. With the incapacity for despair, as with other emotions, it may be that this depends upon irrationalities and defects, including lack of self-knowledge, in the person. It may be that if Van Gogh had passed through a successful psychoanalysis, he would have been a calmer soul; but it is hard to see how he could have painted as he did. Incommensurability enters deeply into moral psychology here, suggesting that some human powers may depend for their exercise on weaknesses, lacks or disabilities. If this is so, incommensurabilities may arise even among the powers that go into making a person autonomous: there may be forms or exercises of autonomy that are constitutively uncombinable.

Within a society or culture, liberal equality irons out the hierarchies that permit a differentiated exfoliation of otherwise uncombinable excellences. Among societies and cultures, liberal universalism disallows all those goods and virtues that depend upon an inherited inequality of status and authority or upon exclusivity in communities that make entry into them and exit from them hard or virtually impossible. Indeed, the liberal project of a universal civilization on which particularistic cultures converge (and into which they vanish) itself incorporates another, subsidiary project – that of levelling down all the forms of stratification and exclusivity that are distinctive or constitutive of particular cultures, and which give them their peculiar identities. It is difficult for liberals to see in this process – undoubtedly real, though fortunately not without exceptions – of global cultural homogenization any loss of value. So ingrained is the liberal presumption in favour of equality and universality that liberal modernism cannot perceive, or refuses to admit, the losses entailed in the destruction of societies characterized by such a division of labour among the virtues. Or else, if the loss is allowed to enter subversively into reflective awareness, it is immediately repressed by an unreflective normative individualism which invokes the interests, rights or well-being of the individual against the excellences of the forms of life that cannot coexist with, and so are lost in, liberal regimes. It is to the errors of normative individualism that I shall shortly turn.

It is evident, if the reasonings advanced have any force, that the egalitarian component of liberalism is undermined by strong value-pluralism. It is important to point out that it is *not* here being claimed that any and all kinds of inequality are permissible, or that the variety of allowable inequalities is unlimited. Such cultural relativism is incompatible with the realist orientation of objective pluralism. On the contrary, the generic nature of the human species enables us to identify evils that are not culture-specific, but universal, and which are therefore to be avoided, suppressed or mitigated in any society in which a worthwhile life is livable. In Hampshire's words:

> it makes sense to speak of happiness, freedom, and pleasure as good things as contrasted with unhappiness, imprisonment, enslavement and pain as bad things: states to be pursued for their own sake and states to be prevented and avoided for their own sake. For such states there is no need to appeal to any distinctive conception of the human good, though a distinctive conception of the human good would be invoked when a decision had to be made in some situation between these evils, giving priority to the one over the avoidance of the other.[25]

For Hampshire, then, there is a minimum content to morality that is universal, albeit chiefly negative in spelling out certain evils which prevent or inhibit a worthwhile human life, and possessing an inevitable indeterminacy both in the embodiment of these evils in different forms of moral life and in resolutions of conflicts of priorities among them. Hampshire goes further, and identifies the central element in the minimum content of morality in the practice of procedural fairness or justice. In this he follows a long line of recent liberal theorists in treating justice as the first virtue of social institutions. While endorsing Hampshire's position that morality contains elements that are not culture-specific, I wish to reject his view that it is justice or fairness that is central among these elements. No purely deontic (rights-based or justice-based) conception can be fundamental or primordial in morality. As Raz has shown,[26] political moralities are never rights-based, since rights are themselves never foundational, but rather intermediaries between claims about human interests that are vital to well-being and claims about obligations it is reasonable to impose upon others in respect of these interests. Rights, in other words, gain their content from the requirements of human well-being – and they will be variable as the demands of human well-being vary. So, analogously, with the broader idea of justice. As Hampshire himself recognizes,[27] practices of justice and of procedural fairness will differ according to the underlying conceptions of the good which animate them. For these reasons, it is extremely implausible to suppose that justice is at the bottom of the universal dimension of morality. Rather, it is the minimum requirements of human well-being that identify the bottom line in political ethics. Accordingly, for example, the evil of slavery – at least in its worst, American, variety of chattel slavery – resided, not in any distributional inequality in liberty which that institution incorporated, but in the injuries to the well-being of the slaves which it constantly inflicted. It is by an assessment of the harms to vital human interests done by different regimes that we will identify those that transgress the universal and minimal requirements of political morality.

Except in limiting cases – in our times, the regimes of Pol Pot, of Hitler, Mao or Stalin – such assessments will never be easy or uncontroversial. In part this is because incommensurabilities break out among generic human evils, as well as among generically human goods. Is a regime in which there is pervasive fear and invasive political control of individual life, but little or no actual violence or threat to life (such as Czechoslovakia in the 1970s and 1980s, where totalitarianism was sustained chiefly by economic sanctions) better or worse than a regime, such as Pinochet's Chile, which incurred far more violence, including violent deaths, but in which the invasive impact of political power on individual liberty was far smaller? The matter is evidently undecidable by reason. Even if we could rationally compare and evaluate such regimes, our evaluations would not be transmissible, by further comparisons, to other regimes. For, as Raz has shown, the most distinctive mark of incommensurability is a breakdown of transitivity in reasoning: 'The test of incommensurability is failure of transitivity. Two valuable options are incommensurable if 1) neither is better than the other, and 2) there is (or could be) another option which is better than one but is not better than the other'.[28] Raz's account of incommensurability in terms of the intransitivity of reasonings about valuable options applies, equally, to judgements about evils. Even where two bad regimes, in which the minimum requirements of human well-being are lacking, can be ranked, our ranking will in virtue of incommensurabilities among their constitutive evils often be untransmissible to other bad regimes.

Incommensurability as a breakdown in transitivity occurs in many areas of ethical life. Sometimes it is innocuous. It is a commonplace that intransitivities occur in friendships: you may be a friend of mine, but your friends may not be my friends. Sometimes the breakdown of transitivity in ethical judgement is more subversive in its results. Consider justice, the ruling fetish of recent liberal thought. It is an unreflective supposition of recent liberalism, stated explicitly by Nozick,[29] that justice is akin to deduction in that injustice cannot arise from justice. But this is false on any view of justice that is less parsimonious, and more in accordance with universal practice and sentiment, than Nozick's. In practice, prescription arising from long possession, say, over many generations, everywhere yields an entitlement (not necessarily unqualified) to the property in question. If, however, as is often the case, the original taking was unjust, we have a breakdown of transitivity in justice. Unjust takings yield just entitlements. Analogously, just takings may yield unjust entitlements. If the distribution of holdings has any weight in judgements of justice, however slight, then the upshot of many just transfers of justly taken holdings may be unjust. The implication of the intransitivity of justice is that the demands of justice may be complex rather than monolithic. If justice encompasses intransitivities, indeed, its demands may be deeply conflicting: they may be conflicts among incommensurables. As Berlin has noted,[30] conflicts among incommensurables may arise within liberty, even negative liberty, itself: we may have no means, save in limiting cases, of assessing on-balance liberty in any disciplined fashion, and so no means of determining a uniquely or most rational resolution of a conflict among liberties. Radical value-pluralism, accordingly, affirms incommensurability not only among ultimate values, but also within them.

There is an analogy here with incommensurability in the arts, as discussed earlier. As between different artistic traditions, we may be able to make comparative judgements – we may be able to judge *this* a better example of a Gothic church than *that* is of Baroque church architecture; yet we may be unable to make a judgement between the Gothic church and an example of Byzantine church architecture, which we *can* judge to be better than the Baroque church. Transitivity has again broken down. It has broken down within a recognizable artistic and cultural tradition, even as it breaks down between traditions. And it does so, even when we can firmly identify the traditions at issue as all of them traditions of high civilizations, superior to those found in other cultures.

Liberal universalism and liberal egalitarianism founder on the incommensurability of divergent forms of human flourishing and on incommensurabilities among obstacles to human flourishing. There are many forms of human flourishing that depend upon inequalities that any liberal view must reject, and for that reason, if for no other, the liberal universalist thesis that all human beings are entitled to the same stock of rights or claims must be false. It will have force, only in respect of a minimum content of morality that massively underdetermines liberal values and which is met by many societies and regimes that are not liberal – which do not acknowledge fundamental equalities in liberty, and so forth. Of course, against the argument that there are valuable ways of life which cannot flourish in liberal regimes, there is an inevitable liberal reflex response: that, because such forms of life may impose significant costs on individuals, and because they deny or render costly individual exit from them, such forms of life do not deserve to survive.

This knee-jerk liberal response may come in two forms, each of which presupposes a deeper doctrine. It may be claimed that forms of life which depend upon, or have among their necessary conditions, involuntary subordination, are somehow necessarily lesser (that is to say, less valuable) forms of life than those that do not. It is difficult to see how such an absurd claim could be rendered credible. Is the claim being made the claim that the life of the Greek gentleman-scholar, whose contemplative leisure was made possible by the institution of slavery, is necessarily worse than that of the self-supporting sweatshop worker in the period of *laisser-faire*? Or is it the (only slightly less incredible) claim that the best life is necessarily one that does not depend upon enforced subordination of others? If the latter, then it is merely the old Socratic claim, which nothing in actual experience has ever supported, that the life depending on injustice cannot ever be as good as the life of the just man. Or else, perhaps, and second, the liberal response trades on the claim that, however valuable a form of life may be, its pursuit is constrained by deontic limitations of justice or rights. But, as has already been argued, the content and weight, together with the very justification of all such deontic constraints, must be spelt out in terms of their contribution to human well-being. In other words, invoking such deontic constraints against forms of life involving involuntary subordination begs the question as to the possibility of human well-being being promoted within (or by virtue of) such forms of life. (Is it self-evident that the life of someone who is the subject of involuntary subordination to another is always worse from the standpoint of well-being than one who stands in a relation of equal freedom to others? It is, after all, an obvious objection to Rawls's theory of justice as fairness that the principle of greater equal freedom and the difference principle may conflict in practice: the serf in a medieval order may be better off, if his lord discharges his duties, than a free labourer. And, if the two principles conflict, why rank the greatest equal liberty principle over the difference principle?) Both standard liberal responses derive their real content from their presupposition in the deeper liberal dogma that only individuals and their states of mind, feeling and action can have intrinsic value. It is to this response, with its invocation of the fourth element in the liberal syndrome, normative individualism, that I now turn.

NORMATIVE INDIVIDUALISM AND THE INTRINSIC VALUE OF FORMS OF LIFE

By normative individualism, I shall intend (following Raz) any moral theory that does not recognize any intrinsic value in any collective good. Normative individualism holds that collective goods have instrumental value only. Accordingly, moral theories which hold that all values are agent-relative values will all be varieties of normative individualism. In a more positive formulation, one may say that, for a normative individualist, only states of individual human lives can possess intrinsic value, with collective goods having value only in so far as they make a contribution to the good life of the individual. Though this is a large and deep question I cannot address here, it is worth noting that normative individualism is a species of humanism – the theory that 'claims that the explanation and justification of the goodness or badness of anything derives ultimately from its contribution, actual or possible, to human life and its quality'.[31] I mention this fact, since I wish to make clear that my argument against normative individualism, although it borrows heavily from Raz's, is unlike Raz's in that it does not presuppose humanism. Indeed, my view is that humanism is indefensible without resort to the Judaeo–Christian tradition which grounds *the supreme value of human personality* in its kinship with a divine personality which animates the universe. In the forms in which it is found in secular liberalism, humanism is merely an atavistic anomaly, a curious relic of theism that has suppressed awareness of its genealogy in Judaeo–Christianity. (Note here that normative individualism is not ethical subjectivism. An ethical subjectivist may be a normative individualist, in that he affirms that only the preferences of individuals confer value on anything; but a normative individualist may be an ethical realist, who believes – as did Kant – that it is a moral truth that only persons have intrinsic value. Normative individualism appears to be neutral on the issue of the objectivity or otherwise of values.)

The thesis of this section of the paper is that normative individualism is false. Individualism must be regarded as merely a particular form of life, in which certain distinctive excellences are achieved, but in which others are excluded. On the view defended here, individualism is one form of human flourishing among a variety of others, and has no special privileges, even if (as I shall suggest) it is our historical fate – at least for those of us who are heirs to a Western inheritance. Why, then, are we to reject normative individualism as a basic position in ethics? Let us follow Raz and consider the value of autonomy. Among us – the inhabitants of modern Western societies characterized by a high degree of social mobility, pluralism in lifestyles and individualism in ethical culture – autonomy is a constitutive ingredient in any form of the good life. If we lacked even a modicum of autonomy, if we were not even part authors of our lives – if our jobs, our marriages or sexual partners, our place of abode or our religion were assigned to us or chosen for us – we would consider our individuality stifled and the goodness of our lives diminished. This is not to say that maximal autonomy, if there could be such a thing, would be a good thing. Perhaps autonomy is a fungible good, consumed in the choices, often irreversible, in which it is embodied. Perhaps it is a positional good, in that the array of options available to an autonomous person in a culture of heteronomous or less autonomous people, but containing enclaves of autonomous life, is richer than any he might have in a society, like that envisaged in *On Liberty*, in which all are highly autonomous. Perhaps, again, maximal autonomy is as much of a mirage as the greatest liberty, since autonomy may have incommensurable dimensions or forms such that comparative on-balance assessments of the greatest autonomy are rendered impossible. (There is a further possibility that different forms or exercises of autonomous choice may be constitutively uncombinable.) Again, it is not here assumed that autonomy is a necessary ingredient in any good human life, nor that the best human lives are necessarily the most autonomous ones. As Raz has put it:

> I think that there were, and there can be, non-repressive societies, and ones which enable people to spend their lives in worthwhile pursuits, even though their pursuits and the options open to them are not subject to individual choice. Careers may be determined by custom, marriages arranged by parents, childbearing and child rearing controlled only by sexual passion and traditions, part-time activities few and traditional, and engagement in them required rather than optional. In such societies, with little mobility, even friends are not chosen. There are few people one ever comes in contact with, they remain there from birth to death, and one just has to get on with them. I do not see that the absence of choice diminishes the value of human relations or the display of excellence in technical skills, physical ability, spirit and enterprise, leadership, scholarship, creativity or imaginativeness, which can all be encompassed in such lives.[32]

In the neo-Aristotelian view presented here, the virtue of autonomy is a local affair. It is left open whether a form of life in which autonomy is inconspicuous or lacking – the form of life of medieval Christendom, or of feudal Japan in the Edo period – may be better from the standpoint of human flourishing, or else simply incommensurably different, by comparison with the form of life of autonomous individuals. Finally, in contrast with Raz, it is not even assumed that autonomous individuals will necessarily, or even generally, flourish best in open, pluralist societies. Perhaps, as the example of recent Asian immigrants in the United Kingdom suggests, social or ethnic groups in which autonomy is not greatly prized will do better on most dimensions of human flourishing, when compared with autonomous individualists, in a society that contains both. On a global, historical scale, it may well be that the linkage between an individualist moral culture and a prosperous market economy is an historical accident, which in its ultimate development proves to be self-limiting in virtue of its comparative disadvantage against other market economies (such as those of East Asia) whose moral inheritance is not individualist.

All that is required for my argument against normative individualism is that autonomous lives be intrinsically valuable lives. Or, at the very least, that autonomy be a necessary, constitutive ingredient of some valuable lives in our society. The central argument against the truth of normative individualism is that valuable autonomy presupposes *as one of its constitutive elements* a rich public culture containing a diversity of worthwhile options. By contrast, consider the exercise of autonomous choice in a Hobbesian state of nature. What would its value be? The Hobbesian autonomous chooser could not marry, adopt a religion or engage in any of the arts of commodious living; the choices of such an agent would be made in an impoverished cultural environment – indeed, an empty one. Conversely, a multitude of conventions, institutions and social forms is necessary for valuable autonomous choice. As these forms wax, so does the value of autonomy; as they wane, so does autonomy, so that at the limiting point of Hobbesian anarchy, autonomy, barely exists. The vital point is that a rich public culture is not an instrumental condition of a valuable autonomous life, but an essential element in it. The lives of autonomous choosers who live in a culture without art, science, friendship, religion or romantic love are poor lives, even if they do not know what they are lacking and so cannot regret its absence. To say this is to restrict the agent-relativity of value and to affirm that forms of lives may themselves have intrinsic (which is to say, agent-neutral) value. To deny this by asserting the agent-relativity of all value, by denying intrinsic value to forms of life, seems tantamount to an endorsement of unrestricted cultural relativism.

If the elements of a rich cultural environment enter into autonomous choice constitutively, not instrumentally, then the inherently public goods[33] that they comprise will also be intrinsically valuable. It follows that art, and scientific inquiry, are intrinsically valuable activities or practices, independently of the contribution they make to the good lives of individuals.[34] A world without them is the poorer, even if (or especially if) no one notices their absence. This argument establishes that, whatever has ultimate value, it is not *only* states of the lives of individuals. A further step in the argument is needed to show that it is forms of life or activity that are ultimately and intrinsically valuable, so that it is from these forms of life that the value of the lives of the individuals in which they are instantiated is derived. This step is provided by the argument that choices, autonomous choices in particular, have value only if they range over options that are themselves choiceworthy. Such options can be provided only by activities and forms of life that are intrinsically valuable. Inasmuch as worthwhile forms of life are what make valuable autonomy possible, it is they, and not the individual lives in which they are instantiated, that are ultimately and primordially valuable. Whatever variations individual choice adds to common forms of life, it is these forms that are the sources of the values expressed in autonomous individual choice. Without them, individuals cannot be even part authors of their lives.

This suggests a perspective on rights that differs greatly from the standard, conventional liberal perspective. It suggests a theory of rights that is non-individualist in character. If scientific inquiry, say, is an intrinsic collective good, then we may seek to protect it by an entrenched right, where the right protects the activity, not its individual practitioners. There may be collective rights to collective goods, if these are intrinsically valuable themselves, and if they are elements of a common life or public culture that also has intrinsic value.

It is important to note that, since it recognizes that intrinsically valuable forms of life and activity are instantiated only in individual lives, this view does not license the wanton sacrifice of individual well-being for collective good. Forms of life are not Platonistic entities which exist independently of their practitioners. If a form of life is a type that can have indefinitely many tokens in the lives of individuals who subscribe to it, it nevertheless cannot exist unless it is instantiated in individual lives. Further, on this view, since most of what constitutes a man's well-being is constituted by elements in the form of life in which he partakes, there will not be any general conflict between his well-being and his form of life. Indeed, in the individualist form of life we are here considering, in which autonomy is a central feature, we will be protecting and enhancing the form of life when we protect and promote the individual's well-being. It is not, however, asserted that there will always be this coincidence. In some cases, the form of life an individual inherits will be injurious to the vital interests he has as a human being. To say this, on the view presented here, is to say that these generically human interests, or components of human well-being, can only be protected in forms of life to which the individual is denied access. The American chattel slave's most vital interests were injured, inasmuch as he was denied access to the form of life of American free men. To affirm that forms of life may injure generic human interests is therefore compatible with the claim that it is only in forms of life and activity that intrinsic value is to be found.

Since cultures vary as to the intrinsically valuable collective goods they contain, so will the collective rights they may wish to recognize. These rights may not be very highly determinate in their content, and they may protect collective goods that are incommensurables. On the view presented here, these are not difficulties that are fatal to this view, since (unlike fundamentalist liberalism) it acknowledges and is founded upon the cultural variability and diversity of the forms of the good life. In its application to the theory of justice and rights, it is conventionalist (but not therefore arbitrary). It implies that the requirements of justice and the content of rights be contoured by reference to the collective goods that are manifested variously in the different cultures. This view, while it affirms the objectivity of human well-being, acknowledges that justice is special, in that (like the institution of any right) it is artefactual and conventional in character. A man or woman may live well, if he or she is ruthless and lucky, without the virtue of justice, providing most of his or her fellows possess it; he or she will not live well if he or she lacks courage, self-command and good judgement. If the account of well-being and flourishing advanced here is Aristotelian in its realism, the view of justice presented is Humean in its conventionalism. Justice is theorized as a convention depending for its authority on general acceptance and reciprocity. In its applications to collective goods, justice demands protection for those that are intrinsically valuable. Freedom of religious worship will on this view be protected as a central element in the good life for human beings, or, at the very least, as a collective good in our culture. It will also, no doubt, receive protection by way of the individual rights we protect – rights of voluntary association, for example. Equally, both collective goods or forms of intrinsically valuable activity and individual claims may be accorded respect and protection in traditional societies that have not yet adopted (or succumbed to) the discourse and practice of rights. The argument as developed so far suggests that, though rights may be explicated in terms of their contribution to individual well-being, it is not the individual that is the bottom line in the theory of rights. For the well-being of the individual is owed to his participation in a form of life or activity that is intrinsically valuable and worthwhile. It may be that, while in practice individual and collective aspects of the practice of rights are mutually complementary rather than competitive, the ultimate source of rights (if we are to engage in rights discourse at all) is in forms of life, rather than in individuals and their claims.

Individualism is never the bottom line in what has value. What has value (in the human world) is the form of life – even if, paradoxically, it is an individualist form of life. This is true, even as forms of life interpenetrate, and are not easily individuated. Few, if any, of us are Sandel's[35] radically situated selves, whose lives are constituted by membership of a single, exclusive community. Yet, even in this post-modernist context, the ultimate sources of value are the diverse forms of life in which we move, and which introduce complexities and even incommensurabilities into our identities and perspectives on the world, rather than the choices of individuals. Like the first language we speak, the parents to whom we are born and the religion we inherit, the post-modern condition of deep pluralism is for us unchosen. (I shall argue later that there is a valid Berlinian argument from pluralism to liberalism, but one that is historical and local, not universal, in its application.) If Raz, Berlin and others[36] are right, value-incommensurability is a universal feature of the human condition, suppressed or veiled in most philosophies; it is far less easily deniable by us, for whom the irreconcilable diversity of human inheritances is a daily fact of life.

Normative individualism, along with the other elements of the liberal syndrome, runs aground on the reef of incommensurability. At the very least, as between pluralism and liberalism, pluralism is the deeper truth. (Our condition is a peculiar, and perhaps novel one, in that, recognizing that our individual identities are constituted by participation in forms of common life, we at the same time find ourselves in the interstices of many such forms. Our situation is perhaps akin to that of the sceptic about meaning in Kripke's Wittgenstein, who in speaking a language that is necessarily public perceives that the attribution of meanings depends ultimately on primordial judgements that are made by individuals.) This is to say that, whereas there is a powerful Berlinian argument, which I shall later develop, from the truth of incommensurability among ultimate values to the liberal prioritization of liberty, that argument has no universal validity. It applies to those historical contexts, such as our own, that are marked by a diversity of incommensurable conceptions of the good and perspectives on the world. The universal implication of radical value pluralism, on the other hand, is that no one political regime can be privileged as having a claim on reason. This is an inexorable result of the thesis of incommensurability among ultimate values.

Incommensurabilities arise, not just between values that are elements in a conception of the good, but between whole conceptions of the good, suggesting that the Millian naturalistic epistemology of ethics, which is grounded on the prospect of an ideal convergence on value-judgements, must be substantially qualified. The Piercean prospect of ethical consensus has but little leverage on experience or practice. Rather, the prospect appears to be that of ultimate divergence among incommensurable value-perspectives, both individual and cultural. Here it is Nietzsche, not Mill, who has most contemporary resonance. As Skorupski has put it: 'The Nietzsche/Mill polarity goes to the anthropological root of ethical and political life; its charge has the power to disorientate and disturb all but the most dogmatically entrenched on either side'.[37] It is important to try to specify more precisely the kind of breakdown of convergence that occurs in an objective pluralist epistemology. The position is that, though convergence is expected on judgements as to which forms of life embody human flourishing and which do not, there will not be convergence as to which among these is to be adopted, since the conceptions of the good they express are incommensurables. Further, within any conception of the good or the form of life it animates, there will be convergence on its component goods and excellences; but not on what is to be done when they come into conflict with one another. Objective pluralism, then, postulates an underdetermined world of values, which can within limits be construed and shaped by human decisions, but whose components are a matter of human knowledge. (It is not, of course, being suggested that there can be knowledge of the varieties of human flourishing that is definitive and final; since, contrary to Aristotle, there are indefinitely many forms of human life, as yet uninvented by the species, in which the human good will be realized. Of these we can have knowledge only when they are embodied in practice.) I shall not here inquire whether, as I have already intimated, an analogous failure of Peircean convergence may occur in the sciences.[38] My argument is neutral on this issue. What I have argued is that radical value-incommensurability, together with the strong indeterminacy in liberal principles I have argued for in other places,[39] spells ruin for fundamentalist liberalism. No determinate set of principles about liberty, rights or justice has been stated which is not disabled by deep indeterminacies – such as afflict both Mill's Principle of Liberty, Rawls's Greatest Equal Liberty Principle and the set of basic liberties, and all theories of rights. (Such indeterminacies are clearest in cases of conflicts of liberties or rights, but are by no means confined to them.) The upshot of this present argument is that recognition of a pluralism of forms of human flourishing, each objective, of which only some can exist in a liberal regime, destroys the authority of liberalism as a universal, trans-historical and cross-cultural ideal. It is in order to reject the inevitable counterclaim about the costs of non-liberal forms of life to the individuals that instantiate them that I have argued for the falsity of normative individualism.

A final point needs to be made as to the import of my argument for the objectivity of human well-being for the evidences of revealed preference. It is often, and sometimes with truth, held that the propensity of people to seek exit from a non-liberal regime is evidence of its detrimental impact on human well-being. This certainly applies to the totalitarian regimes of our century. It is far less clear that exit from a traditional to a modern society demonstrates the superiority of the latter: denizens of a traditional society may be ignorant of the conditions if their well-being and their revealed preferences may only express the untransparency of values in their lives. In practice, again, traditional forms of life are often simply driven out by modern modes of production: there is no question of their practitioners *choosing* exit from a way of life that will otherwise remain viable. Even where exit is chosen, it may entail unnoticed losses, incur benefits that prove delusive, entail the extinction of a superior form of life and adoption of a lesser one. It is an implication of my argument that the universal privileging of individual choice that is a feature of fundamentalist liberalism (and which entrenches the modernist prejudice that good lives cannot be unchosen lives) may sanctify the erosion or destruction of forms of common life from which individual choices and the lives they eventuate in gain much, if not all, of their meaning and value.

THE LIVING KERNEL OF LIBERALISM: CIVIL SOCIETY

The result of the argument thus far is that none of the four elements of the liberal syndrome withstands the force of radical value-pluralism. If there is an ultimate diversity of forms of human flourishing, embodied in ways of life only some of which can be accommodated within a liberal regime, then liberal orders have no general superiority over orders that are not liberal. In short, value-pluralism of this radical sort dictates pluralism in political regimes, and undermines the fundamentalist liberal claim that liberal regimes alone are fully legitimate. We may say of liberalism as a doctrine with aspirations for universal prescriptive authority, then, that it is dead – a result tacitly acknowledged in the most recent theorizings of the later Rawls.

What is still living in liberalism, if its philosophical foundations have collapsed? I shall maintain that what is living in liberalism is not any doctrine or comprehensive theory, but instead the historic inheritance of civil society that has now spread to most parts of the world. It is civil society, with its key guarantees of liberty and the limits on government they imply, that remains alive, not liberalism. In civil society, the four constitutive elements of liberalism specified earlier are preserved, not as universal principles, but as constitutive aspects of civil life. It is civil society that should be the object of theorizing, not 'liberalism' or any abstract conception of liberty. I shall maintain, further, that the only form of liberalism that remains defensible is the Berlinian form, which encompasses a full acceptance of value-pluralism. For most, if not perhaps for all, modern states, civil society is the only sort of society in which the prosperity and values of a modern civilization can be reproduced, and it is the only form of society in which incommensurable conceptions of the good life can coexist in peace. What are the arguments for this view, and what is meant by civil society?

By civil society is meant a number of things. Civil society may be defined contrastively, by noting as one of its contraries the *weltanschauung*-states of both ancient and modern times. A civil society is one which is tolerant of the diversity of views, religious and political, that it contains, and in which the state does not seek to impose on all any comprehensive doctrine. Thus, Calvin's Geneva was not a civil society, and none of the twentieth-century species of totalitarianism encompassed civil societies. Indeed, as I have elsewhere argued,[40] totalitarianism in its Communist varieties is (or was) a Westernizing, modernist project of destroying or transcending civil society, so that totalitarianism is in general to be defined by reference to its enmity to civil society, not to liberal democracy. In a civil society, then, diverse, incompatible and perhaps incommensurable conceptions of the world and the good can coexist in a peaceful *modus vivendi*.

A second feature of civil society is that, in it, both government and its subjects are restrained in their conduct by *a rule of law*. A state in which the will of the ruler is the law, and for whom therefore all things are permissible, cannot contain or shelter a civil society, or, if it does, it will be one that is weak and disordered. (An example of the latter might be Duvalier's Haiti.) One implication of this feature of civil society is that it presupposes a government that is not omnicompetent, but limited. In any civil society, most social and economic activities will take place in autonomous institutions that are protected by the rule of law but independent of government. Civil society and unlimited government are, for this reason, incompatible. This is only another way of saying that civil society has as one of its conditions the limitation of government by the same rule of law that civil society is constituted and governed by.

A third feature of civil society is the institution of private or several property. Societies in which property is vested in tribes, or in which most assets are owned or controlled by governments, cannot be civil societies. The importance of several property for civil society is that it acts as an enabling device whereby rival and possibly incommensurable conceptions of the good may be implemented and realized without recourse to any collective decision-procedure – a recourse which, in any pluralist culture, would inevitably occasion conflict. There is a *Hobbesian argument* for a civil society containing the institutions of several property – the argument that, given pervasive value-pluralism, it is such a society that is most likely to enjoy civil peace. This Hobbesian argument depends on the recognition that civil war or strife is a great evil, threatening all modes of commodious living, so that to conceive of political life as the unending pursuit of a provisional *modus vivendi* is a mark of humility and realism, not of ignobility. The central institution of civil society – the institution of private or several property – has its rationale as an *enabling device* whereby persons with radically discrepant goals and values can pursue them without recourse to a collective decision-procedure that would, of necessity, be highly conflictual. One may even say of civil society that it is a device for securing peace by reducing to a minimum the decisions on which recourse to collective choice – the political or public choice that is binding on all – is unavoidable. Such, I take it, is the Hobbesian argument for civil society, often echoed in Oakeshott's account of civil association. This will not, however, be the most fundamental argument that will be advanced for civil society, which will be defended instead by reference to the varieties of human flourishing it shelters.

A few words are apposite regarding the history and diversity of civil society. Societies having the characteristics specified appear to have emerged in the wake of the Wars of Religion – in the Low Countries, in England and Scotland and in subsequent centuries throughout most of Europe. There can be no doubt that Tsarist Russia was a civil society for the last fifty or sixty years of its existence, just as was Bismarckian Prussia. Whig England had all the characteristics of a civil society. The ultimate historical source of civil society is, most likely, to be found in the dissolution of the European medieval order that began in the thirteenth century. The varieties of civil society so far enumerated should allow us to perceive that civil societies may go along with a variety of political institutions. Civil societies need not have the political and economic institutions of liberal democracy; most, in historical terms, have not. Nor need they contain the moral culture of individualism. The authoritarian civil societies of modern East Asia – South Korea, Taiwan and Hong Kong, for example – have not embraced Western individualism (a fact that may go far to explain their extraordinary economic success).

Nor, finally, is civil society to be identified with market capitalism. Several or private property may come in a variety of forms, each of them artifacts of law, and the institution of the capitalist corporation is only one species of the private or several property institution on which a civil society rests. This last point is of no small contemporary significance. As James Buchanan has pointed out in a seminal paper,[41] the post-Communist regimes, especially that which is emerging in Russia in the wake of the coup of August 1991, will go badly astray if they seek only to replicate the forms of Western capitalism, as advocated by most Western economists. What is needed in Russia, according to Buchanan, is not the transposition of Western economic institutions, but instead a *radical deconcentration* of economic activity, to municipal, village and cooperative levels, in which native Russian traditions of cooperation can be revived. Equally, the Western, and especially the American, project of forcing liberalization on Japanese economic life, though it is bound to fail, is thoroughly and dangerously misconceived. It neglects the embeddedness of economic transactions in an underlying culture that is not, and is most unlikely to become, individualist. In both Russia and Japan, Westernization (or further Westernization) would only involve injury to valuable social forms, with few, if any, corresponding advantages.

It is important that these points be borne in mind, so as to distinguish the argument here from that of those – most absurdly, the American writer Fukuyama[42] – who perceive in the collapse of the Communist regimes 'the triumph of the Western idea', 'liberal democracy as the final form of human government' and 'democratic capitalism' as the universal form of political economy. On the view advanced here, though civil society may be an invention of Western cultures, its adoption by other cultures need not, and in all probability, should not, involve the adoption of Western values. The record of Western cultural imperialism – the near-destruction by Communist totalitarianism of Chinese and Russian traditional cultures, the deracination of Africa by over-rapid modernization and the triggering of fundamentalist movements in Iran and elsewhere by hubristic projects of social engineering – suggests that the emergence of civil societies where they had not hitherto existed, and their re-emergence where they had been suppressed, is a process that should occur at its own pace, subject to the constraints of local cultural traditions.

There is another argument for civil society, which I shall term the *Hegelian* argument, which characterizes it as the institutional infrastructure of modernity. This is an argument that remains forceful, even if, as I have maintained, liberalism conceived as the political theory of modernity is no longer credible. It is an argument which points to the division of labour, the definition of property rights and their embodiment in private institutions whose power and immunities are protected under a rule of law as necessary conditions for the reproduction of a modern society. This Hegelian argument is supported both by theoretical reasonings and by the evidences of modern history.

The evidence of the past decades indicates (what economic theory had suggested) that without the institutions of a market economy a modern industrial society cannot successfully reproduce itself. For this reason alone, the institutions of private property (not necessarily in the form of the Western capitalist corporation) and of contractual exchange are essential elements of any viable civil society. They are possible, in turn, only if their scope and content are defined and protected by a rule of law. This, in its turn, confers upon the subjects of civil society a set of immunities and liberties. These are not just the liberties of buying and selling, but the liberties of voluntary association, of occupation, of travel and so forth. Because by its very nature a civil society cannot coexist with a *weltan-schauung*-state, civil societies will practice tolerance in respect of personal belief-systems, even if (as in the United Kingdom) they retain an established religion. The liberties guaranteed in civil societies are, on this view, necessarily not very determinate, but they must at the least incorporate those sketched above. In all their varieties, civil societies approximate to the Oakeshottean ideal-typical conception of *civil association*[43] – that form of human association in which we are bound together in no common enterprise, but perceive each other as *convives*, each pursuing their own projects, and respecting those of others. Whatever their varieties, civil societies are the only ones in the modern world which reproduce themselves stably as prosperous and peaceful communities. Attempts to reverse the modernist movement toward civil society – in Nazism, communism and fundamentalism – have everywhere issued in barbarism and poverty. It is therefore to the minute particulars of our inheritance of civil society, and not to the delusive vistas of liberal philosophy, that the friend of liberty should therefore address himself.

Civil societies come in many varieties. The political regimes which shelter them may be liberal-democratic, or they may be authoritarian. Civil society will, however, always be voluntarist. The moral culture that animates it may be individualist, or (as in East Asia) it may not. It will be true of any civil society, however, that it will embody the historic inheritance (perhaps exported elsewhere in the world) that 'liberalism' theorized – the inheritance of the *practice of liberty*. In so far as any kind of civil society exists, it will posses the constitutive institutions of civil society – such as the rule of law, private or several property, and the civil liberties of voluntary association, conscience, travel and expression. On the view presented here, a civil society shelters the practice of liberty, whether or not it tolerates democratic freedoms. The only form of equality necessitated by a liberal civil society is, not political or economic equality, but equality before the law. For the essence of the practice of liberty is that, in a civil society, individuals and voluntary associations are bound together by no common end or enterprise but live in peaceful coexistence under a regime of non-instrumental rules. The civil condition, so conceived, is fully compatible with a variety of political regimes, but presupposes always the rule of law and equality before the law.

On the view presented here, civil societies, in all their legitimate varieties, are the living kernel of what was 'liberalism'. Even when their political institution are authoritarian, or their moral culture not individualist, civil societies of all kinds embody a voluntarist conception of human association, and thereby express (or soon come to be animated by) *a culture of liberty* – a culture in which individuals are free to come together in pursuit of shared purposes, but need have no enterprise in common. In this sense, whatever their differences, all civil societies are liberal civil societies. Once the fundamental liberal project of achieving an Archimedean point of leverage on practice is abandoned, theorizing can turn to the institutions, conventions and traditions that comprise the practice of liberty. Criticism and reform of existing civil societies may then proceed, but it will be immanent criticism, internal to the life of each specific civil society, which does not pretend to be governed by any abstract conception of freedom. Freedom is on this account *constituted* by the practices of civil society, which it is the task of the theorist to illuminate. Any such understanding of the practice of liberty is bound to be an historical understanding – one that conceives of civil society as an historical artefact – but one that, in the context of the condition of late modernity (or early post-modernity) offers the best, if not the only prospect for the reproduction of civilized life.

The four constitutive elements of liberalism as a doctrine here re-emerge as characteristics of civil society. The legal structure of a civil society is bound to be *individualist* since none of us is (in the jargon of recent communitarian theory) a radically situated self whose identity is constituted by membership of a single community. On the contrary, we are, each of us, members of a host of communities, sometimes overlapping but often conflicting in their claims, roles and statuses. In this historical context of deep cultural pluralism, in which traditions and forms of life interpenetrate and are not easily individuated, and in which most of us have access to incommensurable conceptions and perspectives of human life and the world, the fundamental legal structure of a civil society is bound to be individualist. (It will, no doubt, contain corporate legal persons; but these will not typically possess the powers and immunities possessed by individuals.) It has been noted that the *justification* for rights of freedom of religion or of scientific inquiry need not be, and in the end cannot be, an individualist one; but this is not to deny that, in any modern pluralist culture, the principal bearer of rights (or of the various immunities contained in the English common law) will be the individual, and not any collectivity. Here individualism is affirmed, not as any set of universal normative claims about the species, but instead as a necessary feature of a modern civil society.

Similarly with *egalitarianism*. Though a civil society presupposes neither political nor economic equality, it does require equality before the law. For it is a necessary feature of a civil society that, just as no one in it is above the law, so no one is denied the protection of the law. Again, inasmuch as civil society is not a *weltanschauung*-state in which one set of beliefs is enforced on all, but rather an association in which all subscribe to common procedures in which no belief or objective need be shared, it confers upon all the same basic immunities and entitlements. Accordingly, every member of a civil society, unless disqualified by special circumstances, has the immunity from arbitrary arrest and the entitlement to a fair trial, freedom to acquire and alienate property, liberty of occupation, travel, conscience and so forth. Since they have the *same* immunities and entitlements under the rule of law, they may be said to enjoy *equality under the law*. Such equality need be neither absolute nor exceptionless: it may be abridged by the institution of preventive detention for suspected terrorists, or (as with Peers of the Realm in the United Kingdom) be qualified by special privileges and disabilities. Legal equality will nevertheless be the general condition in civil society. It is so, not in virtue of any doctrine of universal moral equality, but because the absence of any shared hierarchy of ends in a civil society precludes ranking or prioritizing of any one's freedom over that of anyone else, save in limiting cases.

What of *meliorism*? We have seen that radical value pluralism undermines the idea of progress as a category applicable to human history globally. Within the history of any particular civil society, however, it makes sense to talk of improvement or decline and to frame projects of reform. The standards whereby such projects are conceived and assessed will be to a considerable extend dictated, not by the ideal-typical notion of civil association, but by the specific circumstances and traditions of the various civil societies. Thus, in a civil society defined by a written constitution, such as the United States, reform of current practice may appropriately be conducted by reference to the interpretation of that constitution, while in the United Kingdom discourse will be conducted by reference to the tradition of the Common Law and other forms of precedent. It is not that an ideal type of civil society in the most abstract sense cannot be invoked in any specific historic context; rather that such invocation will not (given the different traditions and narratives of the various civil societies) result in convergence on a single model. The Oakeshottian ideal-typical conception of civil association has value in capturing the essential characteristics of civil society shorn of its historical contingencies; but, for that reason, it will not as a rule be invoked in practical political discourse. Discourse as to amelioration or decline will in general be governed by standards that are imminent in the specific histories and traditions of the diverse civil societies.

The *universalist* element of liberalism survives, not by civil societies converging on any single model, but in virtue of the universality, or near-universality, of civil society itself as a condition of prosperity and peace for any modern civilization. Without the constitutive institutions of civil society specified earlier, no modern society can expect to enjoy peace or commodious living. It may be that, nevertheless, few modern, or post-modern states can achieve a stable civil society for long: there is nothing to support the hope that civil society will be universal *in fact*. Its universality is that of a necessary condition, in virtually all contemporary historical contexts – which are contexts of cultural pluralism in varying degrees – of a common life for those with divergent values and conceptions of the world.

The four constitutive features of doctrinal liberalism return in a contextualized form in the institutions of civil society. It has been affirmed, also, that any contemporary civil society will be animated by a culture of liberty. It remains to connect the Oakeshottian idea of civil association with the idea of liberty as it is supported by value-pluralism in Berlin's theorizing.

AFTER LIBERAL POLITICAL PHILOSOPHY: THEORIZING THE PRACTICE OF LIBERTY

In the post-liberal theoretical perspective advanced here, the project of giving the historic achievement of civil society a universal foundation has been abandoned. Once the foundationalist project of liberal political philosophy is abandoned, what then are the tasks of the theorist? It should be noted, first of all, that the position defended here preopposes acceptance of a thesis in axiology – the thesis of objective value pluralism and incommensurability – and that, since this thesis is one within philosophy, the view I defend diverges from the currently fashionable one, advocated most notably by Richard Rorty,[44] in which philosophy itself seems to have been abandoned. The view defended here, however, radically restricts the ambitions of 'philosophy' by denying to it any prescriptive authority; it concurs with Wittgenstein, in his remark on philosophies of mathematics, that philosophy should not (and indeed cannot) engage in the 'bourgeois' project of founding any specific practice. This is not to deny that philosophical inquiry may have definite results, still less, absurdly, to assimilate philosophical argument to conversation.

The task of philosophy, properly conceived, is to clear away the illusions that obstruct a clear vision of practice. Its task is then principally prophylactic – as exemplified in Berlin's work on liberty, which shows the delusiveness of any fixed set of determinate and harmonious liberties and thereby the impossibility of a libertarian calculus. Once this prophycatic against philosophical hubris is achieved, the theorist returns to his own inheritance and tradition – in our case, to the practice of liberty. Once we cease to be liberal political philosophers, we are free to become theorists of liberty – and to return to a great tradition of such theorizing, which encompasses the thought of the Scottish School, of Constant and Tocqueville, and of Maine and Dicey. The conception of theorizing advanced here has affinities with that of Oakeshott,[45] in that the theorist seeks to discover the postulates of practice. But it has also a content derivable from social theory, in that it will not forswear the illumination of our practices that comes from well-developed explanatory theories. In this the theorist only renews a tradition of discourse broken, in our times, by the fragmentation of the disciplines of the humanities that is a symptom of the broader decomposition of the common culture. For the theorist of liberty, the study of the practice of liberty need not, and should not, be divided neatly into normative and explanatory disciplines: it is the task of theory at once to illuminate the values that animate the practice of liberty and the structure of the institutions in which it is embodied.

It is an important feature of this approach to theorizing liberty that it does not, after the fashion of the anachronistic method of philosophical analysis, seek to elucidate liberty as a *concept* or *definition*, nor does it (in fundamentalist or foundationalist style) try to state fixed and determinate 'principles' about the restraint and distribution of liberty. Rather, it looks to the practices and institutions which embody liberty in any particular historical context and which, in truth, constitute 'liberty' for human beings. This mode of theorizing involves a reversal of method in regard to that practised in the dominant schools of post-War Anglo–American liberal political philosophy, in which free-floating abstractions are deployed in a void, having no concrete institutional, cultural or historical embodiments. The process of abstraction advocated here goes in the opposite direction, from the investigation of the various autonomous institutions that go to make up any concrete civil society to the life of the autonomous agent that such institutions facilitate. We move from the autonomy of institutions to autonomous individuals, where the former are constitutive conditions of the latter.

Liberty returns as the animating value of civil society, not in virtue of its foundational place in any liberal doctrine, but as a characterization of a form of life that can be realized fully only in a society constituted by autonomous institutions and activities. Liberty is prioritized (as a characterization of the status of autonomous agents) because it enables such agents to chart a course among incommensurables which the various forms of life by which they are surrounded present to them. On the view here presented, 'liberty' understood in 'negative' terms as a condition, status or sphere of action protected from interference or coercion derives its principal value from its contribution to 'autonomy' – the partial self-creation of human beings by choices among incommensurables that occur within and between forms of life. Such negative liberty may be valuable for other reasons, in historical contexts other than our own, in which autonomy is itself not especially valuable. For us, negative liberty is an essential, constitutive condition of autonomy, with the autonomous institutions of civil society supplying the array of choiceworthy options which are autonomy's other constitutive condition. Let us see how this connection among autonomy's constitutive conditions is further worked out.

FROM RADICAL VALUE-PLURALISM TO LIBERALISM VIA AUTONOMY

As has already been noted, the historicist argument for civil society here advanced has an early statement in Hegel. It differs from Hegel in denying to history, or to civil society, any teleological character. There was nothing inevitable in the emergence of civil society, and there is nothing that guarantees its survival. Its potentially (but unlikely) universal spread (in its many varieties) means an unavoidable loss of those excellences that civil society drives out. On the value-pluralist view presented here, there can be no *universal* argument to the superiority of civil society. There is nevertheless a powerful case that, for the family of societies having our historical context, in which incommensurable forms of life are deeply interpenetrated, it is a liberal civil society that best promotes human flourishing.

The argument is essentially Berlin's, but is reinforced by Raz's theorizings on autonomy. Berlin's argument is that, if there is an irreducible plurality of objective values that are sometimes incommensurable, then liberty may reasonably be privileged among these values, since when they possess liberty men and women may freely choose between uncombinable ends and make their own combinations of those conflicting values among which a balance may be struck. The argument here has two prongs, negative and positive. Negatively, it trades on the truth that, since there is no one rational ordering or combination of incommensurables, no one could ever provide any *reason* for a particular ranking or combination of incommensurables. More positively, the argument invokes the value of autonomy, both when we are choosing our own mixture of incommensurables that are combinable, and when we are choosing between goods that are constitutively uncombinable. In both cases we are part-authors of our lives, and part-creators of our selves, as we chart our own course among incommensurabilities between which reason cannot arbitrate. And in both cases, our status as autonomous individuals is made possible only by our having available to us autonomous institutions and practices which generate options among which we may freely choose.

Individual choice among incommensurables occurs, accordingly, at two levels. As individuals, we choose (not always, or often, with full reflective awareness) not to explore forms of life or modes of experience that cannot coexist with others we prize: we thereby curtail, often irreparably, a whole range of goods in our lives. If we adopt the life of the devoted family man, we cannot (at least in our day) enjoy the goods of the life of a voluptuary: we deny them to ourselves, as being constitutively incommensurable with the form of life we have chosen. Once this radical choice has been made, we have still many others, often no less difficult, to make, among the incommensurable (but often variously combinable) options that remain. How much of my life will I devote to my family, and how much to my career, or to charitable works? The virtue of a liberal regime is that in it individuals (and, also, groups, associations, cultural traditions and communities) can, each of them, adopt different mixtures of incommensurable values, thereby achieving across the society a variety of forms of human flourishing that could not be achieved within a single human life.

This objective-pluralist argument for a civil society that is liberal in the sense that it accords individuals a wide space for freedom in styles of life is strengthened if one accepts Raz's view that autonomy is accepted by most of us as a vital ingredient in the good life. If, using the texts we find in the forms of common life around us, we wish to be part-authors of our lives, then we will have good reason to demand that choices among incommensurables be made by us, freely and on our own initiative. Even if the life that issues from these choices is not itself an especially autonomous one, the fact that it was autonomously chosen makes it a narrative that one has chosen for himself. And a society that contains a diversity of such self-chosen lives will have a more complex (but not for that reason necessarily or always a more valuable) moral ecology than one dominated or unified by a simple traditional way of life.

For us, then, for whom the practice of autonomy is an essential part of the good life and for whom individualism and pluralism are an historical fate, a liberal civil society is the one in which the richest diversity of forms of flourishing is most likely to be achieved. This result is avowedly culture-specific, and it is not meant to be universalized. Its culture-specificity is no weakness in it, if with Oakeshott we acknowledge that:

> A man's culture is an historic contingency, but since it is all he has he would be foolish to ignore it because it is not composed of eternal verities. It is itself a contingent flow of intellectual and emotional adventures, a mixture of old and new where the new is often a backward swerve to pick up what has been temporarily forgotten; a mixture of the emergent and the recessive; of the substandard and the somewhat flimsy, of the common-place, the refined and the magnificent.[46]

At the same time, the argument from value-pluralism to a liberal civil society has in our time a force that is near-universal. For, given that no modern culture is sealed off hermetically from others, and that in our time the forms of life of different cultural tradition interact and interpenetrate with one another, there will in every modern society be intimations of incommensurable values and perspectives on the world. A liberal civil society has the advantage, for virtually all modern peoples, that in it *epistemic freedoms* are protected – freedoms of inquiry and expression – whereby these intimations of incommensurability can be explored and pursued. Societies that are overtaken by the project of reversing the late modern tendency toward interaction among cultures – societies that are overtaken by religious fundamentalism or fundamentalist political ideologies, such as Marxism – infallibly fall into a barbarism in which all prospects of commodious living, or of peaceful coexistence among men and women, are lost. As Berlin has put it, with respect to the twentieth-century political religions:

> The conviction that, once the last obstacles – ignorance and irrationality, alienation and exploitation, and their individual and social roots – have been eliminated, true human history, that is, universal harmonious cooperation, will at last begin, is a secular form of what is evidently a permanent need of mankind. But if it is the case that not all ultimate human ends are necessarily compatible, there may be no escape from choices governed by no overriding principle, some among them painful, both to the agent and to others. From this it would follow that the creation of a social structure that would, at the least, avoid morally intolerable alternatives, may be the best that human beings can be expected to achieve, if too many varieties of positive action are not to be repressed, too many equally valid human goals are not to be frustrated.[47]

Berlin's restatement of liberalism is a humbler and far more realistic one than could be made by any fundamentalist liberal, such as Mill. Unlike Mill, Berlin does not suppose that there is, or could be, any single measuring rod, on which the merits of different cultures or epochs could be ranked. Nor does he indulge the fantasy that determinate principles are statable and rationally demonstrable which arbitrate conflicts among liberties and between liberty and other values. And he nowhere accords liberal regimes the apodictic superiority over all others that they have in all doctrinal liberalisms. Though it is not a relativistic argument for liberty, Berlin's objective pluralism carries with it an historicist element, when it is applied to societies, such as ours, in which incommensurabilities among values and world-views are pervasive and undeniable. Unlike Mill's or other liberalisms,[48] with their antique echoes of progress, personhood and the religion of humanity, Berlin's is one that can stand the test of our time, which includes radical and tragic choices among goods and evils of which Millian liberalism knew nothing.

Nor does Berlinian liberalism (at least on my account of it) privilege over all others that form of life in which individuals make choices among incommensurable conceptions of the good. On my account, forms of life in which conflicts among incommensurables are resolved by tradition or precedent may be no less forms of human flourishing than ours. That our way of life is ours gives us good enough reason to defend it; we do not need the spurious and illusory support of a theory such as Mill's. The view presented here, unlike Mill's, respects the diversity of modern civil societies, each with its own forms of (perhaps partly incommensurable) immanent criticism, and espouses no paradigm of civil society, to which all must approximate. It does not suppose, as Mill did in his *Considerations on Representative Government*, that there is a form of government that is ideally best for all. Rather, as in the work of Hume as reinterpreted by recent revisionary scholarship,[49] it is assumed that each civil society will understand itself by reference to a distinctive historical narrative, in terms of which criticism and reform of its institutions will proceed. Civil societies are most unlikely, then, to converge on any one model; indeed on the pluralist view developed here, the very notion of such a paradigm is incoherent. This in no way weakens, but ought instead to strengthen, our disposition to defend the civil society we have, each of us, inherited or adopted. Our way of life will survive and prosper, not because we devise a comprehensive theory of it – for, on Berlin's view as on Oakeshott's and mine, moral and political life is in any case not fully theorizable – but only if we are steadfast in our commitment to it. And that commitment is manifested in the realm of practice, not that of discourse or philosophy.

The development of a comprehensive liberal ideology is dangerous, in any case, for this reason. It obscures our perception of the virtues and excellences that liberal society drives out, and so dulls our sense of the undoubted losses that the transition from traditional to civil societies incurs. At the same time, liberal ideology represses the (often pre-liberal) virtues and excellences on which liberal culture itself depends – including forms of common life that liberal individualism tends to corrode. In both these respects, liberal ideology blurs our sense of the historical singularity of liberal civil society.

LIBERAL IDEOLOGY VERSUS LIBERAL CIVIL SOCIETY

We recognize, then, that civil societies are not without losses and costs. Many forms of life that are intrinsically valuable are lost, or weakened, in them. Perhaps the forms of flourishing they allow are not the best our species has achieved, or can achieve; or perhaps we are back in the realm of incommensurables, when we ponder that hard question. We know, however, how terrible are the costs of destroying civil society, of wrecking it in a frenzy of ideological or religious fervor. For us, in any foreseeable future, no form of the good life can be lived outside a civil society. The subtle and humble approach suggested by Berlin, and, in a very different mode, by Oakeshott, in which we seek a *modus vivendi*, never stable or complete, in which we can pursue the intimations of our divergent and incommensurable values without waging war on one another, may appear a dull one to those whose perceptions have been distorted by the hallucinatory horizons of hubristic philosophy – liberal and otherwise. For those who have a sober appreciation of the likely course of the coming century –

a course that, virtually inevitably, will encompass fundamentalist convulsions, near-apocalyptic ecological catastrophes, Malthusian wars and
the spread of technologies of mass destruction in an increasingly anarchic
world – the defence of liberal civil society will appear a more attractive
(and demanding) commitment. Nothing in the reasonings developed here is
meant to imply the inevitability of liberal civil society in our times. Present
trends suggest the opposite, with the fragile institutions of civil society
being increasingly threatened by recent fundamentalisms and by the re-
emergence of atavistic ethnicities. The likely prospect, for most of the
world in the coming century, may well be terror and new forms of
barbarism, not any species of civil society.[50] In this regard, Spengler may
prove to be a better guide to our likely future than the Panglossian fantasies
of Fukuyama. Nothing suggests, in other words, that we can take the
inheritance of civil society for granted. The argument is only that, for us,
the loss of civil society means the loss of civilization.

Further, we ought not to neglect the prospect of a slow decline in our
own civil societies, as traditional practices of law and civil association are
eroded by the inordinate demands of abstract conceptions of equality and
rights. Over the longer run of history, these assaults on civil societies may
yet prove as destructive of it as the more dramatic and explicit attacks of its
avowed enemies among religious and political fundamentalists. It is,
indeed, an implication of my argument that, if civil society is among us in
danger, it is in virtue precisely of the hubris of fundamentalist liberalism –
the liberalism of those (such as Ackerman, the early Nozick and Rawl, or
Dworkin[51]) who seek to use the hallucinatory perspectives of uncritical
philosophy to distract us from the practice of liberty. We are not far from
the point at which the mass availability of hubristic philosophy imposes
impossible strains on the institutions and practices from which it illicitly
derives all its genuine content.[52] It is the argument of this essay that it is
only by abandoning such false philosophy and re-situating ourselves within
our inheritance of practice that that practice can be successfully renewed.

The danger we confront in the established civil societies of the West is
that of the corrosion of liberal practices by liberal ideology. This is a danger
that is ubiquitous in the West, but especially severe in the United States,
where liberal ideology (especially as it is found in academic institutions)
exhibits a hostility to virtually every aspect of civil society, particularly the
market economy. There is a further danger that it is the destructive hubris
of liberal ideology, rather than the inheritance of civil society, that will be
transmitted to the emergent post-Communist world. It is only by deflating
the pretensions of fundamentalist liberal ideology that we can hope to curb
or slow the frittering away of our patrimony of civil institutions that is
presently well under way in the West.

CONCLUSION

> I once said, perhaps rightly: The earlier culture will become a heap of rubble and finally a heap of ashes, but spirit will hover over the ashes.
>
> L. Wittgenstein[53]

Liberalism was the political theory of modernity. As we enter the closing phase of the modern age, we confront the spectre of renascent atavistic barbarisms, which threaten to ruin the modern inheritance of civil society. Our task, as post-moderns no longer sustained by the modernist fictions of progress, rights and a universal civilization or by classical conceptions of natural law as embodied in Greco–Roman and Judaeo–Christian traditions, is to preserve the practice of liberty that is transmitted to us by the inherited institutions of civil society. The task may be a daunting one, but it is one which our circumstances and prospects impose upon us, if we retain any sense of the worth of our inheritance, and any perception of the nature of the alternatives to it. In the past, there may have been viable alternatives, in which civilization and civil society did not go together. Our argument has been to that conclusion. At present, and in any foreseeable future, we have no such options. In the contemporary Western world, a self-denigrating guilt inhibits the discourse of civilization and barbarism that informed the Scottish Enlightenment (the only episode of enlightenment from which, if I am not mistaken, we have anything to learn); yet it is the lesson of our century that, if the claims of commissars or mullahs, Nazis or clerical fascists are conceded, civilization is lost along with the civil societies they seek to subjugate, and barbarism supervenes. We will best serve what remains alive in liberalism, if we come to see liberal civil society as a particularistic form of life, spreading throughout the world, but everywhere threatened by modernist fundamentalisms and atavistic ideologies.

A commitment to the preservation of civil society is, for us, a commitment to the maintenance of civilization. For, though it may be only one of the diverse forms of flourishing our species has achieved, a liberal civil society is the form of society in which we have made our contribution to the human good; and, in defending it, we defend the best in our cultural inheritance, and the best that the species can presently reasonably hope for.[54]

Notes

1 HOBBES AND THE MODERN STATE

1 *Leviathan*, (New York and London: Dent and Sons, 1949) 50.
2 Michael Oakeshott, *Hobbes on Civil Associations*, (Oxford: Basil Blackwell, 1975) 73.
3 *Leviathan*, 49.
4 Quoted in *Hobbes*, (London: Macmillan, 1904) by Sir Leslie Stephen, 139.
5 *Leviathan*, 79–80.
6 *Leviathan*, 103–4.
7 Oakeshott, op. cit., 55.
8 Bernard Gert, in his Introduction to *Man and Citizen* by Thomas Hobbes, (New York: Doubleday, 1972).
9 B. Gert (ed.), *Man and Citizen* by Thomas Hobbes, 48–9.
10 Elias Canetti, *The Human Province*, (London: Picador, 1986) 115–16.
11 On this, see Donald Livingstone's *Hume's Philosophy of Common Life*, (Chicago and London: University of Chicago Press, 1984).
12 B. Gert, op. cit., 42–3.
13 See Isaiah Berlin, *Vico and Herder: Two Studies in the History of Ideas*, (New York: Viking Press, 1976); and 'Vico's concept of knowledge' and 'Vico and the ideal of Enlightenment', in Isaiah Berlin, *Against the Current*, (London: The Hogarth Press, 1979).
14 Oakeshott, op. cit., 63.
15 A good summary of the work of the neo-Hobbesian Virginia School of Public Choice may be found in James Buchanan and Gordon Tullock, *The Calculus of Consent*, (Ann Arbor: University of Michigan Press, 1962).
16 For example, Gregory P. Kavka, *Hobbesian Moral and Political Theory*, (Princeton: Princeton University Press, 1986).
17 A brilliant explanation of the character of the Soviet system is to be found in Alain Besancon's *The Soviet Syndrome*, (New York, 1976).
18 Oakeshott, op. cit., 74.

2 SANTAYANA AND THE CRITIQUE OF LIBERALISM

1 See T.L.S. Sprigge, *Santayana: an Examination of his Philosophy*, (London and Boston: Routledge and Kegan Paul, 1974) 1.

2 First published by Charles Scribner and Sons (New York), republished by Dover Publications, Inc., (New York, 1955).

3 *Life of Reason, or The Phases of Human Progress*, (New York: Charles Scribner and Sons, 1905–6) 5 vols.

4 *Realms of Being* (New York: Charles Scribner and Sons, 1927–42) 4 vols.

5 *Winds of Doctrine: Studies in Contemporary Opinion*, (New York, Charles Scribner and Son, 1913).

6 *Soliloquies in England and Later Soliloquies*, (New York: Charles Scribner and Sons, 1922).

7 *Winds of Doctrine*, 146.

8 *Soliloquies in England and Later Soliloquies*, 165–6.

9 ibid., 165–6.

10 ibid., 207–8.

11 *Dominations and Powers: Reflections on Liberty, Society and Government*, (New York: Charles Scribner and Sons, 1951) 340.

12 *Soliloquies in England and Later Soliloquies*, 184.

13 *Dominations and Powers*, 438.

14 ibid., vii.

15 ibid., 158.

16 'Alternatives to Liberalism' in Santayana's *The Birth of Reason and Other Essays*, (New York: Columbia University Press, 1968) 114.

17 *Dominations and Powers*, 211–12.

18 ibid., 450.

19 ibid., 452.

20 ibid., see 440.

21 ibid., 454–6.

22 'Alternatives to Liberalism', op. cit., 108–9.

23 P.S. Schilpp, *The Philosophy of George Santayana*, (New York: Tudor Publishing Company, 1951) 559.

24 'A long way round to Nirvana' in Santayana's *Some Turns of Thought in Modern Philosophy*, (Cambridge: Cambridge University Press, 1935) 94.

25 'Alternatives to Liberalism', op. cit., 115.

3 HAYEK AS A CONSERVATIVE

1 F.A. Hayek, *Constitution of Liberty*, (Chicago: Henry Regnery Company, 1960).

2 F.A. Hayek, *Law, Legislation and Liberty: a New Statement of the Liberal Principles of Justice and Political Economy*, vol. 2: *The Mirage of Social Justice*, (London: Routledge and Kegan Paul, 1976).

3 Hayek's epistemology is most systematically presented in his treatise on philosophical psychology, *The Sensory Order: an Inquiry into the Foundations of Theoretical Psychology*, (London: Routledge and Kegan Paul, 1952), and in the earlier essays collected in his *Studies in Philosophy, Politics and Economics*, (London: Routledge and Kegan Paul, 1967).

4 For the intriguing idea of a meta-conscious rule, see Hayek's Studies in *Philosophy, Politics and Economics*, ibid., 60–3.

5 Saul Kirpke, *Wittgenstein on Rules and Private Language*, (Oxford: Basil Blackwell, 1982) 88n.

6 Hayek acknowledges the inevitability of legislation in the modern state in his response to the most interesting and original criticism of his views in Bruno Leoni's Freedom and the Law, (Princeton, New Jersey: D. Van Nostrand, 1961). See Hayek, *Law, Legislation and Liberty*, vol. 1: *Rules and Order*, 168, 35n.

7 F.A. Hayek, *The Road to Serfdom*, (London: George Routledge and Sons, 1944).

8 I refer, most especially, to Oakeshott's *Human Conduct*, 274–8, for its masterly evocation of the sources and character of the modern European sense of individuality.

9 For Hayek's conception of an unviable morality, see *Law, Legislation and Liberty*, vol. 2: *The Mirage of Social Justice*, ch. 11.

10 On the Platonist and Christian roots of Marxism, see L. Kolakowski, *Main Currents of Marxism*, vol. 1, ch. 1.

11 For a conservative criticism of Hayek's Mandevillain argument, see Irving Kristol, 'When Virtue Loses all her Loveliness – Some Reflections on Capitalism and "The Free Society"', *The Public Interest*, (Fall 1970) 3–15.

12 For a profound interpretation of contemporary moral inversion, see Michael Polanyi's *Personal Knowledge: Towards a Post-Critical Philosophy*, (Chicago: Chicago University Press, 1958) ch. 7, sections 9–16.

4 OAKESHOTT AS A LIBERAL

1 *Rationalism in Politics and Other Essays*, (Indianapolis: Liberty Press, 1991) 439–40.

2 The paper is 'Michael Oakeshott as Liberal Theorist' by Wendell John Coats, Jr, *Canadian Journal of Political Science*, (December, 1985, xviii: 4) 773–87. Oakeshott expressed his admiration of Coats's paper in a conversation with the present writer.

3 The two books are: *Oakeshott* by Robert Grant, (London: The Claridge Press, 1990) and *The Political Philosophy of Michael Oakeshott*, By Franco, (New Haven and London, 1990).

4 John Rawls, *A Theory of Justice*, (Cambridge, Mass.: Harvard University Press, 1971); Ronald Dworkin, *Taking Rights Seriously*, (London: Duckworth, 1978).

5 Michael Oakeshott, *Rationalism in Politics and Other Essays*, new and expanded edn, Timothy Fuller (ed.), (Indianapolis: Liberty Press, 1991).

6 See note 2, above.

7 *Rationalism in Politics and Other Essays*, 452.

8 Robert Grant, *Oakeshott*, 85.

9 See *Rationalism in Politics and Other Essays*, 384–406.

10 Henry C. Simon, *Economic Policy for a Free Society*, (Chicago and Cambridge: Chicago University Press and Cambridge University Press, 1948).

11 *Rationalism in Politics and Other Essays*, 443.

12 See Oakeshott *The Voice of Liberal Learning*, (New Haven, 1989).

13 See Franco, note 3 above.

5 BUCHANAN ON LIBERTY

1 See my book, *Liberalisms: Essays in Political Philosophy*, (London and New York: Routledge, 1989) ch. 10, 'Contractarian method, private property and the market economy'.

2 Michael Sandel, *Liberalism and the Limits of Justice*, (Cambridge: Cambridge University Press, 1982).

3 James Buchanan, 'The Constitution of Economic Policy', Nobel Prize Lecture, (1986) reprinted in *Public Choice and Constitutional Economics*, J.D. Gwartney and R.E. Wagner (eds), (Greenwich, Conn. and London: Jai Press, Inc.) 112.

4 ibid., 113.

5 Jan Narveson, *The Libertarian Idea*, (Philadelphia: Temple University Press, 1988).

6 Such a thin veil of ignorance is also deployed by G. Kavka in his excellent *Hobbesian Moral and Political Theory*, (Princeton, NJ: Princeton University Press, 1986).

7 I am indebted to Zbigniew Rau for conversation on this topic, and for allowing me to read his forthcoming paper, 'The East European-challenge to dual contract orthodoxy: replacing the state of nature with the state of enslavement', where these questions are illuminatingly discussed.

8 See my 'Totalitarianism, reform and civil society,' ch. 12 of this collection.

9 See Nelson Goodman, *Ways of World-Making*, (Indianapolis: Hacket Publishing Co., 1975).

10 James Buchanan and Geoffrey Brennan, *The Reason of Rules: Constitutional Political Economy*, (Cambridge: Cambridge University Press, 1985).

11 Jeffrey Paul, 'Substantive Contracts and the legitimate basis of political authority', *The Monist*, 66 (4), (October 1983).

12 For an exposition of actual-contract methodology see Gilbert Harman, 'Rationality in agreement: a commentary on Gauthier's *Morality by Agreement*', *Social Philosophy and Policy*, vol. 5, issue 2, (Spring 1988).

13 See Michael Oakeshott, *Hobbes on Civil Association*, (Oxford: Basil Blackwell, 1975).

14 For the best account of Hume's social philosophy, see D. Livingston's *Hume's Philosophy of Common Life*, (Chicago: University of Chicago Press, 1984).

15 For G.L.S. Shackle's account of invincible human ignorance in a kaleidic world, see his masterpiece, *Epistemics and Economics: A Critique of Economic Doctrines*, (Cambridge: Cambridge University Press, 1972).

16 This paper has benefitted from conversations over the years with James Buchanan, Charles King, F.A. Hayek and G.L.S. Shackle. Responsibility for its argument, including its interpretation of Buchanan's thought, remains mine alone.

6 BERLIN'S AGONISTIC LIBERALISM

1 Joseph Raz, *The Morality of Freedom*, (Oxford: Clarendon Press, 1986).

2 Isaiah Berlin, *The Crooked Timber of Humanity: Chapters in the History of Ideas*, (London: John Murray, 1990).

3 'Two Concepts of Liberty', in *Four Essays on Liberty* (Oxford: Oxford University Press, 1968) 118–72.

4 John Stuart Mill, *On Liberty*, in John Gray (ed.), *On Liberty and Other Essays*, (Oxford: Oxford University Press, World's Classics Series, 1991).

5 Edna and Avishai Margalit (eds), *Isaiah Berlin: A Celebration*, (London: The Hogarth Press).

7 THE SYSTEM OF RUINS

1 Eugen von Böhm-Bawerk, *Karl Marx and the Close of his System*, (Clifton, NJ: A.M. Kelly Publishers, 1973).
2 Tom Bottomore (ed.), *A Dictionary of Marxist Thought*, (Oxford: Blackwell, 1983).
3 Gérard Bekerman, *Marx and Engels: A Conceptual Concordance* trans. Terrell Carver, (Oxford: Blackwell, 1983).
4 David Felix, *Marx as Politician*, (Carbondale: Southern Illinois University Press, 1983).
5 Ernest Nolte, *Marxism, Fascism, Cold War*, (Asson, Netherlands: Van Gorcum, 1983).
6 Ernest Nolte, *Three Faces of Fascism*, (London: Macmillan, 1965).
7 Nolte, op. cit.
8 ibid., 84.
9 Alan MacFarlane, *Origins of English Individualism*, (Cambridge: Cambridge University Press, 1976).
10 G.A. Cohen, *Karl Marx's Theory of History: A Defence*, (Oxford: Clarendon Press, 1978).
11 Alex Callinicos, *The Revolutionary Ideas of Karl Marx*, (London: Bookmarks, 1983).
12 ——, *Marxism and Philosophy*, (Oxford: Oxford University Press, 1983).
13 David McLellan (ed.), *Marx: The First Hundred Years*, (Fontana, 1983).
14 Paul Craig Roberts, *Alienation of the Soviet Economy*, (Albuquerque, New Mexico: University of Mexico Press, 1971, 1st edn; New York and London: Holmes and Meier Publishers, 1991, 2nd edn).
15 Norman Fischer, Louis Patsouras and N. Georgopoulos (eds), *Continuity and Change in Marxism*, (Brighton: Harvester, 1983).
16 Susan M. Easton, *Humanist Marxism and Wittgensteinian Social Philosophy*, (Manchester: Manchester University Press, 1983).
17 Jorge Larrain, *Marxism and Ideology*, (Macmillan, 1983).
18 Jean L. Cohen, *Class and Civil Society: The Limits of Marxian Critical Theory*, (Oxford: Martin Robertson, 1983).
19 Michael Burawoy and Theda Skocpol, *Marxist Inquiries: Studies of labor, class, and states*, (Chicago: University of Chicago Press, 1983).
20 Barry Smart, *Foucault, Marxism and Critique*, (Routledge and Kegan Paul, 1983).
21 George C. Brenkert, *Marx's Ethics of Freedom*, (Routledge and Kegan Paul, 1983).

8 THE DELUSION OF GLASNOST

1 Goldfarb, Jeffrey C., *Beyond Glasnost: The Post-Totalitarian Mind*, (Chicago: University of Chicago Press, 1989).

9 THE ACADEMIC ROMANCE OF MARXISM

1 Martin Jay, *Fin-de-Siècle Socialism and Other Essays*, (Routledge, 1989).
2 F. Laclau and C. Mouffe, *Hegemony and Socialist Strategy*, (Verso, 1985).

3 A.W. Gouldner, *Against Fragmentation: Origins of Marxism and the Sociology of Intellectuals*, (Oxford University Press, 1985).

4 John E. Roemer, *Free to Lose: An Introduction to Marxist Economic Philosophy*, (Century Hutchinson, 1989).

10 PHILOSOPHY, SCIENCE AND MYTH IN MARXISM

1 'Theses on Feuerbach', VI, in Lewis S. Feuer (ed.), *Marx and Engels: Basic Writings on Politics and Philosophy*, (London: Collins, Fontana Library, 1969) 285.

2 In *Karl Marx: Early Writings*, introduced by L. Colletti (Harmondsworth: Penguin Books, 1975) 328–9.

3 S. Ryazanskaya (ed.), *The German Ideology*, (Moscow: Progress Publishers, 1964) 31.

4 F. Engels (ed.), trans. Samuel Moore and Edward Aveling *Capital*, I, (Moscow: Progress Publishers, 1965) 179.

5 *Economic-Philosophic Manuscripts*, in *Karl Marx: Early Writings*, 328.

6 L. Kolakowski, *Main Currents of Marxism*, III, *The Breakdown*, (Oxford: Clarendon Press, 1978) 277.

7 *Capital*, I, 79–80.

8 On this and other points in my analysis I have learnt much from *Marx's Theory of Exchange, Alienation and Crisis* by Paul Craig Roberts and Matthew A. Stephenson, (Stanford: Hoover Institution Press, 1973).

9 The term 'catallaxy' I borrow from F.A. Hayek's recent use of it. See his *Studies in Philosophy, Politics and Economics*, (London: Routledge, 1967) 164.

10 'The Obsolescence of Marxism', in N. Lobknvicz (ed.), *Marx and the Western World*, (Notre Dame: University of Notre Dame Press, 1967) 411.

11 ibid., 411.

12 ibid., 411.

13 ibid., 411.

14 ibid., 411.

15 'Repressive Tolerance', in *A Critique of Pure Tolerance*, (with Barrington Moore and R.P. Wolff) (London: Cape, 1969) 93.

16 *One-Dimensional Man*, (London: Sphere Books, 1968) 200.

17 *An Essay on Liberalism*, (London: Allen Lane, 1969) 85.

18 *One-Dimensional Man*, 201. See also Marcuse's *Counter-Revolution and Revolt*, (London: Allen Lane, 1972).

19 E. Kamenka, *Marxism and Ethics*, (London: Macmillan, 1969) 26.

20 L. Kolakowski, *The Socialist Idea*, (London: Weidenfeld and Nicholson, 1974) ch. 2, 'The myth of human self-identity'.

21 G.A. Cohen, *Karl Marx's Theory of History: A Defence*, (Oxford: Clarendon Press, 1978) 151.

22 ibid., 151.

23 ibid., 134.

24 ibid., 134.

25 ibid., 135.

26 ibid., 156, 155, respectively.

27 ibid., 153.

28 ibid., 152.

29 ibid., 153.

30 ibid., 153.

31 ibid., 151.

32 See on this R. Rhees, *Without Answers*, (London: Routledge, 1969) 23–49, for a critique of Marxism from which I have learnt much.

33 I owe this example to D.Z. Philipps and H.O. Mounce, *Moral Practices*, (London: Routledge, 1970).

34 I am indebted to the writings of John Anderson, and especially to his *Marxist Ethics*, in *Studies in Empirical Philosophy* (Sydney, 1962), for these points.

35 Cohen, op. cit., 24.

36 All of the preceding quotations occur on p. 50 of Cohen.

37 On p. 353 Cohen asserts that the theses of the labour theory of value are not presupposed or entailed by any of the arguments he advances in the book. The productivity criterion may presuppose some elements of the labour theory of value; but I am not concerned to argue this there.

38 Cohen, op. cit., 248.

39 Cohen, op. cit., 155.

40 Cohen, op. cit., 169.

41 Cohen, op. cit., 206.

42 Cohen, op. cit., 223.

43 Cohen, op. cit., 160–66.

44 Singer, *New York Review of Books*, (20 December, 1979) 46–7). In reply to Singer, Cohen has insisted that Darwinian theory has a functionalist aspect. I am not persuaded by his claims, but their cogency would not affect the main line of my argument.

45 Cohen, op. cit., 159.

46 In Berlin's *Against the Current: Essays in the History of Ideas* (London: Hogarth Press, 1979), 296–322.

47 Lukács, *History and Class-Consciousness*, (Cambridge, Mass.: Massachusetts Institute of Technology Press, 1971).

48 Alasdair MacIntyre, *A Short History of Ethics*, (London: Routledge, 1968) 268–9.

49 For a systematic statement of Cohen's more recent views, see his *History, Labour and Freedom: Themes from Marx*, (Oxford, 1987).

50 I have not forgotten those neo-Kantian Marxian thinkers who treat Marxist social theory as purely explanatory. I would contend that their writings sacrifice that unity of theory and practice which is distinctive of the Marxian standpoint.

51 I am particularly grateful to Gerry Cohen, David Miller, Bhikhu Parekh and Bill Weinstein for their comments on previous versions of this paper.

11 AGAINST COHEN ON PROLETARIAN UNFREEDOM

1 For their comments on an earlier draft of this paper, I am indebted to Scott Arnold, Gerry Cohen, Jen Elster, David Gordon, Andrew Melnyk, David Miller, Ellen Paul, Jeffrey Paul, G. Pincione and Andrew Williams. Responsibility for this paper, including its interpretation of Cohen's argument, remains mine.

2 'Capitalism, Freedom and the Proletariat' in Alan Ryan (ed.), *The Idea of Freedom*, (Oxford: Oxford University Press, 1979); 'Illusions about Private Property and Freedom', J. Mepham and D. Ruben, (eds), *Issues in Marxist*

Philosophy, vol. IV (Hassocks, Sussex: Harvester Press, 1981); 'Freedom, Justice and Capitalism', *New Left Review*, vol. 125, (1981); 'The Structure of Proletarian Unfreedom', J. Roemer (ed.), *Analytical Marxism*, (Cambridge University Press, 1986); and 'Are Workers Forced to Sell Their Labour-power?', *Philosophy and Public Affairs*, vol. 14, no. 1 (1985).

3 Cohen, 'Capitalism', 12.
4 Cohen, 'Illusions', 227.
5 *ibid.*, 226–7.
6 Cohen, 'Capitalism', 11–12.
7 *ibid.*, 11.
8 *ibid.*, 16–17.
9 *ibid.*, 17.
10 The 'negative' view of freedom as non-interference shifts easily into a view of freedom as non-restriction of options. On this see John Gray, 'Negative and Positive Liberty', John Gray and Z.A. Pelczynski, (eds), *Conceptions of Liberty in Political Philosophy*, (London and New York: Athlone Press and St Martin's Press, 1984) 321–48; reprinted in John Gray, *Liberalisms: Essays in Political philosophy*, (London and New York: Routledge, 1989), ch. 4.
11 Cohen, 'Structure', 250, 21n.
12 On Berlin's conception of freedom, see Gray, 'Negative and Positive Library', op. cit.
13 See H. Marcuse, 'Repressive Tolerance', in *A Critique of Repressive Tolerance*, (Boston: Beacon Press, 1968); and H. Arendt, 'The Revolutionary Tradition and its Lost Treasure', M. Sandel (ed.), *Liberalism and Its Critics*, (New York: New York University Press, 1984) 239–63.
14 George G. Brenkert, 'Cohen on Proletarian Unfreedom', *Philosophy and Public Affairs*, vol. 14 (1985) 93–8; John Gray, 'Marxian Freedom, Individual Liberty and the End of Alienation', *Social Philosophy and Policy*, vol. 3, no. 2 (1986) 170–4.
15 I do not mean to suggest that Cohen's is the best statement of a liberal negative view of freedom, but only that it is Cohen's that I shall deploy in may argument against him.
16 Cohen, 'Structure', 244.
17 *ibid.*, 245.
18 *ibid.*, 242, 7n.
19 *ibid.*, 242.
20 *ibid.*, 244.
21 *ibid.*, 241.
22 *ibid.*, 248.
23 *ibid.*, 250.
24 *ibid.*, 250.
25 *ibid.*, 248.
26 *ibid.*, 248.
27 C.B. Macpherson, *Democratic Theory*, (Oxford: Clarendon Press, 1973) 154.
28 Cohen, 'Structure', 248.
29 *ibid.*, 248.
30 *ibid.*, 249.
31 *ibid.*, 251.
32 Cohen comments approvingly ('Structure', 245, 10n) on Elster's perceptive observation that 'such structures [of collective unfreedom] pervade social life.'

33 Cohen, 'Structure', 244.
34 Cohen, 'Capitalism', 18–19.
35 Cohen, 'Illusion', 228.
36 Cohen, 'Structure', 238.
37 Robert Nozick, *Anarchy, State and Utopia*, (Oxford: Basil Blackwell, 1974) 30.
38 Cohen, 'Structure', 243, 8n.
39 *ibid.*, 243.
40 Cohen, 'Freedom', 10.
41 Cohen, 'Illusions', 224.
42 Cohen, 'Structure', 242.
43 *ibid.*, 244.
44 *ibid.*, 241.
45 For example, Felix Oppenheim. See his '"Constraints on Freedom" as a Descriptive Concept', *Ethics*, vol. 95 (1985) 305–9, and *Political Concepts: A Reconstruction* (Chicago: University of Chicago Press, 1981).
46 Joseph Raz, *The Morality of Freedom* (Oxford: Clarendon Press, 1986), 14.
47 *ibid.*, 16.
48 For an argument that power is best theorized value-neutrally, see John Gray, 'Political Power, Social Theory and Essential Contestability', D. Miller and L. Siedentop (eds) *The Nature of Political Theory*, (Oxford: Clarendon Press, 1983); reprinted in this collection, ch. 15.
49 The idea of a moral notion is explored in J. Kovesi, *Moral Notions*, (London: Routledge and Kegan Paul, 1971).
50 See, on this, Raz, *The Morality of Freedom*.
51 Cohen, 'Capitalist', 15.
52 Cohen, 'Illusions', 232.
53 *ibid.*, 233.
54 On this see John Gray, 'Liberalism and the Choice of Liberties', T.A. Hig, D. Callen, and J. Gray, (eds), *The Restraint of Liberty*, Bowling Green Studies in Applied Philosophy, vol. VII (1985) 1–25; reprinted in John Gray, *Liberalisms*, op. cit., ch. 9.
55 See J. Rawls, *A Theory of Justice*, (Oxford: Oxford University Press, 1972).
56 With reference to Rawls's later writings, I refer especially to 'The Basic Liberties and Their Priority', *Tanner Lectures on Human Values*, (Salt Lake City: University of Utah Press, 1981).
57 See John Gray, 'Marxian Freedom, Individual Liberty, and the End of Alienation', *Social Philosophy and Policy*, vol. 3, no. 2, (1986) 180–5.
58 F.A. Hayek, *The Constitution of Liberty*, (Chicago: Henry Regnery, 1960) 121. The central context of Hayek's argument is stated in somewhat Marxian fashion by Jeffrey Reiman, *Philosophy and Public Affairs*, vol. 16, no. 2, (Winter, 1978), 41: 'The space between a plurality of centers of power may be just the space in which freedom occurs, and conflicts between the centers may work to keep that space open . . . as a material fact, state ownership might . . . represent a condition in which people were more vulnerable to, or less able to resist or escape from, force than they are in capitalism. It follows that, even if socialism ends capitalist slavery, it remains possible, on materialist grounds, that some achievable form of capitalism will be morally superior to any achievable form of socialism.'
59 Leon Trotsky, *The Revolution Betrayed*, (New York: Pathfinder Books, 1937) 76.
60 Cohen, 'Capitalism', 258.

61 Hayek, *The Constitution of Liberty*, op. cit., 126.
62 For the argument that private property maximizes the liberty even of those who have none, see John Gray, *Liberalism*, (Milton Keynes: Open University Press and Minnesota: University of Minnesota Press, 1986) 66–8.
63 Cohen, 'Illusions', 224.
64 On positional goods, see John Gray, 'Classical Liberalism, Positional Goods and the Politicization of Property', Adrian Ellis and Krishnan Kumar (eds), *Dilemmas of Liberal Democracies*, (London: Tavistock, 1983) 174–84.
65 A mass of evidence exists as to the extent of politically enforced social stratifications in the USSR. A useful survey of some of it is to be found in S. Simis, 'The Machinery of Corruption in the Soviet Union', *Survey*, vol. 23, no. 4 (Autumn 1977–8).

12 TOTALITARIANISM, REFORM AND CIVIL SOCIETY

1 For the use of the word 'totalitarian' by Italian theorists of fascism, see L. Schapiro, *Totalitarianism*, (London: Macmillan, 1983) 13–15; and E. Nolte, *Marxism, Cold War*, (Assen, The Netherlands, 1982) 137–8.
2 A good compilation of the post-War literature may be found in C.J. Friedrich (ed.), *Totalitarianism*, (Cambridge, Mass., 1954).
3 For a good survey of the literature that argues against the concept of totalitarianism in Soviet and East European context, see A. Gleason, 'Totalitarianism', *Russian Review*, vol. 45, (1984) 145–59.
4 For an argument that modern capitalist societies are totalitarian, see H. Marcuse, *One Dimensional Man*, (London: Sphere Books, 1964) 105, et. seq.
5 See M. Heller, *Cogs in the Soviet Wheel: The Formation of Soviet Man*, (London: Collins Harvill, 1988).
6 R. Pipes, *Russia under the Old Regime*, (London: Weidenfeld and Nicolson, 1974) 317.
7 Barrington Moore, Jr, *Social Origins of Dictatorship and Democracy*, (London: Penguin Press, 1967) 206.
8 Leonard Schapiro, *Totalitarianism*, (London: Macmillan 1972) 23.
9 E. Nolte, *Marxism, Fascism, Cold War*, (Assen, The Netherlands: Van Gorcum, 1982) section B.
10 The economical exposition of the five-point totalitarian syndrome appears in C.J. Friedrich, 'The Unique Character of Totalitarian Society' in Fredrich, op. cit., 47–59.
11 Perhaps the best defence of this view may be found in Pipes, op. cit.
12 A. Walicki, *Legal Philosophies of Russian Liberalism*, Oxford: Clarendon Press, 1987.
13 Norman Stone, *Europe Transformed*, 1878–1918, (London: Fontana, 1983) 200; and John J. Dziak, *Chekisty: a History of the KGB*, (Lexington, Mass.: Lexington Books, D.C. Heath and Company, 1988) appendix, 173–6.
14 I owe this, and other statistics, to M. Heller and A. Nekrich's magnificent *Utopia in Power: The History of the Soviet Union from 1917 to the Present*, (New York: Summit Books, 1986) 15, et. seq.
15 N. Stone, ibid., 197.
16 N. Stone, ibid., 200, et. seq.

17 D. Lieven, *Russia's Rulers under the Old Regime*, (New Haven and London: Yale University Press, 1989) 290.
18 Heller and Nekrich, ibid., 15.
19 Dziak, ibid., 173, et. seq. The term NKYU refers to the People's Commariat of Justice.
20 Dziak, ibid., 35.
21 Cited in Dziak, ibid., 33.
22 R. Pipes, op. cit., 301–2.
23 A. Besancon, *The Soviet Syndrome*, (New York: Harcourt Brace Jovanovik, 1976) 56.
24 The significance of the Shakhty trial of engineers, see Heller and Nekrich, ibid., 211–12.
25 Heller and Nekrich, ibid., 213.
26 Heller and Nekrich, 701.
27 *New York Times*, July 31, 1989.
28 See E.H. Carr, *The Russian Revolution from Lenin to Stalin, 1917–29*, (London: Macmillan, 1964) and M. Dobb, *On Economic Theory and Socialism: Collected Papers*, (London, Routledge and Kegan Paul, 1955).
29 P. C. Roberts, *Alienation and the Soviet economy*, (University of New Mexico Press, 1971); T. Remington, *Building Socialism in Bolshevik Russia*, (University of Pittsburgh Press, 1984); S. Malle, *The Organization of War Communism, 1918–21*, (Cambridge University Press, 1985).
30 Dziak, ibid., 32–3.
31 Dziak, ibid., 25.
32 Dziak, ibid., 29.
33. A. Nove, *An Economic History of the USSR*, (London: Penguin Press, 1969, 198.
34 Nove, ibid., 266.
35 Nove, ibid., 180.
36 Nove, ibid., 379.
37 Heller and Nekrich, ibid., 264.
38 Heller and Nekrich, ibid., 235–6. It is not intended by Heller and Nekrich, I take it, to equate the Communist genocides with the Nazi Holocaust, since the latter clearly has dimensions that are incommensurable with other twentieth-century genocides. The intention is simply to note that the Stalinist policy of collectivation was genocidal in character.
39 On this, see Robert conquest's excellent book, *The Nation-Killers*, (London: Macmillan, 1960).
40 Eugene Lyons, *Assignment in Utopia*, (New York: Harcourt Brace and Co., 1937) 572–80.
41 On this, see N. Bethell, *The Last Secret*, (London: Fontaine, 1974).
42 See the path-breaking study by C. Andreyev, *Vlasov and the Russian Liberation Movement: Soviet reality and emigre theories*, (Cambridge: Cambridge University Press, 1987).
43 The nuclear Gulag is that portion of the Soviet system of concentration camps in which prisoners are required to service nuclear installations and devices.
44 Dziak, ibid., 52.
45 See Dziak, ibid., 47.
46 *Ibid.*, 49. Further data about the 'Changing Landmarks' movement and the Trust operation are to be found in Heller and Nekrich, *Utopia in Power*, 148–9; C.

Andreyev, *Vlasov and the Russian Liberation Movement*, 175–77; A. Golitsyn, *New Lies for Old*, (London: Bodley Head, 1984) 12; Edward Jay Epstein, *Deception*, (New York: Simon and Schuster, 1987) 25.

47 Epstein, *Deception*, 25.

48 Dziak, *Chekisty*, 49–50.

49 A. Golitsyn, op. cit., 12. Golitsyn's predictions for the next stage of Soviet development, made no later than 1983, are perhaps worth quoting in full:

> Political 'liberalization' and 'democratization' . . . [in the USSR] would be spectacular and impressive. Formal pronouncements might be made about a reduction in the Communist party's role; its monopoly would be apparently curtailed. An ostensible separation of powers between the legislative, the executive, and the judiciary might be introduced. The Supreme Soviet would be given greater apparent power and the president and deputies greater apparent independence. The posts of president of the Soviet Union and first secretary of the party might well be separated. The KGB would be 'reformed'. Dissidents at home would be amnestied; those in exile abroad would be allowed to return, and some would take up positions of leadership in government. Sakharov might be included in some capacity in the government or allowed to teach abroad. The creative arts and cultural and scientific organizations, such as the writers' unions and Academy of Sciences, would become apparently more independent, as would the trade unions. Political clubs would be opened to nonmembers of the Communist party. Leading dissidents might form one or more alternative political parties. Censorship would be relaxed; controversial books, play, films, and art would be published, performed, and exhibited. Many prominent Soviet performing artists now abroad would return to the Soviet Union and resume their professional careers. Constitutional amendments would be adopted to guarantee fulfillment of the provisions of the Helsinki agreements and a semblance of compliance would be maintained. There would be greater freedom for Soviet citizens to travel. Western and United Nations observers would be invited to the Soviet Union to witness the reforms in action. . . .
>
> 'Liberalization' in Eastern Europe would probably involve the return to power in Czechoslovakia of Dubcek and his associates. If it should be extended to East Germany, demolition of the Berlin Wall might even be contemplated.
>
> Western acceptance of the new 'liberalization' as genuine would create favorable conditions for the fulfillment of Communist strategy for the United States, Western Europe, and even, perhaps, Japan.

I do not intend to endorse Golitsyn's theories, but simply to note the respects in which his expectations have been corroborated by events.

50 For an explanation of the term, 'the sixth glasnost', see Epstein, ibid., 279.

51 See, for data on the WIN operation, Dziak, ibid., 49–50.

52 Dziak, ibid., 5.

53 P.C. Roberts and M. Stephenson, *Marx's Theory of Exchange, Alienation and Crisis*, (Stanford, Calif.: Hoover Institution Press, 1973) 94.

54 For an excellent account of the Austrian calculation debate, see D. Lavoie, *Rivalry and Central Planning: The Socialist Calculation Debate Reconsidered*, (Cambridge: Cambridge University Press, 1985).

55 See Michael Polanyi, *The Logic of Liberty*, (Chicago: University of Chicago Press, 1951).

56 On the Lange–Lerner model, see Lavoie, ibid., ch. 5.

57 I have criticized the market socialism of competing worker-cooperatives in my book, *Liberalisms: Essays in Political Philosophy*, (London and New York, 1989) ch. 10.

58 James Sherr, *Soviet Power: The continuing Challenge*, (London: Macmillan, 1987) 27.

59 P.C. Roberts, *Alienation in the Soviet Economy*, (Albuquerque, New Mexico: University of New Mexico Press, 1971).

60 Peter Rutland, *The Myth of the Plan*, (London: Hutchinson, 1985, 183).

61 Sherr, ibid., 30.

62 Sherr, ibid., 31.

63 Simon Leys, *The Burning Forest*, (New York: Henry Hold and Co., 1985) 167.

64 Alexander Zinoviev, *The Reality of Communism*, (London: Paladin Books, 1985).

65 H. Arendt, *The Origin of Totalitarianism*, (London: Macmillan, 1958).

66 See V. Havel, *The Power of the Powerless*, (New York, M.E. Shase, Inc., 1985).

67 A. Zinoviev, *Homo Sovieticus*, (London: Paladin Books, 1985).

68 Francois Thom, *Gorbachev, Glasnost and Lenin: Behind the New Thinking*, (London: Policy Research Publications, 1988) 12.

69 For an analysis that runs in parallel with mine, see L. Sirc, *What Must Gorbachev Do?*, (London, Centre for Research into Communist Economies, Occasional Paper Two, 1989).

70 As far as I know, the term 'Ottomanization' was first used in the context of Soviet affairs by Timothy Gartan Ash. See his book, *The Uses of Adversity*, (Cambridge: Granka Books, 1989) 188, 227–31. Details of the secessionist movements in Lithuania, see *Radio Free Europe Research*, January 5, 1989; for similar developments in Soviet Moldavia, see *Radio Free Europe Research*, February 9, 1989.

71 As reported in *The New York Review of Books*, (August 17, 1989) 24.

72 See Walicki's contribution to *Totalitarianism at the Crossroads*, E.F. Paul (ed.), (New Brunswick and London: Transaction Books, 1990).

73 L. Kolakowski, *Main Currents of Marxism, Volume One: The Founders*, (Oxford: the Clarendon Press, 1978) ch. 1.

74 See Eric Voegelin, *The New Science of Politics*, (Chicago: University of Chicago Press, 1952) 107, et. seq.

75 Michael Polanyi, *The Logic of Liberty*, (Chicago: Chicago University Press, 1951) 93.

76 See N. Berdyaev, *The Origin of Russian Communism*, (London: The Centenery Press, 1837).

77 See Alain Besancon, *The Rise of the Gulag: Intellectual Origins of Leninism*, (New York: Continuum, 1981).

78 See A. Solzhenitzyn, *The Red Wheel*, (London and New York: 1989).

79 See, especially, Dostoyevsky's great novel, *The Possessed* (1871–2).

80 For a brilliant demystification of the French Revolution, see Rene Sedillot, *Le Cout de la Revolution*, (Paris, 1987).

81 See Besancon, ibid., ch. 12 as the Jacobin aspect of Leninism. J. Talmon's *The Regime of Totalitarian Democracy*, (London: 1952), is also relevant here.

82 Theodore H. von Laue, *Why Lenin? Why Stalin? A Reappraisal of the Russian Revolution, 1900–1930*, (New York, Lippincott Company, 1971) 213.
83 For their comments on this paper, I am indebted to Fred Mill, Zbigniew Rau, Roger Scruton, Stefan Sencerz, Andrezej Walicki. I am particularly indebted to Ellen Paul for her detailed written comments.

13 WESTERN MARXISM: A FICTIONALIST DECONSTRUCTION

1 L. Revai, *The Word as Deed: Studies in the Labour Theory of Meaning*, G. Olsen and J. Kahn (eds), (Helsinki: Praxis Press, 1988).
2 L. Wittgenstein, *Philosophical Investigations*, (Oxford: Basil Blackwell, 1972) 5e, section 2.
3 *Concerning Marxism in Linguistics*, IV, 1, 3.
4 G. Olsen, *Sense and Reference in Marxian Semantics*, (Oxford University Press, 1980).
5 P. Reimer, *Analytical Foundations of Marxian Microlinguistics*, (Berkeley, 1982).

14 POST-TOTALITARIANISM, CIVIL SOCIETY AND THE LIMITS OF THE WESTERN MODEL

1 Francis Fukuyama, 'The End of History?', in *The National Interest*, no. 16, (Summer, 1989) 3–18.
2 See my 'Totalitarianism, Reform, and Civil Society' in *Totalitarianism at the Crossroads*, Ellen Paul (ed.), (New Brunswick and London: Transaction Books, 1990) 97–142, reprinted in this volume, ch. 12.
3 Fukuyama, op. cit. 3.
4 On this, see *Utopia in Power: The History of the Soviet Union from 1917 to the Present* by M. Heller and A. Nekrich, (New York, summit Books, 1989) 15, et seq.
5 See my 'Totalitarianism, Reform, and Civil Society', 102–5.
6 See F.A. Hayek, *Individualism and Economic Order*, (London: Routledge 1949); and P.C. Roberts, *Alienation in the Soviet Economy*, (Albuquerque: University of New Mexico Press, 1971). Michael Polanyi's analysis (which Roberts develops) may be found in his book *The Logic of Liberty*, (Chicago: University of Chicago Press, 1951).
7 For an excellent introduction to the Public-Choice perspective, see James Buchanan, *The Limits of Liberty: Between Anarchy and Leviathan*, (Chicago: University of Chicago Press, 1975).
8 For a good account of the New Economic Policy, see Heller and Nekrich, op. cit., 108, et. seq.
9 For the analysis of 'Z', see 'To the Stalin Mausoleum', *Daedalus*, (Winter 1990) 295–344.
10 I have set out the argument against market socialism in greater detail in my *Liberalisms: Essays in Political Philosophy*, (London: Routledge, 1989) ch. 10. For a powerful and scathing indictment of market socialism, see Antony de

Jasay, *Market Socialism: a Scrutiny – the Square Circle*, (London, Institute of Economic Affairs, Occasional Paper 84, 1990).

11 The best defence of market socialism is to be found in David Miller's *Market, Community and State*, (Oxford: Oxford University Press, 1989).

12 I have developed the idea of the New Hobbesian Dilemma in my *Limited Government: a Positive Agenda*, (London, Institute for Economic Affairs, 1989).

13 The distinction between classical and revisionist liberalism is spelt out in my *Liberalism*, (Minnesota and Milton Keynes: Open University Press, 1987).

14 I have discussed Buchanan's work in my paper, 'Buchanan on Liberty', in *Constitutional Political Economy*, vol. 1, no. 2, (Spring/Summer 1990) 149–68, reprinted in this volume, ch. 5.

15 I have criticized Hayekian conceptions of cultural evolution in the Second Edition of my *Hayek on Liberty*, (Oxford: Basil Blackwell, 1986).

16 The term civil association derives from Michael Oakeshott. See his *On Human Conduct*, (Oxford: Clarendon Press, 1975) 108–84.

17 See Arendt's classic, *The Origins of Totalitarianism*, (New York, Harcourt Brace Jovanovich, 1979).

18 For a good account of Lagowksi's neo-liberal views, see A. Walicki, 'Liberalism in Poland', *Critical Review*, vol. 2, no. 1, 8–38.

19 I criticize Rawls' account of the basic liberties in my *Liberalisms*, ibid., ch. 10.

20 See, especially, Buchanan's *Limits of Liberty*, ibid.

15 POLITICAL POWER, SOCIAL THEORY AND ESSENTIAL CONTESTABILITY

1 I refer especially to Steven Lukes, *Power: a radical view*, (London: Macmillan, 1974) and Lukes's *Essays in Social Theory*, (London: Macmillan, 1977); and to W.E. Connolly, *The Terms of Political Discourse*, (Lexington: D.C. Heath, 1974). See W.E. Connolly, *The Terms of Political Discourse*, 2nd edn, (Oxford: Basil Blackwell, 1983) for a response to the arguments of this chapter.

2 The distinction between a concept and its conceptions is made in John Rawls, *A Theory of Justice*, (Oxford: Oxford University Press, 1972), 5–6, and cited by Lukes in *Power*, 27.

3 Lukes, *Power*, 27.

4 For his discussion of the contributions of Parsons and Arendt, see Lukes, *Power*, 27–31. For Connolly's discussion, see Connolly, *Terms of Political Discourse*, 2nd edn, 114–15.

5 This suggestion is advanced in Martin Hollis, *Models of Man* (Cambridge, Cambridge University Press, 1977) 173–80.

6 For this see B.M. Barry, *Political Argument*, (London: Routledge & Kegan Paul, 1965) ch. 10.

7 See Steven Lukes, 'Relativism: Cognitive and Moral', in *Essays in Social Theory*, ch. 8.

8 Lukes, *Essays in Social Theory*, 24–6, asserts that disputes about power and responsibility may in some cases be resolvable empirically. He makes the same claim in his 'On the Relativity of Power' in S.C. Brown (ed.), *Philosophical Disputes in the Social Sciences*, (Brighton, Harvester, 1979) 261–74.

9 Lukes, *Power* 45.

10 Connolly, *The Terms of Political Discourse*, 2nd edn, chs 2 and 4.

11 ibid., 68.

12 I have myself considered (very inadequately as I now think) the question of the lifelong contented slave in D. Robertson and M. Freeman (eds), *The Frontiers of Political Thought*, (Brighton, Harvester, 1980), reprinted as ch. 5 of my *Liberalisms: Essays in Political Philosophy*, (London: Routledge, 1990).

13 Lukes, *Power*, 32–3, and Connolly, *Terms of Political Discourse*, 2nd edn, 107–16.

14 Such Wittgensteinian arguments are invoked in an otherwise very forceful critique of Connolly by Grenville Wall, 'The Concepts of Interest in Politics', *Politics and Society*, 5 (1975), 487–510. See also John Plamenatz's earlier treatment in 'Interests', *Political Studies*, 2 (1954) 1–8.

15 Lukes, *Power*, 52–3.

16 Some difficulties in the attempt to combine these claims are explored by Alan Bradshaw, 'A Critique of Lukes's Power: A Radical View', *Sociology*, 10 (1976) 121–37.

17 The problems generated for their account by the notion of a power structure are discussed, but not resolved, by Lukes, *Essays in Social Theory*, 9–10, and Connolly, *Terms of Political Discourse*, 2nd edn, 116–26.

18 See W.B. Gallie, *Philosophy and the Historical Understanding*, (London: Chatto and Windus, 1964) ch. 8, for a slightly revised version of this article.

19 Stuart Hampshire, *Thought and Action*, (New York: Viking, 1959) 230–1.

20 On this see Alasdair MacIntyre, 'The Essential Contestability of Some Social Concepts', *Ethics*, 8 (1973–4), 1–9.

21 On this see my 'On Liberty, Liberalism and Essential Contestability', *British Journal of Political Science*, 8 (1978), 385–402, where I depart from some of the formulations of an earlier and less satisfactory paper of mine, 'On the Essential contestability of Some Social and Political Concepts', *Political Theory*, 5 (1977) 331–48. A highly relevant and useful contribution to this area of debate is made by Quentin Skinner in his 'The Idea of a Cultural Lexicon', in *Essays in Criticism*, (July 1979) 205–24, especially in 10n on 224.

22 B. Hindess and P. Hirst, *Pre-Capitalist Modes of Production*, (London: Routledge and Kegan Paul, 1975) 33.

23 I am indebted here to W.E. Connolly, *Appearance and Reality in Politics*, (Cambridge: Cambridge University Press, 1981).

24 Hampshire, *Thought and Action*, 233.

25 Lukes, *Power*, 47–9.

26 See S. Milgram, *Obedience to Authority*, (London: Tavistock, 1974) and R.D. Laing and A. Esterson, *Sanity, Madness and the Family*, 2nd edn, (London: Tavistock, 1971).

16 AN EPITAPH FOR LIBERALISM

1 Feinberg, Joel, *The Moral Limits of the Criminal Law*, vol. 1: *Harm to Others*, vol. 2: *Offence to Others*, vol 3: *Harm to Self*, vol. 4: *Harmless Wrongdoing*, (Oxford: Oxford University Press, 1984).

2 Reviewed in the *TLS* of February 8, 1985.

3 *Offence to Others*, vol. 2, x.

4 ibid., xiii.
5 *Harm to Self*, vol. 3, 4.
6 *Harmless Wrongdoing*, vol. 4, 321.
7 ibid., 321.
8 ibid., 322.
9 ibid., 320.
10 Joseph Rax, *The Morality of Freedom*, (Oxford: Clarendon Press, 1986). Reviewed in the *TLS* of June 5, 1987.

17 THE END OF HISTORY – OR OF LIBERALISM?

1 Francis Fukuyama, *National Interest*, Summer 1989.
2 John Gray, *Liberalisms: Essays in Political Philosophy*, (London and New York: Routledge, 1989).

18 THE POLITICS OF CULTURAL DIVERSITY

1 Aurel Kolnai, 'Les ambiguités nationales', *La Nouvelle Releve*, (Montreal, 1946/47_ 533–46, 644–55. Translated by W. Grassl and B. Smith in 'The Politics of National Diversity', *The Salisbury Review*, vol. 5, no. 3, (April 1987) 33–7.
2 On this, see my 'Philosophy, Science and Myth in Marxism', in *Marx and Marxism*; Royal Institute of Philosophy Lecture Series, vol. 14, G.H.R. Parkinson (ed.), (Cambridge University Press, Summer 1982) 71–95; and my 'Marxian freedom, individual liberty and the end of alienation', *Journal of Social Philosophy and Policy*, vol. 3, issue 2, (Spring 1986) 160–87.
3 For an excellent account of the crucial role of Marxist ideology in constituting and reproducing the Soviet system, see M. Heller and A.M. Nekrich, *Utopia in Power: the History of the Soviet Union from 1917 to the Present*, (New York: Summit Books, 1986); and Alain Besancon's brilliant *The Soviet Syndrome*, (New York and London: Harcourt, Brace, Jovanovich, 1976).
4 On this, see *Homo Sovieticus* by Alexander Zinoviev, (London and Toronto: Paladin Books, 1985).
5 L. Kolakowski, *Main Currents of Marxism*; vol. 1, (Oxford: Clarendon Press, 1978) 420.
6 On this, see my paper 'Mill's and other liberalisms', ch. 12 in my *Liberalisms: Essays in Political Philosophy*, (London, Routledge, 1989).
7 See M. Sandel, *Liberalism and the Limits of Justice*, (Cambridge and New York: Cambridge University Press, 1982).
8 Roger Scruton, *The Meaning of Conservatism*, (Harmondsworth and New York: Penguin Books, 1980).
9 Isaiah Berlin, *Against the Current*, (London: Hogarth Press, 1979) 342.
10 Michael Oakeshott, *On Human Conduct*, (Oxford: Clarendon Press, 1985) 320–1.
11 For the late nineteenth-century transformation of France, see Norman Stone, *Europe Transformed: 1878–1919*, (Cambridge, Mass.: Harvard University Press, 1984) ch. III, sec. 5.
12 Kolnai, op. cit., 536.
13 Stuart Hampshire, *Morality and Conflict*, (Oxford: Basil Blackwell, 1983) 138–9.

14 I intend to associate my conception with the rather different view offered by Richard Rorty in his 'Postmodern Bourgeois Liberalism'; *The Journal of Philosophy*, vol. 10, (1983).

15 I am indebted to Isaiah Berlin and the late Michael Oakeshott for conversations on some of the themes of this lecture. Responsibility for the thoughts it expresses remains mine alone.

19 CONSERVATISM, INDIVIDUALISM AND THE POLITICAL THOUGHT OF THE NEW RIGHT

1 For an excellent survey of the New Right, see Norman P. Barry, *The New Right*, (London: Croom Helm, 1987) and David G. Green, *The New Conservatism: The Counter Revolution in Political, Economic and Social Thought*, (New York: St. Martin's Press, 1987).

2 A good account of the role of the IEA in promoting successfully a counter revolution in economic thought can be derived from several of the essays in A. Seldon (ed.), *The 'New Right' Enlightenment*, (Sevenoaks, E. and L. Booth, 1985).

3 So, especially, Hayek's essay, 'Individualism: true and false' in F.A. Hayek, *Individualism and Economic Order*, (London: Routledge, 1976).

4 For an exposition of Tory 'wet' views, see Ian Gilmour, *Inside Right: A Study of Conservatism*, (London: Quartet Books, 1978).

5 See Michael Oakeshott, *On Human Conduct*, (Oxford: Clarendon Press, 1975).

6 Alan Macfarlane, *The Political Theory of English Individualism*, (Oxford, 1978), and Alan Macfarlane, *The Culture of Capitalism*, (Oxford, 1987).

7 Karl Polanyi, *The Great Transformation*, (Boston: Beacon Editions, 1957).

8 C.B. Macpherson, *The Origin of Possessive Individualism*.

9 See J.C.D. Clark's essay in Clark (ed.), *Ideas and Politics in Modern Britain*, (London: Macmillan, 1990).

10 The writings of Paul Craig Roberts are among the best sources of the supply-side argument for the eliminability, or radical reduction, in the business cycle.

11 See B. Parekh, 'The New Right and the Politics of Nationhood', in M. Deakin, *The Next Right: Image and Reality*, (London: The Runymeade Trust, 1986). See, also, R. Scruton's contribution to Clark, *Ideas and Politics in Modern Britain*, op. cit.

12 This point is well developed in Norman Stone's *Europe Transformed 1879–1919*, (London: Fontane, 1984) 201, et. seq.

13 See E. Kedourie, *Nationalism*, (London: Hutchinson, 1960) and K. Minogue, *Nationalism*, (New York: Basic Books, 1967).

14 See Joseph Schumpeter's classic work *Capitalism, Socialism and Democracy*, (London: Allen and Unwin, 1952).

15 I consider some such desirable measures in my *Limited Government: A Positive Agenda*, (London: Institute for Economic Affairs, Hobart Paper 113, 1989).

16 On the failings of Millian individualism, see ch. 12 of my *Liberalism: Essays in Political Liberalisms: Essays in Political Philosophy* (London and New York: Routledge, 1989).

17 For Oakeshott's account of the emergence and character of the the anti-individual, see his *On Human Conduct*, op. cit.

18 M. Oakeshott, *Rationalism in Politics*, (London: Methuen, 1962).

20 WHAT IS DEAD AND WHAT IS LIVING IN LIBERALISM

1 *Culture and Value*, G.H. von Wright (ed.), (Oxford: Basil Blackwell, 1980) 60.
2 On this, see my *Liberalism*, (Milton Keynes and Minneapolis: Open University Press and University of Minnesota Press, 1986).
3 See Pocock's *The Machiavellian Moment*, (Princeton, N.J.: Princeton University Press, 1976).
4 See my *Liberalism*, op. cit., chs 4 and 5.
5 See my *Liberalism*: Postscript, 'After liberalism', (London and New York: Routledge, 1989) 239–66.
6 J. Raz, *The Morality of Freedom*, (Oxford: Oxford University Press, 1986) 194.
7 See 'Michael Oakeshott as a Liberal Theorist' by W.J. Coats Jr, *Canadian Journal of Political Science*, XVIII (December, 1985) 773–87; and R.A.D. Grant, *Oakeshott*, (London: Claridge Press, 199) 62–3.
8 Isaiah Berlin, *The Crooked Timber of Humanity: Chapters in the History of Ideas*, (London: John Murray, 1990) 79–80.
9 Berlin, op. cit., 81–2.
10 Berlin, op. cit., 80.
11 As the Russian fideist L. Shestov puts it, 'History is one thing and meaning another'. See his *Athens and Jerusalem*, (Athens, Ohio: Ohio University Press, 1966) 393.
12 John Skorupski, *John Stuart Mill* (London and New York: Routledge, 1989) 24.
13 J. Raz, *The Morality of Freedom*, 269, et. seq.
14 Hubert L. Dreyfus, *Being-in-the-World: A Commentary on Heidegger's Being and Time*, Division I, (Cambridge, Mass.: The MIT Press, 1991) 262–3.
15 Dreyfus, op. cit., 357, 17n.
16 Dreyfus, op. cit., 280.
17 I owe the term to Bruce Brouwer, from whose unpublished writings on moral epistemology I have much profited.
18 See my *Mill on Liberty: A Defense* (London and New York: Routledge and Kegan Paul, 1983), ch. 3.
19 Stuart Hampshire, *Innocence and Experiences*, (London: The Penguin Press, 1989).
20 The term "the evanescence of imperfection" originates, so far as I can tell, in Herbert Spencer's *Social Statics: The Conditions Essential to Human Happiness Specified, and the First of them Developed*, (London, 1850, 1st edn; republished New York: Robert Schaltenbach Foundation, 1970).
21 Stuart Hampshire, *Innocence and Experience*, 32.
22 Hampshire, op. cit., 33.
23 Hampshire, op. cit., 108.
24 Raz, op. cit., 345.
25 Hampshire, op. cit., 106.
26 Raz, op. cit., chs 7 and 8.
27 Hampshire, op. cit., 108.
28 Raz, op. cit., 325.
29 R. Nozick, *Anarchy, State and Utopia*, (New York: Basic Books, 1974) 151.
30 I. Berlin, *Four Essays on Liberty*, (Oxford: Oxford University Press, 1968) 130.
31 Raz, op. cit., 194.
32 J. Raz, *Facing Up*: A Reply, *University of Southern California Law Review*, vol. 62, March–May, 1989, nos 3 and 4, 1227.

33 I owe this expression to Raz, op. cit., 198.

34 This view was one held by John Anderson.

35 See Sandel, *Liberalism and the Limits of Justice*, (Cambridge: Cambridge University Press, 1982).

36 See, for example, Bernard Williams's *Ethics and the Limits of Philosophy*, (London: Fontana, 1985).

37 J. Skorupski, op. cit., 37.

38 See H. Dreyfus, *On being-in-the-world*, op. cit., in which Heidegger's version of plural realism is both expounded and rendered attractive and plausible.

39 See my *Liberalisms*, last chapter.

40 See my 'Totalitarianism, reform and civil society', in *Totalitarianism at the Crossroads*, Ellen Frankel Paul (ed.), 97–142.

41 James Buchanan, 'Tacit Presuppositions of Political Economy: implications for societies in transition', (unpublished).

42 F. Fukuyama, The End of History', *Natural Interests*, (Summer, 1989).

43 See Michael Oakeshott, *On Human Conflict*, (Oxford: Clarendon Press, 1975).

44 See R. Rorty, *Contingency, Irony and Solidarity*, (Cambridge, 1989).

45 M. Oakeshott, *On Human Conduct*, op. cit.

46 M. Oakeshott, *The Voice of Liberal Learning*, T. Fuller (ed.), (Yale University Press, 1990) 28.

47 I. Berlin, *The Crooked Timber of Humanity: Chapters in the History of Ideas*, op. cit., 235.

48 On this, see my *Liberalisms*, op. cit., ch. 11.

49 See, most especially, Donald Livingston, *Hume's Philosophy of Common Life*, (Chicago: Chicago University Press, 1984); and Nicholas Capaldi, *Hume's Place in Moral Philosophy*, (New York: Peter Lang, 1989).

50 For an astute exploration of this prospect, see E.M. Cioran, *History and Utopia*, (New York: Seaver Books, 1987); and Cioran's *Anathemas and Admirations*, (New York: Arcede Publishing, Little, Brown and Co. 1991).

51 See, especially, Ronald Dworkin's *Law Empire*, (Cambridge, Mass.: Harvard University Press, 1986).

52 Discussions with Donald Livingston have helped me to frame this point, but its formulation is mine alone.

53 L. Wittgenstein, *Culture and Value*, (Oxford, Basil Blackwell, 1980).

54 Conversations with the late Michael Oakeshott, with Isaiah Berlin and Joseph Raz have been of great importance in shaping the thoughts expressed in this essay. Discussions with members of the seminar on the Discourse of Liberty at the Murphy Institute of Political Economy at Tulane in early 1991 advanced my thinking on several of the themes developed herein. I wish particularly to record my indebtedness to conversations with B. Honig, Eric Mack, Jonathan Riley and G.W. Smith. Comments by Tristram Engelhardt, James Fishkin, William Galston, Chandran Kukathas, Kenneth Minogue, Emilio Pacheco and Andrew Williams were extremely helpful in clarifying the thoughts expressed in the paper. Conversations over several years with Nicholas Capaldi and Charles King – often in the context of colloquia conducted by Liberty Fund of Indianapolis – have helped to form some of the thoughts articulated in this paper. Discussions with several people at the Social Philosophy and Policy Center – in particular Eugene Heath, Loren Lomasky, Andrew McInyk, Jeffrey Paul and Fred Miller – helped me frame my arguments more clearly. All the usual disclaimers apply.

Index